Lucien A. Cross

Thomas J. Knight

COLOMBIA

COLOMBIA

Social Structure and the Process of Development

T. Lynn Smith

With a foreword by
Alberto Lleras

University of Florida Press • Gainesville • 1967

A *University of Florida Press Book*
sponsored by the
CENTER FOR LATIN AMERICAN STUDIES

Library of Congress
Catalog Card No. 67-26603

MANUFACTURED FOR THE PUBLISHER BY
ROSE PRINTING COMPANY, INC.
TALLAHASSEE, FLORIDA

for
MICHAEL

Foreword

SEPTEMBER, 1967
BOGOTÁ, COLOMBIA

ESTEEMED PROFESSOR AND FRIEND:

You have asked me to write a foreword for your volume *Colombia: Social Structure and the Process of Development*, concerned essentially with the agrarian problems of my country. In the Introduction you explain that this is the first in a projected three-volume series, with the second examining the demographic aspects of Colombian society, including the subject of urbanization, and the third devoted to social, educational, governmental, and administrative institutions. As anticipated, your work as a whole should be of the same nature and scope as your *Brazil: People and Institutions*.

With much pleasure I accede to your request, but I do so only by means of this letter in order to avoid the pretentious connotations of the Foreword to a highly important and penetrating scholarly work. I would almost like to limit myself to thanking you for the study you have made which surely will be of benefit to my fellow citizens. It is of great value to us that a scientist such as yourself has dedicated so many years to studying the historical and social process of this nation, which you first visited almost a quarter of a century ago. As you know, studies of this type are not numerous in our setting, and only now are the modern sociological disciplines beginning to develop in our universities. For a long while we have had to depend upon the small group of foreign specialists who dedicated their time, their genius, and their scientific experience to following past and present developments in Latin America. From a purely academic point of view, this vast territory lacks attraction for the scientist, and in the minds of your countrymen it does not have the advantages, produce the honors, or arouse an interest to compare with those of other parts of the world. I need not dwell upon the difficulties of investigations in regions where documentary sources are scarce and compilations of data limited, for little has been written upon these subjects and generalizations are substituted for the systematic use of facts. Therefore, we Colombians are indebted to you for assembling and systematizing widely scattered pieces of information as you have done in this volume and as you plan to do in the ones to follow. You criticize and evaluate with good judgment and in a scientific spirit which enables you to arrive at important conclusions relating to our social structure.

I am not the one to examine your conclusions one by one and express an opinion about their importance and validity. Hence, I limit myself to giving my first impressions concerning your book, which I have read with vivid interest.

Precisely at the time the proofs of your book arrived, I was engaged in reviewing data, names, and historical episodes for an autobiographical work which I felt obliged to write to clarify and establish certain facts that the indolence of Colombians in historical matters would allow to be erased and dissipated if we participants did not record them. In this connection what has surprised and satisfied me most in the course of this preliminary examination is the prodigious social, political, and economic change in the Republic which has taken place during the lifetime of my generation. This has been especially great during the last thirty years and most rapid of all during the last fifteen. I believe there are few areas in the world where the transformation of primitive and archaic structures has been taking place with such notable velocity. Perhaps because I was imbued with this spirit I experienced a kind of shock to encounter more than once in your book a focusing upon certain aspects which have disappeared or are changing so drastically that they no longer serve as bases for judgments relating to our social organization, although they prevailed during the first quarter of this century. It is only natural that I would perceive some of the less obvious features of this change because they affected me and because to some extent I had a part in the creation of factors which have been making the changes easier, as for example the two substantial agrarian reforms of our times—to which apparently you attribute less importance—Law 200 of 1936 or *Ley de Tierras,* and Law 135 of 1961 or the Social Agrarian Reform Law. I feel certain that I am now living in another country, absolutely another one, quite different from the one I knew prior to the commencement of my political life in 1930. It could hardly be otherwise if we take into account the influence upon the social process of the recent population explosion, especially through its effects upon the rural violence of the last twenty years, the migration to the cities, and other aspects which you will examine at length with a masterly hand in your next volume. The very pertinent reservations which you make with respect to your propositions and those of others relative to the situations that have been altered by subsequent happenings do not carry the conviction that I myself hold, that there is already a genuinely new country—better or worse, but different— than that you and I knew in 1943. I am sure that we are not dealing with one of those "obstacles to the perception of change in the underdeveloped countries" to which Professor Albert O. Hirschman refers, and as you yourself say in the Introduction, when you can analyze the complete results of the last census you will be able to confirm or modify some of your present opinions. At that time, also, the first results of the efforts of the Colombian Agrarian Reform Institute to bring about some of the objectives which you consider desirable for modification of the agricultural structures of the country will be more evident.

The Colombian Agrarian Reform Institute, for example, has already made some important revisions of previously vague data relative to the division of Colombia's rural property, the distribution of its ownership, and its average size. In 1963 the Institute indicated that, contrary to what previously had been affirmed (in the vast generalizations of our writers), the characteristic landholding is the medium-sized one and the minifundium, the former ranging up to 100 hectares. The latifundium occupies a minor part of the territory in use and generally is made up of lands of inferior quality or is situated in poor zones where roads, trails, and other facilities do not exist. The statement that 3 per cent of the proprietors own 60 per cent of the nation's agricultural and grazing lands is not valid. In the cadastre, according to the Colombian Agrarian Reform Institute, are listed fifteen properties of more than 100,000 hectares, which, when located and inspected, proved to be virgin jungle or properties that some thirty or forty years ago were settled by thousands of *campesinos,* many of them having titles which conflict with those of the cadastral registers. An examination of the distribution of the ownership of the land used in the three most important crops—coffee, tobacco, and cotton—demonstrates very clearly that the medium-sized holding predominates and that unfortunately the minifundium abounds.

But it is clear that even when there exists a "latifundium of paper or of the notaries," as opposed to the actual pattern of ownership, medium-sized and *minifundista,* many of the old judgments persist relative to the distribution of the ownership of the land. In recent years no one has formed additional large holdings; on the contrary, all that has happened politically, economically, socially, and legislatively has been successfully directed toward the dispersion and better distribution of the ownership of useful land. The great mobility that has been produced in Colombian society during the last thirty years— that which the Conservatives call "instability" (*inestabilidad*)—is producing an evolution much more rapid than that which the majority of foreign and Colombian observers are able to see, or willing to admit. In this process not all has been desirable or necessary. Indeed there have been episodes as harsh and bitter as those of violent revolutions; but in any case the old colonial and feudal structure no longer exists and its bases have been disappearing precipitously. It would be presumptuous for me to say in this letter-foreword how this process has unfolded, but there are analyses by highly qualified observers such as yourself and Hirschman, who in his essay "The Problem of Land Tenure and Agrarian Reform in Colombia" makes some keen observations about this latter phase of rural life in Colombia and concludes that the changes completed or in progress probably are a *hidden revolution* of the greatest significance.

I not only greet with special satisfaction this first volume of your work, professor and friend, but even now I attribute exceptional importance to the two that are to follow. As you know there are few well-trained demographers in Colombia, yet the data from the census of population of 1964 (still not available in their complete form) and particularly the consequences of the extremely rapid growth of Colombian society require someone who can analyze the materials and derive from them more definitive conclusions than those which, in a kind of panic, many of us are drawing. We Colombians and all those interested in this type of study, in the academic world and out of it, should have nothing but gratitude for your assistance.

Please receive, Professor Smith, my most cordial congratulations for your work about Colombia. I hope that it may soon be translated into Spanish so that all those interested in sociology and those in governmental service may read it.

/s/ ALBERTO LLERAS

Acknowledgments

A GREAT MANY people in the United States and Colombia are due thanks for the assistance they have given in making this book possible. This is especially true since the studies on which it is based covered a period of almost twenty-five years. Some early support for the work involved came from the General Education Board, largely because of the sympathetic understanding of the late Dr. A. R. Mann, who served as director of that important organization, and Mr. Jackson Davis, who succeeded him as its head. Later on the John Simon Guggenheim Memorial Foundation, through its executive secretary Mr. Henry A. Moe, assisted with fellowships which made it possible for the research to be continued. My most sincere thanks are due these three men and the foundations they directed.

Since 1949, when I joined the faculty of the University of Florida, various officials of this institution have done much to facilitate my research and writing, including that involved in the preparation of this present volume. Thanks are due especially to Dr. J. Wayne Reitz, president; Mr. Robert B. Mautz, vice-president for academic affairs; Dr. L. E. Grinter, dean of the graduate school; Dr. Ralph E. Page, dean of the College of Arts and Sciences; and Dr. Lyle N. McAlister, director of the Center for Latin American Studies.

A number of colleagues also have rendered great assistance, especially by patiently assisting me to clarify basic ideas and by reading and criticizing parts of the manuscript. The list of these includes Dr. Homer L. Hitt, presently chancellor of the Louisiana State University in New Orleans; Dr. Joseph S. Vandiver, now head of the department of sociology at the University of Florida; Dr. Lowry Nelson, professor emeritus at the University of Minnesota and formerly visiting professor at the University of Florida; and professors Irving L. Webber and John V. D. Saunders, both currently colleagues in sociology at the University of Florida.

Many officials of the government of the United States have gone far beyond the line of duty in order to help me with my work in and on Colombia. Foremost among these are Dr. Olen E. Leonard, especially during the years he served in the Office of Foreign Agricultural Relations, and Mr. Kenneth Wernimont, formerly agricultural attaché at the American Embassy in Bogotá and presently vice-president of the Rockefeller Foundation. Many important items in my bibliography, works which played important functional roles in the assembling and analysis of the facts, might have escaped my attention had it not been for the thoughtfulness and consideration of these men.

Great thanks are due hundreds of Colombians who have been helpful in various ways, and a very special type of gratitude must be expressed to three of them. In the course of the field studies and the conversations through which gradually I became acquainted with Colombian society, thousands of persons were met on a strictly informal basis and hundreds more in more formal "structured" types of interviews. The list of these includes large numbers of campesinos in all parts of the nation, *mayordomos* and other bosses and administrators by the dozens, hundreds of landed proprietors especially those holding large estates, and other hundreds of governmental officials (alcaldes of municipios; governors and other departmental officers; senators; deputies; cabinet ministers; and several presidents). Nearly all of those in high places also may be classified as intellectuals. In many cases, I could never have obtained the information I gathered without the tolerant cooperation of large numbers of Colombians in all walks of life, and to them I am deeply grateful.

The three to whom I am especially indebted are: Dr. Justo Díaz Rodríguez, Dr. Luis Roberto García, and Dr. Orlando Fals-Borda. The first two of these were the top officials of the National Departamento de Tierras, or Land Department, during the years 1943-1945, and together we crisscrossed Colombia from one extreme to the other. They have remained friends since then, always assisting during my subsequent trips to Colombia in the collection of materials, briefing me on the situation and changes, and aiding me to establish new and important contacts. The third, whose doctoral work I directed, organized and headed the Facultad de Sociología at the National University. In various positions he has held in Colombia, he assisted greatly in making possible frequent field excursions, did much to keep me informed about new sociological titles, and read and criticized parts of the manuscript.

Over the years my various research assistants have rendered invaluable help in the making of necessary tabulations and computations, construction of maps and charts, and so on. Those who did most in connection with the present work are Mrs. J. S. Vandiver, Mr. Lowell C. Wikoff, Mr. Paul E. Zopf, Jr., and Mr. Harold M. Clements.

Finally, mention must be made of the understanding and encouragement on the part of my wife, and also of my two sons, without which this and my other scholarly endeavors would have been impossible. Words, written or oral, are inadequate to repay the indebtedness involved; but I am deeply grateful to them.

T. LYNN SMITH
Graduate Research
Professor of Sociology
University of Florida

Contents

1

Introduction

THIS VOLUME contains results of my attempts to study the sociological aspects of the development process as it is going on, and
perhaps to some extent as it is being carried on, in the Republic of
Colombia. It is the first of a projected series of three volumes which
eventually, I hope, will cover the same ground for Colombia as
Brazil: People and Institutions did for Brazil. The second will deal
with the demographic aspects of Colombian society, including urbanization; and the third with the basic nucleated social institutions,
namely the family, the educational institutions, the religious institutions, and the governmental and administrative institutions.

For almost a quarter of a century, I have devoted a major part of
my time observing, analyzing, teaching, and writing about various
aspects of Colombian society such as the social structure, the social
processes, and population composition and trends. I spent lengthy
periods of time in that country during the 1940's and also during the
late 1950's as consultant on the various aspects of social organization
once designated as *parcelación y colonización,* or the subdivision of
estates and the establishment of colonies of family-sized farmers,
and now generally referred to as Agrarian Reform. I served as visiting professor at the National University, lecturing frequently at
that great university as well as at several of the others in Bogotá,
and also at the institutions of higher learning in other important
cities such as Cali, Medellín, Barranquilla, and Cartagena. With financial assistance from the John Simon Guggenheim Foundation I have
been able to spend four summers in Colombia and the Andean countries to the south of it studying the spread of settlement down the
eastern slopes of the Andes and out onto the broad expanses of
largely unoccupied lands which stretch eastward from the base of
the mountains.

All of this, which amounts to well over three years, spread over
the period since 1943, has provided an exceptional opportunity to
know Colombian society in all parts of that highly fragmented and

1

diverse country and to observe many of the changes that have taken place during a lengthy period of grievously trying vicissitudes through which the nation has passed. For well over twelve months, for example, during the years 1943, 1944, and 1945, I traveled on journeys through all of the principal regions or sections of the country in company with Justo Díaz Rodríguez, director, or Luis Roberto García, then chief counsel and subsequently director, of the *Departamento Nacional de Tierras* (National Land Department). These trips were designed for the specific purpose of observing *in situ* the wide range of acute problems in man-land relationships, such as faulty land titles, overlapping claims, and squatters, which the officials of the department confronted. A wide variety of transportation modes were used in the course of our travels, for the system of transportation and communication in the 1940's was by no means equal to that in use today. In the large circle surrounding Bogotá, to a distance of 100 miles or so, the department's station wagons enabled us to make dozens of visits to the heavily populated and extremely diverse areas of Cundinamarca, Boyacá, and Meta. Beyond that, the limited network of railroads was used to some extent, extremely primitive auto buses carried us many miles, now and then we were fortunate enough to be able to hire a car, or at least to obtain seats in a car making a scheduled trip between two cities, and with considerable frequency we were able to get transportation on the old motor trucks that even then were threading their ways around the steep precipices of the Andes and through parts of the jungle in the lower altitudes. In some cases, in order to save time in getting from one departmental capital to another, we used the airplanes; and as an official commission, automobiles, small motor-driven vehicles to travel the railroads, and horses were placed at our disposal for local travel by the governors and other officials of the departments we visited. Subsequently, in the course of about 15 additional visits to the country of durations varying from a week to three months, much the same means of transportation were used, as many sections of the country were revisited, some of them time after time. However, as roads were improved and automobiles became more plentiful, this mode of travel and the airplane were used almost exclusively for our journeys within Colombia. The important thing about all this is the fact that almost all of the extensive travels in Colombia were by modes of transportation that enabled us to observe the details of the local scene and in the company of Colombians who knew the people and the society in the areas we were visiting. Thus simultaneously we were able to observe the changes in the rural neighborhoods and communities and to take stock of the tremendous transformations taking place in Bogotá as it swelled from a city of less than 500,000 inhabitants to one with well over 1,500,000, and, in less detail, the simultaneous mushrooming of Cali, Medellín, Barranquilla, Cartagena, and dozens of other important cities.

The fact that this volume is concerned with the rural or agricultural aspects of the development process is due largely to the sequence in which Colombia's recent fundamental compilations of statistical data are becoming available. Although the studies on which this and the forthcoming volumes are based have been going on for almost a quarter of a century, it is not deemed advisable to publish until the results of the most recent censuses have been compiled and published and there has been a year or so for their study and analysis. The census of agriculture was taken in 1959 and 1960, and by 1964 many of its comprehensive tabulations had been published; hence it was possible by this time to complete this part of the work. The census of population, on the other hand, was not taken until July, 1964, and only those entirely unfamiliar with the processes involved would entertain any thought that the essential materials it will furnish, both for the demographic studies and for those of the family and the school, would be ready for release before about 1968. Thus it has been possible to complete the analysis and prepare the discussion of those social institutions, social structures, and social systems to which attention is directed in this book; whereas perforce one must choose between publishing on the other subjects before the results of the census of population are available, which indeed would be ill-advised, or be content to wait several more years before completing the analytical activities and preparing the corresponding manuscripts.

It is especially regretted that neither the process of urbanization nor the studies of the role of education in the development process can figure in this volume, since in many respects they are the moving forces in the drastic social and economic changes presently going on in Colombia. Even so, the subjects that do figure here also are of primary importance in the transformation of Colombian society irrespective of whether it can be described accurately as "directed social change" or is evaluated as being far less telic in nature. Indeed there probably are many who consider the various institutions which govern man's relationship to the land (and especially land tenure and the size of the agricultural holdings and agricultural units), the systems of agriculture, agrarian reform, the community and community development, and the class system as the *sine qua non* of the sociological aspects of the development process. In any case, these are the parts of the study which are covered in this book. Just as quickly as possible, after the new materials are available for study, efforts will be made to complete the analysis of the process of urbanization and that of the role of education in the current transformations of Colombian society. Realistically it does not seem likely that this will be possible much before 1970.

Before proceeding with the substantive portions of this work, it seems advisable to comment briefly upon the basic procedures used in this attempt to report upon Colombian society and its development. These procedures are those of the sociologist utilizing his own frame of reference and what is entitled to be designated as a genuine comparative method of study. By specifying that the approach is that of the sociologist, one denotes (or at least he should denote) that the scientific method is relied upon and that the entire work falls within the compass of a comprehensive and systematic frame of reference. It is true that many journalists and other "writers" may write about social or societal matters. Perforce they also must make use of the two cognitive processes, observation and inference, which are the logical bases of the scientific method; and perchance they may insist to a considerable degree upon the objectivity, impartiality, and empirical testing of tentative conclusions which figure among the essentials of scientific procedures. All of these are indispensable in genuine sociological inquiry. In addition, for the sociologist a comprehensive and systematic frame of reference (a well-organized body of concepts, classifications, previously established relationships, and so forth) is part and parcel of his working equipment; whereas the "writer" tends to improvise his personal ways to observe and organize his materials about the unusual, the startling, the unique, and the novel features of a situation. In brief, in his observations the sociologist looks through a pair of "sociological spectacles" which have been ground to precision by the cumulative results of efforts over a considerable period of time by workers in all parts of the world, while the journalist or other "writer" is guided largely by individual and personal insights as to what he believes will be of interest to his readers. Not infrequently the latter is chiefly absorbed with the ways of combining words and phrases in order to secure a desired effect and not overly conscientious about the extent to which the picture he paints actually corresponds to the reality. The sociologist is entitled to no such artistic or literary licenses.

It also seems advisable to state explicitly what is meant by the genuine comparative method attempted in this study and how it differs from the procedures that traditionally have been called the comparative method. The latter consisted essentially of combing the writings of all types of persons who had visited different parts of the earth and extracting therefrom any sentences or paragraphs touching upon predetermined topics. Apparently the most successful practitioners of this method relied upon corps of readers to discover and excerpt the "grains of wheat" from the masses of materials consulted, a procedure that would guarantee that the works of art coming from the skillful molding of the selected materials by the masters would not be complicated or marred by any basic understanding of the social systems and cultural patterns of the people they were comparing. It is small wonder that this approach has been thoroughly discredited.

The genuine comparative method, however, involves the application by the same observer of the scientific method and the same frame of reference in the study of the social structure and processes of two or more societies. Early in my career I began attempts to secure and disseminate a systematized body of knowledge about the structure and functioning of society in the United States by detailed comparisons and contrasts of regional patterns in the Midwestern, Far Western, and Southern parts of the nation. Later I was privileged to extend this line of endeavor by extensive work in Brazil, Colombia, and other parts of Latin America. Indeed many of the features of the frame of reference I now use (such as that pertaining to the systems of agriculture) were made possible only by careful observation and analysis of phenomena observed in the South American countries. In any case, this is the kind of a comparative method that has been employed in securing, analyzing, and interpreting the materials contained in this volume.

It also seems well to comment briefly upon the order of presentation of the materials contained in this book. The exposition begins with the topic of the size of the land holdings and agricultural units for the simple reason that the large landed estate, the hacienda, is the institution that has done most to shape Colombian society over a period of four centuries. Any genuine development process in the country we are studying must involve drastic changes in this hacienda system and the entire social system to which it gave rise and which it perpetuates. Next comes the discussion of land tenure, the basic legal relationships between men and the land they cultivate, which many sociologists and economists seem to regard as the only institutional pattern involved in a program of land reform or agrarian reform. Colombia's extremely defective system of land surveys and titles is the third topic to occupy our attention, since it is so intimately related to the two preceding subjects. Next comes the chapter on systems of agriculture, for it is almost chimerical to think of substantial social and economic development in a country such as Colombia unless the ways in which the mass of the population goes about extracting a living from the soil can be moved ahead from the most rudimentary and labor-devouring varieties to the efficient ways now employed in many parts of the world. Following these four chapters on the institutional relationships between man and the land it was logical to present the one dealing specifically with agrarian reform. The subject of settlement patterns is, of course, another important feature of man-land relationships, but it also is one which deals with the primary matters related to the structural aspects of the rural community. Therefore it is placed so as to precede immediately the chapter on community and community development. Finally, this part of the studies of social structure and the development process in Colombia is closed with the extremely important topic of social stratification and the class system.

2

The Size of the Holdings

DURING the course of a third of a century of professional work in the study of rural societies I became convinced that the size of agricultural holdings, the extent to which the ownership and control is either concentrated in a few hands or widely distributed among those who live by cultivating the soil, is the most important single determinant of the welfare of the people in rural districts. All of the following seem to be closely associated with a widespread distribution of property rights to the land: (1) strong propulsions to steady work and thrift; (2) high average levels and standards of living among the rural population taken as a whole; (3) relatively little development of social stratification, few class distinctions, the practical absence of caste (inheritance of social position), and, consequently, no significant amount of class conflict and struggle; (4) a fairly high degree of vertical social mobility because there are no important barriers to prevent the individual from attaining a status that is commensurate with his own natural abilities and the amount of effort he personally puts forth; (5) general intelligence of the rural population of a high average level and minimum in range; and (6) in general a rural citizenry possessed of the most highly developed and well-rounded personalities.

The opposite of this, or the concentration of ownership and control of the land in the hands of a few powerful landowners and the consequent reduction of the rural masses to the category of landless agricultural laborers, inevitably seems to produce: (1) extremely low average levels of living, even though the families of the landowning elite may live in fantastic luxury; (2) tremendous class differences between the favored few who occupy positions at the apex of the social pyramid and the toiling masses who lack rights to the soil; (3) relatively little vertical social mobility because caste is strong and the chasm between the elite and the masses is great so that the offspring of persons of low estate, even those endowed with rare natural gifts, find it almost impossible to ascend in the social scale;

7

(4) low average intelligence among the population because the great attainments of the select members of the small upper class are more than offset by the meager development of the personal qualities among the lower classes; (5) a people skilled only in the performance, under the closest supervision, of a limited number of manual tasks and lacking almost entirely in the ability to carry on the self-directing activities involved in managerial and entrepreneurial work; and (6) a society in which a premium is placed upon routine, regulation, and order, rather than innovation, progress, and change.

It would be a mistake to assert that all of the ills of Colombia and the other Latin American countries are due to the large estate, for as one studies societies to the south of the Rio Grande he encounters enough vicious circles to remind him of the workbook of the beginning student of the Palmer Method. Which of these comes first in the complicated sequences of cause and effect cannot, of course, be determined with precision. But to the extent that it is possible to disentangle the confused pattern, there seems to be adequate justification for singling out the concentration of landownership, the *latifundismo* of the Latin Americans, as the one factor that is most responsible for the host of social and economic ills which afflict the southern part of the Western Hemisphere. In no country are the deplorable effects of the maldistribution of landownership and control more evident than in Colombia; and for this reason it seems well to preface this discussion of the size of holdings in that country with a brief consideration of the two basic rural social systems[1] which have as central cores the large landed estate and the family-sized farm, respectively.

Two Sharply Contrasting Rural Social Systems

For the most part, or until recently when an urban and industrial way of life became characteristic of important sections of the earth's surface, the entire history of civilization has consisted of the "natural

---

1. Any long and involved discussion of the nature of a social system seems uncalled for. The important thing about a system of any kind is the organized, integrated, functional relationship between its components, as distinguished from a mere aggregation or physical togetherness. Thus the significance of the word system in the concept of social system is comparable to that which it has in terms such as weather system, organic system, astronomical system, telegraph system, and so on. The modifier which differentiates a *social* system from any other specifies that its components are human beings, groups, institutions, cultural traits, social classes, and so forth.

history" of two sharply contrasting forms of rural social organization. The *raison d'être* of the first of these, or the factor which has determined for the most part the structure, power, processes, and other fundamental characteristics of the system, is the large landed estate. This huge pastoral and agricultural unit, which is known by so many names such as plantation, hacienda, *cortijo, fundo, estancia,* latifundium, and so forth, was the principal one found during ancient times, throughout the medieval period, and until recently in most parts of the earth even during the modern period of man's existence. Furthermore it still persists in large portions of the world where it determines the mode of existence of a large part of the people who are living in this nuclear age. The institution which forms the central cell of the second rural social system is the agricultural unit of moderate size, that which properly is designated as the family-sized farm. This is the social entity which has been so successful during the nineteenth and twentieth centuries in bringing forth the abundance of agricultural and livestock products, in developing the capacities and abilities of the persons making up the masses of the rural population, and in elevating the levels and standards of living in parts of western Europe, Canada, the United States, and a few other countries. The degree, unfortunately high, to which human history is an account of slavery and other forms of servile and semi-servile labor is due almost exclusively to the predominant position that has been enjoyed by the large landed estate and the social system which was integrated with it, whereas the development of genuinely democratic political and administrative organization in the rural districts has gone hand in hand with the evolution and strengthening of a social system based upon the family-sized farm. Indeed it seems fair to say that the one or the other of these two social systems is the universe which determines the opportunities, activities, aspirations, accomplishments, ways of life, levels and standards of living, social interactions, and so on, of the people who live in the rural areas.

In order to indicate in a succinct and specific manner the principal features of the two rural social systems under consideration, Figure 1 has been prepared. In each of the two systems, the size of the agricultural units is taken as the nucleus and the purpose is to indicate that the other characteristics included, and also many others that might be added, are bound up in a cause and effect relationship with it and also with one another. Let us consider briefly a few of the interrelationships involved.

Social Stratification.—Wherever the large estate has a monopoly of the land, it follows that society will be divided into two sharply different social classes. At the one extreme is a small number of families of the large landowners, a social elite, possessed of all the attitudes and qualities of patricians or any other category of aristocrats.

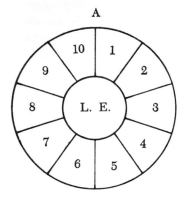

A. BASED UPON LARGE ESTATES

1 High degree of social stratification
2 Little vertical social mobility
3 Caste is an important factor
4 Low average intelligence
5 Restricted development of personality
6 "Order-obey" personal relations
7 Routine all-important
8 Manual labor is degrading
9 Low levels and standards of living
10 Little incentive to work and save

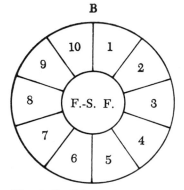

B. BASED UPON FAMILY-SIZED FARMS

1 Low degree of social stratification
2 Much vertical social mobility
3 Caste is unimportant
4 High average intelligence
5 Broad development of personality
6 Equalitarian personal relations
7 Search for improvement, progress, etc.
8 Manual labor considered dignifying
9 High levels and standards of living
10 Great incentive to work and save

Figure 1.—Schematic representation designed to give some of the principal features of the two over-all rural social systems.

They occupy positions at the apex of the social scale, have all the economic, political, and social power in their hands, insist upon an elaborate etiquette of domination and subordination in all of their dealings with persons of the low social order, and so on. At the other extreme, separated by a vast social and economic chasm from the members of the upper class, is the mass of the population made up of vast numbers of families headed by landless agricultural laborers. Living at levels near that of mere creature existence, uneducated and largely unskilled, and with little reason to suppose or even to hope that they or their children will ever be able to better substantially their unenviable lot, they can be classified only as belonging to a lower class.[2] Between the two there is little or nothing that merits designation as a middle social class; there is a lack of agriculturists capable of performing simultaneously all three of the basic economic functions (saving and investment of capital, management, and labor); and it is merely one species of self-deception to consider that an intermediate stratum, such as the very upper level of the lower class, corresponds to a genuine middle-class category.

Very different is the situation in the areas in which family-sized farms constitute the nucleus of the prevailing rural social system. In such zones, regions, or countries, families headed by farmers of middle-class status are in the great majority, hence social stratification is slight and for the most part only the middle social layers are represented. Members of an elite or aristocratic stratum are conspicuous by their absence, and even the most wealthy and most powerful families in such a society do not merit the designation of upper class. It is true that they occupy the highest levels in the society in question, but in reality such farmers lack the mentality, expectations, and behavior patterns of any kind of patricians. They are merely the upper layer of a broad middle class. If now and then a few of them attempt to imitate the ways of life of a genuine aristocrat, many of the things that they do may be utterly ridiculous.

At the same time such a society contains very few persons who actually can be classified as being of lower-class status. Very few heads of households will pass their entire lives in the unenviable socioeconomic positions of wage hands, peons, sharecroppers, or any other type of genuine agricultural laborers. This is to say that a true lower class is practically absent.

Where there is little or nothing corresponding to an upper class,

2. Perhaps it should be indicated that some types of large landed estates exist, such as sugar-cane plantations and huge dairy farms, in which the manufacturing or processing of the products takes place on the farm in fairly close association with the growing or production of the raw materials. In these cases, in effect, the manufacturing and processing activities call for skilled employees who may possess many of the characteristics of a middle social class. Nevertheless the strictly agricultural operations on such estates hardly constitute an exception to the rule.

on the one hand, or an actual lower class, on the other, the existing social stratification consists almost exclusively of the differences between the levels of the various strata which make up the middle-class range. Therefore, it would be just as ridiculous to designate the upper levels of such agriculturists as belonging to an upper class and the least influential and affluent farmers in such a society as being of lower-class status, as it is to attribute middle-class standing to the more fortunate part of the workers who are bound up in a system of large estates. It must be emphasized that in the form of rural social organization in which family-sized farms make up the core, the great majority of the agriculturists are at one and the same time persons who possess and invest modest amounts of capital, workers who themselves take the lead in the performance of all necessary tasks on the farm, and managers who have full responsibility for the planning and execution of all that is done in order to obtain crop and livestock products.

Vertical Social Mobility.—As another consequence of the concentration in a few hands of the ownership and control of the land, on the one hand, or a widespread distribution of the same, on the other, and also inextricably inter-linked with the nature of the class system, is the sharply different nature of vertical social mobility in the two rural social systems under consideration. Even though the system based upon large landed estates perpetuates one small class at the very top of the range and another very large one at the bottom, so that the distance between the two extremes is enormous, there can be very little vertical social mobility in the society involved. It is practically impossible for persons of humble origins to rise in the social scale and almost unthinkable that any of them should aspire to move upward enough to pass the broad gap that separates the one class from the other. At the same time, mutual assistance and the kinship obligations of those in the upper class serve to keep in lordly positions even the most incapable and the least deserving offspring of those of high social positions. Definitely the sons of the patricians, irrespective of how modest their natural endowments may be, do not have to descend the social scale to a status commensurate with their own personal characteristics. In brief the nature and structure of the class system in the rural society that is dominated by the large estates precludes any significant amount of vertical social mobility.

Quite different is the degree of shifting up and down the social scale in the rural social system in which the family-sized farm dominates the landscape and middle-class farmers constitute the population. The range in social position between those who occupy the lower rungs of the middle-class scale and those who are in places near the top of it is, of course, not very great. Nevertheless the amount of shifting, both up and down, that goes on is tremendous. By putting forth greater effort, exercising habits of thrift, taking advantage of the training available in a formal manner, and by experience, each farmer may considerably improve his own position and that of his family. Year after year he can add to the number of acres in his farm, improve his land and outbuildings, better his drains and fences, improve his equipment and livestock, add to the comfort and attractiveness of his home, and elevate his level of living. But at the same time his neighbor who is slightly inclined to work, who is never preoccupied with the problems of management, who makes little effort to save, who allows his land and equipment to deteriorate, who spends money freely on vices of one kind or another, and so on, is soon unable to maintain his position on the social scale. Little by little, or even with great suddeness, he may lose the ownership of his land, be unable to maintain his customary level of living, sink in the estimation of his fellows in the neighborhood and community, and, in a word, fall considerably in rank, power, and prestige. Not even family connections can enable such a person to maintain a favorable social position. In brief, even though the distances involved are short ones, the shifting up and down that takes place within a rural social system that grows out of a dominant role for the family-sized farm is intense; and a high degree of vertical social mobility must be considered as one of the fundamental characteristics of that social system.

Caste.—From what has been said with respect to the fundamental differences in the two rural social systems under consideration with respect to social stratification, it follows as a necessary corollary that the two-class system and the slight vertical social mobility of the one will make the inheritance of social position (or caste) an important characteristic of it, whereas the relatively free circulation up and down through the different layers of the middle-class sector will make caste of little consequence in the other. This difference is given further emphasis by the close association that has existed throughout the history of civilization between the social system based upon the large landed estate and slavery, serfdom, peonage, and all

Colombian farmer examining the coffee crop on his small farm in the department of Caldas. (Courtesy of the National Federation of Coffee Growers of Colombia.)

Family-sized farms in the Colombian highlands. (Courtesy of the Office of Foreign Agricultural Relations, U. S. Department of Agriculture.)

other forms of servile and semi-servile labor. In this connection it is
interesting to take cognizance of the generalizations of one of the
most perceptive of the founders of the science of sociology, Dr. E. A.
Ross, upon the basis of his own personal observations in the Spanish-
American countries of South America. Dr. Ross traveled and wrote
at a time when one could not use jet-propelled airplanes to flit from
one luxury hotel to another, and when, in order to make the journey
at all, it was necessary for one to be in intimate contact with muleteers, drovers, and many other persons of humble social positions.
Among the parts of his trip that were made muleback was that from
Buenaventura to Cali and other parts of the Cauca Valley, and his
interesting and valuable book contains numerous observations made
at the time in this highly favored section of Colombia. The following
comprehensive and accurate generalization was very appropriately
placed in the chapter which he entitled "Labor, Class and Caste":
"Most travelers in South America have no eye for the fundamentals
which make society there so different from our own. One may read
a bushel of the books visitors have written on these countries without
ever learning the momentous basic fact that *from the Rio Grande
down the West Coast to Cape Horn, free agricultural labor as we
know it does not exist.* In general, the laborers on the estates are at
various stages of mitigation of the once universal slavery into which
the native populations were crushed by the iron heel of the conquistador."[3]

Levels of Intelligence.—Wherever and whenever the great majority
of the rural population is restricted to the performance of a few
manual tasks under the watchful eye of some type of "driver," overseer, or *mayordomo,* the lifetime of drudgery that is the lot of the
common man means that most of his human potentialities remain
forever in an undeveloped state. In such societies one finds that the
inhabitants of the countryside remain in a creature-like condition
which bears little resemblance to the state of being of farm people
who have the responsibility for managing and operating the farms
which they own or rent on long-term leases. For this reason a low
average level of general intelligence (defined as the ability to adapt
to new situations) accompanies the features already indicated as
distinguishing the rural social system that is based on the large
landed estate, whereas a comparatively high average level forms

3. Ross, *South of Panama,* p. 144. Italics in original (complete information
concerning works cited will be found in the bibliography).

a part of the system of which family-sized farms make up the central trait.

The Development of Personality.—Also arising out of the two-class system and the relegation of the mass of rural humanity to the unenviable status of agricultural laborers, which are unavoidable features of the rural social system in which large estates monopolize the land, is a highly restricted development of the personality of the typical resident of the countryside, one that contrasts tremendously with the far greater development of human potentialities which takes place in the other rural social system we are considering. This aspect of the subject, of primordial importance for the sociologist, deserves a much more detailed treatment than would be proper for present purposes. Nevertheless it must be indicated and stressed, as is the case time after time in this volume, that in the one rural social system those who cultivate the soil are limited to the performance of only one of the three basic economic roles. They are mere instruments for supplying the labor needed for the preparation of the seed-bed, the planting and cultivation of the crops, the care of the livestock, the taking of the harvest, and the transportation of things on the estate and from the large territorial unit to the market, if perchance the hacienda or other large property is not almost exclusively of a subsistent nature. Stimuli and cultural norms do not encourage them, or, in most cases, even permit them to develop those portions of their potentialities which have to do with the saving and investment of capital, the planning and direction of the enterprises in which their toil is used (often with reckless abandon), and a deep and powerful interest in bettering their own lot and that of their children. As a result a highly restricted development of personality on the part of a large majority of all rural people is almost a "built-in" feature of the rural social system based upon the large landed estate.

How different in its impact upon the human personality is the web of mutually interrelated factors which are involved in the rural social system that is integrated about the family-sized farm. Therein from the moment of his birth the child is subject to conditioning by a drastically different set of forces and very early in his life he acquires the attitudes and behavior patterns having to do with the accumulation and investment of capital, an interest and facility in handling many of the problems of management, and a personal knowledge of and participation in the most skillful and effective

Small farms in the highlands of Colombia. (Courtesy of the Office of Foreign Agricultural Relations, U. S. Department of Agriculture.)

ways of applying labor in carrying on the work of the farm and in increasing its productivity and value. Far from being a mere lackey at the driver's beck and call or subject to the whims and idiosyncracies of any kind of overseer, such a person knows that he holds in his own hands the major responsibility for his welfare and that of his family. In brief he develops not the highly skewed personality of the agricultural laborer, but one much more in accord with the potentialities of the human being and one which represents considerable development of all the skills and attitudes that are required in order to perform the social roles of the owner of modest amounts of capital, those of the administrator or manager, and also those of the agricultural laborer.

Personal Relationships.—Intimately related as cause and effect in each of the respective rural social systems also are the distinctive features of the relationships between person and person in a society which owes its being to the plantation or other large landed estate, or in one in which the family-sized farm gives form and substance to such relationships. Most striking of the differences in this respect are those between the order-and-obey pattern of domination and subordination which arises from the two-class system of the one and the predominantly equalitarian types of social interaction which are produced by the other. In some cases, it is true, the subserviency which is institutionalized among the masses who toil on the great estates may be mitigated in various ways. At least the old adage "misery loves company" finds abundant opportunity for being put to the test in the rural social system in which the great bulk of the cultivators are maintained throughout life in the unenviable status of agricultural laborers; and not infrequently a menial of some lordly master will in his dealings with those from other estates or in other positions try to bask in the reflected glory of the great one whom he serves.[4] Even the phenomenon of leadership within the two rural social systems has little in common, since it is almost a travesty to use such a term as a designation for the compliance with orders that typifies the caciquism of the one; whereas it specifically denotes

4. On this point the observations of Henry Koster, an Englishman who operated sugar-cane plantations in northeastern Brazil during the opening years of the nineteenth century, are especially revealing. He reports: "I frequently visited the plantation of Amparo, which is conducted in the manner that I had attempted at Jaguaribe: but here it is performed with more system. The owner of this place employed constantly great numbers of free workers, of all castes. But the Indians formed the principal part of them. . . . One of these Indians

the capacity of the leader to secure and help direct the thoughts and actions of others of approximately his own social and economic status which is characteristic of the other.

Emphasis upon Established Routine versus Search for Progress.— Largely because the endeavor to secure an adequate input of management in agricultural enterprises is so complex and difficult, routine comes to represent a social value of extraordinary importance in societies that are dominated by the large landed estate. Indeed if such an estate manages to depart from the type in which the production of subsistence crops and self-sufficiency for its own little principality dominates the thinking of those who monopolize the ownership and control of the land, it is almost certain to resort to monoculture and other practices which can reduce to the utmost simplicity the tasks which the peons, slaves, sharecroppers, and other categories of laborers must be responsible for performing, and which the overseers, drivers, or gang leaders must see to it are done in the specified manner. In this situation an innovation of any type is considered undesirable, and the worker who dares depart from the prescribed manner of doing a job is far more likely to receive reprimand and punishment, often with the lash, than to be given a reward of any type. The best laborer is the one who performs hour after hour, day after day, and year in and year out, under the watchful eye of his supervisor, in exactly the same way, the few rudimentary physical activities involved. In such a social system the importance of routine for the successful performance of the work of management and the low esteem in which the laborer and his work are held forestalls even the first steps in the improvement of agricultural methods.[5]

was selling crabs at Pasmado, when a purchaser began to pick out those he preferred; but the Indian stopped him, saying 'Don't begin to pick my crabs, for I belong to Amparo.' Thus even the crabs which were caught by the dependents of this great man were to be respected." *Travels in Brazil*, II, 18-19.

5. This is not to deny that *after* improved implements, sources of power, and techniques in general have been developed in the rural social system based upon the family-sized farms and for the operators of family-sized farms, some of the improved practices may not be borrowed by those who are responsible for large estates devoted to monoculture in various parts of the world. Even in this case, though, there is considerable lag between the time in which such improvements are developed, tried, and tested in the former and the time they become functional in the latter. Thus it was not until the crisis of the 1930's that the machines and implements which began about 1910 to transform life and labor in the midwestern and other family-sized farming sections

How different from all this is the manner in which various forces make for change and progress in the rural social system based upon family-sized farms, one in which the head of each agricultural family is at the same time a capitalist on a small scale, a person who works with his own hands, and, above all, one who must concentrate throughout his lifetime on all the mental activities connected with the performance of the managerial role. The mere fact that the one responsible for planning and directing the various farm enterprises is also the one chiefly responsible for the performance of the required manual labor gives a strong and constant stimulus to the search for less laborious, more effective, and more productive ways of tilling the soil, controlling weeds and pests, taking the harvest, and transporting things from place to place on the farm and from the farm to the market. Moreover, such a system lacks any type of overseer or driver charged with the responsibility of seeing to it that each worker performs each task in the specified, routine way, so that the cultivator is free to study and experiment with alternatives of one kind or another. Essentially for this reason, with very few exceptions (of which the English landlords of the eighteenth and nineteenth centuries, an aristocracy it should be noted who lived on their estates in constant contact with their retainers and their fields and herds, are the principal ones) family-sized farm operators are chiefly responsible for all the revolutionary developments in the ways of getting crop and livestock products from the soil that have taken place in the nineteenth and twentieth centuries.

Attitude with Respect to Manual Labor.—One indelible mark of the large estate, the two-class form of social stratification which it engenders, and the various other features of the rural social system it produces, is the attitude it creates and perpetuates toward manual labor. In brief, wherever large agricultural holdings dominate the rural scene, manual labor is considered to be degrading, to be the mark which identifies one belonging in the lower social class. This,

---

of the United States began to find a place on the cotton plantations of the South; and, as indicated elsewhere in this volume, it was not until after the Second World War that this mechanized system of agriculture began to assume some importance on the sugar-cane, cotton, and rice plantations of Colombia. But all of this involves merely the transplantation to plantation areas of machinery, implements, practices, and skills that were developed in and for a rural social system based upon the family-sized farm. On the role of the family-sized farm in the discovery, invention, and diffusion of agricultural implements and machines, see Smith, "El Desarrollo de Unidades Agrícolas Medianas."

certainly, was one of the principal thoughts in the mind of Sir Richard Burton, perhaps the most observant and widely-traveled person in an age in which to travel meant to be in intimate contact with the daily life of the people visited, when he wrote: "Far below us the Parahybuna brawled down its apology for a bed. Houses and fields became more frequent, and the curse of the great proprietors is no longer upon the land. (Their effect is that which has been in France, which was in the Southern States of the Union, and which is in Great Britain. When will the political economist duly appreciate the benefit derived from the subdivision of land?)"[6]

But be that as it may, the close association that has existed throughout history and in all parts of the earth between large landed estates and slavery or other forms of servile labor is indicative of the cause and effect relationship between the two and of the inevitable tendency for manual labor, the primary role of the slave, serf, or peon, to become the symbol of lowly social position. Moreover, if perchance the slaves or serfs are of different racial or ethnic groups than the masters, the formers' physical characteristics also tend to become symbolic of a mean position in life. It may become almost impossible to eradicate the depreciative connotations of manual labor and certain physical features, such as the color of the skin or the texture of the hair, even after the society in point has passed from an agricultural economy to an urbanized, industrialized basis.[7]

Radically different from the stigmatizing nature of manual labor in plantation areas and other sections given over to large estates, is the attitude toward work with the hands in the zones in which family-sized farms and middle-class farm operators exercise control over the lives and fortunes of those who live in the neighborhoods and communities. In the social systems prevailing in such rural areas, manual labor is considered as dignifying and uplifting, and the stigma is upon anyone who, except on the basis of physical inability to work, attempts to shy away from the performance of his share of the tasks to be done. The middle-class farmer himself performs the labor function and teaches his children from their most tender years to do the

6. Burton, *Explorations of the Highlands of the Brazil,* I, 47.

7. As exemplified by the manner in which the heritage from the plantation system and Negro slavery in the southern part of the United States, keeps the entire nation embroiled in bitter struggles and conflicts involving relationships between white people and Negroes more than a century after the abolition of slavery.

same. Under no circumstances in such a social system can manual labor be thought of as degrading.

Levels of Living.—As a general rule the rural people who are entrapped through birth in a social system dominated by large estates and the two-class type of social stratification have very low levels of living. With a few exceptions, in which the aspirations are conspicuous for the degree to which they are unrealistic, the standards of living of the people are equally low. This feature of one of the rural social systems under consideration is due primarily to the wantonness with which labor is wasted in the production process, the depreciation in which manual work is held, and the relatively small production that legitimately may be attributed to the man-year in such a mode of agricultural organization. It is due also to the tremendous power of the great landowners and the lack of humanitarian qualities on the part of the vast majority of them. Throughout history there has been a close interrelationship between large estates (of which the Mexican haciendas during the regime of Porfirio Díaz may be mentioned as an excellent example) and a subsistence type of agricultural economy, and this has contributed to the small production per man involved in the process. Generally, of course, the powerful landowners have taken the lion's share of everything produced for themselves, but even in the cases in which this is not true, the production per person is very low. Even on the large plantations and other large, commercialized farms, a strikingly low level of living is the lot of the vast majority of all those who must live from agriculture.

All of this is quite different in the rural social system which grows up and becomes integrated about the family-sized farm and the farmer of middle-class status. If perchance, and this rarely has been the case, these middle-class farm operators have possession and control of rich, fertile land, and a few other factors are favorable, the productivity of the farms and the levels of living of the farmers come to be the highest in the world. But irrespective of the fertility of the soil, when it is the general rule for each farmer to be at the same time one who saves and invests capital on a small scale, one who does the manual work on the farm, and one responsible for the management, agricultural production tends to be maximized. This not only brings about an abundance of crop and livestock products, but it also goes far to insure a fairly equitable distribution of the same among all those who have a share in the process. Such a social system lacks any highly favored elite who may take over a major share of the products. However, it should be mentioned that in most countries the rural social system is only one part of the great society, and that in the interchange between the rural and urban portions of any country the problem of distribution may be of primordial importance. Not infrequently the share going to the agricultural sector may appear to be absurdly low, and phrases having to do with overproduction may be on every tongue. Nevertheless, in comparison with the problems of societies in which the dominance of the large estates maintains for generation after generation a very low level of production per man, the problem of the maldistribution of the benefits of abundant output of food and fiber dwindles into relative unimportance.

The Stimulus to Habits of Regular Work and Saving.—As the last of the differences between the components of the two rural social systems to be mentioned in this chapter, it seems necessary to include the radically different nature of the compulsions to regular work and habits of thrift which form integral portions of the two integrated patterns of organization and activity. Very weak indeed is the stimulus to regular work activities in the rural social system based upon large estates and the two-class type of social stratification, and very strong is that stimulus in the other. Deserving to be stressed repeatedly is the fact that in the former the agricultural population must be made up almost exclusively of peons or other agricultural laborers, menial types at least even if they are not held in conditions of actual or semi-servitude. Under such circumstances the individual best serves his own interests if he avoids in every way possible any expenditure of his own energy in the labors on the estate or plantation. His capacities to think for himself are directed in large measure to the ways and means by which he may do the least work possible. Likewise, since he has no reason whatsoever to suppose that either he or his offspring can ascend in the social scale, it would be extremely irrational on his part to save any part of his meager earnings, even in the most favorable situations possible in such a system, that is the fairly rare ones in which the workers are not actually enchained by some type of debt servitude. If by any chance it became possible for the peons and other agricultural laborers, including those classified as sharecroppers, to save significant amounts and to move up the social ladder, such vertical social mobility would have the inevitable consequence of subdividing the great estates in a single generation. But all this is virtually impossible in the social system under consideration, and the workers have neither strong propulsions to work and to save, nor even hope for much improvement of their lot in any manner. As a result, to work the least possible and to lack capital accumulation are fundamental features of the rural society in which the large estates dominate the landscape.

All this, of course, is vastly different with the middle-class operator of a substantial farm. Day and night he is preoccupied with problems related to the management of his land, the maintenance and improvement of his buildings and fences, the best ways to care for his plants and animals, the most effective use of his machines and implements, and so on. From early morning until late night his hours are dedicated to mental and physical activities for which there is never sufficient time. The stimuli which impinge upon him always call for greater effort and never for the best and most effective ways in which to deceive some overseer or driver. The enlargement and improvement of his farm leads him to make maximum efforts to save and accumulate capital, and even within the family budget the multifarious expenditures in the cost of living must face the stiffest of competition with those for farm operations. The addition of a few more acres to the farm, the improvement of barns and sheds, the upkeep of fences and drainage systems, and so on, must be on his mind day and night, year in and year out. Furthermore, he is almost always driven by the aspiration that each of his children will occupy a position in the social scale that is higher than his own, and he tries in every way to make this possible through formal schooling, the enlargement of the farm, the improvement of farm practices, and so on. In brief the stimulus to steady hard work and substantial saving reaches its maximum among the agriculturists who have their being in a rural social system that is integrated about the family-sized farm.

CLASSIFICATIONS

Sociologists and economists have still to devise a classification of land holdings and agricultural units according to size that will be entirely satisfactory, and there is slight chance that this will be accomplished anytime in the near future. However, for the present purposes of analyzing the situation in Colombia it seems necessary to divide the agricultural units into at least three categories: large estates or haciendas; family-sized farms; and small subsistence tracts or estancias. Moreover, it probably is well to distinguish those large estates, or plantations, which are devoted to rather intensive uses for the production of such commercial crops as sugar cane, cotton, coffee, and rice, from the vast majority of all the large holdings or units which produce little or nothing for the market except a few cattle of the poorest quality and on which even the predominantly subsistence activities of the workers yield only the most precarious type of a living. This type of large estate or hacienda is, of course, the one that has predominated in Colombia and most other parts of Latin America for more than 400 years and is the one largely responsible for the opprobrium presently carried by the terms *latifundio, latifundista,* and *latifundismo* throughout Spanish America and Brazil.[8]

8. The ill effects of this prevalent type of large estates in Colombia are documented at many places in this volume, but even so it seems well at this point to present in summary form the report of one high governmental official upon one specific latifundium as it was given in *El Tiempo* of Bogotá, Colombia's great daily newspaper, on October 7, 1943. The report actually dealt with the municipio of Chiquisa, Boyacá, which is situated high in the eastern cordillera between Tunja, capital of the department, and the decadent old colonial city of Leiva. In a rather literal translation this report reads as follows.

"This place, which is improperly called a municipio, consists for all practical purposes of the latifundium called 'Iguaque,' which once belonged to the community of Augustine Brothers, and which occupies the larger and better portion of its territory. The total population does not exceed 2,000 inhabitants, the majority of whom are arrendatarios on the Iguaque hacienda. The president and vice president of the municipio's Council are Señors N. and Y., respectively, it is said through direct hereditary transmission from their deceased predecessor in the possession of the latifundium, because as I was informed by some authorities and residents of the area, it is a long time since there were elections for membership in the Council in Chiquisa. . . .

"That which has been called the village of Chiquisa is nothing more than an old church, a house for the priest, a municipal building, and two huts, rather removed from the other buildings. No more than 20 persons live there. The school officially designated as that of Chiquisa is held in the home of Señorita Anita Rojas, a half hour's distance from the buildings mentioned. The alcalde is entitled to a salary of 10 pesos monthly and the judge to one of 15 pesos, which have never been paid. The employees live at a distance and have never been seen in the municipal building. The treasurer, Señorita X, is not provided for in the budget because the Council never meets; she collects some taxes, but has an order from the *Controlaria* of the department to pay no employees. . . .

"From information volunteered I learned that the employees are maintained from portions of the tithes and church fees which are allowed them for the aid they give in obliging the campesinos to make the annual payment, which amounts to 1.20 pesos for the smallest contributors. The children who attend school have nothing to eat during the ten hours (from 7:00 A.M. to 5:00 P.M. when they return to their homes) except a little corn meal or barley flour mixed with a thin cane syrup."

Of course, since the first Colombian census of agriculture was not taken until 1960, and even many of the essential tabulations were not published until late in 1964, most of the basic analyses of the data, such as those needed to discover the correlates of plantations and of other large estates, are still to be done. However, the principal connotations of the terms "plantation," "hacienda," and "estancia" or "parcela" are generally known by informed Colombians, as are the differences between the first two of them and the high degree to which "hacienda" and "estancia" are merely two features of a single system of large estates in which subsistence activities are the dominating economic objectives in the pattern. The second category, though, needs considerable clarification, especially by anyone in Colombia or elsewhere who attempts to compare the social organization of agriculture in that country with the situation in Canada, the United States, Great Britain, Denmark, West Germany, or any other part of the world in which the "farmer class" is numerically, socially, and economically important. In most parts of Colombia the class structure and class distinctions are such, and the stigma attached to manual labor so great, that only those who have no alternative will engage directly and personally in work on the farm. If a person possesses as much as 100 acres of land, it is almost a foregone conclusion that he will not farm it himself and that he will not even make his home on the land. Rather than to personally accept and execute all three of the functions (investor of capital, manager, and laborer) of the owner-operator of a farm in a rural society in which the middle social class is strong, the Colombian who owns a hundred or two hundred acres of land will delegate the managerial function to some overseer and will have the labor performed by a considerable number of peons. Therefore, as a general rule, the proprietor either possesses enough land so that he can have a number of laborers engaged in its cultivation, or he has so little land that he himself must seek additional employment in order to support himself and his family.

The places that are worked with the aid of agricultural laborers of one category or another are generally called haciendas, or fincas, especially if the crop is coffee, while the small minifundia on which the owners or "renters" grow a few subsistence crops to help feed their families are called estancias. Family-sized units, which to avoid misunderstanding in Colombia and elsewhere in Latin America generally must be referred to as medium-sized farms, or those of an extension adequate to offer full and steady employment to the operator and the members of his family, making use of whatever they can muster in the way of equipment, workstock, and power equipment, and not so large that the bulk of the labor comes from sources outside the immediate family, are a rarity in most parts of Colombia. As a matter of fact, and in spite of the stated objectives of the Agrarian Reform Law of 1961, it probably will be almost impossible for them to be established unless ways and means can be found that will remove the stigma presently attached to working with the hands. However, it should be emphasized that many of the small fincas, most of them given over to the production of coffee, presently operated by the descendants of the hardy pioneers from Antioquia who carved them out of the forests in what is now the departamento of Caldas, are family-sized farms in the strictest sense of the term.

Few efforts by Colombians to classify the nation's landholdings according to size have come to my attention. It is likely, however, that there would be little disagreement on most points with the one by Emilio Cuervo Márquez[9] which is available. The classification in question is given in a brief paragraph, of which the following is a literal translation.

> Relative to their extension, the rural properties in Colombia may be divided into four large groups. To the first belong the latifundios called "concessions," generally of more than 20,000 hectares, which the State ceded to individuals under the title of "baldios," and which they hold without cultivating or exploiting; to the second the properties, or "haciendas," of from 50 to 20,000 hectares which their owners have cultivated in whole or in part; to the third the "quintas" or "casas de campo" of from 10 to 50 hectares, recreational properties which are not devoted to cultivation; and finally, the properties of less than 5 hectares, or "estancias," which are cultivated personally by their owners.

It is to be noted that holdings of from 10 to 50 hectares (25 to 125 acres) enter into consideration only as places of recreation, and that tracts with from 5 to 10 hectares are omitted entirely. For practical purposes the agricultural holdings in Colombia as defined by Cuervo Márquez consist of the large places cultivated by means of employed workers and the small subsistence plots tilled by their owners.

This author's use of the term latifundia also is worthy of comment. Few Colombian's would agree that it should be limited to those un-

9. *La Cuestión Agraria en Colombia,* p. 22.

used concessions which measure more than 20,000 hectares in extent, although most of them probably would accept the proposition that latifundia are not merely large estates. In common with other Latin Americans they seem to regard the latifundium as the large landed property which is deliberately withheld from productive purposes. In this connection it should be noted that where a land tax is practically lacking, as is the case in Colombia and most other Latin American countries, land tends to become an asylum for capital. With impunity its owners may see it lie idle year after year, generation after generation, without fear that taxes will "eat up the property."

To complement the expression latifundia, in Colombia, Ecuador, and Venezuela the very significant designation of *minifundia* is widely applied to the small subsistence tracts owned by the campesinos. These are the small plots which Cuervo Márquez classifies as estancias, little acreages that are too small to support a humble family of peasants even at the pitifully low levels of living to which they are accustomed. That Latin America in general suffers severely from the blighting effects of the hacienda system is widely known, but that Colombia and her Andean neighbors are plagued with acute problems of the minifundia has received practically no mention beyond the borders of the countries themselves.

In the most penetrating analysis of the size of the agricultural estates and farming units that has been done in Colombia, Fals-Borda[10] based his own classification partly on the categories used by Cuervo Márquez and partially on that employed by Smith, Díaz Rodríguez, and García in their study of the municipio of Tabio.[11] This resulted in the following categories: latifundia, which he viewed more in terms of idleness than in those of magnitude; haciendas, or estates of more than 50 *fanegadas;*[12] fincas, or places containing from 5 to 50 fanegadas; and minifundia, or the small parcels of less than 5 fanegadas. Some of the observations made by Fals-Borda with respect to the characteristics of the landed estates and agricultural units of various sizes also are unexcelled in the extent to which they convey insight into the basic nature of the latifundium, the hacienda, the finca, and the minifundio, respectively. Thus he indicates that "the latifundium is a large landed estate which has been withheld from productive uses either because of its location in remote areas,

10. Fals-Borda, *El Hombre y la Tierra en Boyacá*, pp. 141-48.
11. Smith, Díaz, and García, *Tabio*.
12. A fanegada is a unit of approximately 1.6 acres.

or because of agricultural practices of the extensive type in areas where this type is not justified economically. It may include many thousands of fanegadas. This class of holding was predominant in Boyacá during colonial times, and it even grew in importance at the end of the wars for independence, when immense concessions were granted to the generals. For example, the Territorio Vásquez belonged to General Francisco de Paula Santander. However, with the increase of population and the coming of successive generations of heirs it has retreated from the central and mountainous area of the department toward the periphery, that is, toward the llanos, the northern forests, and the Territorio Vásquez."[13]

Haciendas in Boyacá stand in striking contrast with minifundia. "There is an almost invariable rule that the haciendas lie on the beautiful, level expanses of land formed between the Andean ranges, while the small holdings occupy the rugged terrain." Moreover, whereas "the latifundium implies much absenteeism on the part of the owner, the hacienda seems to function on the basis of part-time supervision by the landlord. The owner of an hacienda generally has an overseer, or mayordomo, to look after the menial tasks on the farm, but the owner comes often to the place in order to manage its affairs."[14]

Fincas, or places containing from 5 to 50 fanegadas, "are more difficult to see in the countryside, but they are found throughout Boyacá." They are not associated with any particular type of crop. "The coffee fincas . . ., for example, have little in common with their counterparts in Caldas and Antioquia. They have not permitted the development of a true middle class of farmers. On the contrary, the *arrendatario* system has been transferred to this crop."[15]

One familiar with the rural landscape in Colombia always tends to associate the minifundia with Boyacá. "The campesinos who live on the minifundia, . . . because frequently of the poor soils which are encountered on their steep slopes, to poor seed and rudimentary techniques, or to the lack of water, find it difficult to live from the products of their small tracts, and almost always they are compelled to seek work elsewhere in order to supplement their incomes and be able to live."[16]

13. Fals-Borda, *El Hombre y la Tierra en Boyacá*, p. 143.
14. *Ibid.*, pp. 143-45.
15. *Ibid.*, pp. 145-46.
16. *Ibid.*, p. 146.

DISTRIBUTION OF EXPLOTACIONES AGROPECUARIAS BY SIZE

As indicated in Chapter 3 Colombia at last attempted its first agricultural census in 1960, and the definitive results of that enumeration have now been made available in some detail. Unfortunately the concepts and procedures used in making the census were such that one can neither determine with any degree of accuracy the number and sizes of the farms nor the number of landowners and the distribution of their properties according to magnitude. What we do have is information about what was designated as *explotaciones agropecuarias,* a category that includes farms of all sizes and also all of the subsistence tracts, whether owned by or assigned to the agricultural laborers of various types. By arbitrarily eliminating all of the units of less than a certain size, such as those containing less than two hectares, it may be possible to approximate somewhat closely the number of farms; but the fact that the large landowners may and generally do own a number of estates in different locations makes it absolutely impossible to derive from the census data any reliable information about the distribution of the ownership of the land in Colombia. Some of the data relative to the reported sizes of the explotaciones agropecuarias are given in the analysis of the relationship between size and tenure (see tables 5, 6, and 7), and others are presented here in an endeavor to learn a little more about the number and nature of various kinds of agricultural and stock-raising units.

Land in Explotaciones and Its Uses.—Colombia's agricultural census reports wisely limit the data presented to those for the settled parts of the national territory which have been organized for administrative purposes into 17 departments or provinces. Together these departments include about 579,000 square kilometers of area, or about 51 per cent of the 1,138,000 which is calculated to be the total for the Republic. Even within the departments, however, the major part of the surface is either barren mountain tops, swampland and jungle that have not yet been claimed as private property, or land suitable for agricultural and pastoral uses which have not yet been settled. Thus of some 57,900,000 hectares in the 17 departments, only 27,371,771 hectares (or 47.3 per cent) are accounted for by the land of all types given by the census as the total land in explotaciones agropecuarias in 1960.

According to the uses to which it is put, the census officials divided the land in explotaciones agropecuarias in Colombia into six categories.

These, along with the number of hectares and the percentage of the total in each one of them, are as follows: arable land, cultivated, 1,952,987, or 7.1 per cent; arable land, fallow, 1,578,971, or 5.8 per cent; land in permanent plantings (such as coffee or cacao trees), 1,515,130, or 5.5 per cent; land in pastures, 14,605,954, or 53.4 per cent; land in forests or woodlands, 6,387,024, or 23.4 per cent; and other land, 1,297,761, or 4.8 per cent. These data lend strong support to two generalizations repeated frequently throughout this book and found disseminated throughout the writings of Colombians and others familiar with the Colombian scene. They are the lack of interest in agricultural matters and the concentration of capital and effort in pastoral activities on the part of the Spaniards and their descendants in the New World; and the close association between cattle ranching and latifundismo throughout the history of Colombia.[17] Figure 2 has been prepared in order to show how the amounts of land in "farms," the proportion this is of the total area, and the chief uses of the land vary throughout the departments into which the more settled parts of the Republic are divided.

For present purposes it is sufficient to emphasize only a few points out of the many that could be based upon the data presented on this map. First, one should stress that despite the fact that the parts of Colombia that figure in this portrayal have been occupied for more than four centuries, there still remain huge expanses of unclaimed territory within the limits of the departments into which the settled

17. Perhaps, though, it is advisable to insert a couple of additional items at this point. For example, long before the census of agriculture offered a firm statistical basis for the observation, a report of the head of the National Department of Agriculture indicated that "cattle raising constitutes the nation's rural enterprise par excellence. On the average it is in a ratio of between 13 and 20 to 1, or in other words the *hacendados,* and especially the great rural landowners, and of the latter those who have land in the hot zones, make up from 80 to 87 per cent of the cattlemen." *Memoria del Ministerio de Agricultura y Comercio 1937,* Bogotá: Talleres Graficos "Mundo al Día," 1938, I, 128. On another page of the same report is to be found the following explicit statement of the relationship: "Latifundismo is most pronounced in cattle raising. There are extensive pastoral estates for the breeding, raising, and fattening of cattle in the rich valleys of the Sinú, San Jorge, Lower Cauca, Patía, Cauca, and Magdalena rivers; on the plains of Carmen de Bolívar, Corozal, San Marcos, Valledupar, and Casanaré; and on the llanos to the east and of the Caquetá in general." *Ibid.,* p. 107. See also Bell, *Colombia,* pp. 138-39, who along with other pertinent comments has the following to say: "On the Caribbean coast there are great areas of excellent level lands of alluvial formation which are said to rival those of Cuba for sugar cane, tobacco, rice, etc., but which are planted in Para grass and devoted to cattle raising."

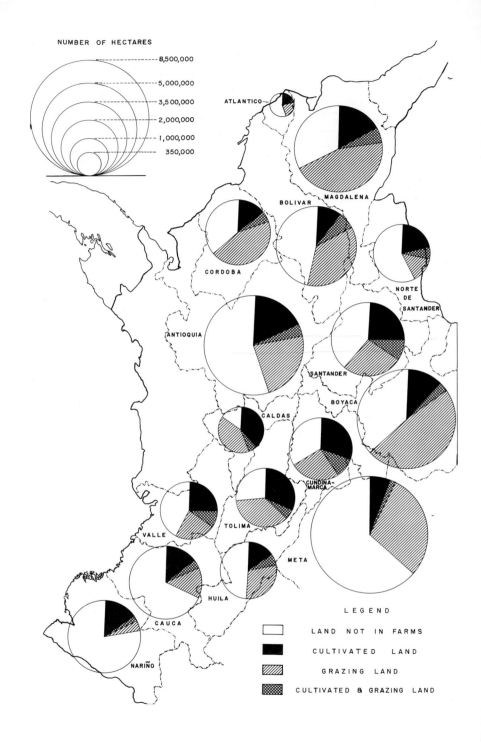

NUMBER OF HECTARES

8,500,000
5,000,000
3,500,000
2,000,000
1,000,000
350,000

ATLANTICO

MAGDALENA

BOLIVAR

CORDOBA

NORTE
DE
SANTANDER

ANTIOQUIA

SANTANDER

BOYACA

CALDAS

CUNDINA-
MARCA

TOLIMA

VALLE

META

HUILA

CAUCA

NARIÑO

LEGEND

LAND NOT IN FARMS

CULTIVATED LAND

GRAZING LAND

CULTIVATED & GRAZING LAND

sections of the nation are divided. In the department of Caldas alone, where the terrain is among the most rugged in the country, is as much as three-fourths of the area included within the limits of the agricultural and stock-raising establishments. Next, of the land that is claimed, legally or illegally, it is important to note that in most parts of the Republic the acreages used or intended for use in agricultural activities are relatively small in comparison with the areas devoted to or reportedly being held for pastoral purposes. Nariño, Norte de Santander, Cundinamarca, Cauca, and El Valle are the departments which either are or come nearest to being exceptions to this rule. Finally, one should not examine this map without observing the tremendous areas—and from all reports many of them are of exceptionally fertile lands—that are devoted to or designed for pastoral activities and the preponderance of the same over those used or intended for crops and plantings in the following departments: Meta, Boyacá, Magdalena, Bolívar, and Córdoba.

One of the more significant compilations of data in the Colombian agricultural census reports is a table in which the explotaciones agropecuarias are classified into the categories of agricultural, pastoral, poultry-raising, bee-keeping, and mixed (almost exclusively agricultural-pastoral, no doubt, and surely mainly pastoral), in cross-tabulation with the magnitude of the areas within the limits of the explotaciones. In its most general aspects this important information confirms the generalization, so frequently encountered in the works of Colombian writers and stressed time and again in this volume, that the Spaniards and their Colombian descendants have been mainly interested in livestock and pastures and that inordinately large shares of all the best land in Colombia have been monopolized by the extensive grazing estates of a relatively small number of large landowners. Thus these 1960 census data indicate that of the total of 1,209,672 explotaciones containing an area of 27,337,827 hectares, the following numbers and proportions were classified as belonging in each of the respective categories: agricultural, 912,662 or 75.4 per cent of the units and including 8,392,039 hectares, or 30.7 per cent of the area; pastoral, 166,676 or only 13.8 per cent of the explotaciones but involving 16,470,914 hectares, or 60.2 per cent of the area; poultry-raising, 51,763 or 4.3 per cent of the establishments but ac-

---

Figure 2.—Amounts of land in explotaciones agropecuarias, proportions these are of total land areas, and principal uses of the land, by departments, 1960.

counting for only 20,707 hectares, or a mere 0.1 per cent of the land; bee-keeping, 143 explotaciones using 143 hectares, both so insignificant that it might have been well to have omitted them from the tabulation; and mixed, 78,428 units, or 6.5 per cent of all, and containing 2,453,805 hectares, or 9.0 per cent of the "land in farms."

In order to present the more significant details of the cross-classification available, Table 1 was prepared. It shows for those explotaciones that were classified as agricultural and pastoral, respectively, how the establishments and the areas within them are distributed in accordance with the size of the units. Observation of these data makes crystal clear the very close association in Colombia between agriculture or the growing of crops and very small farms, on the one hand, and between pastoral activities or ranching and large landed estates, or the holdings that Colombians designate as latifundia, on the other. Among other things, the data given in this table, along with those to be found in the preceding paragraphs, make it possible to show that a mere 26,672 of the explotaciones of the pastoral type, or those in this category which are above 100 hectares in size, include a total of 13,915,947 hectares, or more than one-half of all the "land in farms" in Colombia.

High Degree of Concentration in the Ownership and Control of the Land.—The data from the 1960 census of agriculture now make it possible to demonstrate conclusively a fundamental fact that long has been known upon the basis of far less satisfactory information, namely, that the ownership of the nation's agricultural and pastoral lands is highly concentrated in the hands of the members of a few powerful families. The conventional way of showing the extent to which a few owners and other farm operators have control of inordinately large shares of the land is by means of a tabulation such as is given in Table 2. It shows simultaneously the numbers and proportions of the farmers who have establishments of the various stated sizes and of the amounts and proportions of the land in farms in all of the size categories. From it one can easily see that the official census data show that a mere 1.7 per cent of the "producers," or the 20,595 of them with explotaciones of above 200 hectares in size, account for 55.1 per cent of all the land, whereas the 50.2 per cent of the "producers" with places of less than 3 hectares have the use of only 2.4 per cent of the land and the 62.6 per cent of them with establishments of less than 5 hectares have only 4.4 per cent of it. Fortunately, due to the simple fact elaborated upon in Chapter 3

TABLE 1

NUMBERS AND PROPORTIONS OF THE "PRODUCERS" WITH AGRICULTURAL AND WITH PASTORAL EXPLOTACIONES AND THE AREAS AND PROPORTIONS OF THE TOTAL AREA IN THEIR ESTABLISHMENTS, ACCORDING TO THE SIZE OF THE EXPLOTACIONES, 1960

Size of the explotaciones (hectares)	Agricultural explotaciones				Pastoral explotaciones			
	"Producers"		Areas		"Producers"		Areas	
	Number	Per cent	Hectares	Per cent	Number	Per cent	Hectares	Per cent
Total	912,662	100.0	8,392,039	100.0	166,676	100.0	16,470,914	100.0
Under 0.5	93,849	10.3	26,028	0.3	18,687	11.2	3,319	0.0
0.5–0.9	116,702	12.8	83,636	1.0	6,337	3.8	4,196	0.0
1.0–1.9	173,388	19.0	245,341	2.9	9,196	5.5	13,035	0.1
2.0–2.9	104,576	11.5	246,071	2.9	6,910	4.2	16,466	0.1
3.0–3.9	80,225	8.8	269,383	3.2	6,917	4.2	23,303	0.1
4.0–4.9	49,639	5.4	214,849	2.6	4,968	3.0	21,467	0.1
5.0–9.9	135,382	14.8	926,735	11.0	20,660	12.4	145,817	0.9
10.0–19.9	79,998	8.8	1,090,340	13.0	22,470	13.5	316,467	1.9
20.0–29.9	26,734	2.9	630,925	7.5	12,078	7.3	287,438	1.8
30.0–39.9	14,474	1.6	484,254	5.8	8,726	5.2	294,003	1.8
40.0–49.9	8,323	0.9	360,440	4.3	5,866	3.5	255,119	1.6
50.0–99.9	17,870	2.0	1,171,322	14.0	17,189	10.3	1,174,337	7.1
100.0–199.9	7,603	0.8	992,928	11.8	12,072	7.2	1,644,744	10.0
200.0–499.9	3,165	0.3	868,840	10.4	9,037	5.4	2,685,749	16.3
500.0–999.9	555	0.1	357,046	4.2	3,192	1.9	2,115,298	12.8
1,000–2,499.9	145	0.0	198,258	2.4	1,659	1.0	2,372,198	14.4
2,500–over	34	0.0	225,643	2.7	712	0.4	5,097,958	31.0

Source: compiled and computed from data in Departamento Administrativo Nacional de Estadística, "Resumen Nacional (Segunda Parte)," *Directorio Nacional de Explotaciones Agropecuarias (Censo Agropecuario), 1960.* Bogotá: Multilith Estadinal, 1964, p. 40.

that a large proportion of the farm laborers are included in the "producer" group, this tabulation for Colombia is a much closer reflection of the reality than is generally the case with similar compilations of materials for other countries in which the farm laborers and their families are not counted as being a part of the farmers. Even so, however, in Colombia only the families of "resident" farm laborers are

TABLE 2

NUMBERS AND PROPORTIONS OF THE "PRODUCERS" AND AREAS AND PROPORTIONS OF THE AREAS OF EXPLOTACIONES AGROPECUARIOS ACCORDING TO THE SIZE OF THE EXPLOTACIÓN, 1960

Size of the explotaciones (hectares)	All "producers"		All land in explotaciones	
	Number	Per cent	Number	Per cent
Total	1,209,672	100.0	27,337,827	100.0
Under 0.5	165,652	13.7	38,344	0.1
0.5–0.9	132,419	11.0	93,649	0.3
1.0–1.9	191,347	15.8	270,308	1.0
2.0–2.9	117,005	9.7	275,656	1.0
3.0–3.9	92,001	7.6	309,165	1.1
4.0–4.9	58,181	4.8	251,854	0.9
5.0–9.9	169,145	14.0	1,164,749	4.3
10.0–19.9	114,231	9.4	1,572,076	5.7
20.0–29.9	44,049	3.6	1,043,554	3.8
30.0–39.9	26,500	2.2	890,100	3.3
40.0–49.9	16,240	1.3	705,047	2.6
50.0–99.9	39,990	3.3	2,680,471	9.8
100.0–199.9	22,317	1.9	2,996,152	11.0
200.0–499.9	13,693	1.1	3,994,319	14.6
500.0–999.9	4,141	0.3	2,730,764	10.0
1,000–2,499.9	1,975	0.2	2,808,210	10.3
2,500–over	786	0.1	5,513,409	20.2

Source: Same as Table 1.

included and the substantial part of those who live from agriculture, although not residing on the farms, is omitted from the material given in Table 2.

Nor is this failure to include the important segment of the farmers that is made up of the families of non-resident farm laborers my only reason for stating that now, even after a census of agriculture has been taken and much of its detail published, we do not know, and are likely to continue for some decades to come without knowing with any degree of accuracy, the extent to which the ownership and control of Colombia's rural property is concentrated in the hands of a few large landowners. This is largely because of the ramifications of the fact that an extremely high, although unknown, proportion of the owners of large estates have two, three, four or more haciendas distributed in various parts of the Republic.

It is probable that I, in the course of the years from 1943 on, in which I have traveled in all parts of Colombia, have met the owner and been on the hacienda or plantation of some large landed proprietor who possessed only that one estate. If this is the case, neither my memory nor the copious notes taken at the time enable me to recall that fact. On the other hand, both memory and notes are replete with information about hundreds of cases in which a given hacienda was only one of several large tracts of land owned by its proprietor. Moreover, beginning with all that I have been able to learn about Bolívar and Santander, the books and articles which give information about the lives and activities of the members of Colombia's upper social class are filled with materials about the various haciendas owned by those of elite social positions. Such information does not give us, of course, the divisor we need in order to reduce the slightly more than 20,000 "producers" with places of more than 500 hectares to the actual number of proprietors with places larger than that arbitrarily selected minimum. Nor does it enable us to establish the number and area of those explotaciones of less than 500 hectares which in reality constitute small fractions of the land possessed by those who also are the owners of one or more larger estates. In most cases, of course, these fragments of the holdings of the large landed proprietors are treated as though they belonged to those of the middle range, as though they were places corresponding closely to the farms of western Europe, Canada, and the United States. Obviously, though, the holdings attributed to the largest landowners need to be augmented somewhat to allow for the many tracts of less than 500 hectares that are parts of their total estates. Even if we were to limit our appraisals of the situation to those based upon the census data, if realistic allowances are made for the factors just mentioned, one should probably conclude that the number of Colombians with landholdings of more than 500 hectares is no larger than 10,000 and that it very well may be fewer than 7,500; and one also probably should infer that this small fraction of the "producers," one considerably less than 1 per cent of all, claims and controls at least 60 per cent and probably has possession of no less than 65 per cent of all the land in farms in the 16 departments covered by the agricultural census.

Before leaving this part of the discussion, though, mention should be made of a few other highly significant data which are available and which are directly pertinent to the topic under consideration. As it proceeded to implement the Agrarian Reform Law, Ley 135 of 1961, the Instituto Colombiano de Reforma Agraria made use of its authorization and attempted to assemble data for all of the holdings of more than 2,000 hectares in the 17 departamentos into which the more populated portions of Colombia's national territory are organized. The area involved includes the departamento of Chocó, in which agricultural activities are largely non-existent, as well as the 16 for which the agricultural census materials are available; and the information available is for all places of 2,000 hectares or more, so that it is impossible to compare them directly with any of the size categories employed in the agricultural census tabulations. Even so the results are highly significant.

A total of 1,238 declarations were received from those claiming ownership of land in excess of 2,000 hectares. All together these estates accounted for 7,408,908 hectares of land, of which those claiming ownership asserted that they were making use of only 2,840,347 and that there were "4,568,561 hectares lacking any use whatsoever." In other words these data which were forthcoming in response to a legal procedure showed that the 1,238 largest proprietors were exercizing possession of as much land as the agricultural census reported for all explotaciones of 1,000 hectares or more as shown in Table 2; and furthermore that almost 62 per cent of this land was subject to measures that could cause the title to it to revert to the State.[18]

Minifundia, Family-Sized Farms, and Plantations and Other Large Units.—With the data that have been gathered and the form in which they have been tabulated, it is no easy task to determine, even approximately, the numbers and proportions of Colombia's agricultural and pastoral units that should be classified into the principal size categories, namely, very small farms (or minifundia), genuine farms of the middle-range type (family-sized farms), and plantations and other large units. With the minifundia there are two principal difficulties: first, that involved in making the distinction between the tiny places that actually are farms and those that are merely subsistence plots from which families of farm laborers obtain a few of the foods

18. See Peñalosa Camargo, *et al., INCORA*, p. 41.

that they eat; and second, that which arises as one seeks to differentiate the minifundia which fall near the upper limits of that class from the small places which belong near the lower limits of the family-sized group. Moreover, irrespective of where one draws the line between these two categories, he will not be able to find and classify in the family-sized group any large number of substantial farms operated by sturdy, self-reliant, middle-class farm operators.

Offhand one might suppose that by the time he came to consider the 50,000 predominantly agricultural units involving between 20 and 50 hectares or the 35,000 predominantly pastoral establishments varying in size from 40 to 200 hectares he would be dealing with cases that certainly were not minifundia and hardly could be considered as haciendas or plantations. Hence one might reason that they must belong in the intermediate category of family-sized farms; and certainly these ranges must include, for the most part, units properly belonging in that class. Even with respect to this important part of the middle range, though, certain reservations are necessary. Not infrequently in Colombia, places as small as 40 or even 30 hectares, in the agricultural sector, and those only slightly larger, in the pastoral one, have taken on many of the features of the hacienda system. This is to say that peons or other types of agricultural laborers are relied upon to do the manual labor on the farm, and the proprietor himself attempts to avoid at all costs any participation in such bemeaning activities. In addition, the owner is likely to have his home in some city, from whence he makes only sporadic visits to the farm. Finally, the important work of management is reduced almost to a minimum and that which does find its way into the productive process is mostly of the type that can be supplied by an ill-prepared mayordomo or overseer or caretaker who is left in charge of the activities. In other words many of the agricultural and pastoral units, which from the standpoint of size alone can be considered neither as minifundia nor as plantations and other large agricultural or pastoral units, are merely little haciendas. They are establishments whose proprietors lack the land, the financial resources, and the social standing needed to carry on in the traditional grand hacienda manner, but who definitely do not form part of a sturdy yeoman class. Furthermore it should be stressed that many of the places in these size ranges are merely fragments of the holdings of large landowners and that in truth they are an integral part of the genuine hacienda system.

Irrespective of whether or not they are admitted to the farm category, we may be sure of one thing: very small tracts of land are rapidly multiplying in number and greatly increasing in diversity. Let us consider a few of the aspects of this phenomenon. To begin with, the colonial practice of assigning an acre or two of land to each family of slaves or other retainers, on which those workers could erect rude huts and grow a part of their foodstuffs, survives to this day as an integral part of the hacienda system. Thus by the tens of thousands such estancias, conucos, and so forth, continue to be associated with Colombia's large estates in one expression of the Siamese-twin type of relationship that prevails between large haciendas and a self-sufficient or non-commercial system of production. These retainers, who long were maintained in a servile or semi-servile condition, often are referred to euphemistically as arrendatarios or "renters," so that undoubtedly they make up a large share of all the "producers" classified by the Colombian census as being renters of the small tracts which figure in the tabulations. There were 147,625 "renters" of places of less than 2 hectares enumerated by the 1960 census, or one out of eight (12.2 per cent) of all the "producers" accounted for by that inventory. An undeterminable fraction of them, though, actually are renters or tenants, so that some of these arrendatarios really should be considered as the operators of tiny farms and their places counted as minifundia and not merely subsistence tracts of agricultural laborers. As the size of the explotaciones increases, of course, the proportion of those called arrendatarios who actually are farmers, and not mere farm laborers, rises rapidly. Thus a few classified as renters, even of the smallest explotaciones, and a substantial share of those on places of from 2 to 10 hectares, are one variety of the minifundia category. In the coffee-growing districts, though, the renters having possession of from 5 to 10 hectares frequently are the operators of genuine family-sized farms.

Closely related generically to the subsistence tracts that are assigned to the families who labor on Colombia's haciendas are, of course, the many thousands of little places, mostly located on the steep and badly eroded slopes around the fringes of the large estates, which now are owned by some of the more fortunate of the campesino families. In a large measure these came into existence during the 1930's and 1940's through the *parcelación* projects carried on by private owners in some cases and various official agencies in many more. Just how many of these small parcels should be classified as farms and what proportion of their proprietors should be placed in the farm-operator category are moot questions. Certainly in many cases nothing more than farm laborers and their subsistence tracts are involved; but just as certainly many of the very small pieces of land that blanket the mountainsides in a crazy-quilt pattern and the small plantings of plantains, manioc, sugar cane, and so on, that are spread about in the forested lowlands, are possessed by families who are not tied to the haciendas by tradition, by indebtedness, or in any other manner. Moreover, an added complication in a large number of cases is the fact that the head of the household whose dwelling is on the plot may be constantly away from home working as a peon on some large estate in a distant part of the Republic, leaving his mate and the younger children to grow such crops as they can on the small parcel of land. Under such circumstances it is, of course, impossible to judge with any degree of reliability the number and proportion of the places of less than 2 hectares, or even those of less than 5 hectares, whose "producers" are classified in the owner category, which are mere subsistence tracts of farm laborers and those which properly belong in the minifundia segment of the nation's farms.

The squatters, both those who are occupying in a perfectly legal manner an unalienated part of the public domain and the *colonos* who are "invaders" of lands that are claimed by large proprietors, also make up an important part of the occupants of the large and rapidly increasing number of small agricultural establishments. Furthermore, they are the ones most likely to be missed by the census enumerators, so that any conclusions one may draw with respect to their absolute and relative importance are likely to be understatements of the actual facts. In most cases, of course, the squatters definitely should be classified as farm operators and not as farm laborers, thus obviating one of the most likely sources of error in handling the materials for small units; but, on the other hand, it is extremely difficult to distinguish those squatters who definitely must seek work elsewhere than on their small claims, i.e., true minifundistas, from those who can live on what they can produce on the land they are occupying and thus belong in the class of operators of small family-sized farms.

One who is familiar with the exigencies through which the Colombian countryside has passed since 1947 realizes that the number of squatters or colonos was considerably reduced by the oppression and spoilation the campesinos suffered at the hands of the powerful chieftains and latifundistas of the 1950's. At many places throughout the nation hundreds of their small claims were consolidated into a few additional large estates. Even so, one is hardly prepared to lend credence to the reported number of 46,961, given by the 1960 agricultural census as the total number of "producers" with explotaciones that were occupied without title. Moreover, of the figure reported by the census, 5,536 involved areas of more than 100 hectares apiece and those in the range between 10 and 100 hectares came to almost 20,-000. With the data available, though, one cannot even approximate the number of small places of a largely subsistence nature that are occupied by campesinos who are merely squatting on the land.

Finally, in all of the areas within about 50 or 75 miles of the major cities, thousands of Colombians of upper middle-class status and additional thousands of lower upper-class rank are acquiring small *fincas de recreo,* or week-end places. This is merely the extension to those somewhat lower in the social scale of a modest form of the pattern that long has prevailed among those who occupied firm positions at the top of the social, economic, and political pyramid. In other words the places which now are increasing with such rapidity in the zones adjacent to the large urban centers include only a few hectares apiece; whereas the traditional pattern of Colombia's elite involved the possession of fincas de recreo which were many times larger than that. Moreover, there is an even more fundamental difference between the old pattern and its modern variant. Colombia's elite families traditionally have had the week-end places only as a very small portion of the lands which they owned and controlled, but the small finca de recreo ordinarily is the only rural real estate possessed by the lawyer, the doctor, the businessman who has acquired it.

Perhaps enough has been said to indicate that it is simply impossible to determine with any degree of exactitude the number and proportion of Colombia's agricultural and pastoral establishments that meet the criteria for inclusion in a genuine class of family-sized farms. It is true, as is exemplified by the tabulations in this and other chapters, that there is an abundance of data pertaining to the size of the explotaciones. Nevertheless in a social system that is dominated by the large estate, it still is not possible to determine for Colombia the necessary criteria for separating the largest of the minifundia from the smallest of the family-sized category, nor for distinguishing between the largest family-sized farms and the smallest of the plantations, haciendas, and other large estates. The difficulties inherent in the first of these problems already have been discussed to some extent, and now a few of the more important of those involving the latter may be indicated.

The principal obstacle to the procedure of merely taking an arbitrary limit such as 50, 100, or 200 hectares and considering that as the proper place at which to divide family-sized farms from plantations, haciendas, and other large estates consists of the fact that a large and unknown number of the places containing as few as 100 or 75 hectares actually are parts of the extensive holdings of the large landowners. Furthermore, there is nothing in the system that is even remotely similar to the traditional British pattern in which a gentleman's estate was composed of a number of genuine farms, or places on which tenant farmers operated substantial agricultural establishments. Rather, in Colombia the fincas of the affluent landowners are managed as integral portions of the hacienda system. Moreover, even in the many cases in which places of 50 to 200 hectares are the sole rural landholdings of persons who definitely do not pertain to the landed aristocracy, the cultural compulsions are such that those establishments also tend to be run as though they were merely small haciendas. Their owners generally do not live on the land, but in some city; they visit their places only now and then and certainly would not even consider participating directly in any of the farm work. The management is entrusted to some one selected from the campesino class and numerous unskilled, unmotivated, and inefficient peons are employed to do the work, equipped only with the rudest of tools and implements, and frequently unaided by any draft animals or mechanical power whatsoever. Thus merely because an explotación contains, let us say, 75 hectares, so that definitely it cannot be thought of as a minifundium and, at first glance, at least, hardly seems to qualify as a large hacienda or large plantation, does not mean that automatically it can be placed in the family-sized farm group.

Before presenting our estimates of the numbers of minifundia, family-sized farms, and haciendas and other large estates in Colombia, it seems necessary to discuss briefly the difference between the traditional large haciendas, composed largely of poorly used or completely idle land and frequently consisting of no farm enterprise except a rudimentary type of cattle ranching, and the big agricultural unit on which intensive methods are employed in the production of such crops as sugar cane, cotton, rice, and coffee. In other words it is necessary to the extent made possible by the nature of the data to

attempt the distinction between what properly may be called a latifundium, in the Brazilian or Colombian sense of the term, and the
establishment that qualifies for the designation of plantation.[19]

In recent decades a few of the members of Colombia's landowning elite have ventured into agricultural enterprises such as wheat
growing on a mechanized basis, but even so the vast majority of the
large Colombian estates on which the tractor presently is being used
probably should be considered as belonging in the plantation category. This certainly is the case where the crops involved are sugar
cane, cotton, and rice. In this connection one should note that the
municipio of Consacá, Nariño, is shown by the 1960 agicultural
census to have 4 tractors on its farms, for certainly one or more of
these must be used in the sugar enterprise on the Hacienda of
Consacá which is described in some detail later on in this chapter.
In the temperate climate zones of the Colombian highlands, of

19. This entails, of course, an endeavor to define the concept of plantation,
a task that by no means is an easy one. One of the major difficulties here is
the plethora of definitions that have found their way into the writings of those
who have been dealing with the production of tropical and sub-tropical crops
such as sugar cane, rice, cotton, pineapples, rubber, and coffee, that is to
say with persons who have had little or no occasion to have to take into
consideration the huge agricultural establishments found in some parts of the
world which are devoted to such enterprises as the growing of wheat, potatoes,
or grapes, or that of dairying. Some of these, such as wheat, do not involve
an intensive use of the land and may legitimately be ruled out of the plantation
category on that score alone. It must be stressed, though, that one who deals with
the Colombian scene cannot easily ignore the problem of the large-scale agricultural units engaged in the production of temperate-zone crops, as so frequently
has been the procedure followed by those who have been preoccupied with the
Philippines, Hawaii, Malaya, the West Indies, the Southern part of the United
States, and Brazil. I would define a plantation as a *farm* which is (a) very large,
both in terms of acreage and in terms of the number of workers engaged on it,
and (b) devoted almost exclusively to the intensive cultivation of one or two
highly commercialized crops which may either be sold as they are harvested or
as they are processed on the plantation itself. The qualifications given are intended to exclude all large cattle ranches, haciendas, fundos, *fazendas*, and so on
which are highly extensive in nature and which generally are highly self-sufficient.
Indeed it is the intent to rule out of the plantation group all kinds of large estates
in which the production of one or two crops for sale is not the leitmotiv of those
who control the large acreages involved. It also is hoped that the manner in which
the definition is phrased will effectively exclude all the large wheat farms, such as
those in the western part of the United States, in Argentina, in Australia, and
elsewhere, but will not exclude from the plantation class the "factories in the
fields" and other large, intensively cultivated tracts of land that are called
"ranches" in California and some of the other Western States. Cf. Smith, "Some
Observations Relating to Population Dynamics in Plantation Areas of the New
World," in Rubin, *Plantation Systems of the New World*, pp. 126-27.

Extensive area of minifundia and dispersed settlement, department of Nariño. (Courtesy of L. Eduardo Montero.)

Typical homestead of a small farmer on the Savanna of Bogotá. (Photo by the author.)

course, the presence of a tractor on the hacienda probably means no more, we must stress, than that the proprietor is trying out a little wheat or barley in one of the fertile valley bottoms that has experienced no cultivation whatsoever since the sixteenth century when the Indians' cornfields were replaced by the conqueror's pastures. But the presence of the tractor in large numbers in the Cauca Valley and in some of the northern coastal districts reflects the presence of large sugar-cane plantations in those areas; and the sizeable number of these modern sources of power for the farm that now are present on the plains of the upper Magdalena Valley is due to the large and highly mechanized cotton plantations which now have replaced the extensive cattle pastures which long monopolized the land of the area. Moreover, the presence by 1960 of important numbers of tractors in such places as the area around Valledupar and Augustín Codazzi in the department of Magdalena, in those near Villavencio in Meta, and in the minicipio of Monteria and other locations along the Sinú River in Córdoba, means that many of the large establishments in those areas are genuine plantations.

All told, according to 1960 census data, there were in Colombia 2,637 places of more than 200 hectares reported as being equipped with one or more tractors. Of these, 239 were estates of more than 2,500 hectares, or 30.4 per cent of all the establishments in the largest size category. Another 521 of the explotaciones reporting tractors were places varying in size between 1,000 and 2,500 hectares, or 26.4 per cent of all in this class. Of the establishments containing less than 1,000 hectares, but more than 500, 733 (17.7 per cent) reported tractors; and in the next class, 200-500 hectares, 1,144 or 8.4 per cent did the same. Among these larger places, or in the four size groups in which most of the plantations must come, the average number of tractors per explotación reporting tractors as forming part of their equipment varied as follows: 2,500-over, 3.3; 1,000-2,000, 2.6; 500-1,000, 2.2; and 200-500, 2.2. These low averages mean that caution must be exercised in assigning tractor-equipped large establishments to the plantation category, since some of Colombia's large sugar-cane plantations, such as La Manuelita in the Cauca Valley and Sincerín in Bolívar, each have many of these important machines, and the same is true of some of the large cotton plantations in the Upper Magdalena Valley and other parts of the Republic.

Among the places best entitled to be designated as plantations are the 197 establishments reported by the 1960 census as having plantings of more than 100 hectares of sugar cane, the 64 reported with plantings of above 100 hectares of bananas and plantains, and the 857 fincas reported to be using above 50 hectares apiece for the growing of coffee plants. (This number of large coffee fincas, though, is open to serious question, since all along the western slope of the Eastern Cordillera the practice of calling the resident laborers used by the name of arrendatarios probably means that the acreages worked by many families of laborers were counted as explotaciones. Such a practice of carving up the plantation, for statistical purposes, into many small units credited to renters is about as realistic as that of counting, by the U. S. Census, the plots worked by southern sharecroppers as though they were farms.) The larger units singled out above were responsible for 21.5 per cent of the nation's sugar-cane acreage, 2.6 per cent of the land used for the growing of bananas and plantains, and 8.0 per cent of the area on which coffee trees were growing.

Unfortunately, cotton is omitted from the list of products for which Colombia's agricultural census reports with respect to the magnitude of the plantings. However, the report for the department of El Valle del Cauca, which was prepared by members of the School of Economics of the Universidad del Valle, does supply the comparable information about cotton for that department. This report indicates that in 1959 there were 42 establishments with plantings of more than 100 hectares of cotton (for a total of 7,061 hectares). All of these units certainly should qualify as plantations, and the same no doubt is true of many of the cotton farms having from 50 to 100 hectares of cotton, which were 92 in number and together had plantings totaling 6,620 hectares.

Other than the agricultural units already indicated, and a considerable number of cotton plantations in departments other than El Valle del Cauca, there are very few other explotaciones that should be classified as plantations. Perhaps the 246 places reporting plantings of 100 or more hectares of rice should be considered as such, along with the 26 properties reported as having 50 or more hectares devoted to cacao groves and the 6 tobacco farms of comparable magnitudes. But it probably would not be proper to list with the plantations the 12 establishments on which as much as 100 hectares are planted with potatoes, the 43 growing 100 hectares or more of barley, and the 206 with fields of maize that total 100 or more hectares in size.

Before attempting to give an approximation of the number of Colombia's agricultural units that should be thought of as minifundia, family-sized farms, plantations, and other large estates, respectively, it seems essential to introduce a few data on the size of the establishments that are not based upon area alone. This is because the type of soil, location, topography, rainfall, and so on make the number of acres or hectares alone a very inadequate measure of size. This is as true in Colombia as it is in the United States, and in both countries a favorable combination of such factors may actually make a given place of 200 hectares much more deserving of the designation of a very large farm than another with a less favorable combination even though the latter might embrace thousands of hectares. For example a cattle ranch far out on the Llanos to the east of the mountains might well be considered as a comparatively small establishment, even though it contained a couple of thousand hectares; whereas 100 hectares near Bogotá on the part of the Savanna now being developed for dairy purposes certainly is a rather large farm.

The 1960 census supplies two other series of data that may be used to supplement those pertaining to areas in our consideration of the size of the nation's farms and pastoral establishments. One of these gives the resident farm population in cross tabulation with the size of the explotaciones in terms of area and the second gives comparable information about the number of dwellings per unit. This pertinent information has been assembled, the necessary percentages have been computed, and is presented in Table 3.

Only two comments will be offered relative to these data. First they make it evident that the features of largeness, or the reliance upon labor other than that supplied by the operator and members of his family, are exhibited to a considerable extent on many places of less than 50 hectares of land. Second, they demonstrate rather conclusively that idle, unused or extensively used expanses, and not the intensive monoculture of the plantation, are the dominating characteristics of Colombia's large holdings taken as a whole.

On the basis of the information given above and the other extensive body of observations made in the course of almost a quarter of a century of rather close contact with the rural scene in Colombia, I believe the distribution of Colombia's agricultural and pastoral establishments among the various size categories is about as follows. First, as indicated in Chapter 3, I would relegate about 679,000, or all but about 530,000 of the explotaciones reported, to the category of subsistence tracts used by families of farm laborers, and would not admit them to the class of genuine farms at all. Second, of the 530,000 places entitled to be called farms, I would place about 250,000 in the group of minifundia, that is the places that

TABLE 3

AVERAGE NUMBER OF DWELLINGS AND AVERAGE RESIDENT FARM POPULATION
BY SIZE OF THE EXPLOTACIONES (IN HECTARES), 1960

Size (hectares)	Average number of dwellings per explotación	Average resident population per explotación
Total	1.1	5.4
under 0.5	0.9	5.0
0.5–0.9	0.9	4.0
1.0–1.9	0.9	4.3
2.0–2.9	1.0	4.7
3.0–3.9	1.0	4.9
4.0–4.9	1.1	5.3
5.0–9.9	1.2	5.8
10.0–19.9	1.2	6.4
20.0–29.9	1.3	6.8
30.0–39.9	1.4	7.0
40.0–49.9	1.4	7.2
50.0–99.9	1.5	7.6
100.0–199.9	1.7	8.6
200.0–499.9	2.0	10.5
500.0–999.9	2.7	13.8
1,000.0–2,499.9	3.3	17.4
2,500.0–over	4.1	24.2

Source: Page 59 of source for Table 1

are too small to furnish satisfactory employment and a livelihood to the families using them so that the operator and other members of the family are forced to seek a supplementary income by working off the little farm they own or rent. Third, about 25,000 of the establishments would be placed in the class of large farms and ranches, and of these approximately 2,500 would be thought of as meeting the standards required for classification as plantations. Finally, of the remaining 255,000 units in the middle range, those composed of genuine family-sized farms and the units most resembling them in nature, 55,000 are considered to be nothing more than little haciendas, that is tracts embracing from 50 to 200 hectares held by landowners who lack any other rural real estate and are run as though they were the traditional haciendas of large proprietors, and other miscellaneous acreages which actually do form part and parcel of the landholdings of members of the elite proprietary class. Even the residue of 200,000 explotaciones that is left for the family-sized category after all the sectors mentioned have been subtracted includes a great many places that hardly would be considered as farms by European or North American standards and which would not compare favorably with the family-sized farms one encounters in those parts of Argentina and Uruguay in which a pastoral culture has been replaced during the twentieth century by some well-conceived colonization projects. Nevertheless, the 200,000 establishments involved are Colombia's principal hope as she endeavors to multiply and strengthen a substantial class of genuine farm operators of family-sized units. Given favorable consideration by means of adequate agricultural education, the necessary farm credit, a modern system of agricultural extension, comprehensive programs of community organization, and so on, their proprietors can move substantially in the direction of becoming the sturdy rural element needed to fill the void between the minifundistas and their antiquated hoe culture and the privileged persons who own and control the nation's large agricultural and pastoral establishments.

CORRELATIVES OF THE SIZE OF THE AGRICULTURAL UNITS

Much attention has already been given in this chapter to the specific differences between the rural social systems generated by the predominance of large agricultural and pastoral units, on the one hand, and by the prevalence of family-sized farms, on the other. Likewise, the Colombian data, especially those gathered in the 1960 census of agriculture, have been used to identify and describe various other of the correlatives of various sizes of agricultural and pastoral establishments in the important country we are studying. Before going on to other aspects of the size of the holdings and the size of farms in Colombia, it seems advisable to summarize as succinctly as possible the wealth of statistical material made available on the topics of this chapter by those tabulations of 1960 census data which show for the nation as a whole, and for the one departamento of El Valle del Cauca, how various attributes and variables change as the size of the explotaciones increases. For purposes of this summary, these materials were grouped into four large size groups and the necessary indexes were computed for each (see Table 4).

The four size groups employed are as follows: all places of less than 5 hectares, those embracing between 5 and 50 hectares, those having from 50 to 200 hectares, and those containing more than 200 hectares. The first of these comprises almost all of the subsistence tracts of the farm laborers and the small, inadequate farms of the minifundistas, so that it includes the vast majority of all the explotaciones. At the other extreme, the category made up of places having above 200 hectares of land includes the lion's share of the nation's agricultural and pastoral land and nearly all of the estates that are called variously by such names as latifundia, large haciendas, and plantations. The second group involves most of the places that should be considered as family-sized farms, although some of the features of these all-important agricultural units also help give substance to the figures and indexes for the places having from 50 to 200 hectares.

The tabulation given was prepared to show in some detail the principal correlatives of these four size categories, commencing with various aspects of the land itself, and continuing with materials on tenure, the principal crops grown, the types of livestock on the farms and haciendas, the kinds of power used in the processes of tillage, and even the number of dwellings on the farms, the resident farm population, and the sex ratio of the people who live on the land. In view of the amount of space in this volume that has already been devoted to various aspects of these correlatives, it has been deemed unwise to repeat any of the points at this place. Rather the table is presented as the most convenient way of summarizing the relevant statistical data pertaining to the features that characterize the various sizes of agricultural and pastoral establishments in Colombia.

LATIFUNDISMO

Generally speaking Colombians have not become greatly exercised over the problems of the large estate per se, possibly due in large measure to the extent to which they have been preoccupied with their own principal variety of the concentration of ownership and control of the land. In common with their fellows in many of the other Latin American countries, and especially with the Brazilians, they are acutely aware of what they consider to be the evils of latifundismo. But, as has been indicated above, they do not consider each and every huge landed estate to be a latifundium. The very kernel of their concept of latifundismo involves the idea of huge expanses of privately owned land that is deliberately withheld from productive uses. Consequently, in Colombia, as in many other parts of Latin America, the latifundia are huge landed estates which are either maintained in a condition of complete idleness or else, being eminently suited for intensive cultivation, are partially devoted to the most extensive usages such as grazing. That latifundismo is an "old man of the sea" whose weight is crushing the economy of the nation is widely accepted throughout the Republic.

In addition to the extracts given above a couple of quotations from another Colombian authority will serve to make clear the light in which the latifundium is viewed as well as to indicate that its presence is a factor to be reckoned with throughout large portions of Colombia. For example, in explaining the fact that agricultural production is so low throughout the "Caucauno Nucleus" (the departments of El Valle and Cauca) Ramon Franco R. asserts: "At the bottom of this backwardness there is the problem of latifundismo and the lack of roads and trails. The latifundium paralyzes the development of the activities of the mass of campesinos: it is the Chinese wall which impedes from cultivating the soil the man who can and wants to work it."[20]

The same authority, whose work is indispensable for one who would understand the manner in which the Central Cordillera was settled, describes in some detail the manner in which this latifundismo held back the settlement and development of what is probably the most enterprising section of Colombia. It is well to present at some length a translation of one of the more significant portions of his thesis.

> During the colonial period the Antioquia nucleus was bound like Prometheus to the post of inaction by means of and thanks to the absurd *capitulaciones reales*, [royal land grants] until Mon y Velarde arose and threw off its bonds, oiled its springs, and opened to it a panorama of work in the lands which sufficed for its sparse population.
> But the advent of the Republic generated an identical problem.

20. *Antropogeografía Colombiana*, p. 200.

TABLE 4
SOME OF THE CORRELATIVES OF THE SIZE OF THE EXPLOTACIONES AGROPECUARIAS IN COLOMBIA, 1960

Correlative	less than 5 hectares	5-50 hectares	50-200 hectares	200-over hectares
1. Number of explotaciones	756,605	370,165	62,307	20,595
2. Land in "farms" (hectares)	1,238,976	5,375,526	5,676,623	15,046,702
3. Land in "farms" (per cent)	4.5	19.7	20.8	55.0
4. Arable land (hectares)	578,482	1,367,626	783,057	802,793
5. Arable land (per cent)	16.4	38.7	22.2	22.7
6. Permanent plantings (hectares)	296,179	801,669	247,422	169,860
7. Permanent plantings (per cent)	19.6	52.9	16.3	11.2
8. Pasture land (hectares)	218,662	1,942,000	2,610,258	9,835,034
9. Pasture land (per cent)	1.5	13.3	17.9	67.3
10. Forest and wood lands (hectares)	47,233	948,925	1,773,552	3,617,314
11. Forest and wood lands (per cent)	0.7	14.9	27.8	56.6
12. Level terrain (hectares)*	15,157	43,910	90,011	215,195
13. Level terrain (per cent)*	4.2	12.0	24.7	59.1
14. Rugged terrain (hectares)*	30,763	258,065	222,366	292,480
15. Rugged terrain (per cent)*	3.8	32.1	27.7	36.4
16. Agricultural units: per cent of units	67.8	29.0	2.8	0.4
17. Agricultural units: per cent of land	12.9	41.6	25.8	19.7
18. Pastoral units: per cent of units	31.8	41.9	17.5	8.8
19. Pastoral units: per cent of land	0.5	7.9	17.1	74.5
20. Administrators: number	6,106	17,540	10,773	8,051
21. Administrators: per cent	14.4	41.3	25.4	18.9
22. Administrators: hectares	13,970	344,089	1,093,471	7,993,583
23. Administrators: per cent of land	0.2	3.6	11.6	84.6
24. Owners†: number	446,139	248,260	44,987	15,932
25. Owners†: per cent	59.1	32.9	5.9	2.1
26. Owners: hectares of land	723,158	3,725,555	4,168,249	11,162,623
27. Owners: per cent of land	3.7	18.8	21.1	56.4
28. Renters: number	218,120	59,147	4,144	936
29. Renters: per cent	77.3	20.9	1.5	0.3

TABLE 4—(*Continued*)

Correlative	less than 5 hectares	5-50 hectares	50-200 hectares	200-over hectares
30. Renters: hectares of land	330,740	755,061	390,899	532,574
31. Renters: per cent of land	16.5	37.6	19.4	26.5
32. Squatters: number	16,202	19,421	8,921	2,417
33. Squatters: per cent	34.5	41.4	19.0	5.1
34. Squatters: hectares of land	30,034	346,654	748,405	2,188,982
35. Squatters: per cent of land	0.9	10.5	22.6	66.0
36. Rice: number of "farms"	15,588	23,388	10,639	3,668
37. Rice: hectares harvested	16,108	59,424	63,856	87,404
38. Rice: per cent of harvested	7.1	26.2	28.2	38.5
39. Sugar cane: number of "farms"	113,188	95,610	11,442	2,836
40. Sugar cane: hectares harvested	63,358	148,066	54,344	83,374
41. Sugar cane: per cent of harvested	18.4	41.6	15.8	24.2
42. Barley: number of "farms"	21,158	11,126	914	216
43. Barley: hectares harvested	12,337	23,194	13,184	9,589
44. Barley: per cent of harvested	21.2	39.8	22.6	16.4
45. Maize: number of "farms"	301,578	196,152	32,452	9,069
46. Maize: hectares harvested	231,301	368,409	156,933	114,535
47. Maize: per cent of harvested	26.6	42.3	18.0	13.1
48. Potatoes: number of "farms"	68,841	36,075	2,864	624
49. Potatoes: hectares harvested	39,291	59,737	16,066	8,558
50. Potatoes: per cent of harvested	31.8	48.3	13.0	6.9
51. Wheat: number of "farms"	51,080	28,171	1,418	250
52. Wheat: hectares harvested	39,679	68,031	15,954	6,011
53. Wheat: per cent of harvested	30.6	52.5	12.3	4.6
54. Cotton: number of "farms"*	116	150	98	71
55. Cotton: hectares planted*	4,041	2,065	6,160	6,473
56. Cotton: per cent of plantings*	21.6	11.0	32.9	34.5
57. Cacao: number of "farms"	14,637	16,393	3,640	1,090
58. Cacao: hectares	8,316	27,373	9,484	5,372
59. Cacao: per cent	16.4	54.2	18.8	10.6
60. Coffee: number of "farms"	230,978	166,424	17,304	3,161

61. Coffee: hectares	209,431	557,475	145,494	55,919
62. Coffee: per cent	21.6	57.6	15.0	5.8
63. Cattle: number of "farms"	170,176	207,845	44,748	17,551
64. Cattle: head	576,115	2,207,390	2,200,853	4,659,231
65. Cattle: per cent	6.0	22.9	22.8	48.3
66. Sheep: number of "farms"	85,515	47,203	5,542	2,490
67. Sheep: head	370,010	349,605	90,781	60,879
68. Sheep: per cent	42.5	40.2	10.4	6.9
69. Hogs: number of "farms"	291,508	208,232	40,963	13,954
70. Hogs: head	800,790	764,857	304,482	197,149
71. Hogs: per cent	38.7	37.0	14.7	9.6
72. Horses: number of "farms"	123,779	188,031	40,883	16,558
73. Horses: head	178,839	401,690	153,559	164,702
74. Horses: per cent	19.9	44.7	17.1	18.3
75. Mules: number of "farms"	30,299	81,378	27,214	13,525
76. Mules: head	43,359	149,450	77,981	71,692
77. Mules: per cent	12.7	43.6	22.8	20.9
78. Donkeys: number of "farms"	72,161	51,391	18,721	7,871
79. Donkeys: head	110,116	102,748	52,211	28,840
80. Donkeys: per cent	37.5	34.9	17.8	9.8
81. Manpower only: number of "farms"	537,934	201,786	33,583	8,413
82. Manpower only: per cent of "farms"	68.8	25.8	4.3	1.1
83. Tractors: "farms" having	837	2,504	2,151	2,637
84. Tractors: per cent of "farms" having	10.3	30.8	26.5	32.4
85. Tractors: number	1,144	3,621	4,172	6,424
86. Tractors: per cent	7.4	23.6	27.2	41.8
87. Farm dwellings: number	709,217	455,296	96,865	48,564
88. Farm dwellings: average per "farm"	0.94	1.23	1.55	2.36
89. Resident "farm" population	3,497,412	2,320,735	494,270	253,867
90. Resident "farm" population per "farm"	4.6	6.3	7.9	12.3
91. Sex ratio of "farm" population*	103.0	118.0	137.0	193.0

Sources: Pages 21-59 of source for Table 1; and Facultad de Ciencias Economicas, *Censo Agropecuario del Valle del Cauca, 1959,* Cali: Universidad del Valle, 1963, pp. 31, 69, and 71.

* Departamento of El Valle del Cauca only.

† Includes owners who have administrators in charge of their places as well as those who do not.

How? Unoccupied or "baldio" territory was portioned out in payment of services in the cause of independence, the same as that which recompensed the legitimist chiefs of the War of 1840: to the grants of the Monarchy were joined the feudal concessions of the Republic. Thus the land remained unused in the hands of a few owners, withheld from clearing and planting, in vast latifundia, which, in their hour were a new obstacle to the expansion and progress of the agricultural zone.

The region between the Cauca and the Atrato, for example, all belonged to a few capitalists. The district which lies between the Pozo and the Chinchina belonged to a single proprietor, and that was the rule. The virgin forest was preserved intact, protected by titles and concessions, while the cultivated or arable land was insufficient to feed the population.

On the other hand the people without habitual occupation were caught by the prongs of the "vagrancy laws," severely applied from 1840 on. The consequence? The great masters, the terratenientes of Medellín and Antioquia, filled their labor gangs with persons accused of vagrancy and used them to clear the jungles of the Cauca Valley, but without the incentive of property ownership, in the form of the unpaid colonists who found themselves compelled to give their work under pain of falling under the majesty of the law.[21]

Absenteeism is another item which almost inevitably enters into the concept of latifundismo and which makes that particular form of the concentration of landownership and control seem to be at the very root of most of the evils which afflict Colombian society. In the course of travels throughout all sections of Colombia, at intervals spread throughout three calendar years we made visits to 100

21. *Ibid.*, pp. 178-79. One should indicate, however, that latifundismo in Antioquia did not cease with the colonial reforms nor with the transfer of some of the activities of the Antioqueño terratenientes to other provinces. Consider, for example, the following statements by Alejandro López.

"I have mentioned above the fact, of tremendous importance for whoever pretends to study the problem' to be found in the present state of Antioquia, that the most fertile portion of this territory, and furthermore one that is surrounded on all sides by settlements, is devoted to pastures; this is to say that approximately 100,000 hectares of the best lands and those most favorably situated with respect to markets are almost deserted and do not absorb more than a few thousand hired workers. If the ax of the free antioqueño campesino had not been stayed in its march to the south by the legal fact of the ajudication of these lands, today they would be occupied by between 50,000 and 100,000 families of campesinos, who would live well and free in their own homes, making more dense our well-to-do population and more easily solved all our problems connected with progress. Furthermore, one could point out many other thousands of hectares of good land, or at least land suited for intensive cultivation, which today is dedicated to cattle raising, an industry that perhaps is profitable for the proprietors but not for society." *Problemas Colombianos*, p. 55.

or more haciendas, but in only one case was the owner of the hacienda at home in the casa grande to receive us upon our arrival. Not infrequently we merely accompanied the owner on one of his periodic visits to the estate, but most generally no one was present and in charge but the caretaker. That this sample was not a biased one would seem to be supported by the following generalizations which are to be found in one of the annual reports of the Minister of Agriculture and Commerce:

> If we analyze who it is that in our country ordinarily cultivate the soil and care for the domestic animals, it is easy to deduce that it is the so-called "campesinos," "peones," "arrendatarios," or "aparceros." It is they who regularly live in the country and who personally work the land, sow the seed, do the cultivating, gather the crops, prepare them for sale, and carry them to the market. And on the other hand they are the only ones who care for the livestock, although all of these activities generally are done in the most rudimentary and haphazard manner.
>
> Except in a few cases the owners of the haciendas and above all the great proprietors, when they come to make use of their lands do so without living on them permanently and limit their own activities to informal visits to their inheritances; to give orders to their respective mayordomos (usually ordinary peons of the same haciendas) concerning the fallow fields that should be prepared and planted, the pastures that should be cleared and the animals to be sold, and to receive from them the money secured from the sales that have been made. But never do they work with their own hands or without interruption in the organization and development of the rural enterprises, which they consider to be suited for their peons. Lacking in stability, lacking adequate organization, lacking accounting, lacking personal direction of the activities, and lacking sentiment and sensibility for the country and its way of life, the capitalistic rural proprietors will never succeed in developing for us model rural enterprises nor low costs of production.
>
> This is surely true of the majority of the capitalistic proprietors of the hot lands. Admittedly there are some exceptions among the hacendados engaged in coffee culture and some of those of the tierra fría. The small proprietors, the *minifundistas*, are humble people, without the pretensions of the great masters, and they attend daily to their fields, working personally with their hands and those of their children, and, having their homes in the country, fulfilling the noble mission of stabilizing and augmenting the rural population which the country so badly needs.[22]

22. Restrepo, *Memoria del Ministerio de Agricultura y Comercio*, I, pp. 88-89.

Encomienda and Hacienda

There has been no little confusion with respect to the relationship of the *encomienda* to the large estate (hacienda, fundo, or estancia) which early came to be the dominant element on the cultural landscape south of the Rio Grande. Some of the best informed scholars such as McBride and Simpson have maintained that very quickly the encomienda system lost its original character and became merely a form of land tenure. According to this hypothesis the *encomenderos* soon came to consider the Indians as their serfs and the lands of the natives as their own private property.[23] That the Indians were quickly reduced to a state of serfdom or peonage there can be no doubt, but one should less readily accept the proposition that the large estate in Spanish America grew out of the encomienda.

After a study of the documentary evidence relating to Mexico and the West Indies, the Mexican scholar Silvio Zavala, recipient of one of the Guggenheim fellowships, concluded that the rights of the encomienda "did not include property rights in the land," and that the encomenderos "by grants or purchase, not to mention usurpations, could acquire lands as private property . . . inside and outside the encomiendas."[24]

Even if one merely examines those portions of the regulations which eventually were incorporated into the *Recopilación de Leyes de los Reynos de las Indias,* he should arrive at essentially the same conclusion. Of course one may maintain with much reason that the generality of the practice brought on the prohibition and that the officials and settlers paid very little attention to the law. Nevertheless it is pertinent to note such regulations as the following from *Libro* VI, *Título* IX of the compilation:

1. Ley ix (May 4, 1534) ordering that each encomendero should build a house of stone in the place designated by the Governor.
2. Ley x (March 31, 1583) obliging the encomenderos to have *inhabited* houses in the cities which were the *cabezas* of their encomiendas.
3. Ley xi (October 10, 1618) specifying that the encomenderos "should neither make nor have in the Pueblo of their encomiendas

23. Cf. McBride, *The Land Systems of Mexico,* p. 45; Simpson, *The Ejido: Mexico's Way Out,* p. 10; and Whetten, *Rural Mexico,* pp. 81-82.
24. *De Encomiendas y Propiedad Territorial en Algunas Regiones de la America Española,* pp. 80-81. See also Ots Capedequí, *El Régimen de la Tierra en la America Española durante el Periodo Colonial, passim.*

any house or hut, even though they say it is not for dwelling purposes, but a storehouse or granary, . . . and thus we prohibit the
Encomenderos from sleeping in their Pueblos more than one night,
under pain of a fine of 20 pesos. . . . "

4. Ley xii (November 29, 1563) declaring that the Indians had no
obligation to build houses for the encomenderos.

5. Ley xiii (June 6, 1609) forbidding the issuance to the encomenderos of licenses for staying in the Pueblos.

6. Ley xiv (April 24, 1550) forbidding residence in the Pueblos
on the part of the encomenderos, their wives, parents, children, relatives, servants, guests, mestizos, mulattoes, or Negroes slave or free.

7. Ley xvii (March 31, 1633) ordering that no encomendero
should possess personally or through a second person estancias within
the limits of the Pueblo of his encomienda, and that if he had such
it should be taken from him and sold.

8. Ley xviii (May 28, 1621) indicating that encomenderos were
not to be permitted to have "works" or factories in or near the
Pueblos.

9. Ley xix (May 1, 1549) commanding that the encomenderos
should not keep pigs in the Pueblos of the encomiendas, nor on the
lands pertaining to them which the Indians used for planting.

Also highly pertinent is Ley xxx of Libro VI, Título I (May 14,
1546) which specified that the encomenderos should not inherit the
lands and equipment of their Indians who died without heirs, but
that these should pass to the Pueblo for the purpose of reducing
the tribute and that any extra was to revert to the Crown. And the
same is true of Ley xxii (June 30, 1646) of Libro VI, Título III
which forbade Spaniards, mestizos, and mulattoes to live in the
Indian Pueblos even if they had lands within their districts.

There is little point to the presentation of more evidence relative
to the attempts of the Crown to prevent a series of developments
which might have resulted in the encomienda of Indians developing into an hacienda. In other sections of this same chapter, and
particularly in the one in which is described the long-continued
crowding out of population which accompanied the growth of the
cattle ranches, are presented some of the essential facts pertaining
to the actual origin of the haciendas of Colombia. But mention
should be made of the fact that the bulk of the towns and villages
scattered throughout the Colombian highlands were once Indian
villages and given in encomienda to the conquistadores. They did
not become haciendas. On the other hand of the dozens of Colombian
haciendas whose detailed history has been examined there is still to
be found one that originally was an encomienda.

The Church and the Concentration of Landownership

In Colombia, as in most other sections of Latin America, the priests during Colonial times were the chief champions of the Indians' rights to personal freedom and to the continued enjoyment of the lands which they held at the time of the conquest. Had it not been for them, very few Indian communities would have escaped actual enslavement. But in spite of this, the institution of the church itself came to be one of the principal agencies in the accumulation under a single ownership of huge expanses of landed property; and, since the mayorasgos or entailed estates were not abolished until 1824,[25] in perpetuating the system of large estates for many decades after the control over them had passed into other hands. For example even the partial records which are available seem to indicate that the Jesuits alone had accumulated more than 100 great estates before the covetousness of the political authorities and other factors led to their expulsion in 1767.[26] This and other evidence are sufficient to justify the conclusion that not a few of the haciendas which today monopolize large tracts of Colombia's most fertile lands originally were put together as large estates owned by the church.

Perhaps it would be more difficult to find a better explicit analysis and description of the manner in which the process went on and of its pernicious social and economic effects than that of Antonio Manso, Presidente of the Audencia of the Nuevo Reino de Granada, in his report for the year 1729.

> I have reserved for the conclusion of this report another of the most universal causes of the poverty of the Kingdom and its inhabitants, one so difficult to remove that to the powerful arm of Your Majesty alone is reserved its remedy. It is, my Lord, that the piety of the faithful in these parts is excessive: it has enriched the monasteries and the orders with various gifts, pious works which establish in the churches *capellanías* which are given for the use of the orders; there have been many persons, who finding themselves without legal heirs, have established with a small house, a lot, or a small farm a capellanía for the benefit of this or that convent; with these and industry the orders have built up riches with which they have purchased large haciendas. Next they loan their funds to the people in the community at the honest rate of 5 per cent, taking as security a mortgage on the house or hacienda which they own; and if some time passes without

25. Nieto Arteta, *Economía y Cultura en la Historia de Colombia*, p. 164.
26. Cf. Borda, *Historia de la Compañía de Jesús en la Nueva Granada,* II, 136-40.

the interest and principal being paid the mortgaged property is sold and passes into the hands of the convent; so it is extremely rare to find a house, farm, or hacienda which does not have against it a loan equivalent to its value; in this manner the owners have come to work to pay the interest to the convents, and have nothing left with which to sustain themselves; and gradually all the valuable properties have been made into church lands . . . since that which does not belong to some convent is owned by some secular clergyman who has established there his capellanía.[27]

Resguardos and the Concentration of Landownership

Not all large holdings in Colombia go back to the lavish distribution of lands by the Kings of Spain and their representatives and to the accumulation of land under the control of the church. It would appear that in some parts of Colombia large estates recently were accumulated in the hands of certain unscrupulous officials who used their position and power to cheat the Indians on the *resguardos* out of their lands. On this score much is to be learned by a perusal of the address entitled "Ensayo Sobre la Evolución de la Propiedad en Colombia,"[28] delivered by Diego Mendoza before the Sociedad Colombiana de Jurisprudencia, on November 28, 1897.

What took place is fairly evident from the following: "In the decisions relating to the division of communal properties which we have come to know in our practice of law, we have seen, not without surprise, that the communal owners sold each right in the community for a few cents, without knowing what they were doing; from which it resulted that for a few pesos there were acquired great portions of land. . . . In other times the *corregidores* of inheritances were called *heridepetos*; we do not know what name to give to the *corregidores* of the communities."[29]

The authority from whom we quote attached great importance to this process by indicating: "The social consequence of our agrarian laws has been that we have no *pueblo*, properly speaking, in those departments or in those provinces where originally there were a large number of resguardos or of extensive haciendas expropriated from the religious orders in 1861."[30]

27. Reproduced in Posada and Ibáñez, *Relaciones de Mando*. The extract translated is from p. 13.
28. Published in the *Reportorio Colombiano*, XVII (1897-98).
29. *Ibid.*, p. 116.
30. *Ibid.* For important perspective on the case of one specific resguardo, see Fals-Borda, *Revista Bolívar*, pp. 459-71.

CONCENTRATION OF LANDOWNERSHIP AND DEPOPULATION

The reference to the relationship between the concentration of ownership and depopulation made in the quotation from Alejandro López, given above, deserves elaboration and substantiation. The process began on a wholesale scale in the first years of the conquest when the Spaniards seized as pastures for their livestock the rich and easily accessible valley bottoms which the Indians had from time immemorial been cultivating foot by foot. As the white man's horses, cattle, and swine multiplied, the Indians' plots of corn, beans, and potatoes were crowded back farther and farther into the coves and higher and higher up the slopes of the surrounding mountains. For four hundred years this process has continued, with few if any substantial interruptions, until today most of the lands best suited for agriculture are given over to grazing purposes, while the attempt of hundreds of thousands of Indian and mestizo families to extract a living by cultivating the steep slopes of the hillside is largely responsible for the terrific amount of soil erosion which besets the country.[31]

When the Spaniards arrived on the Colombian uplands after their long climb, they found a pleasant agricultural land rather densely populated by industrious peoples. These aborigines had developed a fairly high type of hoe culture and cultivated numerous domesticated plants of which the Indian corn, beans, and potatoes were the most important. Many of their plantings undoubtedly were on the hillsides, but they were also making intensive use of the level plains, particularly those of the extensive Savanna of Bogotá. As is elaborated upon in Chapter 5, the Spaniards added relatively little to the agricultural complexes of the Chibchas and other native groups, but they did bring along wheat, barley, and oats to add to the native staples. Their great contributions were the introduction of livestock and poultry, among which horses and cattle were by far the most important, although sheep, goats, burros, and domestic fowls were also brought in during the early years. It seems that the Indians especially esteemed the hen.[32] The metal hoe was the princi-

31. Cf. Smith, "Land Tenure and Soil Erosion in Colombia," pp. 155-60.
32. One of the most noted of the early historians, Antonio de Herrera, reports: "An *Indian* of good natural Parts being asked, What was the best they had got by the *Spaniards* in these Parts? answered, That the Spanish Hens Eggs, and the Plenty there is of them was a great Support of Life, being new every Day, and good for Children, and old People, either raw, or dressed;

pal addition the Spaniards brought in the way of agricultural equipment, although the crude oxcart which represented the first appearance of the wheel in this part of the world, and a rude wooden plow little changed from that early used by the Egyptians, also were introduced by the Spaniards. The point is that the Indians' system of agriculture was changed very little by the coming of the Spaniards, and that the Europeans themselves paid relatively little attention to farming. They did not set themselves to the cultivation of the rich heavy soils in the bottoms of the valleys.

But the introduction of the livestock, in which the Spaniards themselves were chiefly interested, had far reaching consequences. The white man immediately began monopolizing the floors of the valleys and the more gentle and accessible of the slopes as pasture lands. The swine, it would seem, constituted the reliable "shock troops" upon whom the conquistadores could depend for forcing the Indians to transfer their subsistence plots to more remote sections. Very quickly the Indians, and the mestizos who were not long in making their appearance, were forced to make their small plantings of corn, beans, and potatoes high on the steep slopes. Today these "indigenes" by the hundreds of thousands are found scattered along the mountainsides gaining a meager subsistence by cultivating their tiny *parcelas* or estancias. Much of the land they use for crops is almost as steep as loose dirt will lie. At the same time down below, on the less abrupt inclines at the base of the mountain ridges and in the bottoms, the lands are given over almost exclusively for the pastures of the hacendados. Even though there are numerous exceptions to the rule it still is accurate to generalize by saying that much of the land now being cultivated in Colombia is best suited for pastures or woodlands, and that substantial portions of the land now in pasture are precisely those which are most suited for agriculture. Naturally the seizing of huge expanses of the best agricultural lands for the horse and cattle pastures of the Spaniards resulted in the virtual depopulation of areas that once were densely settled.

Where, as on the Savanna of Bogotá or on the high plateaus of

because the Hen must be either boiled, or roasted, and does not always prove tender, and the Egg is good every Way. He added, the Horse and Light, because the first carries Men with Ease, and bears their Burdens; and the latter, because the Indians having learnt to light themselves with Wax and Tallow-Candles, and to burn Oil, he said, by means thereof they lived some Part of the Night, and this he thought the most valuable they had got." *The General History of the Vast Continent and Islands of America, Commonly Called, The West Indies,* I, p. 18.

what is now the departamento of Boyacá, the natives were already fairly well organized socially and politically a few brief battles were sufficient to place the administrative controls in the hands of the conquistadores. There the Spaniards merely established themselves in a few new Spanish towns or administrative centers such as Bogotá, Tunja, Pamplona, and Vélez from which they exercised an over-lordship over the Indians assigned to them in encomienda. Most of them had to travel considerable distances in order to reach the community or communities in which their vassals lived, and as indicated above the law was explicit that they were not to remain overnight in the Indian villages. Hence it is easy to see why the conquerors did not pay any great attention to the internal affairs of the communities that were delivered over to them. Except in the areas coveted for their own, and from which they quickly uprooted the Indians, the conquerors probably had very little interest in the lands within the Indian communities. In their relationships with their vassals the Spaniards were mostly concerned with tribute, for themselves, for the King to whom they were obliged to give a royal share, and for the priests and the church. In many cases they were also interested in the levies of forced laborers whom the institution called the *mita* gave them a right to impress for work in the mines. But there is little in the early documents that leads one to believe that the Spaniards paid any particular attention to the claims of a given village to a designated area of land, or that they were greatly concerned about the manner in which the lands of a community were distributed among its members. Indeed the overlords seem to have moved the natives and their villages around pretty much at will, a procedure which undoubtedly contributed greatly to the tendency for the valley bottoms to be taken out of farming and transformed into pastures.

Nearer to their homes in the new towns, however, the Spaniards were greatly interested in lands, and especially in tracts which they could use for grazing purposes. As one examines the early colonial records of an old settlement such as Tunja he discovers that the first documents are largely devoted to five matters: (1) the delineation of the *ejido* or common pasture for the livestock of the *vecinos;* (2) the assignments of town lots or *solares* (four to a block and each surrounded by mud walls); (3) the allotment of *huertas* or garden plots in a tract adjacent to the town plot; (4) the allocation of *caballerías* or grants of land in the territory surrounding the center; and

(5) the certification of brands for use in marking the livestock of the vecinos.[33] The Acta de Fundación of Tunja took place on August 6, 1539, with the nomination of *alcaldes* and *regidores;* and it was only eight days later, and by the fourth official act of the *Cabildo,* that there was "designated the area [ejido] for the use of the conquistadores as pastures for the maintenance of their horses." Apparently this tract included all of the valley bottom, and much of the lower slopes of the hills as well, lying between Tunja and Paipa, a distance of about 30 miles. But it is hardly necessary to multiply the citations; the Spaniards were greatly interested in their horses and cattle and they immediately took over the very best locations, part of them as common pastures and more still as individual assignments or caballerías.

Where the Indians were in a more primitive stage of social organization, and less well organized politically, the individualistic savages accepted the Spanish yoke with less docility. This was generally the case in the great Cauca Valley and throughout the area now occupied by the departments of Antioquia and Caldas. In these sections, however, war and famine quickly cleared the obstreperous natives from the coveted acreages and left the extensive tracts of bottom lands available for the pastures which have continued to occupy them from that time to the present. One could hardly ask for a better description of the process than the one that was left by Pedro de Cieza de León, one of the conquistadores who was alloted a repartimiento at Arma, and who wrote in 1547:

> All this valley, from the city of Cali to these rapids, was formerly very populous, and covered with very large and beautiful villages, the houses being close together and of great size. These villages of the Indians have wasted away and been destroyed by time and war; for, when the Capitan Don Sebastian de Belalcázar, who was the first capitan to discover and conquer this valley, made his entry, the Indians were bent on war, and fought with the Spaniards many times to defend their land, and escape from slavery. Owing to these wars, and to the famine which arose on account of the seeds not having been sown, nearly all the Indians died. There was another reason which led to their rapid extermination. The capitan Belalcázar founded, in the midst of the Indian villages in this plain, the city of Cali, which he afterwards rebuilt on its present site. The natives were so determined not to hold any friendship with the Spaniards (believing their yoke to be too heavy) that they would neither sow nor cultivate the

33. See, for example, *Libro de Cabildos de La Ciudad de Tunja.*

land; and from this cause there was such scarcity that the greater part of the inhabitants died. When the Spaniards abandoned the first site, the hill tribes came down in great numbers, and, falling upon the unfortunates who were sick and dying of hunger, soon killed and ate all those who survived. These are the reasons why the people of this valley are so reduced that scarcely any are left.[34]

From the details supplied by this authority it is abundantly evident that less than a generation sufficed for the Spaniards to convert the once intensively tilled bottom lands into "grazing farms in the plains, where their servants live, and look after the estates." Today the visitors who see the extensive valley given over largely to pastures while the indigenes make their small plantings high above on the surrounding mountainsides should remember that "all these plains and valleys were once thickly peopled, but the natives who survived the wars have retired into the heights and fastnesses which overhang them."[35]

These are only a few of the materials which demonstrate that from Colonial times to the present the pressures have all tended to crowd the subsistence plots out of the valleys and up onto the steep slopes. On the Savanna of Bogotá less than a century after the conquest the concentration of landownership and control had become so great that fully one-fourth of the entire Savanna was in the hands of a single owner. In the meanwhile the population of the Savanna had declined from the several hundred thousand present in 1538—some authorities place the figure as high as half a million—to a maximum of 50,000. From this one tremendous holding, the entailed estate or mayorasgo called the Dehesa de Bogotá, and whose possession gained for two of its owners the title of Marqués, originated most of the haciendas which still make the southern portion of the Savanna, in

34. *The Travels of Pedro de Cieza de León*, pp. 93–94.
35. *Ibid.*, pp. 99, 109, 117. A twentieth-century description of this same area, as given by a North American visitor, is as follows:
"We left Cali at noon, May 13, well provided with riding and pack animals, and half-breed *arrieros,* and started on the well-beaten trail that leads toward the south.
"At first there was no appreciable change in the valley, but by degrees the stretches of absolutely level-appearing land increased in size; instead of extensive cultivated areas there were pastures of large size, covered with a luxuriant growth of grass. Thousands of head of cattle were sprinkled over the velvety turf. We rode an hour through one of these ranches before reaching the river Jamundi. This estate is the property of one Angel Mario Borrero, who is reported to be one of the most influential men in the Department of Cauca, and is only one of his sixteen similar holdings." Miller, *In the Wilds of South America,* p. 18.

common with the parts more to the north, an area of large land-holdings.[36]

Similar were the happenings in other parts of the New Kingdom, but an adequate discussion of the entire matter would involve the full history of rural life in Colombia. Of course the rapid natural increase of the white population, the arrival of newcomers from Spain, and the interest of the Spaniards and Creoles in stock raising rather than in agriculture supplied all the elements necessary to maintain the pressure and to maintain it strongly. From the standpoint of soil conservation it was particularly unfortunate that the strong were interested primarily in their cattle while most of the planting was done by the weak. Perhaps a short extract from the secret report which Jorge Juan de Sancticilia and Antonio de Ulloa made to the King of Spain will indicate the rapidity with which the lands passed from the agricultural Indians to the pastoral white men, and of the measures employed to effect the transfer. Near the close of the first half of the eighteenth century these men wrote as follows.

> One circumstance which, more than any other, awakens our sympathy for that unfortunate people, is to see them entirely stripped of their lands; for although, at the period of the conquest and the laying out of townships, certain portions had been reserved for the purpose of being alloted to the caciques and Indians belonging to the township, avarice has gradually curtailed them to such a degree, that the tracts which remain to them are circumscribed within narrow limits, and the greater part has been wrested from them altogether. Some Indians have been despoiled of their lands by violence; others, because the owners of neighboring estates have compelled them to sell at any price they may choose to give; and others, because they have been induced to surrender them under false pretences.[37]

Not to be overlooked is the contribution of Pedro Fermín de Vargas, friend of Mutis and Caldas, who wrote in the last part of the eighteenth century. Several of his generalizations, including the following one which is presented in a rather literal translation, aid us greatly in understanding how the large cattle estates came to monopolize the lands that should be used for agriculture, and the relation of this to depopulation. "It is true that through a rarity without parallel the coasts of this Kingdom are almost unpopulated, in relation to their extension, and the interior is somewhat more densely populated.

36. Cf. Pardo Umaña, *Haciendas de la Sabana*, pp. 18-19, 131, 210, and *passim*.
37. *Secret Expedition to Peru*, pp. 86-87.

Above all the population is greater in the zones of medium temperatures. The many diseases which prevail in the low, hot zones is the cause, in my opinion, of their scanty population; while in the *tierras frias* the cause is the overly large haciendas which to the extent that they augment the breeding of cattle diminish the number of the people."[38]

At the present time the process seems to have gone on pretty much to completion. Today the pastures of the haciendas monopolize the sparsely populated areas in the valleys and the plains, while the badly eroded slopes of the surrounding mountains teem with people. This is readily apparent to all who will take the trouble to observe. But it seems well to take note of the comments which one of Colombia's keenest observers made about one hundred years ago. This is what Manuel Ancízar, secretary of the Codazzi Commission, wrote in 1850 about the most extensive level tract of land in the Colombian uplands.

> From Bogotá to Zipaquirá it is ten granadian leagues of level road, whose greater part has the same floor which the good Bochica left us when he drained the great lake whose bed constituted the beautiful plain upon which the innocent Chibchas lived and worked. They, according to what we are told by the chroniclers of the conquest, were cultivating palm by palm the entire plain: we have converted it into pastures for fattening livestock, that is to say, we have taken a step backwards, since grazing is the first step in civilization, which is not truly developed except by agriculture. In the ten leagues of plains mentioned, only the Pueblo of Cajicá presents its land carefully cultivated and planted, being preserved there, as in other pueblos of the indigenes, the primitive type of agriculturist in contrast with our lazy industry of stock raising."[39]

Elsewhere during his extensive travels and examination of the tierra fría to the north of Bogotá he observed and commented upon the same maladjustment, including the following extract which might very well be the description of any one of the numerous haciendas which the present writer visited during 1943, 1944, and 1945.

> From Sogamoso to Iza it is something over four leagues of level road, happy and clear through a pretty, green valley occupied by a hacienda called la Compañía, in commemoration of the Jesuits, first owners of that valuable finca. It is the only one in the canton in which the large extension of land included in this valley is concen-

38. *Pensamientos Políticos y Memoria sobre la Población del Nuevo Reino de Granada*, p. 15.
39. *Peregrinación de Alpha*, pp. 12-13.

trated in the hands of a single family, because happily the remainder of its soil is divided into small holdings, the property of many proprietors. La Compañía is simply a pasture for fattening cattle, so that the plantings of the colonos which surround it appear like refugees upon the slopes and sides of the surrounding mountains; and the rich plains possessed by herds of sheep and larger animals, and by numerous troops of mules, are an incontestable sign of the infancy of our country with agriculture dislodged from its legitimate lands by livestock.[40]

Essentially the same process later took place in the hot, sultry plains which occupy the central portions of the great Magdalena Valley, a process that has more than a little in common with the manner in which the large cotton and sugar plantations swallowed up the small holdings which once occupied many parts of the lower Mississippi Valley. Another keen observer described what took place in these *tierras calientes* during the closing decades of the nineteenth century as follows. "The great haciendas of the hot country have put an end to the small estancias with which it once was covered, places which with their small plantings, the pigs which were bred and raised on each of them, and the fruit trees and gourds that surrounded each hut contributed powerfully to hold down the cost of living. In brief they have depopulated these districts to such an extent as to repeat the earlier experience on the Savanna of Bogotá— the poor have no place to live and hands get scarcer day by day."[41]

THE TENA HACIENDA

The case of Tena, one of the large estates in Colombia for which records have been preserved and published in sufficient detail for our purposes, serves to illustrate the manner in which many haciendas came into existence and the vicissitudes through which they passed.[42] The first document in the four volumes of *Títulos de Propiedad* of this hacienda which have been preserved states: "On October 15, 1548 el señor Licenciado Miguel Díez de Arménderiz, conferred upon and granted to General Pedro de Orsúa y Orsúa, Lieutenant General of this New Kingdom of Granada, land for a cattle ranch [*Estancia de ganado*] in the valley of Tena from the

40. *Ibid.,* p. 276.
41. Rivas, *Los Trabajadores de Tierra Caliente,* p. 95.
42. For a rambling account of happenings connected with Tena, and important extracts from some of the pertinent documents, see Rodríguez Maldonado, *Hacienda de Tena (IV Centenario).*

fields of the Bojacá to the village of the Panches which Capitan
Asencio Salinas has there, of the size and area to which he has been
accustomed since the year of Our Lord 1540."[43] Several comments on
this grant are in order. It will be observed that the hacienda of Tena
originated as a grant of land and not in an encomienda of Indians; it
was designed for cattle raising; and it was very large and practically
lacking in determinable limits.

Apparently, Pedro de Orsúa did very little with this extensive
grant of pasture lands, but in 1548 he took possession of the encomienda of the Zuca in the Tena area which in 1540 had first been
given to Asencio Salinas. The same year he led an expedition to the
north and founded the city of Pamplona; and in 1561 he went to
Peru where he was killed during the following year.[44]

As concerns the Valley of Tena, administrative machinery in Bogotá
seems to have moved slowly, but in 1577 the Cabildo conferred upon
Bartolomé de Olaya an estancia for the establishment of a sugar *ingenio,* and he took possession with machinery and plantings. Later, on
May 23, 1581, Governor Lope de Arménderiz, because of the death of
Pedro de Orsúa, granted the lands once held by the latter to Lope de
Céspedes. This was confirmed by the Licenciado Pedro de Zorrila on
July 8, 1581. Twenty years later, March 10, 1601, Lope de Céspedes
and his wife sold the lands to a priest, Gonzalo de Bermúdez, for 150
gold pesos of 13 *quilates.* A short time after this, on February 21,
1603, the records show that this priest sold to Hernán Sánchez Pabón
an estancia 1,800 paces long and 500 paces wide, fronting on the river
and bounded on one side by the lands of the village of the Panches
(those that had been given in encomienda to Asencio Salinas) and on
the other by the lands of the Bojacás.[45]

Early in the seventeenth century Governor Juan de Borja granted
lands rather freely in the Tena area. Thus on January 20, 1603, he
conferred upon Antonio Maldonado de Mendoza a cattle estancia
bounded by that of Bartolomé de Olaya (which an uncle of his, Francisco Maldonado de Mendoza, was "possessing quietly"), running
downstream towards Tocaima, and then towards the top of the Mesa
of Juan Díaz. Nine days later Hernán Sánchez Pabón secured the
grant of another cattle estancia, adjoining the one of Gonzalo de Bermúdez and extending down the Bogotá River. On May 23 of the

43. *Ibid.,* pp. 29-30.
44. *Ibid.,* p. 32.
45. *Ibid.,* pp. 32-33.

same year Juan Melo received grants of two cattle estancias along the Honda ravine, adjoining the lands of Antonio Maldonado de Mendoza. And on September 23, 1606, Andrés López de Escalante was given a cattle estancia at Tocaima bordering on the lands of Hernán Sánchez Pabón.[46]

Immediately after this a dispute arose between Hernán Sánchez Pabón and Andrés López de Escalante over boundaries, although one Royal *escribano* had officiated in giving possession of the grant to the former, and another had given notice to adjoining property owners and conducted the formalities which placed the latter in control of his lands. This was not settled until 1633, after the Jesuits had purchased the lands of Hernán Sánchez Pabón from his heirs. Even earlier, in 1612, Francisco Maldonado de Mendoza had succeeded in ending a dispute with Gonzalo de Bermúdez which began in 1606, by paying the sum of 370 gold pesos.[47]

Soon after Phillip III ascended the throne of Spain in 1598, the Jesuits came to be a dominating force in the affairs of the Valley of Tena, as in many other parts of the Indies. The first Jesuits arrived in Bogotá in 1604, where they enjoyed the favors of Governor Juan de Borja. Of considerable importance is the fact that San Francisco de Boza, who was canonized in the Jesuit temple in Bogotá, was an uncle of the Governor.

The first acquisition of lands by the Jesuits in the Tena valley mentioned by our authority was the purchase on November 27, 1626, from the heirs of Hernán Sánchez Pabón of the estancia of $800 \times 1,500$ paces referred to above. By this time the old order definitely had changed for when, in 1627, Antonio Maldonado de Mendoza applied for an additional eight estancias for cattle adjoining the lands of the Bojacá, only four were granted; furthermore when possession was given the Indians were present supplicating that cattle not be turned loose on the new estancias because the livestock would damage their crops. A few months later, on January 25, 1628, the Governor conferred upon the Jesuit Colegio de Santa Fe eight cattle estancias in the Tena Valley, including the four withheld from Maldonado de Mendoza. And on June 20, 1635, was recorded the sale of the lands of Andrés López de Escalante to one of the Jesuit Fathers.[48]

After giving these data our author became preoccupied with leg-

46. *Ibid.*, pp. 33-34.
47. *Ibid.*, p. 34.
48. *Ibid.*, pp. 34-35.

ends of diamond mines, and failed to indicate the manner in which the Jesuits acquired the remainder of the properties in the area. However, he did transcribe for us the document from the second volume of the *Títulos* which gives the limits of the Jesuit holdings as they eventually came to be. Since this case serves very well to illustrate the inexactitude and indefiniteness of the system of metes and bounds in general use, it is translated in full.

> The boundaries of the Hacienda de Tena, by virtue of which the expatriated regulars maintained and held without contradiction in peaceful possession are: On the upper side as one comes from Santa Fe to the Hacienda, they border upon lands of the Bojacá, the marker being the little bald knob which is there in the opening of the mountain, and from here bearing right to a ravine called La Coyancha, and from here it goes to the Lake, and from here down the mountain to a ravine called Santa Cruz, and from here it borders all of the Lake, as one goes towards La Mesa, to a bare spot of ground on which is a stone bearing the mark of Tena and that of the Hacienda de Cabiedes, with which it adjoins from here to the ravine named Magdalena, where is found a stone on this side which has the two marks before mentioned; from here it goes down to the Zuñiga ravine where there is another stone with the same marks, and from this ravine it extends uphill to the right along the mountain side, always adjoining the lands of the Hacienda de Cabiedes, until it comes out on the heights called Cara Perro, named la Puerta, from which it adjoins the lands of Guayabal to Tena, from this it jogs downhill to to a post which is called Cambulo, and from here it bounds with a place which is called Curares, where there was a palm tree, no longer in existence, and from here downhill along a divide, bordering the Palmar to the Sucia ravine and down this ravine to the Rio Bogotá and from here up the river to the Santa Cruz ravine in the Honda ravine, and up the Santa Cruz ravine to the first marker.[49]

In 1767 the Jesuits were expulsed from Tena; and along with other Jesuit holdings the hacienda was expropriated by the Crown in 1776 and 1777, when it was valued at 30,000 pesos. A few years later, on September 22, 1783, it was purchased by a wealthy Castilian, Clemente Alguacil, for the sum of 28,399 pesos. Our authority states that, following Bolívar's victory at Boyacá, Clemente Alguacil fled hastily from the country and lost his life in a shipwreck in the Caribbean. Since he left no heirs, the hacienda was incorporated into the national domain.[50]

That Tena was one of the choice properties falling to the Republi-

49. *Ibid.,* pp. 49-50.
50. *Ibid.,* p. 55.

can government seems evidenced by the fact that it was given in 1820 to Simón Bolívar and Francisco de Paula Santander, who in turn gave it to their sisters, Juana Bolívar, who lived in Caracas and Josefa Santander, wife of General Pedro Alcantara Briceño Méndez.[51] On December 30, 1845, Juana Bolívar sold her rights in the property to the sister of Santander for 4,000 pesos. Eleven years later the hacienda changed hands once more, passing by sale for the sum of 30,000 pesos to Francisco Javier Zaldúa, who later became president of the Republic.[52]

Javier Zaldúa was beset by numerous law suits concerning the property. He also had the misfortune to lose one of his sons who fell into a vat of boiling syrup at the sugar mill; and his other son entered the priesthood. On February 18, 1884, he sold the hacienda to Pablo and Julio Barriga.[53]

The new proprietors made substantial changes in the order of things at the hacienda. Apparently the lands had been practically abandoned for some time, but they quickly got the cane fields reestablished, and planted substantial numbers of coffee trees. A sugar ingenio was established to grind the cane, replacing the crude old *trapiches*. Each family on the place was assigned a small plot of ground for the growing of subsistence crops, and placed in the status of arrendatarios.[54]

The Barriga brothers kept the hacienda only three years, selling it on April 29, 1887, to Alejandro Urdaneta for 200,000 pesos. Of this sum 74,000 pesos went to pay a mortgage retained by the Zaldúa family. Urdaneta seems to have been a great "playboy," and in 1890 he gave up a substantial part of the property, including the coffee plantations, to a London firm in settlement of debt of $300,000 which he had incurred during a short stay in Europe.[55] By 1892 this part of

---

51. Colonel J. P. Hamilton, a British officer who visited this part of Colombia in September, 1824, included the following item in his published record: "We passed through the pretty village of Tenja on our road to La Mesa, where General Briceño Mendez, then minister-at-war, and his brother, the colonel of the hussars of the bodyguard, had a country-house and large estates in the neighbourhood. The fires we saw in the forests were on this estate, which they were clearing for the cultivation of Indian corn. . . .
"Upon our arrival, we met His Excellency the Vice-President [Santander], who was setting off for the country-house of the minister-at-war, having spent the preceding day at the house of Colonel Olaya. . . ." *Travels Through the Interior Provinces of Colombia,* I, pp. 268-70.
52. Rodríguez Maldonado, pp. 112-13.
53. *Ibid.,* p. 113.   54. *Ibid.,* p. 141.   55. *Ibid.,* pp. 141-42.

the hacienda had passed into the hands of the father of the author of the account we are following who was first administrator and later owner. But after 52 years of peaceful possession, the present owner was plagued by a host of lawsuits instituted by the heirs of Urdaneta, and affairs were in that state when the published story terminates.[56]

Some of the details concerning the portion of the hacienda which comprised the holdings of our author as they were in 1944 aid us in grasping the sense of the magnitude of the latifundium whose story we have been tracing. In addition to the structures necessary for processing coffee and sugar cane and some sawmills, there were "Various spacious and modern buildings, known by the names of '*Mon Repos,*' '*Mon Plaisir,*' '*Mon Trésor,*' '*Mignon,*' '*Désirée,*' '*Beau Séjour,*' '*Micheline,*' '*Zoilo-Emilia,*' '*Petits Plaisirs,*' and others of less importance."[57] This list does not include the old Colonial home which sheltered Bolívar and Santander.

Of much interest to the student of contemporary Colombia's problems are the comments of the master about his own social relationships with the workers on the estate. On this score he comments, "I have had the good fortune of having no problem whatsoever with the more than 250 arrendatarios, healthy workers, whom I have considered my friends."[58] And in the concluding remarks which the owner of Tena appended to his account of that historic latifundium he presents a detailed and idealized version of the relationships between the great landed proprietor and the families on his place under the old regime, and an allusion to some of the bases of conflict in present times, comments which deserve presentation at some length.

> In spite of the fact that the majority of my two hundred arrendatarios on my Hacienda de Tena are illiterate and unable to read my imprudent words, I wish to leave evidence of my loving gratitude to all of these humble campesinos, collaborators whom I have considered as friends, not as slaves.
>
> I have undertaken to understand with a humanitarian spirit their sentiments, respected their plantings, listened to all their troubles, rendered assistance on occasion, and satisfied their last desire: the coffin of wood emanating from the same soil on which they were born, worked, suffered, and which we shall all enjoy some day, rich and poor, eternally, unlimitedly.
>
> Hence my inability to understand the hacendados who have ac-

56. *Ibid.*, pp. 154-55.
57. *Ibid.*, p. 149.
58. *Ibid.*, p. 157.

cused their colonos of taking everything from the dry sticks to the fruit which they have lost, who have established tolls on the interior trails and levied tribute upon the produce harvested through sweat and constant privation. All of these owners of rural properties have harvested the fruit of their avarice.

It gives me great satisfaction to declare publicly that none of my employees, workers, peons, or arrendatarios have caused me any mortification. On the contrary without exception they have given proof of sincere affection. All of them complied fully with their rental agreements on the parcels of land of my property, without my putting any impediment whatsoever in the way of their enjoying completely their improvements and plantings.

In respecting their rights they respected my own.[59]

A Visit to Consacá Hacienda

To conclude this discussion of the size of holdings in Colombia, perhaps the notes taken in connection with a visit to the Hacienda of Consacá in the departamento of Nariño will help bring out some of the little things that make a system of large estates such a powerful determinant in social affairs. This visit was made in company with Dr. Justo Díaz Rodríguez, Director of the Departamento de Tierras of the Ministerio de Economia Nacional, on February 24, 1944. At the time we were on a field excursion to the southern province of Nariño. The following July the same Hacienda and its Casa Grande served as the place in which the President of the Republic, Dr. Alfonso López, was held prisoner during the abortive uprising which did so much to prepare the social and political climate for the disaster in 1948 at the time of the Bogotá Conference. The full details of the day's activities and observations are given, because the fragments would be of little value out of their context in any other place.

"We were out again at 7:00 a.m. to go to Consacá. Before leaving, however, we went to see two *lecherias* in the city (Pasto). Within a block or two of the hotel are the stables for the Holsteins. Here they are milked into glasses which immediately are dispensed to the waiting customers at 3 centavos (about 2 cents) per glass. It is said that the customers will not buy if the milk is drawn into pails and then poured into the glasses.

"After leaving Pasto we soon reached the divide and turned off to cross the deep ravine or canyon into Yacuanquer. This is the oldest town in the departamento. Formerly it was the residence of the *arrieros* (muleteers) who carried on a large share of the freighting in

59 *Ibid.,* p. 231.

this southern province. The coming of the road and the truck put an end to much of this and they now devote themselves to agriculture. The 'bright' spots appearing on the mountainsides among their corn patches indicate that this soon will be much less remunerative than it is at present.

"On leaving Yacuanquer we soon looked over the mountainside, down the slopes of the Galeras Volcano and on down into the hot country along the Guaitora River. Here in this first valley is an excellent example of the way in which inheritance coupled with some topographical features can pulverize landholdings. Formerly this entire valley was one large hacienda which extended from the hot country in the valley bottom, through the temperate zone, and into the tierras frias high on the slopes of the volcano. The hacendado left seven heirs. They divided the land into 21 pieces, one for each of them in all three of the zones.

"As we rode along, the master (Sr. Medardo Buchelli) of the Consacá Hacienda, for which we were heading, supplied a great deal of interesting information. Among other things he stated that in this area, with the coming of Ley 200, hacendados immediately began to get rid of their arrendatarios and to hire wage hands or *jornaleros* to do the work. No attempt has been made to introduce a written contract as a method of preventing the campesinos from acquiring squatters' rights. Nor has there been any provision for the 'casa permanente' as in Brazil. Nevertheless there still remain in the area a considerable number of arrendatarios, i.e., men who are obliged to work three days per week on the hacienda and who in return receive small plots of ground on which they may construct crude huts of wattle-and-daub and thatch and on which they may plant a few subsistence crops and pasture some livestock.

"Soon we were at an advantageous spot for observing the battlefield of Bombona where Bolívar met the forces of the Spanish King. After this come three sugar haciendas, the last of which, Consacá, belongs to Señor Medardo Buchelli. We drove through the pueblo and to the house which lies just below the town. The house is old, known to have been standing for over 300 years, and was used by Bolívar as a hospital for his wounded. It is of two stories, most of the living being done upstairs. Nearby is another large house for the servants, and also the water-driven trapiche in which the sugar cane is ground and the juice made into *panela*. When a decree by the government forbade ingenios to make panela, this family gave up the manufacture of refined sugar entirely and concentrated upon the unrefined brown sugar. The mill turns out about 200 kilos of panela daily and has the cane and the trapiches for more. The furnace, however, is inadequate. Another mill will be mounted just as soon as a new furnace is completed. A large waterwheel supplies power for a small electric dynamo which provides light for the house and for a small sawmill capable of cutting 20 boards per day. It also furnishes the force for grinding cane seven hours per day for five days per week.

"At present the hacienda, which includes 80 hectares of cane land, extensive coffee plantings (25,000 trees), and a large expanse of pasture, is in charge of a mayordomo. He supervises the work of about 40 laborers. Once a week either Sr. Medardo Buchelli (who is 76 years of age) or his son comes to the hacienda to inspect operations and 'fiscalize' affairs.

"Formerly the wheel was used to some extent in the transportation of the cane to the mill. Now the oxcarts are in a bad state of repair and all the cane is packed in on the backs of mules. P. O. J. canes were introduced and did much to revive the industry, but now they are heavily infected with mosaic diseases and the sugar-cane borers. I attempted to get over the idea of trying some selection in planting.

"The alcalde of the pueblo came to the big house to converse with us and to supply information. From that source we gathered the following facts:

"The budget of the municipio (3,851 population in 1938) this year is 3,600 pesos (about $2,400), compared with 7,000 pesos last year. The real property tax is 2 per 1,000 and last year it yielded 800 pesos. In addition the municipio receives some funds from the departamento out of the proceeds of the taxes upon the production and consumption of tobacco. The alcalde receives 20 pesos per month in salary. He has a small finca or hacienda, and it was explained that the free liquor from the 'rentas departamentales' (in Colombia the principal income of the departamentos or states comes from the monopoly on intoxicating drinks which are dispensed through state-operated stores) is among the perquisites that makes it worthwhile to be alcalde. Here, as in all Colombia, the alcalde is appointed by the governor of the departamento. On the other hand the members of the *Consejo* are elected for two-year terms. The Consejo determines the budget, and the alcalde is the administrator.

"There is little migration from the municipio, it is said, but a considerable influx of population is taking place. Local cigar factories are the attractive force. This industry now employs 50 persons, mostly women who are paid 40 centavos per day.

"Wages in agriculture are 50 centavos per day, *seco* (without meals), with work from 8:00 A.M. until 4:00 P.M. and one hour off for lunch.

"The Caja Agraria has only 20 clients in the municipio and has no local office.

"The campesinos take three meals per day, *desayuno* at about seven or eight in the morning, *almuerzo* between noon and one o'clock in the afternoon, and *comida* at 5:00 P.M. For breakfast they ordinarily take two plates of plantain soup to which a little meat or beans may have been added. Lunch consists of "secos sin grassa," i.e., potatoes, yuca, and bananas. For supper they again have soup, which may contain some barley or corn in addition to the plantains. Coffee is taken with all of the meals.

"There have been attacks of malaria which have carried off as many as 25 per cent of the population. According to the master there was only one death on the hacienda.

"There are three schools in the municipio, two of which are in the pueblo. The teachers number 5 (in 1938 there were 1,071 children aged 7 to 14), and they are paid 40 pesos each per month, all of it by the departamento. The average number of students enrolled per school is 120, and the average attendance about 80. An additional school is to be opened soon.

"The only churches are in the pueblo.

"The municipio contains one Indian reservation or resguardo on which about 20 families live. It is said that some of these families are *Indios por negocio*, i.e., for financial reasons.

"The campesinos come to the village weekly, on Sundays, since market day corresponds with church day. However, it was said that a large share of the population do their trading in Sandona, the seat of an adjacent municipio.

"At least 25,000 head of cattle are in the municipio, most of them owned by the few large landholders who have title to the pasture lands on the slopes far above the pueblo.

"There is no doctor in the municipio, but a dentist comes from time to time as his services are called for.

"In the opinion of the alcalde the biggest problem is that of transportation. The leaders of the municipio are greatly upset over a 'diversion' of 70,000 pesos, thought to have been designated for the repair and improvement of their road, for road work in the south near Ipiales.

"While we were at lunch the people of the hacienda were observed erecting an archway decorated with flowers just outside the gate, and lining the approach with the blossoms of the sugar cane. The reason soon became evident. Since the *dueño* was visiting the hacienda, the priest was coming with a procession. At the head came the cross followed by the image of the Virgin Mary from the local church borne by about a dozen girls. This procession had been planned for Saturday, when it was supposed that the master would be coming. His unexpected arrival today caused them to speed up things. Amid the explosions of many firecrackers and other noises, the procession entered the courtyard and continued on into the large central room on the ground floor of the house. Here the image was deposited in state, lighted by the reflections from several gasoline lanterns, and left, along with a pan in which contributions could be placed. This evening the procession will return and carry the image back to the church. In the meanwhile the master, the visitors, and the personnel of the hacienda will make their contributions to the building of a tower on the church.

"Near this pueblo passes the sulphurous stream which issues from the Galerias volcano. This river is crossed on a bridge suspended by cables. Notices posted on each side tells all passengers to get out while the vehicles are passing over."

3

Land Tenure

THOSE conversant with Colombia's recent history and current problems must have concluded that the nature of property rights to the land and the way in which these are distributed among those who depend upon the soil for a livelihood are among the most important features of the nation's social institutions and structures. This chapter is devoted to these fundamental aspects of that country's social organization.

THE DEVELOPMENT OF CHAOS IN PROPERTY RIGHTS

Colombia long has suffered acutely from great confusion relative to the nature and extent of the basic rights which the property owner has in the land. In these significant aspects of the relation of man to the soil, virtual chaos prevails throughout the length and breadth of the national territory; and many of the ills are of such long standing that the trouble must be diagnosed as chronic. Until as late as 1958 the problem seemed to become more rather than less acute with the passage of each decade. Since that time, however, and largely as a result of the agrarian reform program begun in 1961, some improvement seems to be taking place.

The roots of the trouble go back for many years, not a few of them to the colonial epoch. Throughout this long period the lavish granting of large and ill-defined tracts, the failure to provide for systematic land surveys, carelessness and lack of system in the recording of titles, and the occasional wholesale regularization of illegal claims to land set the stage for the tumultous scenes to be enacted in the twentieth century. Little or no improvement accompanied the establishment of the Republic. In fact it might be maintained with much justice that the various maneuvers of this or that administration and frequent political revolutions merely added to the confusion and made more certain that matters would build up to a period of violent crisis. The discordant state of affairs reached unprecedented heights during the great economic depression of the

1930's; and it was one area in which the Liberal Party, flushed with the successes at the polls in which the promise of a better deal for the landless masses had played no small part, attempted radical reforms.

To promise was one thing, but to fulfill was quite another. Great significance should be attached to the decisions of the Supreme Court in 1926 and 1934 which held that the title to land should be voided and the property revert to the state if the owner could not produce the original deeds to show that the estate had actually been alienated. This was like stirring up a nest of hornets; and it would seem that the next move, the adoption of the new fundamental land law, Law 200 of November 30, 1936, was greatly stimulated by the uproar created by that decision of the Court. In retrospect one may surmise that these reforms may only have made a bad situation worse, but then again they may have helped divert the masses from the violent revolution which seemed imminent.

Fundamentally many of the difficulties seem to have stemmed from the attempt to have in effect simultaneously two conflicting philosophies relative to the nature of property rights in land. The conflicts between these two ideological systems were not particularly grave until the twentieth century. By then the growth in the size and density of population, the gradual awakening of the masses to an awareness of some of the rights assured to them by the Republican constitutions, the substantial modification of the status quo in parts of Caldas and other provinces, and the gradual development of some of the members of the lower order of society into beings a little more removed from the level of mere creature existence, brought the fundamental conflict between the two ideologies to a head.

As will be indicated below, early in the period of the conquest Spanish law held that all the land in the territories of the newly discovered countries belonged to the Crown, and that individual property rights to portions of it were to be dispensed at the pleasure of the King. The usual manner of transferring rights to the land from the monarch to the private individual was by *merced* or gift, although in some periods the sale of land was also employed. But at the same time, at least sporadically, the King and his lawyers gave favorable nods to the proposition that land must be used or that the claim to it was nullified; and through the *composición* provisions were made for the adjustment and confirmation of the claims by giving at least some of the persons valid deeds to tracts of ground they had entered upon and occupied without any semblance of authority from the King or his representatives. The doctrine that possession and use of the land, and not merely a paper from the authorities, gave property rights to it grew and flourished as one colonial epoch succeeded another. It also continued to wax in importance in the disturbed period of revolution, and during the disordered times accompanying the frequent civil wars which plagued the Republic during the first century of its existence.

In some sections of the country the illiterate masses long continued to pay, without serious protest, the tribute or rent demanded of them by the members of the elite who possessed legal or other titles to huge expanses of the national territory. If we may believe some of the travelers' accounts, the most idyllic relationships prevailed between the landowners and the peasants who extracted a humble living by working small pieces of the huge estates. For example, Richard Bache gives this picture of the rural scene on the Acosta barony at Guaduas, a famous stopping place on the trail from Bogotá to the Magdalena River.

> April 8th [1823]. Left Villeta at 9, A.M. arrived at Guaduas—four leagues, at 1, P.M. Parts of the road very steep—enjoyed some fine views.
> We presented letters from our friends in Bogotá to Colonel Acosta, who entertained us very hospitably. This gentleman is the Juez-politico of the village of Guaduas, and proprietor of thirty leagues square of mountainous, but fruitful land. He is a well informed, agreeable man, of patriarchial simplicity of manners. In one end of his large house, he keeps a store, containing some foreign fabrics, and the little manufacture of his tenants; principally consisting of straw hats, which are manufactured in almost every house of the village, sandals, baskets, and wooded vessels. He attends to this little shop himself. While sitting with him here, I had an opportunity of witnessing the kind interest he took, as a magistrate and landlord, in the affairs of his clients and tenants; as well as their respectful, yet confiding bearing in his presence. These tenants pay from six to eight, and ten dollars per annum, for as much land as they choose to cultivate. We saw some of them, who came to barter with their patron, dispose of their manufactures, obtain a small loan, ask alms or advice. They were all kindly received, listened to with patience, and dismissed contented.[1]

But other large proprietors, perhaps because they were foreigners, early were plagued with the "problem of colonos" and all the violence

1. *Notes on Colombia*, p. 245.

later associated with the names of El Playón near Bucaramanga or El Chocho near Fusagasugá. Thus according to J. Steuart:

> . . . Mr. Haldane had previously many tenants on his lands, whom he allowed to erect houses, and cultivate for their own use a certain portion, provided they, in return, cleared a fixed quantity of land for the owner (but, since the affray here related, Mr. Haldane has broken up all these settlements); and that the people, instead of confining their cattle within proper limits, allowed hogs, &, to run wild, to the great damage of the different crops; upon which Mr. Haldane, having in vain remonstrated with them from time to time, at last told them that, unless the practice was given up forthwith, he would shoot the first hog he saw at large, which he did. This act drew down their vengeance upon him, and first led to the infamous conspiracy, the intention of which was the murder of the whole family, and then the plundering of the house. . . .[2]

In other parts of the republic, particularly in Caldas, as is indicated elsewhere in this volume, the campesinos were making fundamental progress in shaking off the bonds of custom which obliged them to pay for the use of a modest tract of ground when other land of equal quality was theirs for the taking.

There has been little systematic study of the precise dates at which the campesinos in the various parts of Colombia began to sense that the laws gave them a right to take possession of land in the public domain, cultivate it, and eventually have small tracts adjudicated to them as private property. It came early in Antioquia and Caldas, late in many other parts of the nation; but as early as 1930 it seems to have become rather common knowledge among the humble rural folk who are responsible for the production of most of the nation's food crops. But in 1930 there was no way of telling which unused lands were claimed as private property and which were actually a part of the public domain (*tierras baldías*). It would even

2. *Bogotá in 1836-7*, p. 243. It would seem that eventually Mr. Haldane succeeded in coming to terms with the *campesinos* of the region, for in a later volume is found the following comment upon his estate: "At Palmar, not very far from Guaduas, the estimable Robert Haldane, Esq., has been usefully occupied many years on a vast estate of his own, originally 'tierras baldias.' This gentleman has proved by actual results what a Protestant Christian can do in these wonderfully fertile regions. I met with him a short time many years ago, at the hospitable table of our mutual friend Colonel Acosta, when he told me something of his agricultural plans. Now, he has on his estate no less than 180 families of natives all paying him rent, and his population numbers 700 souls, to whom he ministers usefully, persevering in instructing them not only in arts of industry and civilization but better still, in Protestant Christianity." Leay, *New Granada, Equatorial South America*, p. 102.

seem that the large landholders were opposed to the surveying of lines of demarcation, for this was one of the measures instituted by the Liberal government when it came into power that met with great opposition. Consequently the campesino had difficulty in making sure that he was not on private property, and the government officials were handicapped in trying to direct colonists to unoccupied public lands. According to Francisco José Chaux, the Senator who prepared the exposition of motives for the project which eventually became Law 200, in his address to the upper house of Congress on August 30, 1933, "in many regions of the country, and especially in Cundinamarca, Tolima, Boyacá, and Magdalena, the interference of land titles has formed great latifundia, inhabited by a mass of workers subject to the despotism of an economy of minimum production, immediately consumable." They lack capital and for want of "property rights to the soil which sustains them, never succeed in securing a home for their families, and in place of being factors for the creation of riches, are foci of social unrest. If for a long time these masses have remained tranquil, submitted usually to an ignominious regime of labor, condemned to eternal indigency, their own increase and the awakening of the collective conscience has torn from them that submission and has inspired them to make an urgent and impassioned demand for land."[3] But the negative concept of public lands, the colonial origin of many of the titles, the indefinite boundaries, the lack of care in keeping the records, and the failure of previous administrations to begin the work of marking the limits between the public domain and the adjacent estates, are circumstances the joint effects of which impeded the state from directing the colonists to unoccupied public land.[4]

Under these circumstances it was inevitable that the rural masses would crowd in upon any unoccupied sections; and it was equally inevitable that much ill-will, conflict, and violence would result. One of the main sources of acute disorders was the fact that some of the proprietors would allow the squatters to remain for years, until the land had been cleared and adapted to pasture or cultivation, and then armed with titles and supported by the local police they would appear on the scene and evict the families. At times the colonos may even

3. Martínez E., *Régimen de Tierras en Colombia*, presents all the documents connected with the elaboration of Law 200. The extract translated here is found in I, 53.
4. *Ibid.*, pp. 57-58.

have been deceived into entering on private property. Says the official report of the departamento de Tierras y Aguas for the year 1937: "Many examples could be cited of conflicts originating in the *acciones revindicatorias* [suits to declare the title defective and to return the properties to the national domain] involving extensive zones which were abandoned by the proprietors ostensibly for lack of any economic interest in them, but which they acquired in the highest degree when the work of the colonos who occupied them in good faith, believing them to be baldias, had transformed them into rich centers of production."[5]

Although it is not possible to give all the details concerning the explosive situation that had arisen by the 1930's, the time the Liberal regime gained control of the government, it is hoped that some of of the significant features of the tremendous struggle for the land have been made clear. It is little wonder that Colombians came to think of and to refer to the invasion of a hacienda by squatters as the *problema social*. However, the much abused mass of humble campesinos, once so docile, tractible and obedient, had risen by slow degrees from the creature level to which they had been reduced by both the conquest and the encomienda system and at which they had been held for centuries of vicious exploitation. Some groups of them had developed considerable audacity. Perhaps the factors mentioned above were supplemented by a relaxation of repressive measures, as the members of Colombia's elite class came more into contact with other societies, or perhaps the basic causes were different; but in any case the rural masses took up the practice of occupying and putting to use small parcels of any large tracts of idle land which they knew of. This practice of squatting developed into epidemic proportions during the great economic depression of the early 1930's, and it continued to wax in importance for decades thereafter. Prior to and during the Second World War it was generally thought of as being Colombia's major social problem, an unenviable distinction it retained until supplanted in general public attention by the nationwide eruption of "la violencia" in 1947 and 1948. During the decades preceding 1947, though, the problem of squatters or "colonos" was pre-eminent. From the Banana Zone, near the Caribbean Coast on the north, where the invasions of the highly developed banana plantations paralyzed operations, to Nariño on the Ecuadorian border, a

5. *Memoria del Ministerio de Agricultura y Comercio,* Tomo II, Bogotá, 1937, p. 31.

newspaper headline screaming "Problema Social" was followed by the story of serious difficulties on this or that hacienda because the campesinos had crowded in and taken possession of the land. Aracataca, El Playón, El Colégio, Sumapaz, Fusagasugá, Río Negro, Chaparral, Coyaima, Chicaque, Otún, Pubenza, and Cartago are only a few of the names that figured prominently in the headlines of the 1940's because of the serious clashes there between the colonos and those who claimed ownership of the land.

Law 200 was a serious and a conscientious effort to deal with this problem of squatters. It recognized the basic injustice of permitting the latifundistas to retain the right, generation after generation, to broad acreages which were deliberately withheld from productive uses, while hundreds of thousands of humble country folk lacked the right to use even the acre or two of land necessary to enable them to provide for the meager needs felt by their families. As is indicated below, such a state of affairs was in basic disagreement with the fundamental Spanish law which Colombia, along with most of the other New World republics, had inherited. It was also greatly in conflict with the ideals and aspirations of many of Colombia's young intellectuals, not a few of whom in the decade following the close of the First World War had drunk at the fountains of knowledge in Paris, and some of whom had established the first Communist cells in Bogotá.

The most revolutionary feature of Law 200 is the provision which states that the only valid claim to land is the economic utilization of the same. In literal translation, the legal phrasing of this basic proposition is contained in the following extracts.

CHAPTER I

ARTICLE 1. Presumed not to be public lands, but private property, are the tracts occupied by private persons, it being understood that said possession consists of the economic exploitation of the soil by means of positive actions on the part of the owner, such as planting or seeding, occupation with livestock, and others of equal economic significance.

Inclosure with fences and the erection of buildings do not of themselves constitute proof of economic utilization, but they may be considered as elements complementary to it.

The presumption which this article establishes extends also to the unused parts whose existence is necessary for the economic utilization of the property, or as complementary for the best use of the same, even though the territories involved are not contiguous, or for the enlargement of the enterprise. Together these portions may be of an extension equal to the part utilized and which are reputed to be possessed in accordance with this article.

ARTICLE 2. Rural tracts not possessed in the manner specified in the preceding article are presumed to be public lands.

ARTICLE 3. In addition to the original title conferred by the State which has not lost its legal efficacy, private property over the respective territorial extension is substantiated, and consequently the presumption stated in the preceding article is invalidated, by written titles recorded prior to the date of the present Law, in which are demonstrated acts of possession for the lapse of a period not less than the limit set forth in the laws governing extraordinary prescriptions.

ARTICLE 4. The dispositions of article 3 shall not be prejudicial to persons who two years prior to the promulgation of this law may have established themselves, without recognition of any dominion other than that of the State, and not by precarious title, on lands that were unused at the time of occupation.

In this case, the proof of private property in the respective plot of land may be established only in one of these ways:

(a) By the presentation of the original title, emanating from the State, which has not lost its legal efficacy;

(b) By any other proof, also in full, that the plot has legitimately left the patrimony of the State; and

(c) By the presentation of a title transferring dominion dated prior to October 11, 1821.

ARTICLE 5. The dispositions of the present law pertain exclusively to property rights to the surface of the territory, and have no application whatsoever with respect to the subsoil.

ARTICLE 6. There is established in favor of the Nation the extinction of the right of dominion or property to rural tracts on which possession is not exercised in the form established by article 1 of this law during the lapse of ten continuous years.

When possession has been exercised over a part of the area only, the extinction of dominion shall pertain only to the unused portions which are not reputed to be possessed in conformity with this Law.

The extinction of property rights shall have no effect in relation to the following tracts:

1. One that has a total area of less than three hundred (300) hectares which constitutes the only rural property of the respective owner, and

2. Those belonging to persons absolutely incapacitated or to the adult minors, when they have been acquired through inheritance, and while the incapacitation shall last.[6]

6. A convenient edition of Law 200 is to be found in Maniño Pinto, *Manual de Derecho Civil Colombiano para Uso de los Agricultores*, pp. 201-34. The impact of *Ley* 200 was so great that even an itinerant journalist, with a predilection for bars and cabarets and only a rudimentary knowledge of Spanish, could not escape obtaining a sense of its importance. Cf. Farson, *Transgressor in the Tropics*, pp. 173-74.

The provisions of Law 200 were generally interpreted as meaning that the landowner had a ten-year period of grace in which to demonstrate that he was making economic use of the lands claimed. It was thought to be the equivalent of telling the absentee owner or the other claimant to large unused tracts: "You claim that you own this 10,000 hectares. All right, you have ten years in which to put it to use. If at the end of that time you have developed 4,000 hectares of it into arable lands or pastures, you may keep that 4,000 and an additional 4,000; and the government will take back the re-mainder." Since the ten years did not elapse until November 30, 1946, great uncertainty as to the true state of affairs, and what was in the offing, prevailed all during the period of the Second World War and the years immediately preceding it. Nor was the confusion dispelled following 1946, because for more than a decade after great violence and intermittent civil war plagued the country, now and then flaring up to extreme degrees such as that which disrupted the Inter-American Conference at Bogotá in April, 1948, and that which several months earlier resulted in the leveling of dozens of the pueblos of the Liberals in Norte de Santander, the killing of hundreds of people, and the flight of tens of thousands to a haven of refuge across the international boundary in Venezuela. Amid such chaotic conditions, when the personal safety of large masses of the population was seriously endangered, obviously there was no chance for any serious effort to clarify the basic nature of property rights to the land.

These waves of violence continued for more than a decade, during which two or three hundred thousand people lost their lives. Finally, though, compromises between the leaders of the two major parties were effected, due in a large measure to the understanding and states-manship of Alberto Lleras Camargo, and a government of national union was established in 1958. Thereafter important steps were taken to put an end to the prevailing confusion with respect to property rights to the land. As is indicated in Chapter 6, the measures for agrarian reform had this feature as one of the principal ingredients. Nevertheless, it should be indicated in passing that Law 135 of 1961, *Sobre Reforma Social Agraria,* prescribed in article 22 that "every proprietor of a fundo containing more than *two thousand hectares* (2,000 hectares) must present to the Institute, along with the respec-tive certificate given by the Registrar of Public Documents and the copy of the registry of the title which shows his right to dominion over said fundo, a detailed description of the same, which shall include, moreover, all of the data and explanations the Institute shall prescribe with respect to its location, area, and the ways the land is being used." In accordance with this authorization, the Board of Directors of the Instituto Colombiano de Reforma Agraria in Decree 1,902 of 1962 established the rules for these investigations and the necessary questionnaires were prepared and sent out. On the basis of the information assembled in this manner, from the returns for 1,238 estates, the Institute estimates that there were in the 17 departments into which the more settled part of Colombia is divided a total of 7,408,908 hectares of land in the estates reported, all claimed to be private property. Of this total, however, even those asserting that they were the owners reported that only 2,840,347 hectares (or 38 per cent) were being used, an admission that 4,569,561 hectares (or 62 per cent) were entirely unused, and therefore subject to reincorporation into the national domain. Accordingly, before the end of 1962 the Institute initiated 108 lawsuits seeking the revocation of title or invalidation of claims to 1,128,735 hectares of land in these estates, and it promised that other suits would follow in subsequent years.[7]

THE NATURE OF THE PROPERTY RIGHTS TO THE LAND

In general, prior to 1936, land in Colombia was held under a system of private property essentially equivalent to fee simple; and since 1958 this doctrine once again seems to be becoming the dominant one. Exceptions to this rule have been the communal holdings of the Indian communities, or resguardos, not a few of which continue to exist, especially in Nariño and other southern departments. In these communities the land is owned by the collectivity, and is subject to periodic redistribution by the Cabildo of the Indian community. But except in the far south, the resguardos have almost all been dismantled, and private property in land holds undisputed sway. As indicated above, except for the provisions of Law 200 of 1936, the owners' rights to the land are almost absolute, since relatively few feudalistic restrictions were transplanted to the New World, and those that did get a foothold were abolished about 1850. In common with his fellows in most other American countries, the Colombian owner of cultivated lands and of pastures possesses the soil subject mainly to the right of the state to exercise the privilege of eminent domain and to levy general property taxes. However, on all lands

7. See, Peñalosa Camargo, *et al.*, pp. 38-41.

alienated after October 28, 1873, the state has retained the mineral rights. Since immense pools of petroleum have been discovered in Colombia, with exploration still far from complete, state ownership of mineral rights is of no small significance. Among other things, undoubtedly, it has given rise to a great many efforts to establish fraudulently that certain tracts of land had been patented before 1873. The haphazard manner in which the surveys were made during the early days and the lack of system in the recording of deeds make this field a happy hunting ground for the unscrupulous.

There is little unique in the right of eminent domain as it exists in Colombia. The power of the State to expropriate land for public use, with the payment of a just remuneration, has always been recognized. However, under the basic Law 200 of 1936 it is now permissible to expropriate privately owned land for reasons of social interest, not necessarily involving public use; and by a vote of an absolute majority of each house, compensation for such may be withheld.[8]

EVOLUTION OF PROPERTY RIGHTS IN LAND

The evolution of property rights in land in Colombia has had a long and turbulent history; and the ways in which lands have passed from the hands of the king or the state into private ownership are many and complex. Procedures during the colonial epoch differed considerably from those in effect after Colombia gained her independence. But they were not uniform either during the colonial period or during that of independence.

The Colonial Period.—From the standpoint of property rights in land the entire colonial period falls into three rather well defined parts, namely from the time of the discovery to 1591, from 1591 to 1680, and from 1680 to 1821. It is informative to examine each of these in turn.

To begin with, the King of Spain by virtue of discovery and conquest assumed title to all the lands in what is now Colombia, as he did to those in the other colonies. The Spanish conquistadores were meticulous in the observance of the proper legal forms in taking possession of all the new territories for their lord and sovereign. The lengthy scroll that was read when they first set foot upon newly discovered soil was an indispensable item in the equipment of the

8. Cf. Backus and Eder, *A Guide to the Law and Legal Literature of Colombia,* p. 100.

Spanish adventurers who sought for fame and riches in the New World. Spanish law held that any conflicting claims were not worthy of the slightest consideration, and that by right of conquest all the "lands, plains, woods, pastures, rivers, and public waters" in the newly discovered territories became the property of the crown.[9] Later the sovereign was advised by the best legal minds of the period that, ". . . except for the lands, meadows, pastures, woods, and waters, that through the particular grace and gift of your Majesty have been conceded to the Cities, Villas, or Places of the same Indies, or to other Communities, or private persons in them, all the remainder of this type and especially those which may be broken up and cultivated, is and should be of your Royal Crown and dominion, as anciently we know it was of the despotic and absolute usage of the Montezumas in New Spain, the Incas in Peru, and in the same manner of the other Caciques in the other Provinces. . . ."[10]

This land was parcelled out liberally by the King to those he commissioned to explore and conquer the new territories, and by them to the officers and soldiers who assisted in the tasks. In this connection the precise wording of the *Capitulación* given to Pedro de Heredia (1540) for the discovery of new lands in the Province of Cartagena is illuminating. In a rather literal translation it reads as follows.

> Item, we concede to the persons who go to inhabit the territory that you shall find there, that for the time your government shall last you are empowered to give them caballerías of land and solares on which they may work, and plant, and build, with the moderation and conditions it is customary to give in the Isle of Española; and which, after they have lived on them the required four years, shall be theirs in perpetuity; and that in this way also you may make the encomienda and *repartimiento* of the Indians of said land for the time that is Our pleasure, and obeying the instructions and ordinances that you will be given.[11]

The wording of this authorization is almost identical with those of others given at the time, including that commissioning Sebastian de Benalcázar for the conquest of Popayán.[12] Furthermore the sources clearly indicate the procedures by which these instructions were put into practice. Thus in the account of the travels of Captain

9. Solorzano Pereyra, *Política Indiana*, 1739.
10. *Ibid.*
11. Torres de Mendoza, *Colección de Documentos Inéditos*, Tomo XXIII, p. 57.
12. *Ibid.*, p. 37.

Jorge Robledo in the provinces of Ancerma and Quimbaya (1539) are given some of the details of the settlement of San Juan (called Santa Ana in one copy). The first day was devoted to the establishment of the Cabildo. Two days later "the Señor Captain marked off the solares and assigned them to the resident citizens (*vecinos pobladores*) and the conquistadores, and in the same way he divided the estancias of lands, according to the quality of their persons."[13] Essentially the same pattern was followed at Antioquia in 1541.[14]

Lands also were designated for town sites and for community property, to be used by those who planted themselves in one of the new centers and assisted in the work of dominating the natives and exploiting the resources of the country. Thus there early developed at least four varieties of property rights to the land: (1) that in which the right to the land was acquired by the conquistadores through a concession from the King; (2) that in which those participating in the conquest received one or more grants of land (*caballerías, peonías, estancias de labor, estancias de pan coger, estancias de ganado,* and so on) from the leader of the expedition by virtue of the fact that he was explicitly authorized to divide the new lands among his followers; (3) that acquired by villages, towns, or cities as sites for public buildings and plazas, for communal pastures or ejidos, and as *propios* or community-owned property that could be rented out or otherwise employed, with the receipts being used for community purposes; and (4) that which was distributed among the conquistadores as building lots or solares and for garden plots. After the brief period of four years the citizen of one of the new Spanish towns or cities received the right to his land in what amounted practically to a fee simple. Thus in a royal *cédula* that later was incorporated into the Laws of the Indies the property rights of the settler are set forth specifically: "Having made on them his residence and his work, and resided in those pueblos for four years, we concede to him the right that henceforth he may sell them or do with them freely as he will as a thing of his own."[15] It is to be noted that,

---

13. *Ibid.*, Tomo II, p. 274.
14. *Ibid.*, p. 340. These procedures were strictly in accord with the provisions eventually incorporated in Libro IV, Título XII, Ley i, of the Laws of the Indies.
15. *Las Leyes de las Indias*, Libro IV, Título XII, Ley 1. Jesús María Henao and Gerardo Arrubla make the egregious error, perpetuated by J. Fred Rippy, the translator and editor of their *History of Colombia* (p. 103), of asserting that real property in the New Kingdom dates from 1590 and the

during this epoch, the original title to all land came as a grant or donation. Sale was not among the devices used by the King in transferring the ownership of land to individuals.

With the settlers operating at great distances from the seat of authority, enjoying the privileges of conquerors in relation to the natives who were virtually their slaves, and restrained by no comprehensive and systematic legal provisions, it is not strange that the whites soon possessed, legally or illegally, the lion's share of the desirable lands. Evidence of this is to be found in the laws which were issued, provisions which must generally have come into force only after the rise of the abuses they were designed to correct. Thus in a Royal Cédula dated 1541 notice was taken of the reports that there were in the provinces of Peru (a term often applied to designate the whole northern part of South America) many persons who had occupied a large part of the lands, and who would not permit the building of corrals nor the bringing in of cattle, and who were selling these locations publicly. For this reason the provinces were not growing and prospering as they should. Therefore, upon recommendation of the Council of the Indies the King proclaimed: "We wish and we command that all the pastures, woods, limits (*terminos*) and waters of said Province of Peru, now and henceforth forever, shall be commons, so that all the citizens in it, both those there at present and those who shall come later, may enjoy them freely. . . ."[16]

In another order dated at Valladolid, October 31, 1543, the Prince authorized the Governor at Cartagena to distribute caballerías to the inhabitants of Cartagena and the other pueblos. He specified that the Indians and the other third parties should not be prejudiced by these distributions, and that "the pasture of those cultivated lands, after the

---

government of Don Antonio Gonzalez. The argument is merely that the encomienda system, theoretically, was one in which the Indians were to be fed, clothed, and Christianized in exchange for their manual labor. It was specified that the natives were not to be enslaved, that the lands on which they worked were the property of the King, and that the encomiendas were not in perpetuity. The assertion of these authorities relative to the origin of private property in land in Colombia subsequent to 1590 appears to be based on the fact that Don Antonio dispossessed the *encomenderos* and sold the land on which their vassals had been working, with the arable lands going by preference to the Indians. Until our historians and other scholars recognize that the haciendas and other large estates in Spanish America originated generally in the grants of caballerías, estancias de ganado mayor, and other gifts of lands, and not in the encomiendas or repartimientos of Indians, such misunderstanding of the facts of colonial life are certain to persist.

16. Torres de Mendoza, Tomo XVIII, pp. 5-7.

produce has been harvested, shall be in common."[17] Once again, the principle that pastures throughout Peru should be commons, as had been ordered for the Indies, and everyone prohibited from appropriating them, was specified in an order by King Charles on October 24, 1544.[18]

The second part of the colonial period dates from 1591. As was indicated above it was then that the new governor abolished the encomiendas; and, also from 1591 dates new legislation governing landholding in the Nuevo Reino de Granada. These new laws were the Cédulas del Pardo which were sent out from the metropolis. The need for them was patent.

Although less than a century had passed since the conquest, the relations of people to the land were already in a chaotic condition. (The whole situation has more than a little resemblance to that which prevailed in our own country during the closing decades of the colonial period and the first ones of the Republic, when there was widespread "squatting," mutual recognition by the settlers of the validity of "tomahawk rights," "cabin rights," and the other de facto claims.) As was pointed out above, during the first part of the colonial period in Colombia, the only legal manner of alienating lands was through grants from the King or his representatives, including those made by the cabildo of a new settlement. But the colonists were not content with these gifts, although one may well be surprised at the liberality with which certain conquistadores received one estancia after another (see Chapter 2, in which the size of holdings is discussed). It would appear that all sorts of expedients were resorted to in order to supplement the tracts held through legal grants from the authorities. In some cases the landowners merely occupied and claimed extensions of territory greatly in excess of those specified in the concessions; in others it seems the devices resorted to included either titles granted by those having no authority to dispose of the King's property or even fraudulent claims. As time went on many of the claims, legal and otherwise, changed hands various times so that many people in good faith were occupying properties to which the titles were defective. It was this state of affairs which the Cédulas del Pardo, and particularly the second one which ordered the *composición de tierras,* were designed to correct. These ordinances provided for an examination of all the titles

17. Ministerio de Trabajo y Previsión (of Spain), *Disposiciones Complementarias de las Leyes de Indias,* I, 22.
18. *Ibid.,* III, 296-97.

by which land was being held in the New Kingdom, with a view to regularizing the holding of real property. In effect the composición provided for an adjustment of the claims; it was an attempt to judge each case in the light of the special circumstances and to regularize the titles of deserving claimants even though they were occupying the land without valid deeds. It had the effect of regaining for the crown extensive tracts that had been seized by rapacious land grabbers, but it also provided legal titles for many of those who had been holding land in irregular ways.

Except for the legalization of de facto claims through the composición, the gifts of lands continued to be the only way of transferring ownership from the King to the individual until the year 1617. Then a cédula from Phillip III provided for the sale of state lands at public auction.[19]

The publication of the Laws of the Indies in 1680 marked the end of the second and the beginning of the third and final part of the colonial period. These laws included a comprehensive codification of all the regulations governing the ownership and possession of land in the colonies, including those who held the land by a valid title and also "those who possessed with a just prescription." They prevailed throughout the remainder of the colonial period, or until 1821. Naturally they deserve the most careful study by all interested in land tenure in Colombia and the other Spanish American republics. In fact, an examination of this code, and particularly of Libro IV, Título XII of the Compilation is absolutely essential for one who would understand the property rights which the Spanish settlers acquired in the lands of the New World. This should be evident from a brief indication of the nature of some of the principal laws promulgated by the Crown on this important subject. Consider the following.

Ley i (June 18 and August 9, 1513) ordered that "houses, building lots, lands, caballerías and peonías" should be given to all those who went out to inhabit the new countries. These were to be situated where the Governor should indicate, and the amounts were to vary according to the quality of the settlers. After living and working in the new pueblos for four years the colonists were to receive definitive titles to their properties, and from then on they were to be at liberty to

19. For a knowledge of this and other cédulas, for copies of the texts of many of them, and for much other information about land tenure in Colombia, the author is indebted to Dr. Justo Díaz Rodríguez, formerly Director of Colombia's Departamento Nacional de Tierras.

sell the properties or to use them freely "as a thing of their own."

Ley ii (May 19, 1525) specified that a settler who had received a lot and lands in one settlement could not leave it for another without forfeiting his claims in the first, unless four years had elapsed and his title was definitive.

Ley iii (May 25, 1596) obligated those who accepted caballerías or peonías to erect houses in their solares, to work the lands, and to stock the pastures within a limited time, or else their claims were to be forfeited.

Ley iv (1568) authorized the viceroys to distribute lands.

Ley v (April 4, 1532) specified that lands should be distributed in accordance with plans drawn up by the cabildos, and that the regidores should have preference. It was also ordered that the Indians should be allowed to keep their lands.

Ley vi (June 26, 1523) prescribed that the *procurador* of the place should be present when lands were being distributed.

Ley vii (April 6, 1588) ordered that lands be distributed without favoritism and without prejudice to the Indians.

Ley ix (June 11, 1594) commanded that estancias and lands given to the Spaniards should be without prejudice to the Indians, and that those already taken from the natives should be returned to those to whom they rightfully belonged.

Ley x (October 27, 1535) commanded that lands "without excess" be divided among the discoverers, their descendants, and others, all of whom must remain in the country, and that the land could not be sold to the Church, to a monastery, or to any ecclesiastical person.

Ley xi (November 20, 1536) specified that those receiving land must take possession of it within a period of three months.

Ley xii (March 24 and May 2, 1550) ordered that estancias for livestock should be assigned only in areas distant from the pueblos and fields of the Indians.

Ley xiv (November 20, 1578; March 8, 1589; and November 1, 1591) specified that all lands held without valid titles should revert to the crown. Valid only were concessions from the King, his representatives, or preceeding kings.

Ley xv (May 17, 1631) recognized that many proprietors had taken possession of more land than belonged to them. It also provided once more for the composición de tierras or that new titles should be given to a "moderate" amount of the land being held illegally.

Ley xvii (June 30, 1646) stipulated that these composiciones should not be of land which the Spaniards had acquired from the Indians in disregard of the royal cédulas and ordinances.

Ley xix (June 30, 1646) specified that composiciones should not be allowed to those who had possessed the land less than 10 years, and that preference was to be given to the Indian communities. This is the legislation cited by modern Colombian lawyers as the prototype of the provisions in Law 200 of 1936.

Ley xx (January 10, 1589) authorized the viceroys and governors to revoke the grants made by the cabildos unless they had been confirmed by the King.

The National Period.—No radical changes in the basic rules governing property rights in land came with the attainment of independence and the adoption of a constitution in 1821. This constitution declared to be in force all previous legislation which did not conflict with its own provisions or with the new laws passed by congress. However, a law of October 13, 1821, contained several important provisos. One of these was the abolition of the composición, that is the institution for regularizing illegal occupancy of lands, established by the Cédulas del Pardo; and a second provided for the sale of lands from the public domain. It also stipulated that those who had been occupying public lands from time immemorial should present themselves and receive deeds to their claims. Furthermore Article 12 of the same law ordered the establishment of offices for the registration of land titles, one in Bogotá and another in each of the provinces, and made it mandatory for all landowners to appear and register their titles to the properties claimed; and Article 14 specified that after a lapse of four years, any lands secured through grants or the composición to which the titles had not been registered should revert to the state, and that the government itself was to proceed to register at the owner's expense the deeds to tracts that had been acquired by purchase and in other ways. However, in practice the last provision remained practically a dead letter, since the necessary registries were established only on paper.[20]

No doubt the government of the new nation hoped to use the proceeds from the sale of public lands to pay the liberal grants of funds it made to the officers and soldiers who had fought in the armies of liberation. These bonuses ranged from one of $25,000 for the commander-in-chief, $20,000 for generals of division, and $15,000 for generals of brigade, to $3,000 for second lieutenants, $700 for corporals and $500 for privates.[21]

20. Backus and Eder, p. 99.   21. Walker, *Colombia*, II, 545.

No doubt, too, the multifarious activities and obligations involved in setting the new government in order made it impossible to form a new and adequate land policy overnight. In any case a considerable amount of confusion seems to have been present from the very beginning. Thus from one of the Britishers who was on the scene among the throng seeking concessions of one kind and another, in reward for services in the cause of independence, we learn the defects of a law of June 7, 1823, designed to promote the immigration of Englishmen and other foreigners to Colombia: "The project of *selling* lands [at $2.00 per fanegada in the maritime provinces and $1.00 per fanegada in the interior, as provided by a law of October, 1821] never met with success, and this was the origin of the present law, which would have been more satisfactory, did not the 4th Article of the Vice-President's decree leave it still doubtful how far it is intended to *sell* and how far to *give* the lands in question."[22] Nevertheless, one set of petitioners, Messers. Herring, Graham, and Powles of London, shortly thereafter received a grant of 200,000 fanegadas of land in two Venezuelan provinces and in Chocó,[23] and this was merely the beginning.

Since there was a very close relationship between the desire to promote immigration and the formulation of land policies designed to achieve that objective, the early developments in the handling of the public domain are very closely linked with immigration policy. Therefore it is important to summarize briefly the developments in this field. As outlined in an *informe* dealing with *inmigración y colonización* by Tomás Carrasquilla H. to the Minister of Public Works and Development,[24] the principal legal enactments were as follows.

1. Law 13 of June 11, 1823, was designed to stimulate the immigration of North Americans and Europeans. For this purpose the chief executive was authorized to dispose of 3,000,000 fanegadas of the public domain, but was limited from granting more than 200 fanegadas to any one family.

2. A decree of April 30, 1826, empowered the executive to dispose of 1,000,000 fanegadas more for the purposes stated in Law 13.

3. The convention of the State of New Granada, for the purpose of promoting the prosperity of the Province of Casanare, dictated a decree of March 16, 1832, authorizing the executive power to make use of 500,000 fanegadas of unoccupied lands in that province for distribu-

22. Hall, *Colombia*, p. 70.
23. *Ibid.*, p. 131.
24. Bogotá: Imprenta Nacional, 1906.

tion to foreigners or Colombians who would settle there. Agriculturists might receive between 25 and 200 fanegadas and stockmen between 200 and 3,600. Immigrants were to be exempt from tithes, military service, and all direct taxation.

4. On March 6, 1834, a law was signed making available to the executive power up to 12,000 fanegadas of baldias for each new settlement that might be made in unoccupied or unsettled districts, of which as much as 60 fanegadas might be assigned to a single family. All settlers were to be exempt from military service for 12 years, and the produce of their farms and ranches were to be exempt from the ecclesiastical tithes for 20 years.

5. Law 5 of June 6, 1835, authorized the use of 150,000 fanegadas of the 500,000 in Casanare in grants to persons already in the province.

6. A decree of June 6, 1836, granted the executive power the right to concede to Tyrell Moore up to 100,000 fanegadas of tierras baldias in Antioquia. Moore contracted to settle this area with European agriculturists, factory workers, artisans, and miners, himself bearing the expenses of surveys and titles. The new settlers were to become naturalized in the usual manner, and were to be exempt from the tithes for 20 years, and from military service for 12 years, except in case of invasion by a foreign power.

7. Law 27 of March 29, 1841, supplied the executive power with the authority to cede property rights to each family of Colombians or foreigners which should establish itself in the Port of Turbo and to include as much as 150 fanegadas of the public domain in or about the port. In this case it was specified that mere residence at the port for six years was to be sufficient for one to gain the rights of a naturalized citizen. In addition, the inhabitants of Turbo were to be exempt from the payment of tithing for 20 years, and from military service in times of peace for an equal length of time. The same privileges were also extended to those who should establish themselves in Barbacoas.

8. Law 9, March 12, 1842, introduced a new departure, in that it provided that part of the land adjudicated for a new settlement should be reserved and sold at public auction in order to pay the costs of making the surveys and registering the titles.

9. Law 6 of June 17, 1844, again took up the matter of settling the plains of the Casanare. It stipulated that each family establishing itself in new settlements in the area might receive up to 100 fanegadas, subject to the following conditions: during the first year, from the date of the concession, it must construct a dwelling house and begin to

make use of the land. Neither the one to whom the grant was made, nor those who might succeed to his rights, could abandon residence on the land or fail to make use of it for three years, without forfeiting the claim to the property.

10. A law of May 2, 1845, furnished the executive power authority to cede up to 150 fanegadas of baldias to each family that had established or would establish itself in Caquetá. It specified that the land claimed must be within the limits of the territory itself. All nationals or foreigners who settled in Caquetá were to be exempt for ten years from taxes of every kind. Furthermore, all imports entering the territory by way of the Amazon during the succeeding ten-year period were to be exempt from duties.

11. A law of May 10, 1846, authorized the concession of 60 fanegadas of land to any family that would establish residence in any one of the territories.

12. A law of June 2, 1847, provided that the amount of money appropriated annually for the promotion of immigration should be used by the executive power for the payment of the passages and costs of establishing in the country immigrants from Europe, Asia, and North America. The executive was empowered to enter into contracts with companies that would agree to settle agriculturists and artisans in Colombia. For this purpose it was authorized to make use of 3,000,000 fanegadas of baldias, not more than 10 of which should go to any one person. The immigrants were all to become naturalized citizens, and were not to be liable for military service for 20 years, unless in case of war; they also were to be free from all ecclesiastical taxes, except for the maintenance of their own church, and if they were Catholics they were to be exempt from the payment of the tithes and the *primicias* or first fruits which all other Colombians were obliged to pay; and all the immigrants were not to be liable during the 20-year period for the payment of direct taxes, national, state, or local. This law also provided the authorization for the executive power to contract for the importation of coolies, as workers, and to arrange for their placement with Colombian agriculturists.

13. A law of May 20, 1851, conceded for 25 years, to foreigners who should settle in Goajira, privileges equivalent to those extended by the law of June 2, 1847, referred to above.

14. A law of May 13, 1853, adjudicated up to 80 fanegadas in the settlement of Obaldia to each family that had already established itself in the village or should do so in the future, in accordance with

regulations that were to be promulgated by the Provincial Assembly.

15. Law 80 of July 1, 1870, decreed that the executive power should solicit from the government of the state of Magdalena the cession of the territories of Goajira and Sierra Nevada to be applied for purposes of colonization. It authorized the executive power to make arrangements with the holders of the bonds of the foreign loan, or with other citizens or foreigners, for the organization of companies to engage in the development and colonization of these territories. Conditions to be part of all contracts included the making of a topographic map of the territory, the opening of ways of communication with the coast, or navigable streams, and with other settlements, and the establishment of colonies to foster the cultivation of cotton, cacao, coffee, and sugar cane.

The period covered in this survey is one in which population was slight in relation to the available land, political disturbances and civil wars frequent, and the campesinos still only dimly aware of the rights which they might demand under the constitution. Accordingly there seem to have been relatively few forces pushing for any radical changes in the concept of property rights in the land or for effecting any great redistribution of those rights among the several classes in the population. It is to be noted, however, that increasing emphasis was being placed upon residence on the land and use of the soil as requisites for valid claims to tracts from the public domain. We may be sure that all during this time in many parts of the Republic, more and more humble families of campesinos were discovering the possibilities of gaining relative freedom by settling down on small clearings in the forests and taking possession of small tracts of ground. We may also be sure that those whose claims to extensive acreages of land were based in written titles were allowing the limits of their haciendas to ooze out over adjacent territories so that the boundaries of their estates came to include much more land than that to which their legal documents gave them the right of ownership.

During the nineteenth century in most parts of the Republic there seems to have been relatively little conflict between those claiming property rights through occupation and those possessing documents substantiating property rights over extensive areas. But that was not the case in southern Antioquia and Caldas where a determined peasantry already was engaged in one of the most remarkable bursts of colonization activities, wresting from the wilderness places for their farms and homes, that the world has ever seen. Consider the following rather detailed description of events and developments in Salamina in that portion of Antioquia which later was detached to form the departamento of Caldas.

In 1800 all of the territory included between the Río Buey on the north and that of la Vieja on the south contained only two settlements: the ancient town of Arma, in ruins, and that of Sonson of recent establishment. A trail which parted from Arma, passed by the *tolda* of Guayabo, the heights of Requintadero, the *páramo* of Herveo, and then bore to the north through a wild and difficult country, was the only one which at that time put this part of Antioquia in communication with the old province of Mariquita.

In the year 1801, Don José María Aranzazu made a trip to Bogotá following this route, and as a consequence of this journey that gentlemen came to know and appreciate fully the value and importance of these lands; and thus it was that immediately afterwards he requested of King Charles IV the grant of a large extension of them. The King acceded to the request and ordered that they be delivered, after notice had been given to the owners of the adjacent property; but this matter was not attended to at that time.

In 1806 Tómas Valencia attempted the same operation, but without success.

During the war for our independence all negotiations in this respect were suspended, until in 1824 Sr. D. Juan de Díos Aranzazu, in possession of the pretended rights of his father, asked possession of them from the district judge at Río Negro. This possession was decreed; it was opposed by the citizens of Arma; and there followed an involved lawsuit, which was not decided until 1828 by the Supreme Court, in favor of the opponents. . . .

In the year 1827 the first clearings were made in community by the first settlers. . . .

In 1829 the citizens of Arma concluded a transaction with Juan de Díos Aranzazu, becoming through it owners of the part between the rivers San Lorenzo and Pacora, and of that between the San Lorenzo and the Honda. . . .

In 1833 Aranzazu ceded to the citizens of Salamina some of the lands belonging to him, reserving for himself the more valuable portions; but in 1843 the inhabitants denied the dominion and property rights of the donor, out of which developed litigation which lasted for more than fourteen years, until in the end through the intervention of the National Government it was ended by a compromise. During this tumultuous suit there were assassinations, burnings, imprisonments, dispossessings, and the ruin of interests. Elías González, a relative of Aranzazu and interested in the suit, was killed treacherously while crossing the bridge of Guacaica on the 6th of April, 1851.[25]

25. Uribe Angel, *Geografía General y Compendio Histórico del Estado de Antioquia en Colombia,* pp. 378-80.

These events in Caldas and other parts of the Central Cordillera eventually had their repercussions elsewhere in the Republic, and during the last part of the nineteenth century it became apparent that the old order was passing away. Not to be ignored is the fact that in 1873 the national government asserted its right to the minerals on all lands alienated subsequently; and Law 14 of 1870 established the rules by which occupants of or squatters upon the public domain could obtain definitive titles to their claims. But during this period there also arose, or at least came to be generally accepted, the doctrine that written records dating back for thirty years (bills of sale or other evidences of transfer of property rights) were good and sufficient proof of the ownership of the land. (The absence of tax on land, of course, eliminated one of the proofs so fundamental in the United States.)

The opening quarter of the twentieth century saw the problem that had been building up gradually come to a head, foreshadowing the outbursts that were to come during the subsequent quarter. Before World War I was over, a rapidly expanding population was pressing hard upon resources in the older settled portions of the Republic. The fact that severe erosion was literally washing the economic basis of subsistence from beneath large populations helped accentuate the difficulties. Hundreds of thousands of campesinos found it difficult to know where to turn, and many of them solved their problems by moving onto the unused portions of the extensive estates which blanketed the mountainsides. "Invasions" of the haciendas, or the so-called colono problem, began on a large scale.

At first the government, the controlling Conservative Party, attempted to cope with this situation by purchasing some of the large estates for resale in small plots to the peasantry. Probably these merely whetted the appetites of the campesinos for more. Furthermore, in the government's efforts to obtain lands some of the estates became involved in litigation and it became abundantly clear that many of them were being possessed and held with no title at all, with deeds that were far from satisfactory from the legal point of view, or through claims the legality of which could not be definitely ascertained. By 1926 some of these cases had reached the Supreme Court and the stage was set for one of the most momentous judicial decisions in the history of the Colombian nation. That year the Court handed down a decision pertaining to decisions in cases in which there was a contest between the nation and an individual as to whether or not a given tract of land was private property or belonged to the public domain.

In these cases it was ruled that unless the owner could furnish the original titles or papers or deeds to demonstrate that the property had been legally alienated, the presumption was in favor of the state.

The situation of the landowners in the face of this decision is excellently summarized by Dario Echandia in a paragraph from his able exposition of motives before the lower house of Congress for the project which eventually became Law 200 of 1936: "The diabolical proof demanded by the Court is almost impossible to produce in the major part of the cases, because of the lack of care with which the national archives were kept in the past, and because of the destruction of them during our civil wars; it constitutes a charge that is too onerous and unjustified with respect to the cultivated lands, and is, on the other hand, ineffective with respect to the lands withheld from all economic use if the original title to them is in existence."[26]

The train of events which that decision set in motion is best described by the man who was in charge of the Departamento Nacional de Tierras in the years when the avalanche of conflicts over property rights in the land struck the poorly prepared nation. It seems advisable to translate rather literally a substantial extract from one of the reports of this Director, Dr. Guillermo Amaya Ramírez.

> The doctrine set forth by the honorable Supreme Court of Justice (by virtue of which in order to demonstrate that a tract of land does not belong to the public domain but is private property, it is necessary to demonstrate that it has been taken from the national patrimony in a legitimate way, which may only be done through the exhibition of the original title from the State, which will establish the fact in a concrete and determinable manner) despite being based on elementary principles universally accepted, is producing as a tangible consequence an unbearable situation for the workers in the fields and one profoundly noxious for the national economy. In all parts of the Republic former *arrendatarios* are suspending the compliance with their obligations in the belief that owners lack, as is true in many cases, the respective original titles; and persons from the outside are invading under the same pretext, not only the unused portions of the haciendas, but even the parts cultivated by those who claim ownership; so much so that the latter, fearful of appearing before the judicial power (because of the difficulty of proving private property rights to the estates which they acquired and have possessed in good faith for many years) initiate with the police of the respective municipios, who generally are on their side, actions which frequently amount to genuine ejections.[27]

26. Reproduced in Martínez E., I, 137. The most pertinent paragraphs in the 1926 decision by the court are given in pp. 133-34.

27. "Informe de Jefe del Departamento de Tierras y Aguas," II, 26-27.

As indicated above, out of this and the subsequent ruling of the Court, and the tremendous social repercussions which followed immediately, came the fundamental agrarian reform embodied in Law 200 of 1936. That legislation at the very least served to mollify the situation for a few years, or during the ten-year period of grace given to those who claimed ownership rights in order to demonstrate that they were making economic use of the land. But before the ultimate results could be determined, virtual civil war broke out, a strife which plagued the country for more than a decade. The legislative and judicial processes were re-established in 1958; and the validation or abrogation of claims to landownership came to be a major feature of the agrarian reform program that was initiated in 1961. However, it still is too early to evaluate properly the effects of efforts since then.

Farms, Agricultural Families, Farm Operators and Laborers

The second fundamental part of the sociological study of land tenure consists of the determination of the absolute and relative importance of each of the various tenure categories, and of an analysis of the factors responsible for the variations observed. In other words, after the study of the nature and development of the system of property rights to the land, should come the classification of the population or the families dependent directly upon agriculture for a livelihood according to the tenure status of the worker or the head of the family. In this endeavor it always would be best if the family could be taken as the unit, but, because of the defective nature of almost all censuses of agriculture, usually the individual must figure as the basis for the tabulations actually prepared. Equally grave, moreover, is the defect that is present in the basic tabulations because of the fact that rarely if ever does such a census attempt to include information for the non-resident part of the agricultural population, that is the agricultural families who do not live on the land. This is to say that agricultural censuses tend to ignore entirely all of those who are dependent upon farming and stock raising who make their residences in villages, towns, and cities of various types. Not infrequently, of course, in parts of the United States such as California, Florida, and the Plains States, relatively high proportions of those who work on the farms and who are dependent upon agricultural activities for a livelihood do not live on the land; and the same pattern prevails in many parts of Colombia. Nevertheless neither the Census of Agriculture of the United States nor that of Colombia has made any attempt to take stock of this important component of the agricultural population. Therefore, before attention is directed to the study of farm laborers and farm operators as such, it is well for us to attempt to determine approximately the number of farms in Colombia, the number of families who live from agricultural and stock-raising activities, and the numbers and proportions of such families that should be classified as farm laborers and farm operators, respectively.

Heretofore those interested in land tenure and related matters in Colombia have been limited largely to qualitative analyses and fragmentary attempts at quantitative study because prior to 1960 Colombia had never undertaken a census of her agricultural and stock-raising activities. As the definitive results of her first *censo agropecuario* appear, however, they supply the bases for much more satisfactory appraisals; and, if carefully and intelligently analyzed, they can more than justify the cost of the enumeration and tabulations because of the light that such study can throw upon the entire process of social and economic development. Nevertheless before we make use of these materials in an endeavor to set forth the nature of the various tenure categories in Colombia, the absolute and relative importance of each of them, a few of the ways in which the tenure situation varies throughout the nation, and some of the factors related to the present situation and current trends, it is well to set forth explicitly some of the defects of Colombia's first agricultural census. Those already mentioned, which the enumeration under consideration shares with the long-established Census of Agriculture of the United States, and those of most other countries as well, are, of course, of primary importance. They are particularly important in Colombia, though, because that nation's recent census of population, which will give much essential information about the labor force, or data that can be used to supplement the materials pertaining to the population resident on farms, was not taken until July, 1964, and years must elapse before the detailed tabulations can be published.

Even more important than the defects already indicated, however, is that which comes from the lack in Colombia of the fundamental concept of a farm, the basic agricultural unit which dominates all thinking about agriculture and rural life in the United States and many other sections of the world.[28] As this linguistic deficiency comes

28. The absence of the concept of "farm" and that of "farm operator," and the complete misunderstanding which results from the same in connection with endeavors of sociologists and economists in the United States to com-

to be reflected in the nature of the agricultural census statistics of the country with which we are concerned, it has the most far-reaching consequences. Indeed it must bear a large share of the responsibility for many of the highly questionable generalizations about the distribution of landownership and other tenure matters which since 1958 have commanded much of the time and attention of Colombians of all ranks in society.[29]

Because the fundamental concept of a "farm" is not used in Colombia's census of agriculture, it is essential to indicate rather exactly and fully the nature of the unit that is employed. This is the *unidad de explotación agropecuario*, or the "agricultural-stockraising use unit." Such an explotación is defined for census purposes as "all of the land which a producer uses fully or partially for agricultural and livestock purposes, irrespective of the tenure by which it is held, or its size and location. The unidad de explotación may consist of one or more parcels, provided they are located in the same municipio [county] and that they form part of the same technical entity. The unidad de ex-

municate with their fellows in Colombia and other Spanish American countries, is illustrated by the following specific case. In a paper prepared for a seminar on "Plantation Systems of the New World" which was held in Puerto Rico in 1957, under the auspices of Columbia University's Research and Training Program for the Study of Man in the Tropics and The Pan American Union, the present writer stated: "Since in most countries of the New World the concepts of farm and farm operator are lacking, the definitions given by the U. S. Bureau of the Census are well worth rereading." Then follow the definitions indicated. In the Spanish translation of the same prepared in the Pan American Union, presumably by persons most skilled at such work, the corresponding sentence is rendered as follows: "Como la mayoría de los paises del Neuvo Mundo carece de una definición para los conceptos: *hacienda y hacendado*, es útil releer las definiciones dadas por el Comité de Censos de los Estados Unidos [! ! !]" If the Spanish statement quoted were expressed adequately in English, it should read approximately as follows: "Since the majority of the countries of the New World lack definitions of the large landed estate and the owner of a large landed estate, it is useful to reread the definitions given by the Census Committee of the United States." See Smith, "Some Observations Relating to Population Dynamics in Plantation Areas of the New World," in Rubin, p. 126; and the Spanish edition of the same, *Sistemas de Plantaciones en el Nuevo Mundo*, Washington: Pan American Union, 1960, p. 139. In effect the way in which my words were translated into Spanish, by those who lacked the concepts of farm and farm operator, and apparently were unable to obtain them even while translating the definitions involved, placed me in the preposterous position of telling Spanish Americans that they do not understand such terms as hacienda and hacendado.

29. As reflected, for example, in the address of the Minister of War, General Ruiz Novoa, before a gathering of Colombian agriculturists on May 26, 1964, and that of the Nation's president, the next day, as these were reported in *El Tiempo* of Bogotá, May 28, 1964.

plotación may be known by various names such as finca, hacienda, ingenio, plantación, huerto, huerta, viña, establecimiento rural, and so on."[30] It is hardly possible to identify this unit with any recognizable entity in the United States or Europe; and, on the basis of the data gathered and tabulated with it as the key concept in the frame of reference, it is extremely difficult or impossible to determine even approximately the number of families dependent upon agriculture, the numbers and proportions of these families that are headed by farm operators and farm laborers, the relative importance of owners, cash renters, share renters, and so on, and most of the other indicators needed in order to evaluate the institutional relationships between man and the land. Among all of the shortcomings involved, two are of primary importance: (1) the failure to make use of, or better, to deliberately exclude, the category of administrators or managers; and (2) the grouping together in the one monolithic class of explotaciones, the huge number of small subsistence tracts from which a high proportion of the farm laborers gain substantial parts of the livelihood and the units of various types that could qualify legitimately for classification as small subsistence farms, family-sized farms, plantations, or huge latifundia.

As is indicated in Chapter 2, more than one-third of all the privately owned land in Colombia, along with that occupied by squatters whose claims go back for more than thirty years, is in estates that are in charge of hired administrators or managers. Moreover, it is generally known that these estates include disproportionately large shares of the most productive land, of the soil that is best located with respect to transportation facilities and markets, and of the farms and plantations that are in the most highly developed and productive conditions. Finally, adequate comparisons and contrasts between those estates that are administered by managers and those that are run by their owners or renters are precisely the materials that those most deeply concerned about Colombia's fundamental social and economic problems would most like to have. For example, in 1964, as the data first made their appearance, General Ruiz Novoa, Minister of War, seized upon the information in the one set of tabulations of census materials in which the class of administrators figures, a couple of tables out of the hundreds that already had been published, as the basis for the following statements in his widely publicized address of May 26, 1964: "According to the 1960 Censo Agropecuario . . .

30. Departamento Administrativo Nacional de Estadística, 1962, p. 13.

there are 167,202 [1,167,202] fincas managed by their producers and 42,470 managed by administrators, with the former including an area of 17,892,714 hectares and the latter 9,445,113, which is to say that a number of owners 27 times less and made up of those who do not attend directly to their properties possess a quantity of land equivalent to the half as much as that held by those who manage their land directly."[31]

The second defect, though, is far greater than this failure to make proper use of the category of administrators in the tables which present the detailed information about land tenure in Colombia and in the various departments and municipios into which the nation is divided. It is well to emphasize once more that the fundamental unit used in the enumeration and tabulations, the unidad de explotación agropecuario, includes all of the small subsistence tracts that are used by various types of agricultural laborers as a means of supplementing their meager wages, as well as the farms and other places which call for the use of the time, the managerial abilities, the capital, and the credit of their operators. This comes at a time, furthermore, when those in charge of agricultural census activities in the United States and many other countries are making sustained efforts to enhance the meaningfulness of the agricultural statistics by excluding from the category of "farms" the myriads of small acreages which surround the "country homes of urban workers," the truck-gardening patches of those who reside in the rural-urban fringes, and so on. Unfortunately, though, the damage has been done, and the results of Colombia's one great and costly effort to assemble the data needed for the guidance and direction of her fundamental agricultural policies and of the large agrarian reforms she is attempting, have been vitiated to a large extent by the failure to benefit by experience obtained in other parts of the world in connection with censuses of agriculture. Were it possible for every one of the tables in the publications to include the information about the size of the explotaciones in cross-tabulation with the other materials presented, there would, of course, be no validity to this criticism. Such is not the case, however, nor can it be, because the very bulk of the information makes such a procedure untenable. Even as it is, however, much could be salvaged if two separate and complete sets of tabulations were prepared, one of which would give the information for all places of less than 2 hectares in size, and the other supply the materials for all places containing 2 hectares or more.

31. *El Tiempo,* May 28, 1964.

Until something like this is done, though, the figures for the various departments and especially the tables for the municipios, as well as most of the summary tables for the nation, will consist merely of vast jumbles of information about subsistence tracts, genuine farms, plantations, huge ranches, and immense unused latifundia, all thrown together in one hopelessly inextricable mass.

Thus, even after Colombia has taken a census of agriculture, many of the more important tenure indexes still must be mere approximations or estimates. The classes themselves are not difficult to identify and describe, and that alone is an important step; but it is, of course, utterly impossible to determine with any degree of accuracy the membership of each. Even if Colombia's census procedures were more satisfactory, it would still be exceedingly difficult to know just where to draw the line between the small parcels that should be classified as farms and those that are merely the subsistence tracts of farm laborers; and it also would be practically impossible to determine which of the so-called arrendatarios are genuine farm operators and which are just laborers who receive the use of small pieces of land as the chief payment for their services. All of this should be kept in mind constantly by those who read the following pages, and those who peruse any other discussion of the tenure status of Colombia's agricultural population.

The first classification of Colombia's farmers should be, of course, the fundamental separation of the farm laborers from the farm operators. Each of these consist of various types; and there also are many of the more intelligent campesinos who actually double in both roles, serving as laborers on the estates of the large landed proprietors, and also securing a considerable portion of their support by cultivating small subsistence plots which they own or rent. This makes a hard and fast distinction between farm laborers and farm operators difficult if not impossible, but it does not obviate the necessity of attempting that fundamental classification.

By working with a part of the material gathered in the 1960 census of agriculture, and by making liberal allowances for other factors known to enter but which it is impossible to gauge quantitatively, I estimate that there were in 1960 approximately 1,500,000 families in Colombia who were directly dependent upon agriculture for their employment and their livelihood. Moreover I calculate that about 530,000 (35 per cent) of these were headed by persons who should be classified as farm operators and approximately 970,000 (65 per cent) who belong in the farm laborer category. In arriving at these results, the easiest and most reliable estimate is that of the number of families of farm operators. Thus in order to obtain the figure of 530,000 in this category, it was first assumed that each of the 1,309,942 *viviendas,* or dwellings or households, found on the explotaciones represented one agricultural family. (In estimates as rough as these necessarily must be, little would be gained by any attempt to distinguish one-person households from the others.) Then one family headed by a farm operator was attributed to each explotación containing 10 hectares or more, of which 283,933 were reported. This figure is probably somewhat too high because for each of the cases in which two or more families of those classified as "producers" are involved in connection with a given agricultural unit, there probably are many, many explotaciones in which absentee owners resident in one of the major cities figure as the "producers" who the census assumes are responsible for the operations on the various estates which they own. Actually, from some points of view the 283,933 places containing 10 hectares or more could almost be considered as the number of farms and the equivalent of the number of those truly deserving a place in the category of farm operators. This is because in many sections of the country the estancias, or *conucos,* or other types of the farm laborers' subsistence tracts actually embrace areas greater than 10 hectares in extent, whereas a considerable proportion of the places of from 5 to 10 hectares in size are nothing more than the plots that have been assigned to the campesinos who must serve as laborers on the haciendas for from three to six days per week. Even if such tracts are owned by campesinos and are quite separate from any large estate, their proprietors should not necessarily be considered as farm operators. Inquiries always show, for example, that among the peons one encounters at work upon the sugar-cane plantations, the cotton plantations, or even on ranches far out on the plains to the east of the Andes, are many owners of small patches of land in the mountains on which their families are living. In order to be liberal, though, in attempting to arrive at the number of farms and farm operators, it was decided to attribute two-thirds of the number of explotaciones of from 5 to 10 hectares in size to the category of farms and an equal number of families to that of the farm operators. This procedure adds the figure of 112,820 to the total for each of these. Finally, in order to make sure that the numbers of farms and farm operators are not underestimated, it was considered that one-half of the small places of from 2 to 5 hectares in size should be included in the number of farms and an equal number of families attributed to the class of farm operators. The figure involved in this case is 135,935. By adding all of these together, a total of 530,677 is secured for the number of farms and which is also the number of farm operators. But since it would be ridiculous to think that such a number could be significant to three places, each of these two totals is rounded off to 530,000.

The task of estimating the number of agricultural families who belong in the farm laborer category is even more difficult, and the results obtained are less precise than is true with respect to the families headed by farm operators. One large contingent of the families of agricultural laborers is comprised, of course, of the occupants of the dwellings on nearly all of the small subsistence tracts of one kind or another which are spread throughout the nation. On places of less than 2 hectares in size, the 1960 census counted a total of 438,868 viviendas, which we must assume corresponds to the same number of families or households. Accordingly, irrespective of whether the occupants of these dwellings were included by the census in the category of "proprietors," in that of "renters," or omitted entirely from the group of "producers," all are placed in the class of farm laborers.

Next, following the same line of reasoning as that employed in estimating the number of farms and the number of the families of farm operators, an allowance must be made for the thousands of genuine farm laborers who live on tracts of ground that range in size from 2 to 5 hectares. All together, a total of 270,349 viviendas was reported for the 267,187 explotaciones in this class. Lessening this number of dwellings by a figure corresponding to one-half the number of places of this size, or 133,594, leaves 136,455 as the number of viviendas or families of resident farm laborers attributable to this part of the mixed mass of very small farms and subsistence tracts.

Again, and once more following the line of reasoning used in estimating the number of families headed by farm operators, an additional allowance must be made for families headed by farm laborers who reside on places of from 5 to 10 hectares in size. The census of 1960 reported 169,230 explotaciones in this group and 194,738 viviendas on the same; and this number of dwellings diminished by a figure corresponding to two-thirds the places of this size, or 112,918, leaves 81,918 as the number of dwellings or families of resident farm laborers that should be included, according to our assumptions, in the category of families of agricultural laborers.

The explotaciones containing 10 hectares or more of land, of course, nearly all belong in the class of genuine farms, but not all of them are equipped with viviendas or dwellings. Indeed, in Colombia as a whole, no viviendas whatsoever were reported by the 1960 census for 17,592 of these entities. Nevertheless for the 266,330 places containing 10 hectares or more having one or more viviendas, a total of 415,987 dwellings was reported. Accordingly it was assumed that each one of these 266,330 areas was equipped with a residence for one family of farm operators, and that the remaining 139,657 dwellings were those of agricultural laborers. Summing the four figures indicated gives 796,898 as the number of viviendas or families of resident agricultural laborers on the farms, plantations, ranches, and extensive idle estates in Colombia.

Finally, account must be taken of the greatest unknown of all, that is of the number of families dependent upon work in agriculture and stock raising for employment who do not live on the land but who make their homes in the thousands of hamlets, villages, towns, and cities that are spread over the Colombian landscape. Any estimate of the numbers of such non-resident families of agricultural laborers can be little more than guesswork, but it would be utterly foolhardy to regard it as being inconsequential. Consider the fact that the 1951 census of population showed that well over 10 per cent of all the males actively engaged in agricultural and pastoral occupations was made up of those who lived in those particular villages, towns, and cities that enjoyed the status of *cabeceras,* or heads (in English the expression is seats) of municipios or counties. Hence, one probably would not be overestimating the number of such families if he were to consider that at least 20 or 25 per cent of all those headed by agricultural laborers have their humble cottages, not on the various haciendas and plantations on which they work, but in the population centers of various sizes which are distributed throughout the country. Accordingly, a figure (173,102) equal to slightly less than 22 per cent of the total number of resident farm laborer families was included, so as to bring the grand total of all families of agricultural laborers up to 970,000. This number, in turn, when added to the one of 530,000 representing the families of farm operators, gives 1,500,000 as the sum total of all families in Colombia as of 1960 which depended directly upon agricultural and pastoral activities for a livelihood. On the proportional basis, these materials indicate that about 35 per cent of the agricultural families are headed by farm operators and 65 per cent by agricultural laborers. With the data as they are it is doubtful that any more accurate and reliable estimates can be made. Therefore, as closely as we are able to determine them, the key figures in an inventory of Colombia's agricultural standing are as follows: the number of farms, 530,000; the number of families dependent directly upon agricultural and pastoral activities, 1,500,000; and the numbers and proportions of those families that are headed by farm operators, 530,000 (or 35 per cent), and by farm laborers 970,000 (or 65 per cent), respectively.

FARM LABORERS

The total number of families headed by farm laborers just given does not include tens of thousands of small holders who manage to eke out a meager existence only because they supplement the products of their own tiny farms by work on the haciendas and fincas of Colombia's more affluent families; nor does it include other tens of thousands of families that are squatting on small tracts of land. Nevertheless the arrangements under which the farm laborers are employed vary considerably and this requires their further subdivision into a number of classes.

Peons or Jornaleros.—The peons or jornaleros, that is the casual agricultural laborers who work in return for a meager daily, weekly, or monthly wage, occupy the position at the bottom of Colombia's social scale. They are only a step removed from the *coloni* of the period following the disintegration of the Roman Empire or the Indians who were held in encomienda during the colonial period in Spanish America. The 1938 census assigned 780,152 men, or 32 per cent of Colombia's entire male labor force, to this unenviable category; and the comparable figures for 1951 are 794,075 men, or 26 per cent. Furthermore these totals do not include the hundreds of thousands of campesinos who spend a good share of their time working as peons or jornaleros even though they may own or "rent" small tracts of land. Indeed probably 50 or 60 percent of all male workers in Colombia assume the role of peon for a least a portion of every year. Volumes might be written about the pitifully low levels of existence which are the lot of the bulk of these humble campesinos, with shocking details relative to their inadequate diet, miserable huts, poor clothing, lack of sanitary provisions, and so on, but that is not the purpose of the present paragraphs. Here it is sufficient to point out the exceedingly great numerical importance of these landless masses. It would be farcical to pass them by in any study of land tenure in Colombia.

Peons are used in all types of agricultural and pastoral activities in Colombia, but of course they are the chief reliance for labor on the cattle ranches. In crops such as coffee and cotton these casual laborers find their greatest usefulness during the harvest season, while on the commercialized sugar-cane plantations they are depended upon throughout the year. Generally speaking in the hot sections of the country, whether out on the Eastern Plains or in the humid valley bottoms, peons make up the bulk of the laboring masses; while in the higher and cooler climes where tobacco, wheat, barley, and potatoes are grown, various other types of labor contracts are in use. Since the coming of Law 200 of 1936 not a few landowners have been shifting their workers from a sharecropping basis, and also from the status of arrendatarios, to that of peons or jornaleros. (See the notes on Consacá in Chapter 2.)

The Arrendatarios, Concertados, or Conuqueros.—The second large class of agricultural laborers in Colombia is composed of those who erroneously are designated as arrendatarios or renters. The 1938 census of population enumerated 278,765 males in a category composed of arrendatarios, agregados, and colonos; but the 1951 enumeration lacks this detail. The arrendatarios undoubtedly made up the bulk of these, or not less than 200,000. They work under an arrangement that is little different from that of the coloni of the Roman world in the centuries following the decay of the empire,[32] or from that once employed by the owners of slaves in Cuba and along the Spanish Main. As described by an anonymous visitor in 1823 this system was as follows.

> The agriculturist, in this country, has an excellent method of availing himself of the services of his slaves, almost free of any expense. Each man, or family, receives a certain portion of land, called a *Conuco,* which he cultivated for his own support; for this purpose he is left at liberty a day in each week. A taste for husbandry is hereby acquired, which in the end is beneficial to the estate; five days are devoted to the *hacienda,* and on Sunday they are again free. After hearing mass, in which they are very punctillious, the rest of the day is devoted to dancing, a recreation which the blacks are passionately fond of.[33]

Today from Nariño on the south to Norte de Santander and Magdalena on the north the system is essentially similar, and the workers

32. Cf. Irvine, *The Making of Rural Europe,* pp. 22-23.
33. *Letters Written from Colombia,* p. 88.

engaged in that manner form a large share of the inhabitants of the rural districts. The basic arrangement is as follows: the family of campesinos receives from the landowner a small tract of ground (usually marginal in the sense that it lies on the outskirts of the hacienda and also in terms of productivity) on which its members themselves erect a rude dwelling and on which they grow some subsistence crops, keep a small flock of chickens, and possibly care for a cow or a few head of sheep. In return the members of the family are obligated to work on the hacienda at nominal wages for a certain number of days per week. The exact number of days' service required varies widely, although often it is all six, with only stated periods off during the course of the year, and in other sections of the country only three days of work per week are required.[34]

A few specific cases taken from my field notes and other materials especially prepared for my use will assist in making more definite the arrangements between the laborers who are designated as arrendatarios and the patrons for whom they work. For example, on October 18, 1943, a detailed inspection was made of the homes and parcels of ground occupied by the arrendatarios of the three haciendas in the Samacá Valley, Boyacá, which the Ministry of National Economy had leased for the purpose of demonstrating the use of mechanized equipment in the cultivation of wheat. Notes taken during the day included the following: "Then came the horses and we rode down the side of the valley, observing the houses and 'estancias' of the arrendatarios. The subsistence tracts are all located on the side of the mountain facing the valley, in the ravines which lead into it, and over the top in another little valley or *quebrado*. Most of the lands they occupy are of extremely poor quality, steep slopes badly cut up by erosion, but each of the families has an acre or two that is suitable for planting wheat or barley. Potatoes do not do well on account of the lack of water. Some of the families have a few sheep, a cow or two, and a number of pigs, in addition to the chickens. They construct their own houses of adobe and thatch.

"Our guide, a man of about 50, was born on the place, as was his father and grandfather. The same applies to most of the others. He knew exactly where all the dividing lines lay, the names of all the 'renters,' etc. There are 38 arrendatarios on the place. Formerly this hacienda was devoted exclusively to stock raising and was much neg-

34. Cf. García, "Notes on Land Tenure in Colombia" and Fals-Borda, *El Hombre y la Tierra en Boyacá*, pp. 115-16.

lected. Then the 'renters' were paid 25 centavos per day. Now they are paid 50 centavos per day for seven days per week, although they are not required to work on Sundays. They also have a week off periodically to cultivate their own little plantings. This week they take in turns, family by family, until all have had a week, when the cycle commences again. Thus they get almost two weeks per year for this purpose."

On another hacienda near Paipa, Boyacá, which we visited on October 19, 1943, the laborers also worked six days per week, but around Sogomoso where we were a few days later the three-day variation was noted. Notes taken in connection with a visit to one hacienda in this area include the following: "This hacienda contains about 1,000 fanegadas, of which 500 are in the bottom lands and 500 on the hillsides. The land is valued at 200,000 pesos, and the buildings, equipment, livestock, and so on at another 100,000. The main enterprises are the growing of wheat and the milking of Holstein cows.

"Twenty arrendatarios work on the place, along with 40 'propietarios' who have already secured titles to their small parcelas or estancias. The 'renters' receive 15 centavos per day and are required to work three days per week on the hacienda. The others receive 60 to 65 centavos per day. There is practically no migration, the workers being fixed rather firmly to the soil. Those who have bought their small holdings paid from 800 to 1,000 pesos per fanegada for the plots on the hillsides."

A slightly different arrangement was noted on an hacienda near Toca, Boyacá, visited on August 5, 1944. About 1925 the father (now deceased) of the present owners of the estate pioneered in the first "parcelación" projects in this part of the Republic. Small plots of from two to ten fanegadas were sold on credit to the campesinos, or to those of that class who were the best prospects. The boys have continued the practice begun by their father. Today the municipio of Toca is dotted with little places of four or five fanegadas. At present the hacienda belongs to the widow, two sons, and a daughter. It consists of about 400 fanegadas of which 300 are cultivated. Wheat, potatoes, corn, barley, peas, and beans are the principal crops, and there is some livestock, including 200 sheep, 35 cattle, and 8 horses. In recent years the family has sold 30 tracts totaling 380 fanegadas. Arrendatarios occupy the higher lands in the estate, those up near the páramo. Five families pay a total of 70 pesos per year for 200 fanegadas of land. Those who have plots of ground of their own come to the finca to work only when they care to do so, and the same is true of those who rent the land referred to above.

"There are also *concertados* living on the hacienda. They are assigned about one fanegada per family for crops and allowed the use of a couple more for pasture. They also receive the use of a hut in which to live. They work five days per week, Mondays through Fridays, two weeks out of each month on the finca. For this they receive their board and 15 centavos per day for drink. Workers who come from off the finca are paid 45 centavos per day and their food for the day." On this same hacienda about 40 persons of both sexes and all ages were observed busily working for long hours in one of the fields from which a crop of potatoes has just been taken. It was explained that the custom of the region gave the campesinos a right to glean in the fields from which the crops had been harvested, and that all these people were there to gather in the tubers that had been missed in the digging. They seemed to be acquiring a good many bushels and one of the brothers wryly remarked that the workers sometimes were not above purposely passing by and carefully camouflaging select hills of potatoes in order to have richer gleaning later on.

"Under the system of concertados, those who do not drink can use the 15 centavos per day to feed their families. This leaves them the crops on the little acreages to sell, and in this way they get tidy little sums all at one time. Of course if they drink they must use the crops for food. In any case in this area several hundred campesino families already have attained the ownership of the small tracts of land on which they live."

In the important coffee producing section on the slopes of the Eastern Cordillera above Cúcuta even the old name of conuco is retained. There, according to notes taken on October 25, 1943, "on the coffee estates each worker is assigned a lot or conuco. Such a conuquero or 'renter' lives on this plot, cares for the coffee trees, raises his *pan coger* or subsistence crops, picks the coffee, and carries it to the mill. There it is divided equally between the worker and the landowner." In this area the owner of one large finca, on which there are 1,000,000 trees, allowed the workers credit to supply their needs at the commissary; and they sold him the coffee in the field.

The comparable types of farm labor contracts in the opposite extremity of the nation, the departamento of Nariño, are conveniently described in the words of the report especially prepared for me by one of the officials of the Ministry of National Economy, a capable observer who was stationed in the far southern post for many months. In describing the systems of work this report states: "Leaving out of consideration the system of small holdings in which the Indian works his own land, we find the following types of labor contracts with their respective wages. (a) *The Indian concertado.* In this case the Indian works for the patron almost in a state of semi-servitude, since he receives from him in payment for his work only a miserable daily ration along with the right to work one day out of the week on the small tract which the patron has assigned to him. The improvements that the Indian makes in the course of time that he remains working for the patron do not belong to the worker, as he has only the product of the parcel during the time that he is concertado. (b) *The Indian arrendatario.* This worker gives labor to the owner to pay the rent on a small parcel of land. The amount of rent is stipulated at ten or fifteen days per month. (c) *Aparcería.* This system is one in which the owner of the land gives the land over to the Indian to fence, fertilize, sow, and cultivate with the obligation on the part of the latter to deliver to the former one-half of the entire harvest.

"I should mention that direct rent, that is cash, is almost nonexistent.

"These systems of contract are relative since, owing to the ignorance, timidity, and so forth, of the Indians, the patron abuses them in a heartless manner, even stooping so low as to take from them the smallest portion of the harvest, the house in which they live and the parcel upon which they have worked for long years. . . .

"The case in which the day laborer receives payment in money for his work is extremely rare. Generally he receives part in money and part in food; at other times in food and clothing; and in the sections most removed from the city the patron makes the Indian sign a document in which the latter figures as the debtor for a large sum of money to be repaid in work, which enslaves the laborer for life."

It seems unnecessary to multiply the examples, for the precise number of arrendatarios and all of the variations in the system under which they work could only be determined by a comprehensive census. However, before leaving the subject it is well to refer to the results of the special study made in the municipio of Tabio in the departamento of Cundinamarca, for the situation there is not too different from that in vogue throughout extensive parts of the Colombian uplands, particularly the ones in which the white element makes up the majority of the population. In Tabio we found that "the slopes of the mountains surrounding the valley bottoms, whose fertile soils are monopolized by the *hacendados* for their pastures, are the areas most frequently given over to the laborers as small holdings or as estancias."[35] Of the total of 428 families or households visited in the survey, 187, or 44 per cent, could be classed only in the category of farm laborers, and it is likely that most of the 87 cases of owners with less than 5 fanegadas of land also really belonged primarily in the same class. "Generally in Colombia even the campesinos of this lowest stratum own or are assigned a small tract of ground, an estancia, of an acre or so on which to erect a small dwelling, grow a few subsistence crops, and perhaps raise a hog, a few chickens, or even care for a cow. The tenure arrangements by which the farm laborers hold their small plots of ground also are of interest. . . . Seven out of ten . . . own the small pieces of land on which they live and on which they produce a good share of the food they and their families consume. The bulk of them have purchased their tiny estancias, but about one-third of the total secured theirs through inheritance. One out of eight such families rents the ground on which it lives, two-thirds of them paying cash and one-third working out the rent. Nine families enjoy the privilege of *comodata* (. . . a form of contract in which the use of property is ceded without remuneration upon condition that it be returned in the same state as it was given), and 12 have merely erected their ranchos at convenient spots without bothering about the legal right to occupy the small pieces of ground."[36]

The Aparceros.—Aparcería, the Spanish American and Brazilian equivalent of the English sharecropping or the French métayage, also is fairly prevalent; and the bulk of the campesinos who work the land under various aparcería arrangements probably should be classified merely as farm laborers, although in some cases they may secure enough rights to the use of the land and perform the managerial function sufficiently to justify placing them in the category of tenants and farm operators. It is very difficult to determine how numerous are the workers of this category, but various systems of sharecropping are to be observed as one makes his way from one part of the Republic to another. A few examples may be given.

On February 26, 1944, accompanied by Dr. Justo Díaz Rodríquez, Director of the Departamento Nacional de Tierras, I visited Tucares in the departmento of Nariño. There we found the usual tenure arrange-

35. Smith, Díaz, and García, *Tabio*, p. 23. 36. *Ibid.*, p. 28.

ments to be a form of aparcería in which the owner provided the land and one-half of the seed. The aparcero supplied the other half of the seed and all of the labor. At harvest time the product was divided equally between the owner of the land and the worker. The system was employed in the culture of all the temperate climate crops upon which this earthquake ravaged district depends, namely, wheat, potatoes, barley, and corn.

Near the opposite extremity of the Republic, in the tobacco-growing sections around Piedecuesta, Santander, is another strong concentration of sharecropping of a similar nature. In this case it was estimated by the agricultural officials of the area that as many as 10,000 workers were involved. The typical arrangement is one on which the owner supplies the land and possibly the drying shed. The worker furnishes the tobacco plants, performs all the labor, and harvests the valuable leaves. Then the product is divided with one-third going to the landlord and the remainder being retained by the aparcero.

Since our visit to this section of the country in October, 1943, there have been attempts on the part of the state and national governments to effect improvements in the tenure relationships prevailing in this and other parts of the departamento of Santander. Basically this has consisted of trying to introduce written contractual agreements in which all of the responsibilities and privileges of the landlord and the aparcero are clearly and specifically stated. Those responsible for the programs have asserted that 80 per cent of all the agricultural enterprises in the departamento of Santander are conducted on the basis of contracts of aparcería.[37]

Various other types of sharecropping are found throughout the country, but exact descriptions of them are lacking and it is not easy to determine from the data gathered in the 1960 census of agriculture which sharing arrangements should be considered to be share renting and which are merely payments of a share of the crop to the agricultural laborers who supply the manual labor for the various enterprises. Altogether that census identified 145,056 cases of aparcería, of which 32,022 were reported for Antioquia, 21,392 for Caldas, 20,445 for Santander, 13,113 for Norte de Santander, 12,857 for Boyacá, and 10,979 for Tolima.[38]

37. Pino Espinal, *Conclusiones del Primer Ensayo de Explotación Agrícola por el Sistema de Aparcería de los Cultivos de Tabaco*, p. 20.
38. Departamento Administrativo Nacional de Estadística, 1964, p. 23.

The Minifundistas.—Probably almost as numerous as the arrendatarios are the *propietarios* or owners of the small tracts of ground from which they gather a few subsistence crops. There is some question as to whether they should be classed merely as one type of farm laborers, since they are landowners. However, even though they own a few acres of ground and usually are considerably better off than those who do not, very few of them can live exclusively or even mainly from the small amounts of produce they are able to extract from their pocket-handkerchief plots. Like the arrendatarios and concertados most of them must count on other employment, mostly on the fincas and haciendas, in order to gain a modest livelihood, and for most of them the role of agricultural laborer is the dominant one in their lives. Frequently they must go long distances in order to gain employment. Thus one will find among the laborers far out on the Eastern Plains, in the banana zone, on the coffee fincas of Caldas, among the cotton fields of Tolima, or at the sugar factories in the Cauca Valley, men who own small estancias elsewhere in the distant parts of the country.

As is evident from some of the materials presented above, many of these small owners have only recently acquired their modest little plots. Furthermore, in no small number of cases, the desire to fix the campesinos more firmly to the soil and thus insure an adequate labor supply for the estate has been the principal motivating force leading the hacendado to sell small tracts of ground on the outskirts of the hacienda to the workers. However, it is important to note that the proprietors of the minifundia generally receive a wage considerably higher than those who "rent" subsistence plots, and they also are freer to take other employment in the community or even in far-distant parts of the country.

In several areas I had the privilege of visiting and conversing with many of the former "renters" who had gained the status of owners. Rather typical is the situation among the workers on the once magnificent old Jesuit estate near Paipa, Boyacá, which recently had been subdivided by the state government, with the bottom lands being retained by the state as an experimental sheep-breeding farm and the surrounding hillsides being sold to the campesinos. In these extracts the materials have not been pared to the extent that only those pertaining to tenure and labor are included, for it was felt that these would be more meaningful if given in the general context in which they were taken. The data were gathered on October 19, 1943, and the observations include the following:

"After breakfast . . . we made inquiries about the best way to see the hacienda of El Salitre which has been subdivided by the departamento into a *granja* for the breeding of sheep and into parcels which have been sold to the former arrendatarios. We walked up the road to the headquarters of the granja where we met the director, a young veterinarian in charge of the place. The sub-division of the hacienda is now complete. The bottom lands were reserved for the granja and the lands on the slopes were divided and sold to the 'renters' in tracts up to about 50 acres. Many of the former renters work on the granja at a wage of 70 centavos per day, and they are paid for seven days a week. They also receive free medical services. Formerly, it is said, the men were paid only from two to five centavos per day and for only six days per week. The women were required to render domestic service at the hacienda for one peso per month.

"The director supplied us with horses and accompanied us on a visit to some of the parcelas. We rode out through the granja, which is the only way of gaining access to the parcels, and over several of them. We questioned in detail one young owner of a tract of 13 fanegadas. He had been born here, but had had to go to various de-partamentos now and then in search of work. He had been in both Cundinamarca and Tolima. He is married and has two children. He bought this small tract for one-half down and the remainder in four payments spread over two years, and he has just completed the last payment. The price was approximately 50 pesos per fanegada. On the place are grown wheat and potatoes and he also has a few cattle. At the time of our visit he, his wife, and his parents were harvesting wheat with sickles, similar to those used in Biblical times.

"This young fellow passes weeks without going to town, but his wife goes each market day (Wednesday). They pay one-tenth of the produce to the church. His taxes are 5 pesos per year. When ques-tioned as to his present status compared with the past, his face bright-ened up and he said he was now much better off.

"Next we stopped in a small parcel of three fanegadas. This belongs to an elderly woman and her three sons. They paid approximately 70 pesos per fanegada for the land, and the woman explained in no uncertain terms that it was all paid for and that they were people who met their obligations. She lives in a little thatched, house of mud having only one-room, plus a leanto. Her sons and their families have their own huts. They work on the granja.

"There are quite a number of children of school age among her grandchildren, but none of them are attending school. The old woman does not read and write, but her sons do.

"This family has no cows but they have a few (perhaps 12) sheep and some chickens. The old woman goes to market every week. They pay the one-tenth of the produce to the church. The taxes on this place are 24 centavos per month. Sometimes the old woman buys raw wool in the market and spins it into yarn. To spin three pounds takes her about 15 days, and for this sometimes she realizes 30 centavos. At other times the work results in a loss, for the wool may contain so much oil and extraneous material that it does not work up into sufficient yarn.

"These people eat two or three meals per day. For breakfast they take changua (a hot onion soup), agua de panela (brown sugar dissolved in hot water), and bread. The latter is not always of pure wheat. Sometimes they have chocolate and rarely coffee.

"For almuerzo they eat mazamora (a corn meal soup) and potatoes if they have them. Sometimes, but not frequently, they have a little meat at this mid-day meal. If they have an evening meal it is a repetition of the almuerzo.

"The sons also have been here and there in search of work. One of them spent 20 years in Caldas as an arrendatario or, as it was called there, an *estanciero*. The old woman also stated very emphatically that their lot was much better now that they own this little piece of ground than it was when they were required to work on the hacienda at one peso per month."

Farm Operators

The second major category of agriculturists, the farm operators, are relatively few in numerical comparison with the number of farm laborers. As indicated, in ways that certainly do not understate the number of families that are headed by farm operators, only about one-third of all the households in Colombia whose members are dependent directly upon agriculture for a livelihood are headed by those who could qualify for inclusion in this all-important class. Furthermore, many of the border-line cases, or the families of campesinos who eke out a livelihood by cultivating tiny farms which they own or rent, might very well belong in the farm-laborer category. Also it is well to restate that the data upon which we must rely for the most part in attempting to determine the number, relative importance of, and characteristics of Colombia's farm operators are not those collected about those farmers as such, but rather the information that was secured in the 1960 census of agriculture about those who were identified as "producers." Fortunately, for the nation as a whole, it is feasible to cross classify some of the essential facts about the tenure of these producers with the data on the size of the explotaciones, and this enables one to have the materials for the larger units separate from those for the smaller and more questionable entities (see Table 5).

At first glance the owner-operator in Colombia may seem to be very similar to the farmer who owns his land in Canada, the United States, or a European country such as Germany; and the same may be true of the agriculturist who rents the land he uses for the production of crops or the growing of livestock. The mayordomos, on the other hand, appear to have much more in common with an overseer on a cotton plantation in the southern part of the United States than they have with the managers in charge of estates in western Europe, the English-speaking portions of the Americas, or even in Argentina and Uruguay. Moreover, careful study may also show that there are some striking differences between the entrepreneurs who are responsible for Colombia's agriculture and stock raising and those who operate farms and ranches in Europe and North America.

The first of these differences seems to be the extent to which the members of the elite class include farming, or at least stock raising, among the numerous professional undertakings which they carry on simultaneously. In Colombia it is not unusual to find a hacendado or even a coffee grower who at the same time is a banker, or a merchant, or a manufacturer, and also a lawyer, a university professor, a political figure of some note, and perhaps well established in the diplomatic service of his country. Rare indeed is the possessor of broad acreages who does not share his time between the management of his estates and the pursuit of two or more additional professions. Since this class has the control over the overwhelming part of all the better lands in Colombia, this is a fact of no small importance.

As suggested above the class of farm managers existent in Colombia has little in common with the scientifically trained and experienced professionals one will find in charge of many of the large farms in the United States, Canada, the English-speaking (and also the Dutch-speaking) parts of the Caribbean area, and western Europe. Indeed for the most part they are little more than foremen, merely selected members of the campesino class who have learned about farming and

TABLE 5

OPERATORS OF EXPLOTACIONES AGROPECUARIOS AND LAND IN EXPLOTACIONES
CLASSIFIED ACCORDING TO TENURE, COLOMBIA, 1960

Tenure	Operators of Explotaciones		Land in explotaciones	
	Number	Per cent	Hectares	Per cent
All Farms and Subsistence Tracts				
All categories	1,209,672	100.0	27,337,827	100.0
Owners	755,318	62.4	19,779,585	72.4
Owner operators	712,848	58.9	10,334.472	37.8
Owners with administrators[1]	42,470	3.5	9,445,113	34.6
Tenants—all types	282,347	23.4	2,009,274	7.4
Cash tenants[2]	44,746	3.7	542,133	2.0
Share tenants[3]	145,056	12.0	960,557	3.5
"Personal-service" tenants[4]	23,221	1.9	71,380	0.3
Other tenants[5]	69,324	5.8	435,204	1.6
Squatters[6]	46,961	3.9	3,314,075	12.1
Other and mixed forms[7]	125,046	10.3	2,234,893	8.1
Subsistence Tracts—Less Than 2.0 Hectares				
All categories	489,418	100.0	402,301	100.0

1. Colombian census procedures use the designation of *productor*, or *producer*, for the owner, tenant, or squatter who has the ultimate responsibility for one or more enterprises on the tract of land designated as an explotación. If an owner has land in two or more municipios, as commonly is the case with the affluent proprietors of large estates, each in charge of an administrator, each of his estates is classified as an explotación; and the owner figures two or more times, and the administrator never in the list of productores. In one of the tabulations, however, the explotaciones are classified into two categories, those managed by the so-called "producers" and those managed by administrators. By assuming that all of those employing administrators are landowners, which probably is largely true but subject to some exceptions, the explotaciones of the owners may be divided as is done here into those of owner-operators and those of owners having administrators as the actual operators.

2. The 1,728 tenants who pay in both cash and kind are included here.

3. This category, that of the *aparceros*, includes those who are genuine tenants or renters who pay a share of the crop as rent; but it also includes all of the laborers who are paid on a share-of-the-crop basis. Probably the great majority of the cases included actually are laborers, similar to sharecroppers in the southern part of the United States, and not genuine tenants at all.

4. In census terms this category includes the hands or day laborers on the large estates who receive the use of a small plot or small tract of the owner's land, in exchange for which they are obligated to work without pay for a stipulated number of days per week; and also those who render service to the State or the Church in exchange for the use of land.

5. Includes 8,006 standing renters and 61,318 tenants of an unspecified nature.

6. Includes the squatters on public and private land, except those who have been on their claims for more than 30 years, who were classified with the owners.

7. Includes the 25,690 cases said to represent other unspecified forms of tenure and 99,356 "producers" who had two or more types of tenure.

TABLE 5—(*Continued*)

Tenure	Operators of Explotaciones		Land in explotaciones	
	Number	Per cent	Hectares	Per cent
Owners	294,031	60.1	235,667	58.6
Owner operators	291,085	59.5	232,450	57.8
Owners with administrators	2,946	0.6	3,217	0.8
Tenants—all types	147,625	30.2	118,416	29.4
Cash tenants	26,773	5.5	16,944	4.2
Share tenants	62,757	12.8	59,539	14.8
"Personal-service" tenants	15,164	3.1	10,603	2.6
Other tenants	42,931	8.8	31,330	7.8
Squatters	8,777	1.8	7,405	1.8
Other and mixed forms	38,985	7.9	40,813	10.2
Minifundia—2.0 to 4.9 Hectares				
All categories	267,187	100.0	836,675	100.0
Owners	152,108	56.9	487,491	58.3
Owner operators	148,948	55.7	476,738	57.0
Owners with administrators	3,160	1.2	10,753	1.3
Tenants—all types	70,495	26.4	212,324	25.4
Cash tenants	8,025	3.0	24,298	2.9
Share tenants	41,211	15.4	128,089	15.3
"Personal-service" tenants	5,237	2.0	14,945	1.8
Other tenants	16,022	6.0	44,992	5.4
Squatters	7,425	2.8	22,629	2.7
Other and mixed forms	37,159	13.9	114,231	13.6
Tracts of 5.0 to 49.9 Hectares				
All categories	370,165	100.0	5,375,526	100.0
Owners	248,260	67.1	3,725,555	69.3
Owner operators	230,720	62.3	3,381,466	62.9
Owners with administrators	17,540	4.8	344,089	6.4
Tenants—all types	59,147	16.0	755,061	14.0
Cash tenants	8,150	2.2	113,017	2.1
Share tenants	39,062	10.6	503,915	9.4
"Personal-service" tenants	2,682	0.7	28,832	0.5
Other tenants	9,253	2.5	109,297	2.0
Squatters	19,421	5.2	346,654	6.5
Other and mixed forms	43,337	11.7	548,256	10.2
Tracts of 50.0 to 199.9 Hectares				
All categories	62,307	100.0	5,676,623	100.0

TABLE 5—(*Continued*)

Tenure	Operators of Explotaciones		Land in explotaciones	
	Number	Per cent	Hectares	Per cent
Owners	44,987	72.2	4,168,249	73.4
Owner operators	34,214	54.9	3,074,778	54.2
Owners with administrators	10,773	17.3	1,093,471	19.2
Tenants—all types	4,144	6.7	390,899	6.9
Cash tenants	1,358	2.2	139,053	2.4
Share tenants	1,776	2.9	163,283	2.9
"Personal-service" tenants	118	0.2	10,197	0.2
Other tenants	892	1.4	78,366	1.4
Squatters	8,921	14.3	748,405	13.2
Other and mixed forms	4,255	6.8	369,070	6.5
Tracts of 200 Hectares or More				
All categories	20,595	100.0	15,046,702	100.0
Owners	15,932	77.4	11,162,623	74.2
Owner operators	7,881	38.3	3,169,040	21.1
Owners with administrators	8,051	39.1	7,993,583	53.1
Tenants—all types	936	4.5	532,574	3.5
Cash tenants	440	2.1	248,821	1.7
Share tenants	250	1.2	105,731	0.7
"Personal-service" tenants	20	0.1	6,803	*
Other tenants	226	1.1	171,219	1.1
Squatters	2,417	11.7	2,188,982	14.6
Other and mixed forms	1,310	6.4	1,162,523	7.7

Source: Pages 39 and 42-43 of source for Table 1.
* Less than 0.1 per cent.

cattle raising in a routine manner and have been placed in charge of affairs on the haciendas in the intervals between the owners' infrequent visits. Few, very few, of them could qualify for membership in the American Association of Farm Managers. But they are relatively numerous, and except for the cursory manner in which the owners may contribute to the management of the estates during their occasional visits, they alone must supply such managerial and directing activities as are given to Colombia's farms and ranches. There are exceptions, of course, and the relatively few but highly important sugar-cane, cotton, and rice plantations, and also some of the large coffee fincas, are managed expertly and efficiently. But these exceptions do not negate the general rule—that the system of large estates

controlled by absentee owners and left to the mercy of poorly prepared mayordomos and hosts of unskilled peons is one in which a
paucity of managerial activities are applied in the use of the great
bulk of Colombia's best land.

With these general observations in mind, attention is directed, suc-
cessively, to each of the principal categories of farm operators, namely,
owner-operators, managers, renters, and squatters.

The Owner-Operators.—From what has been said above, it should
be evident that it is not easy to determine the number and proportion
of owner-operators in Colombia. Nevertheless, from the data presented
in Tables 5, 6, and 7 at least a rough approximation may be made.
The first of these is the more general one, and shows for different
size groups of explotaciones, the proportions of the "producers"
and of the land that may be classified as falling into or being
under the control of persons in the various tenure categories. It must
be repeated, though, that in making this tabulation it was necessary to consider that all of the administrators or managers were operating places of those who were classified by the census as being
owner-"producers." Strictly speaking this is not fully justified, since
undoubtedly some of those who rent from estates, financial institutions, religious organizations, and so on, actually turn the management
of those lands over to administrators of more or less competency.
Likewise, the data in this table, along with those in tables 6 and 7,
suffer from some of the assumptions that figured in connection with
the gathering and classification of the data of the 1960 agricultural
census. Even at the risk of being considered repetitious, it seems well
to state somewhat differently the basic defects of these assumptions,
and the ways in which they make it difficult or impossible to use the
materials on explotaciones and producers to determine the essential
facts about farms and farm operators. First, there is the great problem
of the owner-producers. The assumption was made that all landowners, except those who rent their land to others, are entitled to
be included in the producer category; and that if they own land in
more than one municipio, or county, each of those estates is entitled
to be classified as an explotación. This has the effect of counting many
of the landowners time after time, thus greatly swelling the number
of owner-producers; and it also conceals to a high degree the extent
to which the large landowners own and control the bulk of the land,
especially the better land, in the Republic. Secondly, those peons
who work on the estate, under the orders of the administrator or

mayordomo, also are counted as producers, and hence the tracts they occupy as explotaciones, provided they receive the use of small plots of ground as part-payment for their services; or if, over a period of time, in order to help guarantee an available labor supply, they have been allowed to become the owners of small pieces of ground on the

TABLE 6

CUMULATIVE FREQUENCY DISTRIBUTIONS OF THE NUMBERS OF EXPLOTACIONES AGROPECUARIAS CONTAINING TWO OR MORE HECTARES OF LAND ACCORDING TO THE TENURE OF THEIR "PRODUCERS," AND WITH THE DATA FOR ADMINISTRATOR-OPERATED UNITS GIVEN SEPARATELY, BY SIZE OF EXPLOTACIONES, 1960

Size (hectares)	All categories	Owners‡	Renters	Squatters	Mixed tenure	Adminis- trators
Total	720,254†	461,287	134,722	38,184	70,658	39,524†
5 or more	603,249	309,179	64,277	30,759	39,004	36,364
10 or more	283,922	200,737	31,545	24,972	20,687	31,423
20 " "	169,691	122,918	14,240	18,965	10,239	25,961
30 " "	125,642	91,722	9,044	15,598	6,907	22,992
40 " "	99,142	72,651	6,458	13,102	5,108	20,468
50 " "	82,903	60,919	5,080	11,338	4,095	18,824
100 " "	42,912	32,377	2,249	5,536	1,986	12,981
200 " "	20,595	15,932	936	2,417	894	8,051
500 " "	6,902	5,476	248	704	320	3,568
1,000 " "	2,761	2,127	86	348	134	1,620
2,500 " "	786	542	20	154	51	496

Source: Pages 39 and 42 of source for Table 1.

† These totals do not equal the sums of the categories included because: (1) administrators are not considered, by the census, to be producers; and (2) 15,403 cases of "other" types of tenure are omitted.

‡ For places above 10 hectares in size, a figure for each portion of the range shown that roughly approximates the number of owner operators may be secured by taking the number of owner "producers," adding to it the number of those of mixed tenure, and then subtracting the number of administrators.

outskirts of the haciendas. Especially in connection with the totals and with the data for all size groups of less than 10 or 20 hectares, this has resulted in the combination in a hopelessly inextricable manner of the information for farm laborers and that for genuine farm operators. Finally, and most equivocal of all, the managers or administrators are not admitted to the class of producers, even though the census terminology itself, in the one series of tables that supplies information about them, calls them *operadores* or operators. Thus those proprietors who live in the distant city and who visit the farms only occasionally are considered as producers, as are many of those who toil from sun to sun under the supervision of the mayordomos or administrators, providing only that they own or "rent" small subsistence tracts from which they may gain a portion of their livelihood. But those actually in charge of the estates, those who perform the meager amount of managerial activities that actually go into agricultural production, and those who control and direct the work of a

TABLE 7

The Relative Importance of Various Tenure Classes Among Colombia's Agricultural "Producers" for the Different Size Groups of Agricultural Units, 1960

Size (hectares)	All categories	Percentage in each tenure category			
		Owners*	Renters	Mixed tenure*	Adminis- trators*
2 or more	100	64.0	18.7	9.8	5.5
5 " "	100	68.2	14.2	8.6	8.0
10 " "	100	70.7	11.1	7.3	11.1
20 " "	100	72.4	8.4	6.0	15.3
30 " "	100	73.0	7.2	5.5	18.3
40 " "	100	73.3	6.5	5.2	20.6
50 " "	100	73.5	6.1	4.9	22.7
100 " "	100	75.4	5.2	4.6	30.3
200 " "	100	77.4	4.5	4.3	39.1
500 " "	100	79.3	3.6	4.6	51.7
1,000 " "	100	77.0	3.1	4.9	58.7
2,500 " "	100	69.0	2.5	6.5	63.1

Source: Pages 39 and 42 of source for Table 1.
  * For all classes of explotaciones above 10 hectares in size a figure roughly approximating the proportion of owner operators may be obtained by adding the proportion of those in the mixed tenure category to the stated percentage of owners and then subtracting the proportion of administrators from that sum.

large proportion of the so-called "owners" and "renters," do not qualify for inclusion in the category of producers.

Tables 6 and 7 were prepared in ways designed to facilitate the process of estimating the number of owner-operators in Colombia irrespective of whether or not one is inclined to include or exclude the smaller holdings from the category of farms. If, for example, one were to think that only places of 20 hectares or more should be counted as farms, he would probably take the figure of 122,918 "producers" indicated as owners of places of that size, increase it by the 20,637 cases of mixed tenure in the corresponding range of sizes, and then diminish that sum by the 25,961 administrators attributed to places of the category under consideration. The resulting number, or 107,196, might be thought of as the number of farm owner-operators in the country, whereas if the lower limit of the farm category were placed at 5 hectares, a comparable calculation would give 311,819 as the number of such operators. In any case, the final estimate would have counted the larger owners several times apiece, and those squatters who reported that they had been on their claims for more than 30 years would be included with the owners. On the percentage basis, the materials in Table 7 offer some basis for the consideration of about 52 per cent of the farm operators as owners if all places of 5 hectares or more are considered as farms, and 63 per cent as the corresponding index if only places of 20 hectares or more are placed in that category

Irrespective of what is considered to be a farm, or not to be a farm, however, the data in Tables, 5, 6, and 7 indicate that the lion's share of the landowners in Colombia are small holders and merely a slight rung higher on the agricultural scale than the minifundistas. In some of the departments, though, and particularly in Caldas,[39] there are considerable numbers of families who have farms that are large enough to provide incomes commensurate with middle-class social status. It is impossible to determine the number of these very accurately, but if all places of from 40 to 200 hectares in size were in the hands of such farm operators, there were in 1960 about 80,000 of these farmers, of whom some 50,000 were owners; and if the limits are considered to be from 30 to 100 hectares, the corresponding figures are about 83,000 and 55,000. In Caldas, especially, these farmers have many striking similarities with peasants and yeomen in other parts of the western world, and since their efforts are concentrated on the production of coffee (which is not a traditional crop), they are less bound by the age-old routines than is true of those engaged in the small-scale production of most of the other crops.

Socially, economically, and politically the members of the old elite families who possess the country's large estates, and especially the cattle haciendas, are by far the most important group in Colombia. Their number is comparatively small, probably not over 5,000 and certainly no more than 10,000. They certainly are much fewer in number and they control much greater proportions of the land than it

39. Cf. Parsons, *Antioqueño Colonization in Western Colombia, passim;* and Pineda Giraldo *et al., Caldas,* I, *passim.*

would appear from an uncritical acceptance of the 1960 census data, even as those have been arranged in Tables 5, 6, and 7. They do not, as indicated above contribute any great amount of time or managerial activities to the vast, and frequently widely scattered domains over which they exercize the control. That which they do give is sadly lacking in quality, if one judges it from the standpoint of modern scientific knowledge and practice. But due primarily to the absence of any significant tax upon the land, their monopolistic position is secure. Generation after generation, the way the system works, they can hold the land, use it well, use it poorly, or not use it at all, without fear that it will be "eaten up by taxes." Thus, in effect, in Colombia land is an asylum for capital, and it literally is impossible for these old families to become "land poor." Herein lies the basis of much of Colombia's greatest problem, one whose very nature makes difficult any solution by peaceful, evolutionary means. However, some headway was made by means of Law 200 of 1936, and the 1961 Ley de Reforma Social Agraria offers hopes of additional improvement. If, however, substantial reforms are not forthcoming, a huge and violent eruption of the lower social classes is almost sure to ensue; and if this comes about the fact that many of the elite may have deserved no better will be slight solace for the rivers of blood that will flow and the vast destruction of property that will take place.

Administrators or Managers.—Many of Colombia's largest and most highly developed estates are under the direct supervision and management of some kind of administrators or managers, and in the case of some of the sugar-cane, cotton, and rice plantations, these managers are well prepared for their work. Unfortunately, though, the same is not the case with the vast majority of those who are left in charge of the estates which monopolize most of the best land in Colombia. Many of them, including those whose lack of adequate preparation is hamstringing operations on the largest haciendas that I have been privileged to visit, are little better informed about agricultural matters than are the peons who work under their supervision. In this respect in most sections of the broad expanses of the countryside in Colombia there has been remarkably little change during the decades that have passed since Alejandro López wrote: "The gravest illness presently afflicting our agriculture, and in general all of our industry, is the lack of preparation, the crude procedures, and the truly obstinate and reactionary spirit of the intermediary between the patron and the worker. That this post [that of the administrator or mayordomo] is demanding to a high degree and full of responsibilities, there can be no doubt; and it is beyond understanding that such posts should be filled with peons selected from among those who demonstrate some spirit of order and command, and a little of the rudimentary knowledge attained by personal experience and from tradition."[40]

TABLE 8

NUMBER AND PROPORTION OF EXPLOTACIONES AGROPECUARIAS OPERATED BY
ADMINISTRATORS AND PROPORTION OF ALL LAND IN FARMS IN
ADMINISTRATOR-OPERATED UNITS IN 1960,
BY SIZE OF EXPLOTACIONES

Size (hectares)	Explotaciones operated by administrators		Per cent of land operated by administrators
	Number	Percentage of all	
Total	42,470	3.5	34.5
Under 0.5	544	0.2	0.4
0.5–0.9	836	0.6	0.7
1.0–1.9	1,566	0.8	0.9
2.0–2.9	1,029	0.9	0.9
3.0–3.9	1,392	1.5	1.6
4.0–4.9	739	1.3	1.3
5.0–9.9	4,941	2.9	3.1
10.0–19.9	5,462	4.8	5.0
20.0–29.9	2,969	6.7	6.9
30.0–39.9	2,524	9.5	9.7
40.0–49.9	1,644	10.1	10.2
50.0–99.9	5,843	14.6	15.1
100.0–199.9	4,930	22.1	23.0
200.0–499.9	4,483	32.7	34.4
500.0–999.9	1,948	47.0	47.8
1,000.0–2,499.9	1,124	56.9	56.9
2,500.0–over	496	63.1	67.4

Source: Page 39 of source for Table 1.

In order to facilitate the consideration of such data on administrators and their role in Colombia's agricultural and stock-raising activities as were made available by the 1960 census of agriculture, Tables 8, and 9 and Figure 3 were prepared. The first of these tables shows the number of administrators reported for each of the size groups into which the explotaciones agropecuarias were classified, along with the proportions they represented of all those responsible for the operations on such units, and also the proportions of the land in the estates of

40. López, *Problemas Colombianos,* p. 159.

which they had charge. Table 9 supplements this with data showing the number and proportion of places managed by administrators for each of the departments and also the variations in the proportion of the land in farms and subsistence tracts for which they were primarily responsible. Finally, Figure 3 was prepared to facilitate observation and comparison of the manner in which the relative importance of

TABLE 9

NUMBER AND PROPORTION OF EXPLOTACIONES AGROPECUARIAS OPERATED BY ADMINISTRATORS AND PROPORTION OF ALL LAND IN FARMS IN ADMINISTRATOR-OPERATED UNITS IN 1960, BY DEPARTMENTS

Department	Explotaciones operated by administrators		Per cent of land operated by administrators
	Number	Per cent of all	
All departments	42,470	3.5	34.5
Antioquia	7,858	4.6	32.2
Atlántico	769	6.5	41.9
Bolívar	2,006	3.1	35.1
Boyacá	1,723	1.0	31.3
Caldas	5,598	7.0	38.0
Cauca	1,387	1.9	28.8
Córdova	1,117	2.3	28.4
Cundinamarca	4,652	3.2	29.5
Huila	1,068	3.1	24.7
Magdalena	2,814	5.1	38.7
Meta	760	4.8	58.1
Nariño	1,164	1.3	10.7
Norte de Santander	917	2.3	19.0
Santander	1,816	2.0	22.6
Tolima	2,866	4.0	31.3
Valle del Cauca	5,955	11.7	47.3

Source: Page 21 of source for Table 1.

the administrators, the percentage of the farm land for which they were responsible, and comparable information for each of the other principal tenure classes, varies from one part of the republic to another.

These census materials confirm the conclusions formed by many persons, merely on the basis of casual observation, that administrators are of little consequence on the smaller farms (or those up to about 100 hectares), and that they are of primary importance in connection with all of the larger places and especially in all that has to do with the great haciendas and other large landed estates. All of this

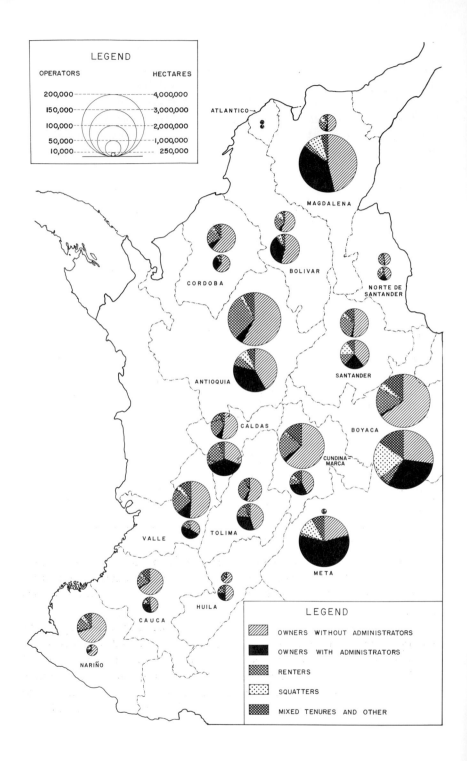

LEGEND

OPERATORS   HECTARES

200,000 ------- 4,000,000
150,000 ------- 3,000,000
100,000 ------- 2,000,000
50,000 ------- 1,000,000
10,000 ------- 250,000

ATLANTICO

MAGDALENA

CORDOBA

BOLIVAR

NORTE DE
SANTANDER

ANTIOQUIA

SANTANDER

CALDAS

BOYACA

CUNDINA-
MARCA

VALLE

TOLIMA

META

CAUCA

HUILA

NARIÑO

LEGEND

OWNERS WITHOUT ADMINISTRATORS

OWNERS WITH ADMINISTRATORS

RENTERS

SQUATTERS

MIXED TENURES AND OTHER

gains greater significance when considered in relation to the other features of the size of the holdings, which are treated in the preceding chapter; but even here it should be stressed that almost two-thirds of the land in the places of 1,000 hectares or more is found within the limits of the estates that are managed by administrators. Were it possible to prepare a tabulation in which all of the land owned by each of Colombia's great proprietors was considered as a single unit, the role of the administrator would be magnified considerably over that which appears from the manner in which the materials have been made available.

The inclusion of tens of thousands of subsistence tracts and the "producers" on the same vitiate largely the significance of any comparisons that may be made concerning the relative importance of administrators among all those counted as responsible for the explotaciones. Even so, however, the range in the proportion of such managers, as shown in Table 9 and Figure 3, from 1.0 per cent in Boyacá, and 1.3 per cent in Nariño, to 7.0 per cent in Caldas and 11.7 per cent in El Valle del Cauca, is striking to say the least. Boyacá and Nariño are justly famed as the strongholds of the small subsistence-type farmers; whereas the relatively high proportion of administrators in Caldas probably reflects a tendency for those of some affluence to place administrators in charge of the relatively small coffee farms that they have acquired. The percentage in El Valle del Cauca, however, is due to a considerable extent to a fairly high development of commercialized sugar-cane, cotton, and rice plantations in considerable portions of the rich, level, and well-watered valley which for centuries was the unchallenged domain of huge, rudimentary cattle ranches. Much more conclusive, though, are the variations in the proportions of the land, included in the places for which administrators have responsibility. In this case, the thousands of small subsistence tracts and minifundia exert relatively little influence upon the indexes for the various departments. On this basis, it will be noted that administrators are in charge of the places containing almost 60 per cent of the land in the new department of Meta, the location of much of the development that presently is going on at a feverish pace on the plains to the east of the Andes, and that they supply the managerial services for almost one-half of all the land in the department of El

Figure 3.—Variations from department to department in the relative importance of the principal tenure categories, 1960.

Valle del Cauca, even though the materials for that major civil division include huge expanses of extremely rough mountainous terrain which is thickly dotted with the small farms and subsistence tracts of the campesinos. In Nariño, it should be noted, the large terrateniente and his mayordomos play relatively insignificant roles, even though several notable exceptions to this rule stand out in my memory; and Norte de Santander, Santander, and Huila also are far below the national average in this respect.

Renters.—Some of Colombia's farms, ranches, and plantations are owned by banks and insurance companies, religious organizations, and private individuals, who rent them to farmers who lack the ownership of the land, or of enough of the land, which they use for their agricultural and stock-raising enterprises. As indicated in Table 6 the 1960 census of agriculture reported that 20 of the very largest places in Colombia, those containing more than 2,500 hectares of land, were in the rented category. Nevertheless, other than the system inherited directly from the days in which the coloni of the last days of the Roman Empire became the serfs of the Middle Ages[41] and under which the campesinos obtain the use of small subsistence tracts and agreements among small landowners and other members of the campesino class, there is little renting of land in Colombia. One may note, for example, in Tables 5 and 6 that the number of those classified as renters by the census of agriculture falls precipitously from 282,347 for all explotaciones, to 134,722 for places containing 2 hectares or more, to 64,227 on units of 5 hectares or more, and to a mere 6,456 for farms embracing 40 hectares or more of land.

This is due, of course, to the fact indicated above that members of the traditional, upper-class, landowning families prefer to retain the actual direction of the enterprises on their properties even though the amount they can perform on their occasional visits to their estates may be merely nominal. As also has been mentioned above, the absence of a significant tax on the land makes it possible for them to carry on in the most lackadaisical manner, free from all fear that taxes may "eat up their land."

There is in Colombia no large number of immigrant farmers possessed of the necessary managerial skills, such as the Italians in

41. In many of the Spanish American countries even the name (colonos) of the workers who till the land in return for a small tract of ground, on which they may live and grow a few crops for subsistence purposes, remains the same. In Colombia, however, as indicated above, the workers under this type of an arrangement commonly are called arrendatarios, or "renters," or conuqueros.

Argentina and the Japanese in São Paulo, Brazil, to bid avidly for leases on various farms and ranches. In fact there seem to be few compulsions indeed that would make it economically desirable for the landowners to transfer, for stated periods, their rights to the land to renters of one type or another, and accordingly any genuine problems of tenancy, such as those afflicting Argentina during the second half of the twentieth century, are still a thing of the future as far as Colombia is concerned. As a matter of fact, it probably would be a godsend for the nation's economy if a substantial number of renters, equipped with twentieth-century agricultural skills and techniques, could have possession for a few decades of many of the vast expanses of potentially rich and productive land that have languished for centuries in the pastures into which the conquistadores converted many of the Indians' cornfields. In this connection, the following case, in an area that was intensively cultivated at the time of the conquest, then passed almost 400 years as pastureland in a rudimentary pastoral economy, and in the twentieth century is once more becoming highly productive agricultural land, is highly suggestive. In the course of a field trip on November 11, 1943, in the area near Puerto Tejada, which is located a short distance south of the city of Cali in the Cauca Valley, I made the following observations.

"Here they plant a mixture of bananas, coffee, and cacao, with possibly a little maize or yuca. There is not much of the latter. . . .

"At one place, larger than the average, we stopped and discovered that it was operated by a Spaniard who had worked for eight years in the western part of the United States. He came to Colombia with 6,500 pesos. This farm of 90 fanegadas he began working several years ago on a share arrangement with the owner, a civil engineer. Since the latter could not give much attention to the farm, this Spaniard is now renting the place. He pays one peso per month for each fanegada. The plantings are corn and bananas, with young cacao trees being set out among the latter. We examined these rather closely, and saw the workers preparing their almuerzo of roasted plantains which for them is a real banquet.

"This fellow has two tractors and considerable farm equipment, including a small four-wheeled farm wagon. He explained that this is extremely useful, but that the workers' lack of experience in hitching and driving animals is a serious handicap. Ordinarily he keeps six laborers, and sometimes there are as many as twelve. Wages here are 1.10 pesos per day without food.

"The main enterprise on the farm is dairying, with 45 milk cows of which 35 are now producing. They are of a mixed native and zebu breed. They represent an investment of 3,600 pesos and produce 150 liters of milk per day. At 10 centavos per bottle, this brings in 15 pesos. Labor for the enterprise costs 2.50 pesos and the entire rent is only 3.00 pesos, so that he gains a neat profit on this enterprise."

This case, though, is highly atypical. A much more representative case of renting in Colombia was encountered in the municipio of Lenguazaque, in the highlands to the north of Bogotá in October, 1943. Notes taken at the time indicate that the landlord was an absentee and that the rent was paid with products. The land involved was a tract of about 300 fanegadas, the property of a man who lived in Bogotá and who was said to be the owner of various other haciendas in different parts of Colombia. At the time of our visit there were 15 renters on the place. They paid three-fourths of all products, mostly wheat, as rent. In case of a crop failure, it was said, rent was still demanded, even though the contract was supposed to be on a share basis.

Squatters or Colonos.—The so-called colonos, or squatters, also must be considered as farm operators, although generally their operations are on a small scale and of a subsistence type. They are considerably more important than their number might seem to indicate, because they have been the cutting edge of the rising tide of discontent that has convulsed Colombia from the 1920's on. More than any other group they have been a challenge to the long-established status quo, in which society was sharply divided into a small group of the elite at the apex of the social hierarchy and a great mass of poverty-stricken, illiterate, malnourished, and lethargic campesinos at the base. Their existence has been even more significant than otherwise would have been the case because almost every arrendatario, and many a jornalero or peon as well, has been a potential colono.

The 1960 census of agriculture classified the "producers" on 46,961 explotaciones as "ocupantes sin título" or colonos. This, though, is certainly a substantial understatement. It does not include those squatters who indicated they had been occupying their claims for more than 30 years, a group that were classified in the owner category. More important than this, however, in reducing the number enumerated is the fact that they are on the frontier, or a little in advance of it, many of them in places that are far out of the way and extremely difficult to reach. Census procedures being what they necessarily must be, in Colombia as in other countries, it is almost certain that substantial numbers of them were missed entirely in the enumeration.

The working definition entered in my notes during the 1940's and which was employed in making observations in all parts of the highly fragmented republic, is as follows. "Colono. The occupant of a tract or area of ground who cultivates or uses it without any legal title. A type of squatter. He does not recognize any one else's title to the land. He may be ejected only by legal procedures and with indemnification for the improvements he has made. (In government colonies the term is used for the small proprietor.)"

The vast majority of the squatters are occupying and claiming modest amounts of land, for according to the 1960 census of agriculture only 5,536 of them had explotaciones of more than 100 hectares in size. Indeed almost 9,000 of them or nearly one-fifth of the total, were claiming tracts of less than 2 hectares. More in line with policies for adequate development of Colombia's unpatented lands and the subdivision of her latifundia, however, is the fact that 19,436 (41.4 per cent of all) of the squatters were on tracts varying between 10 and 100 hectares in size.

According to the census reports the squatters were most numerous in the departments of Magdalena, Boyacá, and Bolívar, with reported totals of 6,558, 6,383, and 6,330, respectively. In terms of acreages involved, though, almost two-thirds of the land occupied by squatters was in two departments, or Meta with 1,250,030 hectares and Boyacá with 769,657 hectares (see Figure 3). In both of these cases recent occupation of large tracts on the plains to the east of the Andes probably accounts for the bulk of the land involved.

Particularly during the period 1930 to 1950, the colonos who were invading or otherwise claiming rights to portions of large haciendas made up a large proportion of all squatters. During these decades the conflicts between the campesinos claiming rights to the land because they were occupying it and making use of it and the large landowners who maintained that they had titles to the property became so numerous and so acute that the problem of colonos generally came to be considered as Colombia's greatest social problem. About 1948, however, the devastating proportions assumed by "la violencia," or virtual civil war, became so great that the colono problem was relegated to a secondary position.

On the basis of the numbers of campesinos involved, the colono problem was especially acute all along the western slope of the Eastern Cordillera from a latitude some 50 miles to the south of Bogotá to the northern extremity of settlement in the department of Norte de Santander. It also was great all along the slopes of the central range from the department of Cauca to Caldas and even into Antioquia. One of the gravest cases I encountered in the course of my travels was in the Cauca Valley itself, near the small city of Cartago. There, one estate of about 500 fanegadas had long been used principally for grazing a few head of cattle. In the 1930's it was invaded by about 150 families of campesinos who built their huts and began growing subsistence crops on small tracts of the land. This invasion was resisted physically by the family claiming property rights to the hacienda, assisted by the local governmental authorities. The officials of the national land department, who were along, were of the opinion that at the expiration of the ten-year waiting period prescribed by Law 200 of 1936 (that is in 1946), this land would revert to the government and then would be parcelled out among the squatters who had occupied it. As noted elsewhere in this volume, the serious internal conflicts which scourged the nation from about 1946 until 1958 precluded the work of regularizing claims and titles to the land, but the current agrarian reform program is giving primary attention to this fundamental problem.

COMMUNITY-OWNED AND COMMUNAL LANDS

Before closing this discussion of land tenure in Colombia it is necessary to mention briefly the communally or collectively owned lands which still are to be found in the Republic. Historically these have been of tremendous importance,[42] and even today they are to be reckoned with in some places and especially in the department of Nariño. Three types of community or communal holdings are to be identified, namely, the *propios* or community-owned lands which were to be rented out, with the proceeds used to help pay local governmental expenses; the ejidos, or common pastures adjacent to the village on which all citizens were privileged to turn their livestock; and the resguardos or Indian communities in which all the land was held in common.

Propios.—There seems to be few remaining vestiges of the liberal grants of land which the Crown gave to the New World towns and

42. Cf. Fals-Borda, *El Hombre y la Tierra en Boyacá,* pp. 72-101.

villages in order that the revenues derived from their use could help defray the necessary expenses of the communities. No doubt they rather quickly passed into private hands; and some of them such as the Dehesa de Bogotá may have formed the nucleus of famous old haciendas. However, a careful survey might reveal that a considerable number of Colombian towns or pueblos still enjoy a substantial income from community-owned lands. At least one comes across in the literature a case now and then similar to that of Corozal.

In a small volume[43] published in 1873 a school master, Domingo Jiménez, gives important details concerning the history and problems of a small community in the departamento of Bolívar. According to this authority, Corozal was founded in the year 1775. Apparently the new settlement was largely the idea and work of the first priest, Juan Antonio Aballe, who, following his death in 1799, received the title of the "*Mas grande benefactor de este pueblo.*" Apparently in the course of the 24 years of his service, this divine had succeeded in getting together a considerable amount of this world's goods. But to his sisters he left nothing except what he had brought from his native Spain. For the community of Corozal he seems to have left the remainder. His herds of cattle valued at $22,545, were used to establish a trust fund whose income was to be used by parishless priests residing in the city for masses in favor of all the inhabitants of Corozal. In addition, although we are not told how he came by the property, he "left to the pueblo more than 60 caballerías of land that should be cultivated as its own property, without the obligation of paying for the use of it."[44] At the time our schoolman wrote, the inhabitants of Corozal still enjoyed the peaceful possession of these lands, except for the inevitable disputes over boundaries to which reference is made in Chapter 4.

How typical the case of Corazal is, or even if that community today retains this community property, is not known to me. I did not have the opportunity of visiting that part of Bolívar, and I know of no contemporary study of the persistence of the propios.

The Ejidos.—Except in the Indian communities, or resguardos, I found little evidence of the survival of the communal pastures, or ejidos, adjacent to the towns and villages, which once were such an essential part of the typical Spanish settlement. In not a few cases it was found that these collectively owned tracts had been devoted

43. *Geografía Física i Política de la Ciudad de Corozal.*
44. *Ibid.,* p. 35.

to other community purposes, including airports, but they were not in evidence in their original form. Nor does one find very much in the literature to indicate that they are still a factor to be reckoned with. A careful survey, however, might reveal that a considerable number of communities still retain this interesting appendage.

The Resguardos.—The abolition of the Indian communities and their communal holdings and the establishment of their inhabitants on an equal plane with other citizens was one of the first reforms attempted by the government of the Republic of Colombia. One of the first North Americans to describe the new nation, Colonel William Duane of Philadelphia, who visited Bogotá and other parts of Colombia in 1822 and 1823, included the whole of the Report of the Secretary of the Interior in his interesting account. The problems of the resguardos and the proposals for their solution are clearly set forth in the following paragraphs from that report.

> The greater part of the Indians of Colombia have been a degraded class, and are yet partially so. The Spanish laws reduced them to perpetual pupilage, and it may be said, without fear of contradiction, that they were the slaves of the priests and the magistrates. Both one and the other commanded them to be whipped publicly for the most trivial faults, and even though [they were along] in years. Thus they lived in a state of debasement and degradation, the energy of their intellectual and physical faculties destroyed. Obliged to cultivate lands in common, they never improved them, and mournfully vegetated in villages, existing in misery, and with difficulty able to pay the sum of from six to nine dollars a year exacted from them as tribute, which all males from 18 to 50 were obliged to pay!
>
> The first general Congress annihilated these cruel oppressions, by placing the natives on an equality with all other men; suppressed the tributes and personal labour wrongfully exacted, and provided that the *resguardos,* or common lands, should be laid out and conferred on them as fee simple estates within five years.[45]

From that time to the present the problems of the collectivist agrarian communities of Indians have continued to preoccupy the authorities, with sentiment strongly divided for and against the preservation of the resguardos. Hundreds of them have been extinguished and the lands deeded to the individuals who composed the communities. But in 1944 there were still 124 of them in existence, not counting 13 others in process of being dissolved, and 5 very similar communal groups, the *Comunidades Civiles Indígenas.* They

45. *A Visit to Colombia,* pp. 533-34.

were most numerous in the southern part of the country, with 50 of them being in Nariño and 46 in Cauca; but there were also one or more in each of the following departamentos: Antioquia, Atlántico, Boyacá, Caldas, Cundinamarca, Magdalena, and Valle del Cauca.[46] Had it not been that the inhabitants of many of the resguardos were deceived into signing papers relinquishing their title to the land, the number still in existence undoubtedly would be far greater than it is. And even today there is sharp disagreement over the question of what should be done about those that remain, some contending vigorously that the rights of the natives can be protected only if the resguardos are retained and others maintaining strongly that the old system must be abolished and the Indians incorporated into national life on a plane of equality with the other inhabitants.[47]

Owing to the importance of the resguardo in the natural history of Colombian society, and particularly of its overwhelming significance in all matters pertaining to the masses of Indians and mestizos, a detailed account of its origin, development, and functioning is highly important. Fortunately such an analysis is available in the writings of one of Colombia's leading social scientists, José M. Samper, from whose excellent study the following paragraphs have been translated:

> The Indian resguardos (guarda de las cosas) consisted in brief of the following: In the first part of the colonial period the encomenderos, on the one hand, by virtue of official title, and on the other, the priests and the missions, in the name of the Church, and the rapacious adventurers by right of personal conquest, had taken possession of all the lands previously belonging to the Indians in the areas surrounding the villages, that is in the most important and valuable locations. The Spanish government wished to assist these millions of pariahs, to return to them their property or a compensation for it, as far as possible, and to assure them the rights, guarantees, self-government, and security of living on their own land. To this end the tribes of Indians were organized into agrarian communities, to form pueblos within society, almost independent of the common authorities. Each tribe or aggregation of natives received its tract of land in the area about or in the vicinities of the villages or places, a tract delineated with the greatest precision possible and more or less extensive, in accordance with the size of the tribe.
>
> The land which constituted the resguardo was inalienable in per-

46. Cf. *Tierras y Águas,* the official publication of the Departamentos of Tierras and Águas of the Ministério de la Economía Nacional, Año 6 (1944), Números 63 and 64, pp. 62-67.

47. See, for example, the discussion by Honorio Pérez Salazar, "Emancipación Jurídica del Indígena."

petuity; each head of a family of indigenes had a right to cultivate a portion of the soil and to establish and maintain his house and field; the rights were equal proportionately, that is according to the number of children; the right was not one of private property but of usufruct, for the property belonged to the entire community, with the character of indivisability. These usufructory rights were hereditary through the head of the family, following the maternal line as a proof of having Indian blood; and in case there were no legitimate heirs, the personal right of usufruct returned to the community. Each tribe or resguardo had a cabildo composed exclusively of indigenes, fathers of families, elected according to specified rules; and this cabildo administered the internal affairs of the resguardo, resolving the problems which arose that did not affect the rights of outsiders or involve the common principles of civil and penal law reserved to the higher authorities.

As is evident each resguardo reestablished in its essence the primitive organization of the indigeneous tribes prior to the conquest. . . .

We add, in relation to the resguardos, as a proof of the benevolence which resulted in their creation, that the laws declared the indigenes to be minors, that is to say privileged before the law, and very particularly placed in charge of the authorities the defense and protection of the rights of the indigenes. In appearance all of this was very benign; but the medal of the resguardos had another side: the tribute (called mita in central Colombia). What sort of thing was the tribute? It was a genuine head tax which, by means of an impost, the Indians had to pay to the state, in addition to the tithes and the primicias and levies for the stole of the priests, and of the heavy contributions which under the name of *voluntarias* they paid by reason of *alferasgos* for the fiestas of the church, which multiplied in proportion to the interminable nomenclature of virgins and saints.

Thus the resguardos did nothing but to give a new form to the servitude of the indigenes: they ceased being serfs of the glebe to the encomenderos in order to become the serfs of the state and of the resguardo, without prejudice to the priests and the Missions. The tribute was clearly unjust, since the impost, in addition to being levied by the head, was not repaid by the state by a direct administration. The indigenes in each resguardo had the responsibility of making their own roads, bridges, constructing and maintaining the parish church, etc., etc. Thus the tribute was a heavy, unrecompensed exaction. The best proof of the iniquity of this tax is the fact that upon the gaining of independence by Colombia and the other republics, their first measures undertook to suppress the tribute and to give citizenship to the protected indigenes, as well as to prepare for the abolition of slavery.[48]

48. Samper, *Ensayo sobre las Revoluciones Políticas y la Condición Social de las Repúblicas Colombianas,* pp. 58-60.

4

Land Division, Land Surveys, and Land Titles

WHEREVER the institution of private property in land prevails, the manner of dividing the area among the inhabitants, the surveying of the boundaries which separate the holdings of one man or one family from those of another, and the ways of recording the titles or deeds to the land are among the most important of the institutional relationships between men and the soil. The three are so intimately interlinked that they must almost be thought of as comprising a single feature of the land system. In Colombia, as in most other parts of Latin America, many of the most acute social problems arise directly out of the prevailing antiquated and inadequate systems of surveying the land and recording the titles. Just as a faulty system of surveys and defective titles have plagued parts of Brazil for many decades,[1] and just as parts of the United States once suffered from virtual chaos because of the lack of system in the occupation and alienation of the public domain,[2] Colombia now is afflicted and is likely to be seriously troubled for some time to come by similar weaknesses in the traditional institutionalized relationships between men and the land. Worst of all, with each year that passes tens of thousands of acres of previously unoccupied land are being surveyed and deeded according to the expensive, inexact, and deficient methods inherited from the Spaniards. It would be difficult to discover a better example of a serious cultural lag.

In analyzing this particular part of the cultural pattern, two distinct features should be kept in mind. The first of these is the extent to which the surveys are definite, determinate, and permanent. The importance in this connection grows out of the need for a simple, accurate, efficient, and economical method of making the surveys and recording the titles. It is a matter merely of adequate national bookkeeping. The second relates to social interaction, community and neighborhood organization, and societal welfare in general.

1. Smith, *Brazil*, pp. 258-76.
2. Smith, *The Sociology of Rural Life*, pp. 246-52.

Where the village form of settlement prevails this second feature is of no great significance; but in countries such as Colombia and the United States, in which scattered farmsteads are the general rule, it is of paramount importance. When each farm family makes its home on the land the extent to which the surveys permit the dwellings to be located near one another is very closely related to the costs of building and repairing roads, of wires for electricity, of telephone lines, and of other facilities. Certain systems of land surveys bring about such dispersion of the families over the landscape that the maximum difficulties are placed in the way of social intercourse; while others greatly facilitate neighboring, mutual aid, and all other forms of social interaction among the people on the land. Finally, the extent to which the settlement pattern and the layout of fields may be adjusted to the topography is largely dependent upon the manner in which the land is surveyed for the purpose of dividing it among the inhabitants.

The nation which lacks a definite, determinate, and permanent system for surveying its lands cannot perfect a simple and efficient method of recording the titles to the same. If surveys are indefinite and indeterminate, the expediency of a resurvey is not easily available for the settlement of the inevitable disputes over property lines. If mere surface phenomena, such as trees, stones, streams, ravines, divides, are the points of reference on which surveys are based, with the passage of time the boundaries of many farms will be altered. In fact the limits of some of them may be entirely unknown.

The most satisfactory manner of eliminating such uncertainties is by the adoption of astronomical bases for the surveys. Such is easily accomplished by the simple expediency of utilizing the lines of latitude and longitude as points of departure. This was the principle which the genius of Jefferson employed as the foundation for the national land system of the United States, and one which has been imitated widely in other parts of the world. However, it should be indicated that many of the advantages which may be derived from such a simple, rectangular, and permanent system of land surveys have been vitiated in this country by the prescription that all of the parallelograms into which the surface of the nation was divided should consist of squares. In spite of this defect, the checkerboard pattern of land division used in the United States and Canada has reduced to a minimum uncertainties about boundaries and the resulting social conflicts over property lines. It also lent itself to the perfection of a highly satisfactory method of registering land titles. This situation contrasts sharply with the confusion along these lines which prevails in much of the Old World and throughout many parts of Latin America. As a nation the United States has benefited immensely because Jefferson and others of the founding fathers saw to it that a definite, determinate, and permanent system for surveying the land early was incorporated into its basic law.

The welfare of man on the land also requires that the system of land division in vogue permit him to build his home in close proximity to those of some of his neighbors, unless, of course, the village form of settlement is used. The benefits derived from close association with his fellows—especially important for children—and the costs involved in the provision of such modern necessities as paved roads, electricity, telephone lines, and school busses make it highly undesirable for farm homes to be widely dispersed over the land. Herein lies the chief weakness of the official system designed by Jefferson and used throughout the bulk of the territory of the United States. The checkerboard pattern, with the farms laid off in the form of squares, has resulted in a dispersal of rural dwellings that is near the maximum, density of population and the size of the holdings being as they are. Had rectangles considerably greater in length than in width been used in the surveys, the system could have retained all its advantages and at the same time the extreme degree of separation of the farm homes from one another could have been avoided. Even this, however, would not have permitted the adjustment of the surveys to topographical conditions; and once the land has been divided and the titles recorded it is difficult and expensive to bring about any substantial change or improvement in the system.

In Colombia there are three principal aspects of the matter under consideration deserving of attention. The first of these is the unsatisfactory nature of the old system of metes and bounds which is in use in the more densely settled parts of the country. The second is the problem of the procedure to be used in laying off the small tracts or farms into which an hacienda is divided when the state, the nation, or a private agency undertakes a *parcelación* project. The third, and last, is the provision of a national system of surveys, similar to those employed in the settlement of the United States and Canada, which can bring some semblance of order into the way in which newly opened sections on the frontier are occupied and settled.

A Defective System of Surveys

The system of surveys employed in Colombia is defective in nearly every major aspect. As a result it has given rise to almost as much confusion and conflict as were engendered by the overlapping claims and "shingle titles" which prevailed throughout Kentucky, Tennessee, and other western states before the adoption of the Ordinance of 1787 which set the pattern for our national system of land surveys.

The chief defects of Colombia's land surveys may be summarized as follows. (1) They are indefinite. It is almost impossible for anyone to state precisely the area included in any given tract of land. The property descriptions almost always must include the phrase *más o menos* (more or less). (2) The surveys are indeterminate. It may be that the limits of some of the fincas, haciendas, or estancias were known with exactitude at the time they were surveyed;[3] but certainly

3. In a large share of the cases even this is doubtful. In addition to the defects inherent in the system, or lack of it, in the surveys themselves a great deal of vagueness and confusion resulted from faults of a technical nature. To begin with there were few trained civil engineers to do the surveying, so that most of the actual work was done by amateurs. In the second place the Spanish measures, linear as well as of area, were quite unstandarized, and varied widely in time and space (see, for abundant evidence on this point, Páez Courvel, *Historia de las Medidas Agrarias Antiguas;* and Ossa V., *Medidas Agrarias Antiguas*). It is true that the laws of the Indies specified precisely what was to be included in a *caballería*, as the grant intended for a conquistador of high estate who fought on horseback was called, and in the *peonía*, as the allotment for an ordinary soldier was designated. Thus Libro IV, Título xii, Ley i declares that ". . . a peonía is a *solar* [town lot] of 50 feet in width by 100 feet in length, 100 *fanegas* of arable land for wheat or barley, 10 for maize, two *huebras* of land for a garden, and eight for orchards, and pasture for ten brood sows, twenty cows, five brood mares, one hundred sheep, and twenty goats. A caballería is a solar of one hundred feet width by 200 depth; and in all other respects it is the equivalent of five peonías. . . ." Obviously such specifications left a great deal to the imagination of the founders of the new settlements, and the conquistadores rose to the occasion. The amount of variation one finds in New Granada alone is almost unbelievable. And, finally, in the early deeds, it was commonplace for only a part of the limits to be specified. Páez Courvel distinguishes three types of such incomplete descriptions: (1) those having an "open perimeter," i.e. only part of a geometric figure specified; (2) the ones in which the description consisted merely of an indication of the extension of the grant along a given stream; and (3) those in which the name of the river on which a claim fronted was given, and also the names of the creeks which marked its limits on the two sides, but no indication of the boundary at the rear. Páez Courvel, p. 206. The early travelers frequently mentioned one or more of these defects in the surveys, of which the following case described in the account left by J. P. Hamilton (I, 72) is fairly representative: "We arrived at six P.M. at Rinconada, a solitary house. . . . We slept here. The master of the house was a Creole, a very industrious man;

with the lapse of time this ceased to be the case. As indicated below it soon became almost impossible for a surveyor to determine the location of many of the property lines. (3) The surveys are impermanent. The surface phenomena on which the descriptions are based are not fixed in time and space. Stream beds shift about considerably in the course of time, and not infrequently a river changes its course radically. Trees die and others of the same species spring up near where the first were growing. Rocks may be moved, and a divide may be changed materially by erosion. Stakes and other markers may be removed or rot away, and A and B, or their heirs, may develop marked differences of opinion as to precisely where the property of the one ceases and that of the other begins. All of these and many others have come about in Colombia; and they have all made for a lack of certainty about land boundaries, and with that the upsurge of wave after wave of conflict over the land. Indeed, Colombia's indefinite, indeterminate, and impermanent system of land surveys has been one of the most fruitful sources of conflict in that sorely troubled country.

The extent to which these defects, and others not enumerated, are encountered in a typical Colombian municipio is fairly well illustrated by the comments made by the author and his colleagues after their intensive survey of Tabio. These are as follows:

> In colonial times, when to a few encomenderos were given huge extensions of land and the natives who resided upon it, slight attention was paid to developing systematic land surveys and simple property descriptions and deeds. Divides, watercourses, stones, trees, and other natural phenomena served as the guideposts for the system of metes and bounds that was employed. As generation after generation of the numerous heirs of the founding fathers have brought about subdivision after subdivision of the original holdings, much the same system has been followed. However, the practice of defining the boundaries of one man's holding by indicating the names of the proprietors on whose lands it adjoined became predominant. This system, which reminds one of the community whose inhabitants made a living by doing each other's washing, naturally proved a fertile field for the development of disputes over boundaries and titles, a phenomenon which constitutes one of the most acute social problems with which

---

he had three years before got a grant of 1,000 yards along the bank of the river, and as much as he could cultivate in the rear, paying the small tithes to the clergy of Mompox. During this time he had erected a sugar-house; a neat building, in nice order; and his plantations of sugar, chocolate, and plantains, were in a most thriving condition."

present-day Colombia is faced. Tabio, greatly subdivided as it is, is entirely cut to this indefinite, indeterminate, and impermanent system of surveys. The following description of the boundaries of the lands within the municipio, which the nation took over for the establishment of a potato experiment station, is typical.

"The Departamento promises to transfer to the Nation, by public deed and destined for the Potato Experimental Farm, the right of ownership that it has over the rural finca designated 'El Chircal' situated in the jurisdiction of the Municipio of Tabio, Departamento of Cundinamarca, in the part denominated 'El Rincon,' composed of two contiguous lots called 'El Muelle' and 'Santa Rita,' bounded as follows: EL MUELLE.—On the one side by the lands of Modesto García, today belonging to his heirs; on the other, with the undivided lands of the heirs of Ramón and Vicente González, of Jenaro Ramírez, of the successors of León Sánchez and Feliciano Vanegas; on the foot by the land of Eustargio García, and at the head, with the lands of the Garcías. SANTA RITA.—On one side, by lands of Feliciano Vangegas; on the other, by lands of Jenaro Ramírez; at the top of the hill, with the land of Dr. Jesús Casas Rojas and with lands of the heirs of Manuel Macias; and finally, with land belonging to the succession of León Sánchez."[4]

It is hardly necessary to say more in order to indicate that Colombia's land surveys and property descriptions are patterned upon outmoded models. It is evident that they are oriented merely with respect to surface phenomena such as streams, washes, divides, trees, stones, lake fronts, and other features of the landscape. All of these are likely to be indefinite and certain to be impermanent. With the passage of time the exact property lines become indeterminate. This was serious even before the discovery of oil and the importance of the subsoil made exact limits a matter of tremendous economic concern. As one Colombian engineer (Dr. Ramón Guerra Azuola in his *Elementos de Ingeniería Legal*) rather jokingly pointed out just before the turn of the century:

A grave difficulty for the engineer may arise from the lawsuits over the boundaries of farms, when an attempt is made to establish exactly their limits as defined in the old documents. As a rule there figure in them as recognized points many things that since have been completely obliterated. The following may serve as an example: "Beginning on the slope of the Viajal and following a straight line to where the spotted bull is grazing, thence to a thorn tree which is growing between two stones, and from there to the highest hill, etc." . . . In addition to this the measures were arbitrary to a certain extent or at least inexact. . . .[5]

4. Smith, Díaz, and García, *Tabio*, pp. 27-28.   5. In Páez Courvel, p. 24.

The dependence upon such a system, with the limits defined in terms of movable and perishable points of reference, makes it impossible to give or receive a simple deed; and of course under such a system it is utterly out of the question to define accurately the limits of a given tract of land so as to insure that the boundaries will remain the same for ten, twenty-five, or fifty years in the future.

Basing the surveys on simple surface phenomena inevitably gives rise to the practice of delineating dividing lines and describing prop-

Metes and bounds surveys in an area of tiny farmsteads, department of Nariño. (Courtesy of L. Eduardo Montero.)

erty limits in terms of metes and bounds. Dr. Guerra probably did not find in the old documents the example he used of the spotted bull, nor even a reference to a place where a hog was rooting, or a horse rubbing itself against a tree. But the principle was the same. Colombian property lines run from tree to tree, stone to stone, peak to peak, or clearing to clearing; they make great use of water courses and divides. With startling frequency they even describe one man's holding merely by saying that it adjoins with that of his neighbor. Naturally great confusion may, and almost always does, arise if A's lands are described as being bounded on one side by the holdings of B, while the latter's estate, in turn, is defined as being limited on the one extremity by the farm of A. Added to all this is the fact that the water courses and dividing ridges follow extremely irregular lines; indeed, it frequently may be almost impossible to determine exactly where they lie. Finally, in colonial times in Colombia it was not uncommon for a part of the perimeter to be entirely unspecified. As a result of all these, the area of a given tract of land may never be determined with any degree of certainty; and as indicated above, since the surveys are indeterminate, practically all figures on areas given in property descriptions in Colombia contain the phrase *más o menos*. This is also generally the case in Latin America.

In addition to the factors described above, there is one other widespread practice which has done much to confuse property lines and titles in Colombia. This is a custom which has prevailed for centuries of a man's heirs keeping *indiviso* the land he left to them. Says P. L. Bell, once United States Trade Commissioner in Colombia: "The chief difficulty encountered is in the case of 'indivisos,' where there are a number of owners in common; such estates have been handed down for generations without any partition proceedings. The disentanglement of an 'indiviso' is a tedious and costly proceeding, dragging on for many years."[6] Even though this problem has not developed to the acute stage comparable to the one which paralyzes activity in many parts of Brazil, and amounts to communal ownership in some,[7] it nevertheless is one to be reckoned with. It is among the most troublesome features of the many cases which come to the attention of the officials of the national land department, and the history of Colombia is full of chronicles similar to the one from which the following extracts are translated.

> For the enjoyment of the youths and a warning to the incautious perhaps it would be well to relate some of the things which happened to me in Guataquicito, and how, in spite of the difficulties and opposition I succeeded in developing a valuable hacienda, which, although it is not mine today, has added greatly to the wealth of the nation.
>
> On the upper Magdalena, on the right bank and across from the village of Guataquí . . . lay a beautiful meadow which remained practically unused until 1857. It had belonged to the former Guataquí Indians who held it in common, they and the persons to whom they had ceded their rights in the course of 50 years. This meadow was called Guataquicito.
>
> The number of those who had rights in these lands was 300; and of these rights 72 were mine. The number of persons who claimed

6. *Colombia*, p. 156.
7. Smith, *Brazil*, pp. 261-63; and Smith, "Notes on Population and Social Organization in the Central Portion of the São Francisco Valley," I, 50-52.

rights to these lands was about 3,000; and to untangle this net an involved lawsuit was necessary. Out of it came enough documents to load a mule. On the day on which the decision was rendered, I secretly sent the papers to the Court for approval, and then embarked for Ambalema in a canoe. Unhappy thought! It was believed that I was taking the papers there, and that the loss of them would cause the decision to be annulled. While I was riding along thoroughly relaxed, contemplating the ripples of the river and given over to pleasant thoughts, horrors! The boatmen swung the vessel about violently and I was catapulted to the bottom of the stream. No one knows how I reached the bank. . . .

When the land was divided and each one given his share, a large part of it came to me and a small one went to the house of Crotheshyway & Co., for whom Colonel Amaya was the agent. That firm was accustomed to receiving a large share of the tobacco produced by the cultivators on Guataquicito, so on the first week when that grown on my land was carried to my factory there was alarm, indignation, and protest. This ended in a fight between Colonel Amaya and Colonel García, who was my agent, and in this struggle many joined in on one side or the other according to their sympathies.

From then on the settlement of Guataquicito became a field of battle; at night one could hear the whistling of the bullets being exchanged between the camps, and at all times the members of both parties went about armed. . . . Finally Mr. Crotheshyway decided to recall Colonel Amaya and to sell us his part of the land.[8]

In order to provide a clearer understanding of the nature of surveys and property descriptions in Colombia a few typical examples are presented for examination. The first of these pertains to a grant on the Magdalena River made to Cristóbal de Pantoja in 1673. The request to the Audiencia at Bogotá, made on his behalf by his brother, asked for 3 caballerías of front lands, "running downstream from the mouth of La Miel River to as far as it will extend on that side; and on the inner side, which is uninhabitable, forested, and very hilly, to the place which my said brother shall designate, or such as may be necessary for the benefit of the hacienda which he shall establish. . . ."[9] The grant was made on June 26 of the same year, in the following terms: ". . . there should be and is granted to Cristóbal de Pantoja, inhabitant of this city, 3 caballerías of land which he requests in the location and places he designates, and according to the limits and boundaries set forth in his petition."[10]

8. Medardo Rivas, pp. 233-36.
9. Quoted in Páez Courvel, p. 180.
10. *Ibid.*

Finally, when the beneficiary was formally placed in possession of the tract on February 9, 1675, the limits were described as follows.

> . . . and requested me to give him possession of said 3 caballerías of land for his own, and in order to do so, I took the said Captain Cristóbal de Pantoja by the hand and walked along a path he had opened, and he, himself, with a machete cut some branches and pulled up some saplings and performed other acts as evidence of possession, of that which I certify embraces the said three caballerías of land, which are suitable for cultivation, extending downstream along the Magdalena River from the mouth of the La Miel River to the Cocorná Ravine and running along the banks of the La Miel inland to the Samaná Ravine, which two said ravines are designated as the boundaries of said lands.[11]

The "open perimeter" of this particular property description is worthy of special mention. Here in the Magdalena Valley such a boundary was assumed to be "closed" by the divide of the first mountain chain inland. In other parts of the Republic similar assumptions were not always as easily made. Consider for example the difficulties confronting the surveyor who would seek to determine the property lines of the grants given at Cartagena. From an official publication in which attention was given to this subject the following property descriptions have been translated.

> The year 1593. On the 29th of November there were conceded to Pedro de Heredia three caballerías of land in the Barrancas de Río Grande, one league above the barranca called Mateo Rodríguez, he being obligated to bring to this city for its use the third part of that which he shall produce.
> The year 1598. February 10 of said year: to Don Bartolomé Aronja (founder of the village of the same name) two caballerías of land adjacent to Curucha (Arjonita Antigua), where his father has an estancia and some cows[. . .].
> The same year, same date: To Captain Luis Polo de Aguila four caballerías of land, from the Arryos de Silo to the estancia of the Mahates.
> The year 1601. On the eighth of January of said year a grant was made to the pastor, Gaspar de los Reyes, giving him a title to two caballerías of land in an estancia which he occupies which adjoins with that of Don Alonso López de Aya and another which belonged to Juan Viloria.
> The year 1614. On April 14, 1614 there were ceded to Don Juan Jurtado del Aguila the lands of Paricuica, which were left uninhab-

11. *Ibid.*

ited when the Indians were assembled at different places by the Visitador Juan de Villabona Subiurre, formerly Visitador of said natives.

After quoting these descriptions from the records the anonymous author adds: "And thus follow the annotations by the thousands."[12]

Similar examples could be multiplied from all parts of Colombia and for all of the epochs. But it should not be presumed that Colombia's antiquated metes and bounds system of land surveys is of historical interest only. Even before the development of the oil industry made the precise location of boundary lines of paramount importance, a well-informed North American observer wrote as follows. "On account of the little known and explored condition of Colombia during colonial times, its broken and tropical nature, and the rather crude means of survey obtaining at the time, boundaries were vague, being described as from one river to another or from one mountain range to another (peaks being designated as corners, etc.); and from this condition there come down to modern times many conflicting titles of lands, which have caused endless litigation."[13] And in more recent years, since the petroleum wells became a major source of the national income, Colombia's crude, vague, and indefinite surveys have given rise to endless quarrels and conflicts. Says the Colombian scholar who appears to have delved most deeply into the subject, in commenting upon the lightness with which an earlier writer had disposed of matters pertaining to unstandardized measures and indefinite boundaries: "Our author writing in 1892 did not suspect that a half century later quarrels over the land, stimulated by the desire for the riches of petroleum, would disturb the dust on the cases in the old archives in a search for these obscure old formulas, so disdained in the past cen-

12. *Geografía Económica de Colombia*, pp. 274-75.

13. Bell, p. 132. The lands which the parish priest left to the pueblo of Corozal as community property provide a good example of the universal and endless litigation which has been brought about in Colombia by the faulty system of surveys and titles. By 1873, in spite of the wars for independence and the many revolutions, the lands donated by the priest upon his death in 1799 were still in the peaceful possession of the pueblo. "But they were subject to frequent litigation because of the loss of titles and from their present limits not being perfectly marked." Numerous attempts had been made to have the lands resurveyed and the titles confirmed, but these had given rise in 1865 to "tumultuous meetings, with exaggerated pretensions and ridiculous menaces against notable persons of this City . . . !" By 1873, when the account closes, the matter was still unsettled "serving as the instrument for many passions, principally of a political nature." Jiménez, *Geografía Física i Política de la Ciudad de Corozal*, pp. 41-42.

tury, which now constitute the source of the rights and the key to the most intricate litigations."[14]

These metes and bounds surveys are of contemporary interest also because they remain almost the sole reliance in the surveying and patenting of lands. Examples galore are not difficult to find since they figure in the current, abundant litigation over the land. One conveniently available for use is found in a case in which the question at issue was whether some titles issued in 1922 and 1923 were definitive or merely provisional. Messers Ernesto Villegas and Arturo Marin Aguirre, in 1936, solicited the National Land Office to give them a definite ruling respecting their property rights to an estate named El Tapir delineated as follows: "Beginning at a stone marker called Conejo on the Zeta divide, and extending along the divide towards the Altamira peak; from there, along the crest which leads down to the El Retiro peak, to the edge of the precipice which rises from the Gallinazo Cordillera; along said precipice to the point at which it intersects with a line from the stone marker Conejo to the point of the landslide at an angle of 3.22 degrees; and from there along said line to the starting point."[15] This property description now figures in all the official documents related to this particular finca, and thousands of others of a similar nature are being added to the national records every year. In the second half of the twentieth century, well along in the atomic age, these outmoded patterns are being imposed upon practically all the areas into which settlers push their way.

LAND DIVISION ON PARCELACIÓN AND COLONIZATION PROJECTS

Until recently the manner of laying off the plots for the individual settlers on Colombia's resettlement or parcelación projects and in the agricultural colonies has had little to recommend it over the haphazard procedures handed down from antiquity. Apparently it has mattered little whether the federal government, that of one of the departamentos, or one of the semi-official agencies connected with the banks was in charge of the subdivision project. The lines were run with slight regard for any considerations other than that of getting the large property cut up into tracts of convenient sizes. Variations in the productivity of the land, the maximum benefit from water courses, the desirability for each family to have ready access to roads and trails, the facilitation of social intercourse between the families, and other

14. Páez Courvel, p. 25.
15. Restrepo, *Memoria del Ministerio de Agricultura y Comercio*, pp. 121-22.

rational features seem not to have entered into the planning. Despite the fact that the officials in charge were "on the ground" and in position to direct matters in details, the resulting surveys have not even been definite, determinate, or permanent. They have merely broken up some large holdings, whose defective surveys and titles frequently were largely responsible for the decisions to subdivide, into smaller tracts whose equally deficient delineation is certain to generate much social conflict in the years which lie ahead.[16]

But there are exceptions to this general rule, developments which lead one to believe that Colombia eventually may learn to profit by the experiences of other countries, such as Brazil,[17] in the rational planning of her projects in the subdivision of large estates. Among examples of this that were observed are the following.

In the Cauca Valley the small farms along the river in the vicinity of Cali and Puerto Tejada have been laid out in a satisfactory manner. The plots are small, but they usually front on the road or the stream. Not infrequently they extend from the one to the other, thus giving them two fairly well established bases. In addition, the fact that they are laid off side by side introduces a considerable amount of regularity into the pattern. These surveys are not as satisfactory as those based on immovable points fixed by astronomical observations, but as compared with the metes and bounds customarily employed in Colombia they have much to be said in their favor.

The lands which have come into the hands of the foreign fruit companies and those on which the oil companies have conducted their operations also have been laid out, as a rule, in a manner quite different from the surveys employed in other parts of the Republic. Of course, in the first case, the lines have not been run for the purpose of separating the holdings of one man from those of another; and in the second, the territory included is for the most part still to be occupied with anything except a little rudimentary agriculture or some haphazard cattle ranching. But in both cases the surveys employed are rectangular in nature, copied closely after the system used in the United States, with the lines of latitude and longitude employed as the bases.

Another example of more systematic land division was observed in the department of Santander on the large estate called El Playón, a

16. Cf. Fals-Borda, *El Hombre y la Tierra en Boyacá*, pp. 62-63.
17. For the details of Brazil's highly perfected methods of laying off lands in her various colonization projects, see, Smith, *Brazil*, pp. 276-82.

hacienda on which there have been numerous outbreaks of armed conflict between the arrendatarios or colonos and those who possessed documentary evidence of ownership. Perhaps in desperation, the proprietors finally decided to dispose of the bulk of the land to the occupants and others at fairly reasonable prices. In laying off the tracts for the purchasers the road was taken as the base of departure and then each holding was made uniform in width throughout its extension. This introduced considerable system into the surveys, and has also resulted in the development of a line village pattern of settlement.

No doubt there have been similar developments in other parts of the country, but they are probably not very numerous. However, as more experience is gained in the organized colonization of new areas, a much greater degree of rationality in planning and executing the surveys is to be expected. Several of the leaders in Antioquia, particularly, have made use of long, narrow tracts laid off side by side and fronting on a road in the conquest and settlement of the highly tropic sections of the department. This has been particularly true in the road through the jungles to the area about the Gulf of Urubá.

SURVEYS FOR COLOMBIA'S UNPATENTED LANDS

A large share of Colombia's most desirable lands have already been surveyed and deeded by the costly and deficient systems of metes and bounds described above; and other huge expanses are claimed by the proprietors who legally possess many of the large holdings. But there remain many hundreds of thousands of square miles of the public domain that are still to be claimed and settled; and in many sections of the country intrepid pioneers are rapidly pushing forward the frontier. Unfortunately, though, as yet Colombia is not profiting by the mistakes others have made in surveying and disposing of their public lands. Whereas in the United States the genius of Jefferson, and the fact that he and another licensed surveyor, George Washington, occupied the presidency for 16 of the first 24 years of our history under the Constitution, early brought order and system into the occupation of our virgin lands, Colombia still has everything to do in this respect. Even during the second half of the twentieth century the indefinite, indeterminate, and impermanent system of surveys is still the only one being used in the transfer of parts of the national territory to private owners.

The case against the continued use of such a deficient system is so strong that its salient features deserve a place in this treatise or any other which attempts a serious treatment of the institutionalized relationships between man and the land in Colombia or any other endeavor to understand and describe the process of rural or agricultural development in that nation. This is especially true since in 1944 a bill, essentially in the form presented below and one that would have corrected the situation, passed the lower house of the national congress and went on for consideration in the Senate. Apparently it had the support, or at least lacked opposition, of nearly all factions in the country. It had been pushed actively by four different ministers of national economy, and seemed certain of final passage in the upper house, when it and about all other constructive legislation was paralyzed by the upsurge of virtual anarchy. A few of the most significant features in the train of events which was involved are as follows: the resignation of Alfonso López as president; the irreconcilable split in the Liberal party into the extremists, led by Jorge Gaitan, and the moderate faction; the election of a Conservative president by a small plurality of the votes; the protracted struggle between a president, holding the very strong powers of the executive under the Colombian Constitution (including the right to appoint the governors of the departments, who in turn appointed the alcaldes of the municipios or counties), and the Liberal majority in both houses of the congress; strife amounting to virtual civil war in those departments in which the president attempted to replace Liberal governors with members of the Conservative party; the assassination of Gaitan and the sadistic and ruinous excesses of the mob during the Bogotá conference; the election which brought Laureano Gómez to power as president, and the upsurge of "violence" throughout the republic; the coup which ousted Gómez and led to the exercise of dictatorial powers by General Rojas Pinilla; the "revolution" which brought the downfall of Rojas, and the attempt to pacify the country; the election of Alberto Lleras Carmago as president by the National Union of Liberal and Conservative forces, and his constructive term; and the election of Guillermo León Valencia, Conservative, as the second National Union president, and the succession of crises which has ensued.

These are but a few of the highlights of the troubled times Colombia has been passing through during the last 25 years, a period in which probably some 300,000 lives were lost in the chaos which has ranged through the misty shadowland which separates what most properly would be called civil war and armed insurrection from pure banditry. In any case the situation has been one in which the development of an adequate land system and nearly all other significant developmental measures were pushed into oblivion. In 1959 the bill itself was reintroduced in the congress, but once more it seems to be lost because of the shattering of the coalition and the extreme struggles for power among the numerous splinters that have broken off from the traditional parties.

The text of the proposed law for the establishment of a national system of surveys is as follows.

THE CONGRESS OF COLOMBIA DECREES

ARTICLE 1: For the purpose of adjudication, occupation, and use of public lands, these are divided into adjudicable and non-adjudicable. Non-adjudicable lands are those reserved by law, or by disposition of the Government, or those destined for special purposes; those which form part of the protected forest zone or which include woods of special interest; and those which the Government shall set aside as a reserve for future agricultural and pastoral enterprises, conservation of forests, distribution of the population, or establishment of immigrants.

On the lands included in public forests the establishments of settlers will not be permitted without the previous authorization of the Ministry of National Economy.

The Government shall proceed to designate in each Departamento the areas of public lands which are adjudicable.

ARTICLE 2: The surveys of adjudicable public lands shall take as a point of departure a vertex of geographic coordinates, that is, the intersection of a meridian and a parallel; [in this way] the square degrees [*grados*] shall be determined; each *grado* [square degree] shall be divided into 121 *cuadrados* [squares] of 10 kilometers per side; each *cuadrado* shall be divided into 25 *secciones* of 2 kilometers per side; the *sección* shall be divided into 4 *lotes* each 2 kilometers by 500 meters, and these in turn shall be divided into 4 *parcelas* each one of which shall have an extension of 25 hectares (see Figures 4 and 5).

This system shall be called the Official System of Colombia.

ARTICLE 3: From the date on which this law becomes effective it shall not be possible to initiate occupations nor adjudications before the public lands have been surveyed into *grados, cuadrados,* and *secciones,* according to the official system.

ARTICLE 4: Before being declared open to settlement each *sección* of public lands must first be classified as: (1) Forest Reserve, (2) Cultivatable lands, (3) Grazing lands, and only the last two may be occupied by settlers.

ARTICLE 5: Public lands shall be adjudicated and adjudicable only in extensions not exceeding 200 hectares for agricultural uses or of 1,200 hectares for grazing purposes to all persons of age who have a right to the adjudication of a portion of this extension. Excepted from this right are those who already are proprietors of lands worth 10,-000.00 pesos and those married persons whose wives or husbands already have obtained adjudications to the extent of either of the established limits.

ARTICLE 6: The lands occupied by a person awaiting adjudication shall be called his *portion,* and no person, from the date of this law, can obtain by adjudication *portions* of less than 25 hectares, and

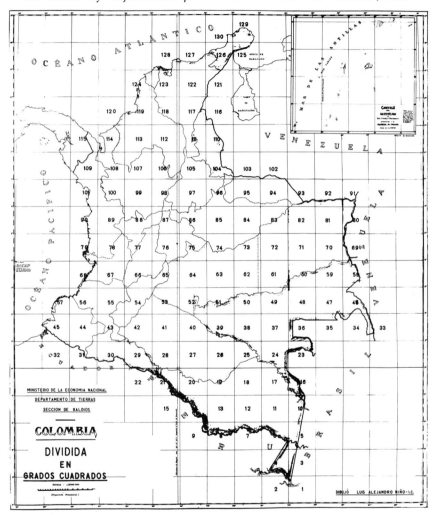

Figure 4.—Map showing the territory of the Republic of Colombia divided into grados.

these must always be taken in entire *parcelas* in accordance with the official system, without its being possible in any case to divide or fragment these *parcelas*.

Each *portion* shall consist of adjacent parcelas of 25 hectares. Every candidate for a *portion* must make his application with the indications and specifications which are treated in Article 2 of this official system.

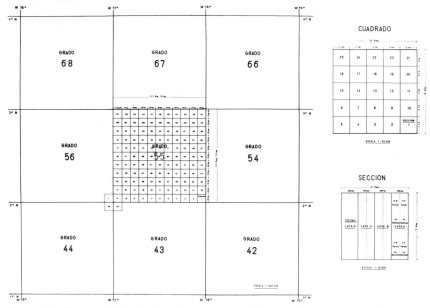

Figure 5.—Proposed details for the division of the grados into cuadrados, secciones, lotes, and parcelas.

ARTICLE 7: When the application is received, if the *portion* applied for has not been given to another, or there is no other application pending, the applicant shall be given a provisional title, it also being possible, in the negative cases, to change the specifications from the *portion* applied for, to another one.

ARTICLE 8: The possessor of a provisional title may change it for a deed to the land after 3 years, if he has complied with all the conditions established for securing the definitive title.

The possessor of a provisional title must in any case comply with all the conditions and exchange the provisional title for the deed to the land within 10 years from the date of the provisional title. If this is not done the applicant shall lose all his rights to the *portion*.

ARTICLE 9: Indispensable conditions which must be complied with in order to obtain the deed to a *portion* are as follows:

1: To build a dwelling house on the *portion*.

2: To live on the *portion* with the family, if the applicant has one, for at least nine months per year for three consecutive years.

3: To enclose and maintain with visible and permanent fences at least one-fifth of the area claimed.

4: Agriculturists must maintain in cultivation at least one fifth of their *portions*, and stock growers must maintain the same proportion occupied by livestock to the degree that the quality of the land permits.

ARTICLE 10: A person who has obtained the adjudication of one *portion* of any type and who has disposed of it, may obtain the adjudication of another one, but it shall not exceed 25 hectares.

ARTICLE 11: Neither the public land to which provisional title has been given nor that that has been adjudicated may be sold or divided in extensions of less than 25 hectares in accordance with the official system, except that which is used for the sites of population centers or for such other public services as the Government shall consider necessary.

ARTICLE 12: Section 15 of each of the *cuadrados* shall be set apart as a patrimony for educational purposes.

ARTICLE 13: After the demarcations established by the law have been made, under no circumstances shall be permitted the occupation or use of the inadjudicable areas, and those who violate this disposition, in addition to being subject to fines, shall be expulsed from the areas occupied or used without being entitled to any indemnification whatsoever for the improvements made.

ARTICLE 14: From the date of this law it shall not be legal to adjudicate public lands in extensions of less than 25 hectares; to those who previously have entered claims to smaller areas, the Government, considering the circumstances in each case, shall designate a period during which they may complete the minimum requirement, or, if justified by study of the economic and physical situation, may grant them the adjudication of an area less than the established minimum.

ARTICLE 15: The settlers already established in zones which are classified as unadjudicable shall not be permitted to enlarge their claims without previous authorization of the Government, and, in order to obtain the adjudication, they must conform in the use of the land to the regulations which the Government shall prescribe.

ARTICLE 16: All the owners of public land bonds or titles of any kind whatever must present them to the Ministry of National Economy within two years from the date of this law to exchange them for provisional titles; those which are not presented during this period shall be considered null and void and of no value whatsoever and those who negotiate or try to use them will be penalized in accordance with the law.

ARTICLE 17: Both the definitive titles and the provisional titles shall carry the specifications of the person in whose favor they are drawn, state whether it is the first or second adjudication, and whether the holder is married or single; and the indication of the *parcela* or *parcelas, lote* or *lotes, sección* or *secciones, cuadrado* or *cuadrados,* and *grado* or *grados,* shall constitute the demarcation of the *portion,* these specifications alone indicating the boundaries of the *portion* without its being necessary to determine them in any other form.

ARTICLE 18: To carry this law into effect the Government shall proceed to make the sketches or maps or plans of the adjudicable areas and of the lots into which they may be divided, and it shall do the same with the unadjudicable area. After the zones of adjudicable public lands have been determined, the Instituto Geográfico Catastral y Militar shall proceed to make areo-photografic maps of them.

ARTICLE 19: In order to carry out the provisions of this law, and to facilitate the occupations and adjudications by small farmers and for the control of the norms specified, the Government shall send to each Departamento the commissions that shall be considered necessary, being obligated to establish for each Departamento at least one commission composed of engineers, agronomists, civil engineers, draftsmen, and lawyers for the adjudication of the public lands and the giving of the title to which the occupation of adjudicable lands has given a right.

In each region these commissions shall have as their functions to study and survey, in accordance with the official system, the areas which are cultivatable and adjudicable. Furthermore, they may work in areas already adjudicated or on private property which is unused or deficiently cultivated. They must send monthly reports to the Governors and the Ministry of National Economy concerning the lands visited with the data specified in the preceding Article, in order to make them known to the interested persons, to whom, through the respective Alcaldes, there shall be fixed the period for them to comply with the specifications.

ARTICLE 20: All official and semi-official credit agencies shall give preference in their credits or loans to the settlers established in the legal manner to facilitate their development of their lands.

ARTICLE 21: The Ministry of Public Works shall make the surveys and construct roads passable by wheeled vehicles to the zones of adjudicable public lands, and these roads shall be considered as part of the National Road System.

ARTICLE 22: The Government shall proceed to include in the budget the sums necessary to carry out this law, and if for any reason the appropriations are not made for the ordinary manner, funds shall be transferred or the necessary credits opened to carry its provisions into effect.

ARTICLE 23: The Government, in regulating this law, shall establish the procedures for adjudication of public lands and for the leasing of the same, as well as for applying the penalties to those who violate these dispositions.

ARTICLE 24: There are repealed all the dispositions which are contrary to the provisions of this law.

Bogotá, August 1944
T. LYNN SMITH
Asesor Técnico

JUSTO DÍAZ RODRÍGUEZ
Director del Departamento de Tierras[18]

The provisions of the proposed act are clear and require no explanation. But it is well to indicate the advantages its adoption would have conferred upon the country. These are several and are discussed briefly in turn.

Such a law would have established, for the guidance of future settlement in Colombia, a definite, determinate, and permanent system of surveys embodying all the advantages of the rectangular one based on astronomical observations employed in the United States. But it would not have imposed a checkerboard pattern, with its many social and economic disadvantages, upon the landscape of New Granada.

The proposed law provided for the regularization of settlement on the frontier by providing some of the basic rules by which land could legally be claimed and patented. It was designed to eliminate the haphazard way in which the occupation of new lands is taking place. For example, once it had gone into effect, the gerrymandering of claims so as to monopolize some particularly significant resource, such as a water course, would have ended. At the same time since the length of the holdings would be considerably greater than their width it would be possible for the settlers to secure many social and economic advantages, by building their houses in fairly close proximity to one another.

Colombia does not have the funds to justify the expending of huge sums unnecessarily in the surveying of lands that are to be patented. As matters now stand when a settler files a claim to a tract from the public domain, specifying its limits in terms of metes and bounds, the government is obligated to send a surveyor to measure the area and establish the markers. This is far more expensive than necessary. Under the system proposed in a day or a week a given surveyor could delineate exactly the boundaries of far more land than is possible under the cumbersome system of metes and bounds.

18. Smith, "Colonization and Settlement in Colombia," pp. 134-39.

5

Systems of Agriculture

WILL IT BE possible for Colombia quickly and effectively to replace its antiquated, labor-devouring, and frequently bemeaning ways of securing and transporting agricultural and livestock products with a system of agriculture that is modern, efficient, and dignifying to those engaged in cultivating the land? What Colombia is to be a decade from now and at the opening of the next century depends largely upon the answer to this question. If the masses of her rural population now knew how to farm as well as did the Canadians of such provinces as Ontario and Saskatchewan as early as 1910, Colombia already would be a model of social and economic development worthy of imitation by all of the other so-called underdeveloped nations. Moreover, it should be stressed that I feel justified in making these statements, even though there are many examples of highly effective agricultural methods in various parts of Colombia, such as some of the magnificent sugar-cane plantations in the Cauca Valley, the cotton plantations on the plains of the upper Magdalena Valley in Tolima and the neighboring departments, the huge dairy farms on the Savanna of Bogotá, and some noteworthy areas of mechanized agriculture on the northern coastal plain. But I am also acquainted with the Biblical and pre-Biblical ways of extracting a living from the soil that are the general rule in the bulk of the heavily populated part of the country, with the almost exclusive reliance of Colombia's rural people upon the hoe (and frequently even upon the digging stick), the sickle, and the ax and fire. Moreover, I know from personal observation in all parts of Colombia the extent to which labor is squandered needlessly in the production process, and the corollary to this, the parsimonious use of management in the agricultural and livestock enterprises. I am familiar with the lack of standardized weights and measures and the chaotic system of marketing which follows, as does night the day, such defects in the organization of the economy. Furthermore I have not been oblivious of the extent to which the backs of men and the heads of women, supplemented at times in some places by troops of pack animals, are relied upon for transportation on the farm and also widely used to move grains and tubers from farm to market. Finally, at the most elementary level at diverse places throughout Colombia I have personally taken stock of the paucity of information and the lack of acceptable practice with respect to such basic components of a satisfactory list of agricultural skills and practices as seed selection, the use of fertilizers and insecticides, the pruning of fruit trees, and the most elementary features of erosion control.

Nature and Significance of Agricultural Systems

In this treatise the designation system of agriculture is given to the highly integrated social system composed of beliefs and ideas, cultural traits and complexes, technical skills and "know how," techniques and practices, prejudices and habits, scientific knowledge and folklore, implements and machines, and so on, employed by the members of a given society in order to gain a livelihood from the soil. The interdependent aggregation or assemblage involved should be designated as a social system, and not some other kind of a system, because the indispensable components involved are persons, groups, social classes, institutions, cultural forms, and other strictly societal elements. As is true of the other social relationships between man and the land discussed in this volume, this portion of the social order is highly institutionalized. In all parts of the world there is a fairly high degree of standardization at the local level in the customary and approved ways of preparing the soil for the seeds, of destroying the weeds, of controlling insects and other predators, of taking the harvest, of caring for the livestock, and of transporting things on the farm and from farm to market. Moreover in general the value system prevailing in each specific rural community is oriented in a manner that is favorable to the preservation of existing ways of growing plants, caring for livestock, and utilizing the products of agricultural and stock-raising activities. Although he has made every effort to do so, the present writer has been unable to discover a more appropriate term for denoting the socio-cultural system under consideration than the *system of agriculture*. This, in turn, seems vastly superior to "agricultural techniques," which probably is the most likely alternative, because it tends to stress the comprehensiveness, the complexity, the systematic integration, and the organic unity of the aggregation or assemblage involved.

Explicitly stated, as is implicit in what is said above, a system of agriculture must be defined broadly enough so that it will include all of the lore, the scientific knowledge, the so-called know how, the practical skills, and even the superstitions, which farm families employ in the growing of crops, the raising of poultry and livestock, and the tasks of transportation. Thus in parts of Colombia the system of agriculture in one of the remaining primitive communities may have as its central core the digging stick manipulated by the women of the tribe, domesticated plants such as maize or manioc, and a set of religious and magical beliefs and practices designed to promote germination and fertility and to ward off harmful influences or entities; whereas in parts of the Cauca Valley or along the Magdalena Valley in Tolima and the neighboring states it may involve the most modern scientific knowledge of seed selection and propagation, the tractor for use in preparing the seedbed and for tillage, the use of the airplane for dusting with insecticides in order to control harmful insects and parasites, and the motor truck for transportation on the farm and from farm to market. Between the agricultural lore of a simple primitive community and the established and intelligently applied scientific principles, the engineering knowledge and skills of contemporary society, and the highly developed managerial abilities of the modern farmer lies the entire range of social and cultural achievement; and all of the segments of this range are involved in one or more of the agricultural systems presently prevailing in Colombia.

Civilization itself could develop only as part of mankind's effort could be spared from the absolutely essential work of securing enough food to meet the basic creature needs of the population and directed into other channels of activity. Therefore, historically the acquisition of a fund of knowledge which now makes it possible for the farmer in Colombia or any other part of the earth to multiply many times the free gifts of nature and to bring forth plant and animal products in great abundance is the greatest achievement of the human race. Only the increasing ability of a small part of the population to meet the needs for food and fiber of all the members of society has made possible the specialization, division of labor, and accumulation of scientific principles and technical skills necessary in order to bring us to the atomic age. Furthermore, the basic task of the Alliance for Progress and all other programs of technical assistance throughout the world is essentially that of bringing the systems of agriculture of what, since the close of the Second World War and the mushrooming of international agencies, are euphemistically designated as "underdeveloped" or "developing" nations nearer to the stage of perfection such systems already have attained in many of the so-called developed nations. The fact that this can be done only as the entire rural social system based upon large estates, and the resulting servile or semi-servile conditions of the rural masses, is replaced by the rural social system based on family-sized farms makes agrarian reform programs the most crucial endeavors in the lines of social and economic development in the "have not" sections of the earth's surface. Indeed, in the decades immediately ahead efforts to improve Colombia's systems of agriculture are sure to be the most significant ways of attacking the hunger, poverty, misery, and disease that still afflict large segments of her population. If such efforts are successful so that the ordinary Colombian agriculturist can be taught to farm with an effectiveness equal to that of his fellows in many other widely separated parts of the world he quickly can make the transition, such as that which occurred in Denmark during the nineteenth century, from his creature-like mode of existence to a position far more commensurate with the potentialities and aspirations of human beings.

The need for the average rural Colombian to learn to farm is patent, and it has been impressed and reimpressed upon my mind in every one of the hundreds of days I have spent in the rural sections of Colombia from 1943 on. The average Colombian who depends upon the land for a livelihood is relying upon a system of agriculture that is less efficient, more prodigal in the use of labor, and generally less "advanced" than that the Egyptians were using at the dawn of history. Still more important, though, is the fact that the customary way of life of the rural masses inevitably shapes many of the children born in the countryside into creatures in which the characteristics of the beast of burden are likely to overshadow those of the human being. If Colombia is to come into her own as a nation, she must develop rapidly and put generally into practice a system of agriculture in which the energies of those who engage in farming are not dissipated with abandon in grossly antiquated work patterns, a system in which men and women cease to function as beasts of burden, and a system in which manual labor no longer is considered to be degrading but thought of as dignifying and uplifting. She must have ways of securing plant and livestock products in which the managerial function is exercised effectively by the majority of those who live from the land, and not relegated to an almost inconsequential position of importance among the factors of production. Her reliance upon hoe culture must give way to practices in which draft animals and motors supply most of the energy needed for the performance of farm tasks. In brief, as quickly as possible, Colombia must shift to a system of agriculture in which each person engaged in agricultural work makes use of considerable amounts of horsepower, many well-designed implements and machines, and efficient vehicles as he goes about his work of producing, processing, and transporting the products of the soil.

SYSTEMS OF AGRICULTURE AND LEVELS OF LIVING

In the so-called underdeveloped countries, which is to say (in terms of the values prevailing throughout the world during the second half of the twentieth century) in the nations that are not highly industrialized, the general level or plane of living is determined to an overwhelming degree by the system of agriculture that is being used. Before considering the systems of agriculture upon which Colombia's people and her society are dependent, it seems advisable to elaborate briefly upon this proposition. Anyone who travels about the world, even though his observations are made in the most cursory manner, is certain to discern that the levels of living vary tremendously from one part to another. In most of Asia, for example, he is bound to be impressed by the fact that the social and economic conditions of the masses of the population are almost unbelievably low. In Europe, on the other hand, in comparison with Asia, he will note that the average levels are very much higher. But even there he will see that the per capita consumption of goods and services by those who live in the northwestern part of the continent is much higher than that by the inhabitants of the southeastern parts of it; and he will observe sharp changes in the plane of living of those residing in fairly close proximity to one another, as, for example, the higher level in Switzerland than in the adjacent parts of France, and the superior condition of those in northern Italy in comparison with the people of southern Italy and especially the inhabitants of Sicily. In America it is readily apparent to all that the general level of living of people in the United States and Canada is much above that of their fellows in the Latin American countries, and that vast differences prevail between the planes of living in the

The process of extracting the coffee beans from the cherries. (Courtesy of the National Federation of Coffee Growers of Colombia.)

various parts of a given country, such as the higher levels of living in the northern and western regions of the United States, in comparison with those in the South, and the vastly superior living conditions in southern Brazil over those prevailing in the eastern and northeastern sections of that vast sub-continent.

Inevitably, because the variations in the levels or planes of living are so evident to so many, numerous explanations have been advanced to account for those variations; and because the primary importance of social and cultural factors was not understood until well along in the twentieth century, the most generally accepted of these explanations have for the most part involved hereditary or racial factors. Such a line of reasoning holds that some populations have higher levels of living than others because of their natural or inherent superiority, or in effect that zoological or racial characteris-

Transporting bags of coffee cherries to the processing floors. (Courtesy of the National Federation of Coffee Growers of Colombia.)

tics are the cause of the more favorable levels of production and consumption. Likewise this widespread way of thinking assumes that populations having low levels of living are in some anatomical or physiological manner inferior to those who enjoy more of the necessities and amenities of life.

Nowadays a very widespread explanation relies upon industrialization as the basic factor responsible for differences in the levels of living in various societies. As indicated above, industrialized nations are rather generally thought of as "advanced" or "developed" ones, and the countries that have not industrialized to any extent are dubbed as "underdeveloped," especially now that storms of protest quickly reach the ears of anyone who presumes to characterize them as "backward." Generally overlooked by those who glibly repeat this

Weighing coffee beans. One step in preparing them for export. (Courtesy of the National Federation of Coffee Growers of Columbia.)

thesis is the fact that such differences greatly antedate the industrial revolution, and that even today there are areas completely dependent upon agricultural enterprises in which the average level of living of the population compares favorably with that to be found in any industrial community. I can accept neither of these explanations, nor others, such as that of climatic determinism, as the ones having validity. Instead I advance and defend the proposition, thoroughly sociocultural in nature, that the differences between the systems of agriculture prevailing in various parts of the world constitute the real key to understanding in this field. If one understands the nature of the system of agriculture and the role played by it in

social and economic affairs, he is well on the way to an explanation of why such sharply contrasting levels and standards of living
have been generated and perpetuated.

Let us elaborate briefly upon this point, and begin by stating that
the analysis of the level of living of any people resolves itself
largely into a consideration of the following three factors: (1) the
quantity and quality of the natural resources available for the use
of man; (2) the output per worker, preferably measured on the
annual basis, since in some cases the output per day or week may
be very high while underemployment holds that per year to a volume
that is entirely inadequate; and (3) the manner of distributing that
which is produced among those who have had a share in the productive process.

Natural resources are of no import until man's cultural heritage
has reached a stage that enables them to be utilized. Colombia's
great iron, coal, and petroleum resources, for example, were of
practically no importance to the hundreds of thousands of Indians
the conquistadores encountered along the coastal plain, in the humid
valley bottoms, and especially on the high plateaus. The cultural
heritage of these natives did not include a knowledge of iron or
petroleum, although their need for the former was acute, and they
quickly borrowed it from the white man in order to make effective
points for their arrows and spears. As a matter of fact, the history
of Colombia, as that of all nations, is filled with developments in
which, as the cultural heritage accumulated, material after material
came to function in the list of significant natural resources.

The annual output per worker is the crux of the problem facing
those who attempt to bring about a substantial increase in the level
of living in any country; and it is precisely in connection with this
output that a change in the system of agriculture in Colombia and
the other so-called underdeveloped nations has so much to offer in
the improvement of the living conditions of mankind. In countries
such as Canada, Colombia, Brazil, the United States, and the Soviet
Union, where the pressure of population upon identifiable natural
resources is very much less than it is in such countries as China and
India, or even in most parts of Europe, the annual productivity per
worker is highly dependent upon the extent to which labor is expended in the productive process. If labor is used lavishly, this is
to say if it is combined freely with relatively small inputs of capital
and management, the output per man is far less than where each

worker makes considerable use of tools, machinery, power, and managerial skills in the work which he performs.

If, as was true for centuries in the southern part of the United States, the tools used in farming have a tendency to be heavy, crudely shaped, and ill-adapted to the functions to be performed, and if the average farm worker employs relatively little horsepower and equipment, the production per man will be low. Under such conditions this production and the level of living which is dependent upon it can never rival those in other areas in which the hand tools are more highly perfected and especially where liberal inputs of power and machinery are combined with the labor of the ordinary farmer.[1] If, as still is the case in huge expanses of South America, Africa, and the Western Pacific, man's only aids in his efforts to wrest a livelihood from the soil are the ax and fire, the

1. This point is illustrated excellently by the following observations of Frederick Law Olmstead, one of the keenest thinkers ever to write about the southern part of the United States: "But here, I am shown tools that no man in his senses, with us [i.e., on the farms of New York state], would allow a laborer, to whom he was paying wages, to be encumbered with; and the excessive weight and clumsiness of which, I would judge, would make work at least ten per cent greater than those ordinarily used with us. And I am assured that, in the careless and clumsy way they must be used by the slaves, anything lighter or less rude could not be furnished them with good economy, and that such tools as we constantly give our laborers, and find our profit in giving them, would not last out a day in a Virginia cornfield—much lighter and more free from stones though it be than ours." *A Journey in the Seaboard Slave States,* pp. 46-47. From Virginia, Olmstead proceeded on down the Atlantic Coast to South Carolina where, after visiting some of the famed plantations near Charleston, he wrote in his journal: "I saw women working again, in large gangs, with men. In one case they were distributing manure—ditch scrapings it appeared to be—and the mode of operation was this: the manure had been already carted into heaps upon the ground; a number of women were carrying it from the heap in baskets, on their heads, and one in her apron, and spreading it with their hands between the ridges on which the cotton grew last year: the rest followed with great, long-handled, heavy, clumsy hoes, and pulled down the ridges over the manure, and so made new ridges for the next planting. I asked a young planter who continued with me a good part of the day, why they did not use plows. He said this was rather rough land, and a plow wouldn't work it very well. It was light soil, and smooth enough for a parade ground. The fact is, in certain parts of South Carolina, a plow is yet an almost unknown instrument of tillage." (P. 397.) Also near Charleston, Olmstead conversed with a man who described "as a novelty, a plow, with 'a sort of a wing, like, on one side,' that pushed off, and turned over a slice of the ground: from which it appeared that he had, until recently, never seen a mould-board: the common plows of this country being constructed on the same principles as those of the Chinese, and only rooting the ground like a hog or a mole—not cleaving and turning. He had never heard of working a plow with more than one horse." (P. 402.)

output per man will be so slight that nothing more than a very low level of living is possible. Or, if, as still the case in many parts of Colombia, Ecuador, Peru, and Bolivia, those who live from agriculture have no tools or implements whatsoever except the digging stick and the crudest of hoes, the level of living inevitably is very low. The fundamental point to keep in mind in this connection is that where the system of agriculture is more advanced, that is where it is of the type in which each worker makes abundant use not only of land and labor, but also of efficient tools, equipment,

Lavish use of labor. Harvesting wheat with the sickle. (Courtesy of Kenneth Wernimont.)

and power—where capital and management are not used parsimoniously in comparison with labor—the output per man is much greater, and given anything resembling an equitable distribution of the product, the level of living tends to be high.

In many ways the role of management is the most important feature of all. If each agriculturist is himself the decision maker (a thinking, deciding, acting agent), as is the operator of a family-sized farm, the managerial function is not relegated to the inadequate position it plays generally on large estates throughout the world. Where the man who performs the manual labor also receives substantial return for the performance of managerial activities, much has been done to insure a relatively high average level of living for all of the families who participate directly in the agricultural process. On the other hand, almost inevitably, in all types of large-scale agricultural enterprises, there is a tendency for managerial skills to be used sparingly while labor is employed without stint. This is particularly the case in those countries where the absence of a general property tax, or a ridiculously low rate of taxation of land, enables land to become an asylum for capital.[2] Such a poor combination of the factors of production, along with the failure of the mass of those who work in agriculture to receive any return for managerial activities, dictates that the average level of living will be very low. Colombia's haciendas share in the sparse input of management that is characteristic of large-scale agriculture throughout the world. Even the few of these large estates that are highly commercialized, such as the few dozen sugar ingenios, the rice and cotton plantations, and the great coffee fincas, hardly enjoy the benefits of adequate inputs of management. The vast majority of these haciendas, huge in size, devoted largely to pastoral activities of the most rudimentary type, and featured by their subsistence roles in the national economy, share in the paucity of management that is characteristic of the haciendas of the other Spanish American countries, the plantations of the English-speaking world, and the state and collective farms of the Communist countries.

ABORIGINAL BACKGROUNDS OF COLOMBIA'S SYSTEMS OF AGRICULTURE

The systems of agriculture presently found in Colombia and the dietary patterns intimately related to them, which in combination give much of the meaning to ways of life in general, retain many features that were characteristic of aboriginal cultural and societal patterns in the northwestern part of South America. This is to say that in what is now Colombia, the principal economic bases of existence found among the peoples of the New World by the discoverers from the Old World prevailed almost side by side at the time of the conquest. In fact the area now occupied by the Republic of Colombia was the principal line of contact, and probably the arena of conflict, between the ways of living which had become organized

2. Cf. Smith, "The Cultural Setting of Agricultural Extension Work in Colombia," pp. 241-42; Smith, "Notes on Population and Rural Social Organization in El Salvador," pp. 377-78; Smith, *Brazil*, pp. 352-56; and Smith, *Current Social Trends and Problems in Latin America*, pp. 30-32.

and crystallized about the two great food and agricultural complexes that had developed in the Americas. Here, immediately to the north of the Equator, and in a terrain which makes it possible for modern Colombians to go in a few hours from a hot, humid tropical climate to one in which the spring or fall of the temperate zone prevails throughout the year, the utmost variety in land use, tillage practices, crops grown, and foods eaten was present at the time of Columbus. From the north, or from Mexico and Central America, had come all of the influences of the cultural patterns and societal activities of the "seed planters," in which corn or maize, in close association with beans, gave form and substance to production and consumption patterns of the societies involved; from the south had come one of the principal expressions of the "vegetative planters," an "Andean" way of life adapted to cold climates, in which the potato was the staff of life and its production the principal agricultural activity; and the lowlands of Colombia itself may well have been the center of origin and dispersal of the aboriginal forms of life and labor characteristic of those "tropical vegetative planters" who had manioc and other tubers as the central elements in their agricultural, economic, and social systems.[3]

3. The utmost variety and complexity of the social and cultural heritages of the aborigines who lived in what is now Colombia is evidenced even by the rather superficial work of such anthropologists as Clark Wissler (*The American Indian*, pp. 17, 20); but it is shown much better in the writings of more careful and thorough investigators such as Carl O. Sauer ("Cultivated Plants of South and Central America," in Steward, editor, *Handbook of South American Indians*, VI, pp. 487-543; and, especially, Sauer, *Agricultural Origins and Dispersals*, Chapter III). Basilio Vicente de Oviedo, who spent a long lifetime as a priest in various highland pueblos in what are now the departments of Cundinamarca and Boyacá was in a position to observe and report on happenings along the line of scrimmage between these great American food and agricultural complexes. About the middle of the eighteenth century he reported as follows: "The yucas that they produce with little trees, and the fruit is the roots, are ready in the hot climates at the end of six months and remain in the ground for a year, and in zones that are not so warm are ready to eat at the end of a year, and stay in the ground for two years, when they are best. They are the most common food of everyone and at all meals. In the *llanos* they produce another species of yuca, from which cassava is made, and it is the daily bread of those lands. . . .

"In the cold zones and the medium ones as well, but with greater frequency in the cold ones, they plant and harvest other roots of great use and benefit to all, which last throughout the year, and which are called *turmas*, and in Quito and other parts are called *papas* [potatoes]. They are of two species: some are called creoles, and they produce more quickly and are more tasty; and the others are called *turmas de año* [year potatoes]. These also are the regular food of all and at all meals. . . .

Despite the close geographical proximity of these radically differing social and cultural forms, however, one should not jump to the conclusion that it was easy for them to intermingle and blend. Whereas, as stated above, it is not difficult for the present-day Colombian to go from a cold climate, through one adapted to the growing of coffee and sugar cane, on down into the torrid zone, and back again to the mountain tops in a few hours, such is not the case with domesticated plants and the cultural and social complexes associated with them. After centuries of what appears on the maps to be existence side by side, those who depend heavily upon the potato in addition to maize differ in many fundamental respects from those who rely largely upon maize without the potato, and both have patterns of life and work that contrast sharply with those of the remnants of the manioc eating groups who once occupied a large part of what is now Colombia. In other words even during the second half of the twentieth century the uses to which the land is put, the crop combinations, the ways the campesinos go about extracting a living from the soil, and the foods the rural families consume is determined largely by whether or not they inhabit a part of Colombia in which the basic aboriginal part of the cultural heritage was derived from a system oriented almost exclusively about maize, around the potato along with maize, or about manioc, respectively. This is to say that the large populations of Antioquia and Caldas have the use of corn in the form of the *arepa* as their basic breadstuff; those of Nariño, Cundinamarca,[4] Boyacá, and the highest sections of the Santanders

---

"Above all else the main food, especially of the poor and of the Indians and country people, is the maize, which is the wheat of the Indies, and which is planted in all parts of this Kingdom, in the hot, intermediate, and cold zones; and in the hot lands they produce two crops a year, with great abundance. . . ." Luis Augusto Cuervo, editor, *Cualidades y Riquezas del Neuvo Reino de Granada* (by Vicente de Oviedo, pp. 48-49).

4. Fals-Borda, *Peasant Life in the Colombian Andes,* p. 147, says that the "usual dinner" of the *campesinos* in the community "consists of two different soups, called *cuchuco* and *ajiaco,* served one after the other." The perceptive author of this careful study of a typical highland neighborhood then explains that the former is made by boiling ground corn, barley, and wheat to form a thick soup, and that the latter is made of finely sliced potatoes, along with peas, tubers called *arracachas,* manioc, and broad beans. Boiled potatoes along with other tubers, eaten about five o'clock in the afternoon, make up the customary evening meal.

This pattern is not essentially different from the one my associates and I found in our study of Tabio in Cundinamarca, in what appears to have been the first sociological survey of a community made in Latin America. The practices in Tabio, in turn, correspond closely to those prevailing throughout the entire

grow and consume large amounts of both potatoes and maize (and also wheat, barley, and other temperate zone crops which were introduced by the Spaniards during Colonial times);[5] and that the sparse native populations to the east of the mountains are the rem-

---

tierra fría zone north of Bogotá as they were observed and recorded in my journal during the years 1943, 1944, and 1945. For Tabio, on the basis of an interview at every home, the following generalization was made. "The upper classes of Tabio eat freely of home-produced foods supplemented by those brought from the tropical sections of Colombia and those imported from abroad. The humble campesinos, on the other hand, have a very restricted diet. Its standard form is about as follows:

"Breakfast is usually quite early, at about 6:00 A.M. It consists of *changua*, *agua de panela*, and *cacao*. The first of these is a thin soup of water, salt, and onions, with perhaps a bit of another vegetable added. The second is a thin syrup made with water and panela (a brown-sugar cake from which none of the molasses has been extracted) and served hot. The third is chocolate mixed with corn flour and molded into small balls.

"From about 11:00 A.M. to noon comes the second meal of the day, *almuerzo*. At this time, the indispensable plate is *mazamorra*, a thick corn-flour soup, and the native beer called *chicha*, a potent fermented beverage, is generally consumed at this meal. The few who are able to eat meat or bread once or twice a week may also partake of them at this time.

"In the late afternoon, around 3:30 P.M. comes the third repast, called *la comida* or *puntal*. It consists of potatoes and *chicha*. The final meal of the day, *cena* is eaten about 6:30 P.M., after the *campesinos* have returned from work in the fields. It consists of *mazamorra* and *chicha*.

"In addition to these meals, the practice of munching parched corn throughout the day is quite common. Few of the campesinos make any regular use of meat or bread. Milk and eggs are rarely eaten by them. Many of the humble rural folk produce these highly desirable foods but only for sale." Smith, Díaz, and García, *Tabio*, pp. 61-62.

5. The role of wheat in the patterns of life and labor of the people living in the tierra fría zones of Boyacá and neighboring departments is well described in the following translation of a paragraph from one of the basic sources of information about Boyacá: "This cereal [wheat] was unknown to the indigenes of America. The Spaniards introduced it into New Granada in the year 1540, and it was first cultivated in the Tunja region, where Captain Aguayo made the first attempts to grow it. The success he had resulted in it becoming one of the principal crops of the cold zones of Boyacá. Since then wheat has been the favorite crop of the campesinos of the Boyacá altiplano, because of the ease with which it is grown, the constant demand in the markets for this grain, and its low cost of production. It is the crop grown by the poor campesinos, for it does not require constant attention and it permits them, therefore, to seek other uses for their labor as day laborers or peons on the rich haciendas. After planting, wheat needs only one weeding per year before it is cut and threshed . . . wheat does not find its market for consumption in Boyacá. The people of this department do not eat it, using instead maize, plaintains, potatoes. The markets which take wheat are those of the other departments, hence this grain has come to be the principal medium for paying for the merchandise imported by Boyacá." Medina R., organizer, *Boyacá*, pp. 416-17.

nants of the once numerous peoples who were largely dependent upon manioc to supplement the results of their hunting and fishing activities. To a considerable extent, of course, maize, beans, and manioc or yuca have become incorporated into the dietary patterns and systems of agriculture of those living in all parts of Colombia, but it is remarkable to note the absence of the potato (and barley and wheat) in the highlands of the Central Cordillera at altitudes corresponding to those in which they flourish in Nariño and all along the Eastern Cordillera.[6]

It is important to consider in this connection some of the results from Colombia's first census of agriculture which provides data for 1960. At that time a total of 108,404 "explotaciones," or 9.1 per cent of all those (1,209,672) enumerated in Colombia, were reported as producing potatoes. All together, however, these potato plantings involved the use of only 123,652 hectares (or about 309,000 acres), an average of slightly less than three acres per cultivated unit, and included only 3.5 per cent of the arable land.[7] Thus, despite the fact that here and there in the cold highlands of the Eastern Cordillera to the north of Bogotá, and especially near the mountain tops in the departments of Cundinamarca and Boyacá, one may find extensive haciendas with fairly large fields of potatoes, potato growing is largely confined to the small farms and subsistence plots of the campesinos. As a matter of fact, computations based on the 1960 census data indicate that explotaciones of less than 20 hectares in size, of which 98,751 reported plantings of potatoes, accounted for 65.9 per cent of the total acreage devoted to this crop. The average for the group amounts to only 0.8 hectares, or only slightly more than one acre per "farm." On the other hand, the 163 estates containing more than 500 hectares apiece on which potatoes were grown

6. In this connection an entry made in my journal the day I had my first opportunity to ascend the eastern slope of the Central Cordillera is of some significance. Thus on November 9, 1943, the following note was made: "Leaving Cajamarca we ascended rapidly to La Línea, which is on the divide and the boundary between Tolima and Caldas. This area is newly colonized and from Antioquia. Most of the forest has already been destroyed, with large stumps still hanging on the hillsides. Little of the land is used for agriculture although there is some cane (at the lower altitudes), corn, manioc, etc. No wheat was observed even when we passed the 3,000 meter mark and neared the summit. This makes me think that probably the 'maicero' cognomen of the Antioqueños may be one of the more significant differentiating characteristics in the country."

7. For census purposes lands devoted to coffee, cacao, and bananas were excluded from the arable land category and placed by themselves in one designated as "permanent cultivations."

accounted for a total of only 2,611 hectares, or an average of 16 hectares per farm.[8]

Anyone who has traveled extensively throughout Colombia can hardly have failed to observe the distribution of potato growing (and of wheat and barley with which it is closely associated) has some very interesting and peculiar features. It is, of course, strictly confined to the high intermountain valleys and the mountain slopes or the regions known in Colombia as the tierras frias.[9] But not all sections of Colombia having climatic conditions and terrain favorable to potato growing (and wheat and barley, as well) make use of this fundamental crop and foodstuff. Potato culture has persisted only in those parts of the Colombian highlands which at the time of the conquest were densely populated by rather highly civilized peoples. Therefore it is strictly in accord with expectations to find that the census reports potatoes as a crop on 13,110 explotaciones in the department of Nariño which adjoins Ecuador on the north. All of these potato patches are, of course, high on the slopes of the Andes and in the great intermountain trough which separates the two ranges of these mountains in Ecuador and on northward into southern Colombia. As a matter of fact, if one drives northward from Ipiales, just a few miles from the international boundary, through Tuquerres and Pasto and on to La Unión near the line which separates Nariño from the department of Cauca, from the various vantage points he enjoys during the journey he is able to see close at hand or on the distant slopes almost all of the potato fields in the department. Furthermore, in such a drive along the spine of the continent one is merely following the age-old route traced by peoples and cultures in their movements to the north and, to a small degree, from higher to slightly lower altitudes. Apparently such a northward thrust of peoples and cultures was going on in considerable force at the time of the conquest, and it continues today. With potato culture as a central complex in their basic social and cultural pattern, representatives of this highland society, who

8. These data and those for the other crops given in this chapter, are based upon figures given in Departamento Administrativo Nacional de Estadística, 1964.

9. To distinguish them from the páramos or frigid zones, which begin at an altitude of about 9,500 feet; the *tierras templadas,* or intermediate zones best adapted to coffee growing, at altitudes which range from about 2,500 to 7,000 feet; and the tierras calientes, or torrid zones, the coastal plains, the low valleys (such as the Magdalena), and the plains and jungles which occupy the eastern three-fifths of the national territory.

long have occupied the tierra fría zone of Nariño, continue their thrust to the north, keeping to the high slopes of both the Western and the Central Cordilleras, after these part company in order to allow space for the Cauca Valley. In these latitudes with no high, cold intermountain valleys to afford living space for large numbers of people, the strength of these migrations naturally is greatly reduced. Nevertheless they continue until on the slopes high above the small city of Buga, they meet head-on with the sustained drive southward of the Antioqueños and their distinctive cultural and societal patterns. From there on to the north throughout the vast highland portions of El Valle, Caldas, and Antioquia, very few potato patches (and practically no plantings large or small of wheat and barley) are to be found. But if one crosses the torrid bottoms of the Magdalena Valley and ascends the western slope of the Eastern range to altitudes above 7,500 feet just to the south of Bogotá he again will encounter regions in which potatoes, wheat, and barley are central elements in patterns of life and labor of the campesinos. Furthermore, this pattern extends from there to the north, all throughout the realm once occupied by the Chibchas (through the high, cold, and densely populated parts of the departments of Cundinamarca, Boyacá, Santander, and Norte de Santander) and on into the high, Andean portions of Venezuela. Throughout this large and elongated area potatoes, along with wheat and barley, are the basic ingredients in the subsistence-crop combinations and dietary patterns of the humble masses whose huts and pocket-handkerchief-size tracts (some of which qualify as farms) blanket the mountainsides with their crazy-quilt arrangements. In all of these sections the minifundia of the campesinos, some of whom own their small tracts and others who secure the use of subsistence plots in return for their labor on the haciendas, are the sources of the foodstuffs on which the masses subsist and for most of the potatoes that find their way to the markets.

The 13,110 explotaciones in Nariño reported as producing potatoes in 1960 average only slightly more than one hectare of planting per "farm" or a total of 14,454 hectares. As one passes northward along the routes mentioned above, however, the number of "farms" growing potatoes amounts to only 2,382 (3,729 hectares) in Cauca and to a mere 130 (764 hectares) in El Valle. Farther to the north, only 824 farms in Caldas reported potatoes as a crop, but the area involved came to 5,581 hectares, indicating that potato growing in this enterprising offshoot of Antioquia is for the market and not for subsistence purposes. In Antioquia itself, to supplement the basic use of maize as a breadstuff, 10,846 explotaciones with a total of 8,569 hectares of potatoes were reported. In addition, before presenting data for the other principal region of potato culture, it seems advisable to give the basic information about wheat and barley culture in the areas just mentioned. In Nariño itself, the number of explotaciones reporting wheat growing combined with the number reporting barley[10] totals 18,550 and the number of hectares involved is 63,843, indicating the subsistence nature of wheat and barley production in that department. Immediately to the north, in Cauca, the number falls to 3,902 plots and 4,352 hectares used for these crops, and in El Valle the "farms" total only 129 and the hectares used 1,195. In Caldas the number of places reporting wheat or barley is only 27 and the combined area involved only 226 hectares; and in Antioquia none of the 169,299 farms and subsistence tracts reported any land being used for either wheat or barley.

Due to the cultural influences carried by the migrants pushing northward along the high slopes of the Central Cordillera some potato plantings (1,017 in number) are found on the subsistence tracts and farms that are located in the department of Tolima, but there are practically none (only 90) across the Magdalena River in the department of Huila, even though the crest of the Eastern Cordillera forms its eastern boundary. Likewise the number of explotaciones in these departments on which wheat or barley is grown is insignificant, the total for the two combined being only 226 in Tolima and zero in Huila.

To the north of Huila is the department of Cundinamarca, with Bogotá near the center of its limited area of tierras frias; and to the north of Cundinamarca is huge, highly rural Boyacá, whose great expanses of torrid lands in the Magdalena Valley and to the east of the Andes are separated by the high, cold, and densely populated "backbone" of the department. Together Cundinamarca and Boyacá made up the heartland of the great Chibcha dominions. Therefore, we should expect the carriers of the potato cultural complex (and the complementary wheat and barley culture as well) to be in the ascendancy in the cold zones of these two important departments; and this is exactly what is indicated by the results of the 1960 census

10. The way the data are tabulated does not permit one to determine how many places grew both crops.

of agriculture. In Boyacá alone the subsistence tracts and farms reporting potatoes as a crop amounted to 44,171 (38,039 hectares) and in Cundinamarca they totaled 28,503 (37,674 hectares). Together these two departments accounted for 67 per cent of all the potato-growing explotaciones and 61 per cent of the potato acreage in Colombia. Likewise the two contained 71 per cent of all the places reporting wheat and barley and 69 per cent of the land devoted to these two temperate-climate crops. Even so the average size of the wheat and barley fields was only 2.9 hectares in Cundinamarca and a mere 1.1 hectares in Boyacá, data which once more indicate the high degree to which the plantings of these two important grains are limited to the subsistence tracts of the campesinos. Despite the large fields of these grains that one may see on the haciendas on the Savanna of Bogotá, on the plains of Ubaté, and in such favored spots as the Sogamosa Valley and the Samacá Valley, the fact remains that wheat and barley culture is highly restricted to the subsistence activities of the campesinos and the grains themselves destined, for the most part, for use along with potatoes in the *sancochos* and other typical dishes of the rural masses.

North of Boyacá the department of Santander is oriented about its capital, Bucaramanga, which is located in the intermediate zone in which such crops as coffee, tobacco, and sugar cane thrive; and its neighbor, Norte de Santander, has an economic and political life that revolves about a capital, Cucutá, situated at the eastern base of the Andes in one of the most torrid parts of Colombia. Nevertheless, all along the high slopes of the Andes and in the high intermountain valleys, such as that of Pamplona, the subsistence crops are potatoes, wheat, and barley, and the way of life of the campesinos is similar to that of their fellows in the highlands of Boyacá and Cundinamarca. Thus in Santander the 1960 census reported that there was a total of 4,154 subsistence tracts and farms producing potatoes, and in Norte de Santander a total of 2,382, and explotaciones with plantings of wheat and barley totaled 7,425 in the former and 2,638 in the latter.

The efforts made in the preceeding pages to elucidate some of the distinctive features of production and consumption patterns in Colombia should not obscure the fact, however, that maize is by far the most ubiquitous crop in Colombia. This "Indian wheat" is grown on 45 per cent of all the subsistence tracts and farms in Colombia, with this proportion varying 63 per cent of all those in Boyacá and 58 per cent in Cauca, to 26 per cent in Caldas and 28 per cent in

Tolima. Likewise it is found frequently alongside plantains as an ingredient in the sancochos of the lowlanders as well as a supplement to the potatoes in those of the highlanders, but, of course, its principal use is as a breadstuff out of which is made the *arepas* of the antioqueños and also the less palatable ones of the campesinos who are carriers of other cultural heritages.[11]

THE SPANISH CULTURAL HERITAGE AND COLOMBIAN SYSTEMS OF AGRICULTURE

Two additional factors, both involving the cultural heritage carried to the New World by the Spaniards, have played and continue to play heavy roles in the life and labor of the people of Colombia. The two are intimately interrelated, but in the interests of clarity of thought it is essential to consider them separately. The first is the fact that, at the time of the conquest, the Spaniards were a pastoral people and not an agricultural one; and the second is the historical reality that the conquistadores seized the lands which the Indians were cultivating intensively in the production of the corn, potatoes, beans, and

11. The following extracts serve to bring out the importance of maize in the diet of the population in many parts of Colombia: "In Colombia maize occupies an exceptional position in human sustenance, as it is the nutritional base of the entire population; from which comes the great economic importance which this cereal has for us. It has been the practice to joke about the maize-eating Antioqueños, alluding to the part played by maize in their daily diet; but they are not the only ones in Colombia who eat corn, nor perhaps the ones who use it to the greatest degree. One who has seen the loading of maize destined for Medellín at El Blanco and Gamarra may have come to believe that Antioquia truly is an exceptional consumer of this product; but if he knows that the Antioqueños have to go far out in search of it in order to supplement the deficient production on their own poor lands and if he also has seen the campesino of the central plateau eating his bowl of *mazamorra*, his arepas, and his serving of parched corn, and if he knows in addition what maize means for the diet of the inhabitant of the Cauca Valley or of Tolima, for example, will come to think, and not incorrectly, that all Colombians are *maiceros* [maize eaters] and many of them to a greater degree than the sons of Antioquia. What happens is that the latter extol the high qualities of maize with a degree of presumptiousness, while the others eat it silently. Oh that the *fiesta del maíz* which is celebrated periodically in Sonson should be converted into a national fiesta!

"In Tolima maize is an essential part of the general diet. *Hard* maize is eaten, while still green (*choclo*), on the cob, and when more mature it is prepared by roasting or cooking in the husks, or fried after husking; when ground it is used in mazamorra, arepas (*sarapas*), and cakes; it is eaten dry, after being pulverized by pounding (*peto, mote*), after soaking (*cuchuco*), or after grinding (mazamorra and the various kinds of arepas, cakes, and cookies). *Bland* maize, or *maíz capio* is eaten after it had been made into flour and then toasted, in mazamorra, and more commonly in *chucula*, or as people sometimes say, chocolate flour." Paris Lozano, *Tolima*, pp. 206-7.

so forth, which formed the staples of the aborigines' diet, and transformed them into extensive pastures for the horses and cattle that the new overlords had brought from Europe. This, in turn, forced the intensive agriculture of the natives back into the nooks and coves of the mountain fastnesses, up onto the steep slopes of the mountain chains, and out and away from the more fertile and accessible areas and onto less desirable lands of all types. As a result there quickly was established the pattern that has continued ever since, which throughout the entire upland sections of Colombia is one in which the lands best suited for farming are devoted almost exclusively to pastures, whereas the intensively cultivated crops are grown mostly on the steep hillsides, that is on terrain suited only for pastures or forests.

The Pastoral Nature of the Spanish Cultural Heritage.—As one who had a passing acquaintance with Roman history, many perplexities arose in my mind as I gradually came to know the general pattern of man-land relationships in Colombia. I knew that Spain as an integral part of the Roman Empire had been to a large extent the granary for the same; and I knew and admired the knowledge of agriculture that guided the writings of such famous Romans, and also Spaniards, as Seneca and Columella. Therefore I was not prepared to understand the almost complete neglect of farming by the Spaniards and their descendants in the New World, and the overwhelming degree to which they had been and continued to be preoccupied solely with horses and cattle. My observations in Peru had shown the disasterous results in that country which had followed the superimposition of a pastoral culture upon the intensive agriculture, based upon remarkable achievements in terracing, irrigation, and other aspects of agricultural engineering, in the land of the Incas. Far from preserving and building upon the fantastic farming accomplishments of the great Andean civilization, the conquerors have laid them waste and substituted in their stead a rudimentary set of pastoral activities, that is to say the type of rural economy that would prove most destructive of terraces and irrigation systems the natives had constructed. The Indians, of course, if they were to survive at all, had to find some place where they could plant their subsistence crops of maize, potatoes, beans, manioc, and so on. In brief in the land of the Chibchas as in that of the Incas they retained their agricultural tradition. In this way agricultural activities became sharply differentiated from livestock enterprises, and even today in Colombia and the other Spanish American countries it is not common to find farms which consist of a combination of livestock and crop enterprises. Therefore in Colombia and elsewhere in Latin America one must not assume, as is the practice in such countries as the United States, Canada, and England, that the term agriculture automatically embraces livestock enterprises as well as the growing of crops. Always the thinking must be in terms of *agricultura* and *ganaderia,* with the former the concern largely of the more humble portions of the rural population and the latter the preoccupation of the affluent and powerful families who own the large estates. Furthermore, the latter generally have their principal residences in the national capitals or other large cities, whereas the farmers live in the villages or on their small holdings.

But although these facts of rural social organization became apparent to me as the years passed in which Colombian society was one of the principal objects of my studies, it was not easy for me to understand why the Spaniards had little or no interest in farming. Nor was anyone with whom I conversed in Colombia or elsewhere in Latin America, or in the United States for that matter, able to offer any help in the solution of the puzzle; and an extensive reading about the development of Latin American civilization likewise failed to offer any help in understanding why the once great agricultural people and civilization of the Iberian Peninsula had become, by 1500, almost wholly unable or unwilling to transfer an agricultural way of life to America. Only a personal visit to Spain and the discovery of the analyses of some outstanding Spanish social thinkers, and especially the works of Gaspar Melchor de Jovellanos (1744-1810),[12] furnished the key to the cultural process that actually took place. In order to explain the backwardness of Spain's agriculture, Jovellanos first focused attention upon the effects of the large estates, or the high degree of ownership and control of the land, which "after having ruined the agriculture of Italy proceeded to ruin that of the regions subject to the empire."[13] The disastrous results of the large estates were not corrected during the era of Gothic domination, for these conquerors seized two-thirds of the land for themselves "which they abandoned in part to cultivation by their slaves, and devoted in part to the breeding and grazing of cattle, as the sole kind of riches known in the

12. See especially his *Informe de la Sociedad Económica de Madrid al Real y Supremo Consejo de Castilla en el Expediente de Ley Agraria.* I have used the second edition of this work published in Madrid in 1820 by the Imprenta de I. Sancha.

13. *Ibid.,* p. 4.

climate in which they were born. . . ."[14] Then Jovellanos presented the proposition that in the course of the 800 years of hit-and-run struggle between the Christians and the Moors, the Spaniards were transformed from agriculturists into persons who were almost exclusively interested in horses and cattle. This transition, which has had such far-reaching consequences in the development of society in Colombia and the other Spanish American countries, deserves description in detail.

> Such agriculture as there was all perished in the irruption of the Saracens, and many centuries had to pass before the rebirth of what we properly may call our agriculture. It is true that the Andalucian Moors established the culture of the vine in the most appropriate portions of their dominions, and rooted it strongly in our eastern and southern provinces; but the despotism of their government, the harshness of their exactions, and the disputes and civil wars which agitated them, would not have allowed it to flourish, even if it had not been for the inroads and conquests which we continually made upon their frontiers.
>
> When by means of these incursions we had recovered a large part of the national territory, it was very difficult for us to restore it to cultivation. Prior to the conquest of Toledo there was no agriculture except that of the northern provinces. That on the level plains of León and Castile, exposed to the continuous raids on the part of the Moors, was forced to shelter itself in the vicinity of castles and strong points, and preference was given to the raising of cattle, a movable form of wealth, and one that could be saved from the accidents of war. After that conquest had given more stability and extension to the area beyond the Guadarrama mountains continuous agitations interfered with cultivation and distracted the hands engaged in it. History portrays our estates, already stripped in support of their masters on the great conquests, which recovered the kingdoms of Jaen, Córdova, Murcia, and Sevilla by the middle of the fourteenth century, soon turning their arms one upon the other in the shameful divisions which were inspired by a desire for favors and advantages. What, then, could be the fate of our agriculture prior to the end of the fifteenth century?[15]

It was this way of life, characterized especially by dexterity in the use of arms and a pastoral economy, which the Spaniards transferred to America, and which quickly set in motion the forces that monopolized the best lands in Colombia and the other countries for the livestock enterprises of the conquerors and forced the agricultural under-

14. *Ibid.*, p. 6.
15. *Ibid.*, pp. 6-7. See also pp. 19-21.

takings of the natives in Colombia and elsewhere onto lands that never should have been cultivated.

Pastures in the Valleys and on the Plains and Cultivated Crops on the Hillsides.—Since the close of the Second World War, the mechanization of agriculture and the expansion and commercialization of the growing of such crops as cotton, sugar cane, and rice are bringing into agricultural production extensive areas of fertile, level land in such places as the Cauca Valley, the plains of Bolívar, and the plains of the upper Magdalena Valley. Until recently, however, all of these, along with the most fertile, level, and accessible areas in other parts

The motor truck is now important in moving cotton from the gin to the mill. (Photo courtesy of Alice Fray Nelson, Editor, *Foreign Agriculture.*)

of the Republic, were devoted almost exclusively to a rudimentary pastoral economy, whereas the nation's food crops were produced for the most part on the small subsistence tracts which blanket the steep slopes of the mountains. In brief, throughout more than four hundred years of history since the conquest, all throughout the densely populated tierra fría zone, only now is any substantial headway being made to reverse the situation in which the land that should be cultivated is monopolized for the pastures of the powerful landowning families and the cultivated crops are grown on the hillsides on slopes so steep that under no circumstances should they be used for anything except pastures and forests.

That even today the pastures of the haciendas occupy the valleys and plains of the tierra fría zone, that is in the area containing the bulk of the rural population, is readily apparent to all who will take the trouble to observe. Hence to help document this proposition it is well to refer again to the translations of a couple of observations made in 1850 by Manuel Ancízar, secretary to the Codazzi commission, and one of the keenest observers ever to report upon the Colombian scene. The first pertains to a portion of the Savanna of Bogotá, perhaps the most extensive tract of level land in the entire Colombian highlands.[16]

The second extract might very well relate to any one of numerous haciendas which I have had the privilege of visiting since 1943.[17]

Because societal patterns once established are so highly resistant to change, even in cases such as that under consideration at present in which the policy maker and administrator may think and act as though the physical aspects of the complex were the major elements involved, it should be stressed that the illogical and pernicious inversion of land uses in Colombia goes back for many decades before it was described so succinctly and accurately by Ancízar. Thus in the report he prepared for his successor, in compliance with regulations of the Laws of the Indies, Antonio, Archbishop of Córdova, who headed the ecclesiastical hierarchy in Colombia and who doubled as Viceroy of New Granada for more than ten years ending in 1789, had the following to say.

> This ["the general sluggishness of our colonies, the proportionately slight fruits which the metropolis has received from them, and the general disorder in all respects" described in the previous paragraph], which in general may be said of all America, is evident in a most terrible manner in this kingdom. One sees the most fertile valleys, whose abundance implores the hand of man, more to harvest than to work, which nevertheless are found empty and without a single inhabitant, at the same time that the steep and sterile mountainsides are peopled with criminals and fugitives who have escaped from society to live without law or religion. . . . Men of moderate wealth are those who, through a lack of safeguards to prevent the concentration of landownership in the hands of a single person, have been

16. See p. 68 above.
17. See pp. 68-69 above. See also A. C. Veatch, *Quito to Bogotá*, pp. 27-28.

able at vilely low prices to acquire immense territories on which in general they keep as serfs those who are less fortunate. The former cling tenaciously to their holdings for the profits they receive from the parts that are used; but the latter, who constitute the mass of the free inhabitants form a vagabond and wandering population, who forced by the mania of the landowners, move about with the facility permitted by the slight weight of their possessions, the small value of their huts, and the lack of affection for the fonte in which they were baptized. They have the same where they die as they had at their birthplace, and at any place they find the same as that they have left.[18]

The results of having the interests of the powerful devoted almost exclusively to livestock, with agriculture left to the humble, and of having the pastures in the valley bottoms and on the plains and the cultivated crops on the hillsides, have been disastrous to the extreme. In other chapters of this volume, some of these are explored in more detail. Here, however, the role of these factors in connection with soil erosion must receive mention, for as is the case in many other parts of Latin America, in Colombia soil erosion has literally washed away what was the base of support for hundreds of thousands of people; and as one year succeeds another the forced depopulation continues of what once were among the most prosperous sections of Colombia. This deplorable situation is most acute in the temperate zones to the north of Bogotá, the lands that were so attractive to Jiménez de Quesada and his followers; but one need not be an agricultural engineer or soil expert in order to see the tragic results of the process throughout Antioquia, in Caldas, in Cauca, in Nariño, and other departments. Severe depopulation produced by erosion has already taken place in large sections of Cundinamarca, Boyacá, Santander, and Norte de Santander; and what may be evaluated as even worse, many communities in these areas still retain large numbers of families, or the less able and vigorous members of families, long after practically all hope has vanished that the soil can afford them anything remotely resembling a satisfactory level of living. Hopeless misery and abject resignation to poverty characterizes the remaining inhabitants of numerous pueblos in these sections of Colombia, of which those of Leiva and Lenguazaque may be mentioned as unenviable examples. In fact, one would probably search in vain were he to attempt to find other

18. Antonio, Arzobispo Obisbo de Córdova, "Relación del Estado del Nuevo Reino de Granada, . . . , Año de 1796," in García y García, editor, *Relaciones de los Vireyes del Nuevo Reino de Granada,* pp. 215-16.

areas in which soil erosion, in combination with a host of other social and economic factors, has wrought greater havoc upon people and society than may be readily observed in the portions of Colombia to which attention is directed in these paragraphs.

When the Spaniards arrived in these Colombian highlands after their long climb, they found a pleasant land densely populated with agricultural peoples. Apparently this section of the New World had been supporting a large population (the Chibchas and their neighbors) for a lengthy period; and nothing I have discovered in the early records indicates in any way that the Indians' intensive use of the soil had in any way diminished the carrying capacity of the land. But how different is the situation today! In the course of more than 400 years, huge expanses of this once verdant territory have been converted into "badlands" which probably are absolutely beyond reclamation, and the destructive process seems to be continuing at an accelerating rate. Already the havoc that has been wrought in the lands about Leiva, Pamplona, Tunja, Samacá, Lenguazaque, and scores of other pueblos almost defies description. Hundreds of thousands of acres that once were covered with a productive top soil and a lush vegetation were, after the Spaniards arrived, planted to wheat, barley, potatoes, and other cultivated crops. Now, as mentioned above, they are far beyond redemption. The lesson they teach, however, should produce the most strenuous efforts on the part of all who have Colombia's welfare at heart to speed up the work of getting the long-established pattern reversed, to get the valley bottoms and plains into crops and the hillsides into pastures and forests.

Present-Day Systems of Agriculture in Colombia

During the third quarter of the twentieth century Colombia's systems of agriculture are undergoing modifications that are more drastic than those experienced at any time in her history with the exception of the ones that took place directly after the conquest. Great changes occurred, of course, immediately following 1536 when Jiménez de Quesada began his famous march. He and his handful of followers installed themselves as the overlords of areas inhabited by the Chibchas and their neighbors, the lands were parcelled out among the conquerers in *repartimientos*, and the Indians assigned to the new masters in encomiendas. Because of the cultural heritages brought by the white overlords, European grains, such as wheat and barley, gained space in the fields alongside the corn and potatoes of the natives; and the hoe, the crude wooden plow, the oxcart, the ox himself, and the mule were introduced to take on significant roles in the system of agriculture of Colonial Colombia. These innovations were truly dramatic. But thereafter modification was slight and slow. As late as 1878 one of the most perceptive Colombians of all time, in an address given on the occasion of the installation or founding of the Sociedad de Agricultores Colombianos, could generalize accurately as follows.

> In our country the plow is not used, except in the vicinity of a few cities. After felling the virgin forest or the shoots that have grown up on the old fields, in the ashes of the fire and without any working of the soil, the reproductive seeds are confined to the breasts of the earth. The hoe and the digging stick, managed by hands that are not always expert, then engage in a desperate struggle against the noxious plants for the preservation of the crops. With rare exceptions the period of stubble is the only rest given the soil. Fertilizers are used only in insignificant amounts and that only in a few localities. . . . Each year the cultivator seeks virgin lands for a crop of corn, and the felling of the forests, reaching to the headwaters of the streams, causes them to dry up and creates a waterless land uninhabitable by man, a terrain exposed to the irresistible winter torrents which spreads the detritus from the uncovered mountain tops over the lands in the valleys. I know of great expanses of once-fertile bottom lands that now are unused, converted in this way to infertile, stony, and sandy areas, habitable only by rattlesnakes. . . . One may come to doubt that our agriculture at present is superior to that of the Muiscas, our grandfathers, who at least maintained on the tops of the Andes in Cundinamarca a population much larger than the present one, to judge by the accounts of the conquest, the oral traditions handed down to the present by the conquered race, and the vestiges of the ancient fields, which in great parallels show the forms of the rows on the slopes of the great mountains, erie and solitary at present.[19]

Such remarks also serve to support the adequacy and the veracity of the observations of the numerous foreigners who after decades of residence in Colombia have sought to inform people in other parts of the world about systems of agriculture and other aspects of the social scene in New Granada. Consider, for example, some of the advice given to the English bondholders who in 1861 had agreed to accept, as payment of the debt owned to them by the government of Colombia, 1,724,420 hectares of public lands. The committee representing these bondholders planned to develop in Colombia the production of cotton that would insure a supply of fiber for Britain's textile mills

19. Camacho Roldán, "La Agricultura en Colombia," I, 648-49.

at a time when the Civil War in the United States was threatening the very existence of those mills. Robert Haldane, an English planter who had lived and worked for thirty years near Guaduas, or about halfway up the western slope of the Eastern Cordillera, on the trail between the Magdalena River and Bogotá, responded to one of the queries of the committee as follows: "As respects agricultural implements—if an intending colonist were to ask me what he required to take out with him, I would answer, 'By-and-by the plough, easily sent out; but for the present, hatchet, bill-hook, fork (grape), hoe, shovel, pick, and a *spade.*'"[20]

These data, and hundreds of similar observations and generalizations that might be assembled, all point to the fact that, prior to the rapid changes which recently have got underway, the ways of getting products from the soil in Colombia relied for the most part upon the ax and fire, upon the digging stick and the hoe, and, in the most advanced situations and to a very limited extent, upon the primitive wooden plow and the lumbering ox. In order to pursue this subject in more detail, though, it seems advisable to introduce and discuss in turn, with specific reference to Colombian life and labor, the frame of reference that I have developed in my attempts to deal systematically with this all-important aspect of rural social organization. According to this arrangement, all of the ways man has developed for the purpose of extracting a living from the soil may be classified into six basic systems of agriculture, which are designated as follows: (1) riverbank plantings; (2) fire agriculture; (3) hoe culture; (4) elementary plow culture; (5) advanced plow culture; and (6) mechanized farming.[21]

Riverbank Plantings.—Before it is pertinent to talk about a system of agriculture, it is essential to distinguish between an agricultural and a purely collecting stage of existence. This involves the question as to precisely what is involved in the transition to agriculture from the purely collecting economy which generally is thought to have preceeded it? And how are pastoral activities related to the two? Should we accept without question the widely diffused ideas constantly repeated by those who write about agricultural origins which assume that agriculture began with the use of the digging stick or crude hoe? For example we may easily discover many equivalents for the follow-

20. Bowles, *New Granada*, p. 151.
21. Cf. Smith, *The Sociology of Rural Life*, pp. 330-56; and Smith, *Brazil*, pp. 360-90.

ing lines on the beginning of agriculture which appear in one of the most popular sources. "A stick was the first hand tool used to scratch the surface of the ground before planting, and a forked stick, held in the ground by the plowman while the oxen dragged it ahead, was the first plow."[22] But one may very well question, "from whence all of the knowledge, engineering skills, and 'know-how' that these statements take for granted?" The practice of saving seeds for planting instead of consuming them as hunger arises, certainly is no spontaneous behavior pattern; the idea of tillage is still to occur to hundreds of peoples widely scattered about the earth's surface and it certainly was not present in the thought-patterns of thousands of others in the past; nor should the keeping of oxen, and all of the complex arrangements involved in yoking them to a vehicle or implement, be accepted uncritically as spontaneous or instinctive activities of mankind. It is hardly possible that any of these behavior patterns could have developed except as a result of thousands of years of experience and the slow and gradual accumulation of culture.

Probably the first agriculture was merely a slight transition from the customary collecting activities out of which it grew, and undoubtedly it was woman and not man who was responsible for that transition. She very well may have commenced her interference in the processes of nature by pulling out or thinning, some of the plants from a cluster from which she had learned to expect gifts of seeds or tubers. But this alone did not make her into a farmer. However, when she got and applied the idea of taking some of the seeds or tubers and placing them in a spot where they could sprout, take root, and grow, she had entered into the first stage of her long history as an agriculturist. The fact that this transition probably occurred only in places where one crop season followed immediately upon another may have helped reduce the temptation to give immediate satisfaction of wants the priority over the needs of the future. In any case, among the first places she selected for her plantings were the soft, mellow loamy deposits left on its margins by a receding stream, places in which the womenfolk of many primitive peoples probably learned to plant merely by dropping seeds and sinking them into the ground with the ball of the foot. It is important to stress, however, that such a farming process does not rely upon any tools whatsoever, not even the digging stick.

This elementary system of agriculture, which may be called the riv-

22. *Compton's Pictured Encyclopedia and Fact-Index*, I, 47.

erbank type, is still extensively used throughout the great Amazon Basin in South America, an area which probably shares with the banks of the Nile, those of the Tigris and Euphrates, and those of the rivers of Southern China, the distinction of being the ones in which agriculture was first practiced. The Amazon sections of Colombia are ones in which the aboriginal population has been almost entirely decimated, so this most elementary and rudimentary system of agriculture does not have the importance there that it does in the Brazilian, Peruvian, and Bolivian sections of the Basin, nor along the banks of the Orinoco and its tributaries in Venezuela. Historically, though, in Colonial times it probably played a fairly important role in the huge section of Colombia that lies to the east of the Andes.[23]

Fire Agriculture.—In some places tillage by means of the digging stick, or the improved digging stick called a hoe, may have evolved directly out of the riverbank plantings just discussed. This is to say that hoe culture may have developed directly out of the most rudimentary of all systems of agriculture, the one in which the action of nature's rivers is solely responsible for the preparation of the seed bed. Indeed it is likely that the first combinations of crops and livestock were ones in which, as the Nile and other rivers receded, oxen were employed to tread into muddy surfaces the seeds that had been broadcast by hand.[24] But in South America, and especially in Brazil and the neighboring portions of Bolivia, Peru, Colombia, and Venezuela, another system of agriculture developed long before the digging stick evolved into the hoe, and it still persists side by

23. Nevertheless, specific descriptions of this system of agriculture are not prevalent in the accounts left by the naturalists who spent long years in the area. That they knew and took for granted such a way of getting products from the soil, though, seems apparent from the writings of Alfred Russell Wallace, who indicates that in the course of some of the "dull and dreary evenings" he spent at Javita, a small village on the Orinoco, near the passage which links it with the Amazon system, he amused himself by describing in blank verse the life of his Indian hosts. Their system of agriculture inspired the following lines:
> The women dig the mandiocca root,
> And with much labour make of it their bread.
> These plants the young shoots in the fertile earth—
> Earth all untill'd, to which the plough, or spade,
> Or rake, or harrow, are alike unknown.

Travels on the Amazon, p. 177.

24. Maspero, *The Dawn of Civilization,* p. 66, has written as follows: "As soon as the water of the Nile retires, the ground is sown without previous preparation, and the grain, falling straight into the mud, grows as vigorously as in the best-ploughed furrows." See also, Gosse, *The Civilization of the Ancient Egyptians,* p. 28.

side with ways of getting products from the soil which have as essential components the tractor and even the airplane.[25]

Wherever fire finds a liberal supply of dried limbs, branches, and trunks of trees on the surface, it leaves in its wake a soft, mellow, pliable patch of earth. Such a burned-over area in a virgin forest also is almost entirely lacking in plants or weeds to compete with any seeds that might be deposited there by a woman or a man. Hence it is merely a short and easy step from the point in which the river is depended upon to prepare a seedbed to plantings in burned-over portions of the forest, and even to the use of a hatchet or an ax to supply the fuel for the fire. Before the coming of the white man, throughout most of the South American continent, with the exception of the temperate zones in the Andean highlands, a system of "felling and burning" was the principal manner of preparing the soil for the seeds of beans and maize, the tubers of the manioc, and the other plants which the natives depended upon for their foodstuffs. And as one decade succeeds another during the course of the second half of the twentieth century, tremendous areas of Brazil, Colombia, Venezuela, Peru, and Bolivia, as well as large sections of Africa, Asia, and Oceania, are still occupied by peoples who have not passed beyond this elementary, wasteful, prodigal, and destructive stage of agricultural production. The terms "wasteful," "destructive," and "prodigal" are used advisedly, since the mere existence of what the Brazilians designate as *derrubadas e queimadas* and the Spanish Americans call *rozas* is sufficient proof that a section of virgin forest, or at least a second growth that has been standing for decades, has been destroyed merely in order to produce a few pecks of maize, rice, beans, or tubers. The statement by J. C. Willis that "vast areas of good forest land have been ruined in southern Asia by this destructive practice" is fully supported by my personal observations in extensive portions of Colombian, Brazilian, Peruvian, and Bolivian territory. The system involved, which still competes with hoe culture for supremacy in the vast lowland expanses of tropical South America, I have designated as "fire agriculture."

This attempt to introduce a neologism was made deliberately and despite the innovator's low esteem of the practice generally. I justify it in part by the need to "shock" agricultural specialists and other

25. For an analysis and description of this system of "fire agriculture" see especially Smith, *Brazil*, pp. 364-72.

visitors to South America into the realization that the felling and burning they see on a wholesale basis are playing entirely different roles than those carried by the same activities in clearing the land and creating new farms in the United States and Canada. Briefly in the latter, the work of chopping down the trees and burning the tangled mass of fallen timber has been in preparation for the plow and the extraction of the stumps. In Brazil, Colombia, and the other South American countries, on the other hand, the process of felling and burning is a *substitute* for the work of the plow and there is no thought of attacking the stumps.[26] Another reason for designating the process as "fire agriculture" is the deceptive and misleading nature of the other terms that have been used by North American and European writers to denote the pattern involved. These include such names as "slash and burn," "shifting cultivation," and the *"milpa* system." Definitely something more than "slashing" is required to fell the virgin forests of tropical South America.[27] Likewise the process of cutting down the giants of the rainforests with the ax, allowing them to dry, and then firing the lot, has little in common with the Central American milpa. In the latter the campesinos wield the machete to cut the brush and shoots that grow up each year in the hillside corn or bean patch. These, then, are piled and later on they are burned. Even more egregious is the practice of employing the designation of "shifting cultivation" to the derrubadas e queimadas under consideration. How can one possibly justify the use of "shifting cultivation" to designate a process in which no cultivation whatsoever is involved?

Prior to about 1850, when planted pastures of Guinea and Pará grasses enabled the Colombian upper classes to extend their cattle haciendas into the forested areas in the lowlands, the aboriginal

26. I have observed in a few settlements made by European farmers since the close of the Second World War, such as the Dutch colony of Hollambra, near Campinas in São Paulo, Brazil, the work of removing the stumps from areas that were felled over a century ago. The lands involved served for many decades as coffee plantations, and then as cattle pastures, and only now are they coming into their own as rich, productive, cultivated fields.

27. Consider, for example, the following description of the actual process: "The work commences: the file of peons begin the felling of the forest; the small trees submissively give way to the stroke of the machete, the small shoots bow miserably like the masses before a dictator; but the towering giants, the *diomates* and the *guayacanes*, fearlessly resist the ax, but they always fall, with a thundering crash that terrorizes all the wild animals and reverberates throughout the forest." Medardo Rivas, p. 58.

system of fire agriculture appears to have been about the only way of securing agricultural products throughout the vast Magdalena Valley and other tropical rain forest sections of Colombia. Maize was the principal crop grown and the operations were confined to the subsistence farming of the masses. Here and there, especially in proximity to the river towns and cities, and as close to Bogotá as altitude permitted, were to be found a few plantings of sugar cane, with each collection of fields centered about a small, primitive mill for the making of syrup. This syrup, in turn went up the mountainsides to Bogotá and the numerous other cities and towns in the highlands on the backs of mules which carried salt from the mines of Zipaquirá and temperate climate products on the return journey. Then, as now, though, the many thousands of campesino families got their corn, their staff of life, by the rude, primitive, destructive, and inefficient processes involved in fire agriculture. This required hard work for many months in felling with the ax an acre or two of virgin forest, allowing the tangled mass to dry, firing the lot, and then, often while the trunks of the fallen timber were still smoldering, dibbling in with the aid of the big toe, or at most a digging stick, a few seeds of maize in the soft, pliable earth as it had been left by the fire. As indicated by Medardo Rivas, for example, "Cultivation [more accurately, the substitute for cultivation] was reduced to felling the forest and planting the maize, and as the ears were gathered the second growth already had sprung up; and soon the woods again took possession of the land, without leaving anything for the future."[28]

Colombia's system of fire agriculture has never been described more accurately or more completely than it was by P. L. Bell, who once was a "Trade Commissioner" with the United States Department of Commerce. Consider the following extracts from one of his comprehensive and enlightening reports.

> With the exception of the wheat lands of the table-land of Bogotá, the two large sugar estates mentioned, and a few individual efforts in modern agriculture, there is, in general, little cultivation of the soil in Colombia. . . .
> Throughout the coast regions and in the Magdalena Valley and other valleys of the interior, there is little attempt at cultivation or the use of modern agricultural implements or machinery. The principal field crops of corn and cotton are handled in the following man-

28. *Ibid.*, p. 34.

ner: the land, if new, is first cleared of the underbrush with the machete and then the larger trees are cut down at waist height with the
ax. This work is done during the dry season, and the dry brush and
other growths are burned off just before the rains begin—leaving the
land encumbered with an assortment of stumps, partly charred trunks
of hardwood trees, etc., and incapable of being plowed in any case.
The burning over kills the seeds of all weeds, as a general thing, and
the corn or cotton seed is planted in holes dug with a sharp stick
or iron bar at the beginning of the rains. During the growth of the
plants nothing further is done, with the exception of periodically
chopping out the larger weeds with the machete.[29]

This destructive and inefficient system remains as the principal
reliance of the campesinos throughout the extensive tropical forests
of Colombia, although the hoe to some extent is coming into use in
connection with the planting of the seeds. This means that among
the humble classes the fire agriculture of the lowlands rivals the
hoe culture of the uplands in importance as the system by which
the subsistence crops of the rural masses are produced. However,
two important related developments must be mentioned. One of
these is the extent to which the plantains and bananas have come,
since colonial times, to be basic in the diet of the lowland masses,
and the other is the spread of the cattle haciendas throughout the
tropical lowlands.

The first of these, the use of plantains as the principal staple in
the diet, frequently to the displacement largely of maize, really
called for no substantial improvement of the system of agriculture.
It merely meant that the plantings made in the clearing were more
permanent. Less frequent fellings and burnings are required when
plantains are the staff of life, than when the chief reliance is upon
maize.

The second is far more significant. About 1850 the Guinea and
Pará grasses came to be known by the upper-class, landholding families of Bogotá and the other cities. Very quickly they began the
practice of sowing the seeds of these, along with the maize, in the
freshly burned-over rozas in the zones lying between sea-level and
the 6,000-foot mark. Says Rivas:

> He that carried to these regions the grass of Guinea deserves a
> statue on Gaucana hill as high as the Statue of Liberty in New
> York, one that, illuminated at night, would be viewed throughout the
> vast extension of territory that it has made productive. . . .

29. Bell, p. 175.

It is said that during the government of General Santander, he had some plants brought, which, as a curiosity, he gave to the agriculturists.

A true miracle, this Guinea grass!

Previously the forest was felled, the roza was burned, and the maize was planted; and, as we have said, when it was harvested, the second growth already was disputing the field with the cultivator, and the land remained as it had been before. Now the marvelous seed is sown at the time the maize is planted, and when the ear of corn is ready, a green blanket already covers the soil; and little by little this pasture is being extended to cover the entire hot zone, where thousands of cattle are brought to feed and fatten, and on which are supported all of the pack trains of mules that carry the goods to the interior.[30]

The process is by no means complete as yet, though, despite the huge clouds of smoke that regularly obstruct the vision of one who flies from Bogotá to Medellín, or over many other parts of the lowlands. Throughout my journal, for example, are numerous entries which were stimulated by observations such as the following made on February 23, 1944, while on a visit to the Sibundoy Valley on the eastern slope of the Andes in the extreme southern part of Colombia.

The land about the edges of the Valley is nearly all occupied; the swampy central portions constitute a national reserve; and the *colonos* are rapidly felling the trees on the mountain sides, burning them, sowing one crop of corn, and then making the slopes into pastures. . . . Land on the plain is valued at about 200 pesos per hectare; and that on the slopes at 100-120. This is cleared and in pastures. *Desmontes* [felling and burning] come at 12-15 pesos per hectare, and an additional 5 pesos is necessary for clearing and preparing the pastures. All of this is rapidly exhausting the forests of the area, even before the lumber industry has a chance to begin. Today I saw many acres covered with the long, charred trunks of trees, acres that yesterday were forests, tomorrow will be corn patches, and next year will be pastures.

It should be stressed, though, that the bulk of those who inhabit the humid lowlands of Colombia do not fell and burn the forest and plant small patches of corn and other crops as a prelude to sowing grass for pasture lands. Instead they rely upon the destructive and inefficient system of fire agriculture for the production of the foodstuffs upon which they depend, deserting the clearing as soon as the harvest has been taken and elsewhere making another

30. *Ibid.*, pp. 35-36.

roza for the subsequent planting. Throughout the extensive lowlands and also on the slopes up to the level of about 6,000 feet, this system prevails on a scale that makes it rival in importance in the production of Colombia's basic foodstuffs, the age-old hoe culture of the uplands, and the mechanized farming that now is developing swiftly in certain favored locations. As will be indicated below these include the valley bottoms which are close to the principal towns and cities, such as the Savanna of Bogotá and the Cauca Valley, and some of the grassy plains, such as those on the Llanos

Trials at replacing the hoe and pointed stick in seed planting in Colombia. (Courtesy of the Rockefeller Foundation.)

near Villavicencio and Florencia east of the Andes, and those on the northern coastal plain.

Hoe Culture.—Once it was established by vast amounts of trial and error that soft, clean, spongy surfaces favor the growth of seeds, man was on the verge of another basic step in his halting climb to civilization. Many groups throughout the primitive world independently hit upon the idea of using sharpened sticks for stirring the soil preparatory to depositing seeds which they expected to multiply. In all probability the idea for such tillage came from the use of sticks and shells to help spare the fingers and nails in digging for tubers, but in any case the selection, preservation, improvement, and use of a digging stick do not depend upon any great intellectual development. When the early agriculturists got and applied the idea of adding a flat piece of bone, shell, or metal to the end of the digging stick, the hoe came into existence; and then only an elementary knowledge of fertilization, such as placing a fish in each hill of corn, was needed in order for genuine cultivation and permanent agriculture to develop.

Digging sticks of one kind or another may have been the principal implements used by the Chibchas and other highland groups when the Spaniards arrived, although in some cases at least the curved nature of the sharpened stick and the fact that it was operated by a pulling motion, rather than by pushing, justify denoting the instrument employed as a wooden hoe. Fals-Borda, citing the chroniclers Pedro Simon and Pedro de Aguado, states that "among the tools which they [the Chibchas] developed, a large wooden hoe made from a crooked branch and stone axes (*macanas*) were the highest achievements."[31] Moreover, in my own travels throughout the mountainous districts of Colombia I frequently have seen the digging stick in use, although not to an extent that would rival that of the now ubiquitous hoe. On one occasion in 1944 just south of La Unión in Nariño I observed a gang of about 50 men working in unison with digging sticks at the task of "spading" a large hillside. On this same trip, on a hacienda situated between Pasto and Ipiales, I was given "a demonstration of preparing furrows and rows with the 'palito'— a curved stick equipped with an iron point. Three strokes, one on each side and then one in the middle! All the potato rows one sees in this broad expanse of territory are prepared with this instrument." In the northern sections of the Andes probably not many of the pre-Colombian digging sticks were equipped with the prong, which enables the pressure from a foot to supplement that by the hands in forcing the point of the instrument into the ground, as were those of aboriginal Peru and as are those used today in much of Peru, Bolivia, and Ecuador.

Most of the essential features of the hoe culture which still function as the dominant system of agriculture throughout the densely populated temperate zones of Colombia have been described accurately and in detail by Fals-Borda in his careful sociological study

31. Fals-Borda, "A Sociological Study of the Relationships between Man and the Land in the Department of Boyacá, Colombia" (Ph.D. dissertation, University of Florida, Gainesville, 1955, pp. 210-11; this study was published in Spanish, *El Hombre y la Tierra en Boyacá, Bases Socio-Históricas para una Reforma Agraria*).

of Boyacá. Although his field observations were limited to this one department, and largely to the thickly settled (i.e., upland parts) of it, his conclusions apply almost equally well to the extensive sections of the departments of Cundinamarca, Santander, Norte de Santander, and Nariño which are similar to it in climate and terrain. He first dismisses fire agricultural practices as being of slight importance in the areas studied, although not entirely absent even in the growing of potatoes. Specifically, he states: "Fire agriculture is practiced, to a limited extent, in sections of mountains which are covered with heavy growth. This is done, among other places, in Puebloviejo, Belén, Ventaquemada, and Arcabuco. Toward the end of the dry season, the farmers cut down trees and bushes, let the branches dry for about fifteen or twenty days, and then set the vegetation afire with matches or charcoal. Planting, usually corn or potatoes, is done three days after the firing, while the ashes are still warm. This planting is done with a wooden stick which stirs the ashes as well as the soil below."[32]

With much reason Fals-Borda indicates that the hoe with the metal blade quickly came to compete seriously with the digging stick soon after the arrival of the conquistadores, and cites authorities to show that Jiménez de Quesada himself brought the first ones. Nevertheless during colonial times these improved instruments were expensive and scarce, sometimes costing as much as a horse or a house;[33] and he confirms my observations that widespread hoe culture of the northern Andes by no means has reached the point at which the crude, aboriginal wooden hoe has been entirely supplanted by the one equipped with a blade of metal. "The large wooden hoe apparently used by the Chibcha, now called *gancho,* is still used in Boyacá, especially for the harvesting of potatoes. The gancho is employed preferably for soft and porous soil. The women of the *vereda* of Chorroblanco near Tunja use a gancho which is more like a wooden pick-hoe, an instrument closely resembling the small Inca *corana* drawn by Guaman Poma in the sixteenth century. An early adaptation of the native stick with a steel point has survived in Socha."[34] Thus as Colombia moves well along into the second half of the twentieth century the hoe culture on which the millions of her campesinos, living and working in the cool climate along the high

32. *Ibid.,* pp. 212-13.
33. *Ibid.,* pp. 213-14.
34. *Ibid.,* pp. 214-15.

slopes of her great mountain chains and in her great intermountain valleys, are dependent for a livelihood is in the stage wherein the metal hoe itself has not entirely replaced the digging stick as the central element in her principal system of agriculture. However, at the intermediate altitudes (2,500 to 6,000 feet) at which the coffee trees thrive, the metal hoe is the chief reliance of the system through which the nation's great export crop is produced.

Fortunately, the agricultural census of 1960 supplies some of the quantitative data needed for the most effective study of the relative importance of and distribution of hoe culture and the other more improved systems of agriculture used in the production and transportation of the crops upon which Colombia's people and economy depend. Some of the most pertinent of these have been assembled, along with some essential computations, in Tables 10 and 11. The first of these tables indicates that almost two-thirds of all the agricultural units (that is the farms and subsistence plots which it is impossible to separate in the census tables) enumerated in the 1960 census were solely dependent upon manpower for the performance of all the work on the farm, including the transportation of the products from the fields to the storage places. The data in this compilation indicate that neither mules, oxen, tractors, or power equipment of any type, were used in the agricultural tasks on more than one-half of the "explotaciones" of every size group up to the one involving farms having more than 200 hectares of land. Of the total number of 1,309,942 dwellings reported on the "farms," only 48,564, or 3.7 per cent, were on these places of 200 or more hectares. Therefore, even if we were to suppose that the major share of the non-resident agricultural laborers were employed on the larger places, it still would appear that well over one-half of all Colombian families who gain a livelihood from agricultural activities have nothing except their hands, aided in extensive areas only by the ax and fire, and in most of the more densely populated sections, almost exclusively by the hoe and the pick, for use in their struggle with nature.

The lack of an adequate definition of the farm, failure by the census to secure most of the more essential facts about the agricultural laborers, and absence in the tabulations for the various departments of cross-tabulations featuring the size of the agricultural units, such as are available in some of the tables for the nation and which made possible the compilation in Table 10, greatly handicaps anyone who would try to understand the way in which reliance exclusively upon manpower varies from one part of Colombia to another. The best that can be done is to assemble for each of the departments, as has been done in Table 11, the number and proportion of the "explotaciones" of all sizes solely dependent upon human energy. Even so, however, the tabulation that is possible is not entirely lacking in interest and significance. Note, for example, that

TABLE 10

Numbers and Proportions of the Explotaciones Agropecuarias in Colombia Reporting no Power Except Manpower, by Size, 1960

Size of explotaciones (in hectares)	Number of explotaciones	Explotaciones dependent solely upon manpower	
		Number	Per cent
Less than 0.5	165,652	144,236	87
0.5–0.9	132,419	96,059	73
1–1.9	191,347	131,054	68
2–2.9	117,005	75,630	65
3–3.9	92,001	56,216	61
4–4.9	58,181	34,739	60
5–9.9	169,145	94,579	56
10–19.9	114,231	60,849	53
20–29.9	44,049	23,362	53
30–39.9	26,500	14,204	54
40–49.9	16,240	8,792	54
50–99.9	39,990	21,872	55
100–199.9	22,317	11,711	52
200–499.9	13,693	6,233	46
500–999.9	4,141	1,536	37
1,000–2,499.9	1,975	551	28
2,500–over	786	93	12
Total	1,209,672	781,716	65

Source: Page 56 of source for Table 1.

in all of the departments on the northern coastal plain, almost none of the "explotaciones" are operated in ways that call for the use of the ox, the mule, the tractor, or any other source of power except that of the peons. The extreme is, it will be noted, in the department of Bolívar where almost 62,000 agricultural units, or 97 per cent of all, depend exclusively upon the power that can be supplied by men and women; but in these respects Bolívar is closely rivaled by its neighbors along the coast, or by Magdalena, Atlántico, and

Córdoba, to be specific. Nor do the many thousands of families who produce vast amounts of coffee to sell and maize to eat in the departments of Caldas and Antioquia have much to work with other than the ax and the hoe. These people, who come nearer to being genuine middle-class farmers than those in any other part of Colombia, have practically no draft animals and machines, not even the lumbering ox nor the wooden plow, to magnify the power of

TABLE 11

NUMBERS AND PROPORTIONS OF THE EXPLOTACIONES AGROPECUARIAS IN COLOMBIA REPORTING NO POWER EXCEPT MANPOWER, BY DEPARTMENTS, 1960

Department	Number of explotaciones agropecuarias	Explotaciones dependent solely upon manpower	
		Number	Per cent
Total	1,209,672	781,716	65
Antioquia	169,299	135,861	80
Atlántico	11,902	11,431	96
Bolívar	63,827	61,823	97
Boyacá	169,282	47,273	28
Caldas	80,424	68,495	85
Cauca	73,753	42,758	58
Córdoba	48,393	42,230	87
Cundinamarca	145,003	73,327	51
Huila	34,683	16,332	47
Magdalena	54,989	52,007	95
Meta	15,835	9,060	57
Nariño	90,285	55,630	62
Norte de Santander	39,069	24,222	62
Santander	89,972	44,393	49
Tolima	72,133	51,795	72
Valle del Cauca	50,823	45,079	89

Source: Page 32 of source for Table 1.

their arms. Even in the fabulously rich and productive lands of the department of El Valle del Cauca, where in 1960 the farmers owned 3,080 tractors, in a total of only 13,138 on all the farms in Colombia, 85 per cent of the families living on the land had only their hands, the ax and the hoe, or the most rudimentary and inefficient systems of agriculture, to help them in gaining a livelihood. Most conspicuous of all is the Municipio of Palmira in this department, home of one of the most famous and modern sugar-cane plantations in the entire world. The estates in this municipio alone reported a total of 501 tractors in use in 1960, with 306 farms having one or more of the machines which make up the central core of a mechanized system of agriculture. But in spite of this, the vast majority of the families in the municipio who depended upon agriculture for a livelihood were still in the hoe culture stage of existence: 2,168 of the "explotaciones" of a total of 2,928 in the municipio indicated a reliance exclusively upon manpower.[35]

Interestingly enough, dependence solely upon human energy is at its minimum on the farms of Boyacá, the department which figured in Fals-Borda's fundamental study of man-land relationships. In it only 30 per cent of the "explotaciones" indicated the use of neither tractors nor draft animals. This, of course, may be attributed largely to the fact that in its densely populated highland districts, the hoe culture inherited from the Chibchas has been blended to a considerable extent with the rudimentary plow culture brought by the Spaniards. Thus, in comparison with the 47,273 "explotaciones" entirely upon human power, there were 121,409 reporting some use of draft or pack animals in connection with farm tasks. The same situation prevails in the highland sections of Santander, Norte de Santander, Cundinamarca, and Nariño, and this helps to make the absence of anything other than manpower in their systems of agriculture less pronounced than otherwise would be the case.

Rudimentary Plow Culture.—Long before any part of mankind had perfected an alphabet, so as to make written records possible, some of the world's agriculturists had hit upon the idea and use of the plow. A forked stick shaped so that one person could apply force by pulling while another was thrusting was, of course, the fundamental instrument in this momentous discovery, but in some places a rudimentary plow may have evolved from the crude hoe. In any case, though, as the curtain went up on the written history of human society the crude wooden plow, sometimes even equipped with a rough metal point and drawn by oxen, had already become the central feature in the systems of agriculture in use by the agricultural peoples of Egypt, Mesopotamia, and probably, other cradles of civilization.[36] This early

35. The Universidad del Valle, aided by the Rockefeller Foundation, the United Nations, and other agencies, assembled much more information and published the census tabulations in far greater detail than has been done for the other departments. These facts for the Municipio of Palmira are from the Facultad de Ciencias Económicas, pp. 153-55.

36. Cf. Tylor, "On the Origin of the Plough and Wheel-Carriage," pp. 74-82.

plow, like its modern counterpart in Colombia, the Iberian Peninsula, and many other parts of the world, was exceedingly primitive and inefficient. Drawn by the lumbering movement of the ox, it laboriously rooted along tearing the ground, instead of gliding smoothly, lightly cutting and turning the soil, as is the case with the modern, improved instrument which constitutes the central core of the system of agriculture denoted as advanced plow culture. Nevertheless the mere fact that draft animals were used to pull such plows was a revolutionary achievement, even though several persons still were needed to keep the sharp prong of the stick in the ground, control the direction of its movement, and manage the oxen that pulled it along. As I have had abundant opportunity of observing on the Savanna of Bogotá, on other

The central elements of the rudimentary plow culture as practiced in Colombia. (Courtesy of Kenneth Wernimont.)

plains in Colombia that are level as a table top, in many other parts of Spanish America, in Brazil, in Spain, and in Portugal, awkward oxen, with their jerky movements, can never be hitched effectively to the modern, turning plow. Even more unsatisfactory are the results when, with a complete disregard of the abc's of agricultural engineering, they are harnessed to more complex and finely integrated mechanical systems such as the mowing machine or the grain harvester.

Rarely, or probably never, were horses hitched to the rudimentary plows in Egypt, Mesopotamia, and other parts of the ancient world, nor to those of the Iberian Peninsula and others of the Roman world from which Colombia and other parts of Latin America received the European portions of their cultural heritages. As a matter of fact, throughout the vast expanses of the Roman Empire the horse shared the upper-class status of the master whose chariot he drew, or for whom he served as charger, and with whom, frequently, he was buried. Even the thought of bemeaning such a noble steed by forcing him to draw a plow, or to perform any other work connected with agriculture, probably would have been abhorrent to the rural masses in Spain, Portugal, and other parts of the Empire's heartland.[37]

The wooden plow drawn by oxen near Bogotá. (Photo by U. S. Department of Agriculture.)

When the Spaniards arrived in the part of South America that now is the Republic of Colombia, Spain was dependent upon two basic systems of agriculture: hoe culture, which was discussed in the preceding section, and rudimentary plow culture. The central features of the latter system of agriculture consist of the primitive, wooden, rooting plow, the use of oxen as draft animals, and the rude, two-

37. Such a social and cultural value, though, apparently did not dominate in full force the thinking of some of the peoples on the margins of the Roman world. Thus, "as late as the tenth century, farmers in England were forbidden, by law, to harness the horse to a plow." Ellis and Rumely, *Power and the Plow*, p. 25. Obviously such a law would never have been promulgated until after the old Roman mores governing the matter had begun to lose their force.

wheeled ox cart; and, as mentioned above, temperate zone grains, such as wheat and barley also were important components of the system. In addition, the breeding and use of mules, not as draft animals, but for riding and packing purposes, were practices brought by the Spaniards which came to play important roles in the transportation

In the North American settlements by the English, Dutch, Swedish, and French, the horse was used as a draft animal. (From a print of 1600.)

of things on the farm and from farm to market in Colombia. Unlike their Dutch, English, and French counterparts in North America, the Spaniards lacked familiarity with, and hence were unable to carry to America, a turning plow equipped with a moldboard, the highly important four-wheeled farm wagon, and the horse collar, which alone made possible the effective use of horses (and mules as well) as draft animals. In brief, the European parts of the cultural heritage of Colombia and the other Latin American countries had elementary plow culture as the highest accomplishment connected with the basis of their economies, whereas Canada and the United States started from a level in which an advanced plow culture was already well on the way to perfection.

The introduction of the wooden plow, the ox cart, and the ox itself, such grains as wheat and barley, mules for packing purposes, and horses and mules to ride, had far-reaching effects upon the system of agriculture. Perhaps had the Spaniards themselves been interested in agriculture, rather than principally concerned with pastoral activities,

In the conquest and settlement of Colombia and Spanish America in general, the horse served only as a war charger. (From a drawing by Theo. de Bry.)

the ways in which the farmers went about getting products from the soil, moving them from field to store house, and from farm to market, would have been even more improved. As it actually was, though, everything concerned with farming was left largely in the hands of the Indians, and the mestizos, who quickly came to constitute a significant part of the population, while the Spaniards, from their residences in their new administrative centers and garrison towns, devoted themselves largely to stock raising, the supervision of mining activities, and other non-agricultural pursuits. The systems of agriculture in vogue changed little after the first few decades of Spanish occupation, with fire agriculture remaining dominant in the heavily forested zones at the lower altitudes and hoe culture, partially fused with rudimentary plow culture, being the system relied upon in the densely populated upland areas from Nariño on the south to Norte de Santander on the north. The same is largely true today, although, as will be described below, mechanized farming is reaching significant proportions in certain limited parts of the Republic.

Some of the best evidence of the relatively weak position of elementary plow culture in Colombia (and likewise the slight development of advanced plow culture and mechanized farming) is that presented above which shows the overwhelming extent to which Colombia's farms and subsistence tracts are dependent solely upon human beings for all the energy applied in the performance of farm tasks. This may be supplemented, though, with some additional information based upon other data collected in the 1960 census of agriculture. See Table 12. This material shows merely the number and proportion of all farms and subsistence tracts in Colombia which make some use of animal power in connection with agricultural and processing operations. Probably transportation activities, such as the use of mules, burros, and oxen as pack animals on the farm and from farm to market, also are involved, but the explanations of the categories employed do not enable one to be sure on this point. In any case, the important thing is that on one-third, only, of all the "explotaciones" in Colombia is there any use of draft or pack animals in connection with farm work. Moreover, this one-third of the agricultural units, which totals 398,040 in number, includes 119,920 which report the use of animals to drive small, old-fashioned *trapiches* to express the juice from the sugar cane; but it is impossible to tell how many of them employ animals solely for this purpose, and how many of them use mules, oxen, burros, and perhaps horses for other farm tasks as well.

For the most part, the indexes showing the variations in the importance of draft and pack animals on the farms and subsistence tracts from one department to another are merely the percentages which added to those representing the proportions relying upon manpower exclusively will bring the total almost to the 100 per cent mark. For example, in Atlántico, Bolívar, and Magdalena, almost complete dependence upon the arms and backs of men and women for all the energy applied to farm tasks (as shown by the materials in Table 11) is merely another way of expressing the almost complete lack of oxen, mules, and donkeys (as reflected in Table 12). However, in a few departments, such as Meta, Tolima, El Valle del Cauca, and Cundinamarca, the use of tractors and other mechanical sources of power is sufficiently important to have a significant influence upon the indexes.

Advanced Plow Culture.—The tremendous and speedy improvement of each of the major components of the system of agriculture,

TABLE 12

NUMBER AND PROPORTION OF THE EXPLOTACIONES AGROPECUARIAS IN COLOMBIA
REPORTING THE USE OF ANIMAL POWER, 1960, BY DEPARTMENTS

	Explotaciones using animal power	
Department	Number	Per cent of all explotaciones
Total	398,040	33
Antioquia	32,085	19
Atlántico	157	1
Bolívar	1,616	3
Boyacá	121,408	72
Caldas	7,103	9
Cauca	30,694	42
Córdoba	5,733	12
Cundinamarca	65,585	45
Huila	17,608	51
Magdalena	2,379	4
Meta	6,432	41
Nariño	33,875	38
Norte de Santander	14,401	37
Santander	45,048	50
Tolima	12,901	18
Valle del Cauca	1,015	2

Source: Page 32 of source for Table 1.

which the present writer designates as advanced plow culture, and perfection of the system itself is the supreme achievement of the nineteenth century. For several centuries the necessary cultural base had been accumulating in the northwestern part of Europe, but in the "breakthrough" itself, one of the most important in the entire history of civilization, the great roles played by Great Britain, Holland, northern France, and western Germany were even excelled by those carried by the United States and Canada. This revolutionary development, in turn, was the indispensable prelude for the industrial revolution, the rapid growth of towns and cities, the universalization of general education, and the flourishing of the sciences which made the twentieth century appear almost as a sport in the evolutionary process of acquiring a knowledge about and a control over the processes of nature. Advanced plow culture is one of the principal keys to an understanding of these and the related developments which have brought us into the age of the atom. With much reason one can contend that this system of agriculture is primarily responsible for the alternatives to slavery and serfdom that have proved to be so successful, and for freeing the vast majority of the people in the societies involved from the imperative of passing their entire lives in the drudgery required merely in order to produce enough food and fiber to sustain and clothe the population. By 1910 it had reached the stage of perfection at which, by the application of mechanical power to farm equipment, only a few decades would be required to achieve the system of mechanized farming which today, in a few parts of the world, enables about ten per cent of the population to produce an abundance of food, fiber, and other raw materials for the people of the countries involved, their tremendous industrial plants, and for export as well.

It is my considered opinion that if one of Colombia's neighbors, Brazil, now had a rural population who knew how to farm as well as did the farmers in England, the northern and western parts of the United States, and parts of Canada as early as 1910, Brazil today would be one of the great powers of the world.[38] Likewise, if Colombia's farmers were able to make use of an advanced plow culture in their work of extracting products from the soil, this is to say if her dominant system of agriculture were organized about the use of the turning plow, horses and mules as draft animals, the four-wheeled farm wagon, and the thousands of other implements, devices, and machines (single trees, double trees, "eveners," mowing machines, grain binders, potato diggers, potato sorters, corn huskers, harrows, rollers, corn planters, drills, and so on for many pages), that nation's position domestically and internationally would be enhanced manifold. But such is not the case, nor is it likely that advanced plow culture will ever become of primary importance in Colombia's rural scene. Instead, mechanized farming likely will develop rapidly in the areas devoted to the production of such commercial crops as sugar cane, cotton, and rice; hoe culture will continue to be the chief reliance in the

38. On this point, see, Smith, *Brazil,* p. 357.

It is said that steel turning plows and discs do not work well in Colombia. (Photos by U. S. Department of Agriculture.)

care of the acreages devoted to coffee; and hoe culture, with a slight infusion of some features of rudimentary plow culture, and to a much lesser degree the even more primitive and wasteful system of fire agriculture, will continue to be the ways in which the millions of subsistence farmers produce their crops of maize, plantains, potatoes, wheat, barley, manioc, beans, and so on.

This is not because there have been no efforts to introduce the use of the steel turning plow and other components of the system of advanced plow culture into Colombia. Thus all of those in the flock of visitors who made their way to Bogotá at about the time Colombia gained her independence seem to have been preoccupied with the need for the plow and the ways in which it might be brought to the aid of the Colombian farmer. For example, Captain Charles Stuart Cochrane of Britain's Royal Navy, who ascended the Magdalena River and climbed the trail to Bogotá in 1823, had the following to say.

> It is the custom of the country to use the plough in the cold districts, and the hoe in the hotter, or lower level; but I feel convinced that were our English ploughs introduced here, it would be practicable to use them for the land in general; and I am happy to find that many of these most useful instruments are on their way to this country, where only industry, enterprise, and capital, are wanting to reap a golden harvest. I should advise, that men experienced in agriculture, and skilled in the best methods of managing land, should go out, amply provided with the best instruments of husbandry; and with the machinery for winnowing and grinding the corn in a superior manner to that now practiced in the country, where the grain is badly sifted and worse ground.[39]

At about the same time a military man from the United States, Colonel William Duane of Philadelphia, ever ready to defend Colombia and the Colombians from the barbs of critics, such as the Frenchman Mollien, resorted to more direct action in his endeavors to correct deficiencies in the manner in which Colombian farmers were expending their efforts. While on the trail between Cucutá and Bogotá he observed and described in detail the common wooden plow used in the community of Crenza in what is now Boyacá.

> It differs in nothing but being larger, and the cattle much larger, than the plough of Hindustan, and that of Egypt.
> The *paisano* was very inquisitive, and heard my account of our

39. *Journal of a Residence and Travels in Colombia during the Years 1823 and 1824*, II, 5-6. See also, Hamilton, I, 245.

ploughs with attention, and, with a pencil, I gave him a rough sketch, and explained the power gained by two handles in directing the line of the furrow; the uses of the soil-board, and the turning over of the sod. He expressed a wish, *if it were possible*, to obtain an American plough. I gave him a side sketch, and a separate sketch of the coulter, and the soil-board.[40]

Despite all efforts, a century later the need for a modern plow was still greatly impressing those who traveled about in Colombia, for, as the International Cotton Mission indicated in 1926, plows were being used only in the Cauca Valley, on the Savanna of Bogotá, and on some cotton plantations on the northern coastal plain. Elsewhere throughout Colombia the hoe was still "the common agricultural implement."[41]

From what has been said above, it is obvious that the good intentions of the early visitors left little or no lasting effect. If we can learn anything at all from their efforts and the endeavors of hundreds of perceptive Colombians who have tried to improve the farming practices of Colombian agriculturists, it is that efforts to introduce new traits and practices are successful only to the extent that the new elements readily find places in one of the established systems of values and procedures. Thus, the bringing of Guinea and Pará grasses during the nineteenth century produced tremendous expansions of Colombia's pasture lands simply because they enabled the existing pastoral culture, with its deep-seated and all pervasive values and procedures, to be extended into huge parts of the lowland forested area. They affected the system only by allowing its spread to additional territory, not by requiring a basic readjustment and rearrangement of its various parts. With the steel turning plow, however, the attempted use of an instrument precisely adjusted to use in the less developed stages of advanced plow culture, such as still prevails in the southern Appalachians and a few other parts of the United States, results in disappointment. The same has been true of dozens of "experiments" with animal-driven mowing machines and grain harvesters which I have experienced the agony of witnessing.

The basic difficulty is, of course, or at least so it appears to me, that the implement or feature whose introduction is attempted is adapted to and forms an integral part of a system whose interrelated components, finely adjusted to one another, are quite different from those into which it is injected in Colombia. The gears of the mowing

40. *A Visit to Colombia*, p. 408.
41. Pearse, *Colombia with Special Reference to Cotton*, p. 56.

machine or grain harvester, for example, are made to fit the pace of the horse or mule, and not to that of the slower ox. As a result in Colombian trials the cutting blades or knives grab and pull rather than cut with swift, clean movements, as they do in the system in which they were perfected. Likewise, the uneven pace of the oxen introduces a fatal forward and backward swing into the movement of the cutting bar. Even the plow, to work successfully, must be used as part of a complex in which the power is applied evenly and smoothly and with the proper length of the tugs, and so on, so as to achieve the balancing of forces that makes it glide, cut, and turn the soil. It is a far different instrument than was its European predecessor of the seventeenth and eighteenth centuries, which was merely in the process of transformation from a tearing implement into one that would turn the soil with the minimum expenditure of energy. Definitely it will not support for long the application in jerks of great amounts of ox power such as it is subjected to when it is incorporated into the rudimentary plow complex. Hence the disappointing results of the sustained efforts of one of the most perceptive Colombians of modern times, after years of endeavor to assist his humble friends in the settlement he had studied intensively, to improve their agricultural system. "The first steel plows easily broke, and later models were defective in the angle and blade-catching mechanisms. Therefore, the farmers assessed these innovations negatively."[42] No better have been the results in those parts of Colombia in which the attempt has been made to move directly to advanced plow culture from the older hoe culture and fire agriculture systems. Thus Bell reports that in the lush, northern coastal areas "American plows were first tried out at Monteria, on the Sinu River, but proved a failure because of the lack of knowledge in their use. Local planters argue that plows are not necessary in this region, the land being so rich as to need no cultivation. The introduction of modern agricultural implements and machinery into this district will be difficult, and considerable demonstrating will have to be done in order to convince the people of the advantage of modern methods."[43]

It is highly improbable that any national or international agency

42. Fals-Borda, *Facts and Theory of Sociocultural Change in a Rural Social System*, p. 20. For a detailed study of the prevailing system of agriculture and other aspects of rural social organization in the rather typical upland district in which these experiments took place, see Fals-Borda, *Peasant Life in the Colombian Andes*.

43. P. 221.

working in Colombia will undertake the simultaneous introduction at one time and place of all of the components of a genuine system of advanced plow culture. Rather, they will concentrate their efforts upon the mechanization of agriculture, which certainly, from the standpoint of the proprietors of the large estates at least, will give much more effective results. Nor, at the time of writing does there seem any likelihood that Colombia will come to be the home of any community of European farmers, such as the Dutch settlers in Hol-

Cattle from the costal plains on their way to the market. (Courtesy of the Office of Foreign Agricultural Relations, U. S. Department of Agriculture.)

lambra and in a few other new colonies in Brazil. These new Brazilians, although making use of tractors, bulldozers, and other mechanized equipment for clearing and terracing the land, rely upon draft horses and all the other features of a highly perfected advanced plow culture for the bulk of the work on their highly productive farms, a lesson that could be of prime importance throughout Brazil and other parts of Latin America. Hence, as stated above, there is small likelihood that Colombia will ever enter a stage of development in which advanced plow culture will play any significant part in her basic agricultural economy. Unfortunately, the evaluation and recommendation of the Mission headed by Lauchlin Currie and sponsored by the International Bank for Reconstruction and Development seems to be having little or no effect. To one who has been in contact with the Colombian scene since the report was published in 1950 there is little evidence of any tendency to consider "more important than mechanization in terms of tractors and tractor equipment" the unspectacular "shift from hand labor and the almost exclusive use of pack animals on small farms to practicable types of animal-drawn machinery and wheeled vehicles, possibly two-wheeled carts or even four-wheeled wagons."[44]

Mechanized Farming.—The modern, light, well-balanced, strong, and relatively large implements and machines characteristic of the mechanized system of agriculture presently are entering rapidly into use in some of the more important and productive parts of Colombia. Nowadays one who visits the tableland on which Bogotá stands, or the Cauca Valley, or the northern coastal plain, or the upper part of the Magdalena Valley, or even the prairie lands to the east of the Andes no longer will be surprised by the absence of the tractor and its associated plows, harrows, cultivators, and other implements. In the wheat and rice growing sections he will see combines for threshing the grain as it is cut, or, at least, small threshing machines which are replacing the ancient practice of using animals to tread the threshing floor. In the cotton producing areas he may even see the airplane engaged in the work of dusting the fields of growing plants. All of this represents a revolution in agricultural methods, which, although slow in coming, now is moving ahead with great speed. Fortunately, Colombia has an ample supply of petroleum, so that once the machinery itself is available at reasonable prices and the system for stocking and supplying parts is developed adequately there will be relatively few major obstacles to the mechanization of agriculture on most of the larger holdings throughout the country. Even many of the humble campesinos may be expected to participate in the process, by acquiring the skills essential to manage the machines and keep them in running order, by securing tractors of their own which they use on their own tracts and in custom work for their friends and neighbors, or at least by hiring those who do have tractors to do the plowing on the

44. Currie, *et al.*, *The Basis of a Development Program for Colombia*, pp. 394-95.

About 1940, a few small steam-driven threshing machines were introduced into Colombia. (Photos by U. S. Department of Agriculture.)

(*Above*) Early stage in the traditional process of threshing wheat. (*Below*) The same threshing floor later in the day. (Photos by the author.)

small plots for which they are responsible. In general, though, the mechanization of agriculture is likely to redound more to the favor of the large landowners than it is to the masses of Colombian rural society, that is to help maintain the social and economic differences that have always been the principal feature of Colombian society. It is not likely to promote a wider distribution of ownership and control of the land.

The 1960 census of agriculture came at a date that enables us to secure a general picture of the rural scene exactly at the time the process of developing a mechanized system of agriculture was just getting well underway. That census reported a total of 15,361 tractors in possession of the "producers" responsible for the 1,209,672 "explotaciones" which figured in the enumeration. Roughly we may consider that there were at the time about 1.3 million Colombian families or households residing on the land and directly dependent upon agriculture and stock raising for a livelihood, since the total number of dwellings on the "explotaciones" was found to be 1,309,942. These

The mechanization of the wheat harvest in Colombia in its opening stages. (Courtesy of the Rockefeller Foundation.)

data enable us to calculate that in 1960 there was about one tractor in use for each 85 agricultural families in Colombia. It is true that the number of families dependent upon agriculture is considerably larger than the number residing on the land, since probably at least 20 per cent of all the agricultural families make their homes off the land in hamlets, villages, towns, or cities. But this is offset, to some extent at least, by the custom work that is done on the land by tractors owned by those who do not live on the "explotaciones." Thus one tractor for each 85 families of agricultural workers, or perhaps one tractor for 100 such families, probably is as close to the actual ratio as it is possible to get. It would seem to be the best possible indicator of the degree of development of the mechanized system of agriculture.

We would expect, of course, a very close positive relationship between the size of the agricultural unit and the degree of mechanization of agriculture as indicated by the ratio between number of tractors and the number of agricultural households. Fortunately, the 1960 census data were tabulated in a manner that makes it possible to calculate the necessary ratios (see Table 13). It would be difficult to conceive of a series that would show more clearly the tendency for the use of the tractor to increase directly as the size of the farm enlarges; and the data would make it appear that the places of 200 hectares or more already are mechanized to a considerable degree. Unfortunately, though, the reality does not correspond as closely to the indicated relationship as these data seem to show. Here again we encounter one of the basic defects in the census tabulations that follows from the lack of an adequate definition of a farm, or, at very least, the failure to prepare two entirely separate and distinct sets of tabulations, one for places of less than two or three hectares and the other for places larger than the minimum selected. The difficulty is that many of the families of farm laborers, who are attached to and work upon the large estates, are called "arrendatarios" or even "propietarios" so that they help swell the number of households per tractor in the categories of "explotaciones" having less than 3 hectares, and they do not figure in the ratios for the larger places, mostly above 200 hectares, on which they actually work. A substantial, although undeterminable, allowance must be made for this factor.

It also is possible to show in a rough way how the ratio of households per tractor, or the degree of mechanization of agriculture, varies from department to department. See Table 14 and Figure 6. This variation is tremendous, the range being from only one tractor for each 503 resident farm households in the rough terrain of Antioquia, to one for every 20 such households in El Valle del Cauca. Were it possible to separate the thousands of subsistence tracts located on the mountains which rim the Cauca Valley from the farms on its rich productive bottom lands, the ratio for the latter might be found to be as low as five households per tractor. The development of a mechanized system of agriculture having the tractor as its core element also has made relatively little headway in the cool, densely populated, and tradition-bound departments of Santander, Nariño, and Boyacá; nor on the small coffee farms which cover the hillsides of Caldas, or on the variegated, but remote, sections of Norte de Santander. On the other hand, in Atlántico, closely surrounding the city of Barranquilla, and in Meta, in the first reaches of the plains which lay to the east of the Andes, the use of the tractor and the associated implements and machines is almost keeping pace with the developments in El

TABLE 13

THE RELATIONSHIP BETWEEN THE SIZE OF THE EXPLOTACIONES AGROPECUARIAS AND THE NUMBER OF HOUSEHOLDS PER TRACTOR IN COLOMBIA, 1960

Size of explotaciones (hectares)	Number of dwellings	Number of tractors	Number of dwellings or households per tractor
Less than 0.5	154,599	71	2,177
0.5-0.9	112,628	150	751
1.0-1.9	171,641	353	486
2.0-2.9	113,327	208	545
3.0-3.9	94,823	214	443
4.0-4.9	62,199	148	420
5.0-9.9	194,738	762	256
10.0-19.9	142,691	1,054	135
20.0-29.9	58,676	728	81
30.0-39.9	36,369	600	61
40.0-49.9	22,822	477	48
50.0-99.9	59,228	1,930	31
100.0-199.9	37,637	2,242	17
200.0-499.9	27,670	2,540	11
500.0-999.9	11,191	1,705	7
1,000.0-2,499.9	6,516	1,380	5
2,500.0-over	3,187	799	4
Total	1,309,942	15,361	85

Source: Pages 56 and 59 of source for Table 1.

Valle. Moreover, the broad plains of the upper Magdalena, in Tolima, Huila, and Cundinamarca, devoted extensively to cotton plantations, and the Savanna of Bogotá itself, are experiencing a burgeoning of mechanized methods of agricultural production. Finally, in the other departments on the northern coastal plain, Magdalena, Córdoba, and Bolívar much activity presently is underway in which the tractor is being used to transform rich level tracts long devoted exclusively to a rudimentary pastoral economy into cotton, rice, and sugar-cane plantations.

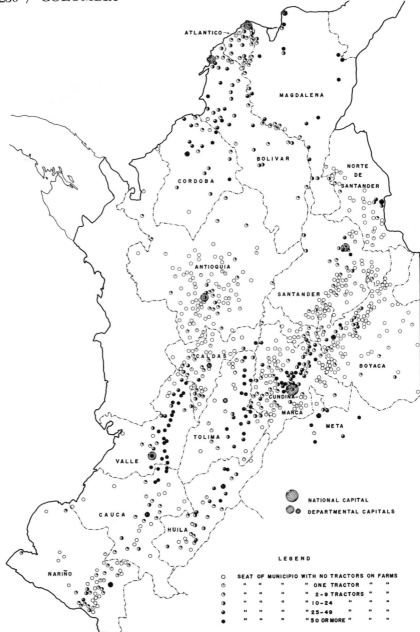

Figure 6.—Distribution of tractors in Colombia in 1960, by municipios.

A little additional light on the distribution of tractors and the system of agriculture in which they are the central components may be secured by an examination of the extent to which they have made their appearance, or failed to make it, in the various municipios (or counties) into which the departments are divided. See Table 10. One who makes use of these data, though, should realize that there are certain conspicuous incongruities in the materials from which they were assembled in comparison with those on which the preceding

TABLE 14

NUMBER OF AGRICULTURAL HOUSEHOLDS PER TRACTOR, BY DEPARTMENTS, 1960

Department	Number of dwellings or households	Number of tractors	Number of households per tractor
Total	1,309,942	15,361	85
Antioquia	171,604	341	503
Atlántico	6,935	236	29
Bolívar	61,752	795	78
Boyacá	192,324	751	256
Caldas	89,593	359	250
Cauca	78,830	626	126
Córdoba	56,723	863	66
Cundinamarca	167,652	3,036	55
Huila	36,275	511	71
Magdalena	61,289	1,340	46
Meta	15,145	523	29
Nariño	87,556	263	333
Norte de Santander	43,993	187	235
Santander	102,935	290	355
Tolima	75,290	2,203	34
Valle del Cauca	62,046	3,037	20

Source: Pages 33 and 35 of source for Table 1.

tables have been based. Thus the "Resumen Nacional (Segunda Parte)" of the census materials published in 1964 gives the total number of tractors owned by the "productores" responsible for the agricultural enterprises as 15,361, or the figure employed in Table 14. In sharp disagreement with this, and with no explanation offered anywhere in either of these official reports, the "Resumen Nacional" published in 1962, the one in which the materials for municipios is given, states the "number of tractors owned by the productores" to be only 13,138. For most of the departments the differences are not particularly great, as, for example, those pertaining to El Valle del Cauca for which the first report gives a total of 3,080 tractors and the later report one of only 3,037. In the case of Cundinamarca, however, the disparity between the totals is tremendous: 1,599 being the figure given in the tables published in 1962 and 3,036 that in the ones published in 1964.

In spite of the deficiences in the basic data, there seems to be little reason for questioning the basic finding presented in Table 15 which is that the tractor as a source of power for agricultural operations has now made its way into more than one-half of all the county-like subdivisions of Colombia (see Figure 6). This means that a demonstration of its power and utility has come within the realm of vision of most of those engaged in agriculture, and especially that its existence and applicability under Colombian conditions is constantly called to the attention of those who own and control the bulk of the best land in all parts of the country. The use of the tractor is most widely diffused in all of the departments that front on the Caribbean coast, most closely rivaled by those (Meta, Huila, El Valle del Cauca, and Tolima) in which level plains make up large proportions of the areas included within departmental boundaries. On the other hand, the departments in which densely settled mountainous sections account largely for the land in farms and the rural population (Boyacá, Antioquia, Norte de Santander, and Santander) are the ones in which the large majority of the municipios in 1960 still were awaiting the coming of the tractor and the mechanized system of agriculture.

At the stage reached by 1960 in the adoption of the mechanized system of agriculture by Colombian farmers, the distribution of the tractor was still very spotted throughout the various departments into which Colombia is divided. As a matter of fact, a mere 10 of the 824 municipios account for 23 per cent of all the tractors on Colombia's farms, although they are the homes of only 1.8 per cent of the resident agricultural population. See Table 16. Within these 10 municipios the total number of tractors owned by the ones responsible for the farming activities varies from 501 in the municipio of Palmira, in El Valle del Cauca, to 182 in the municipio of Pradera in the same department. If this type of analysis is extended somewhat, as may be done with the materials in Table 16, it will be observed that 20 municipios, containing a mere 4.2 per cent of the resident agricultural population, are the locations of one-third of all the tractors on Colombia's farms; and that 40 municipios, with only 8.4 per cent of the resident agricultural population, account for almost one-half (47.7 per cent) of all the tractors on the "explotaciones" in the nation. Of these 40 municipios, it is easily seen that 11 are in the single department of El Valle del Cauca, whose rich, productive and level lands, after 400 years of use in a very rudimentary pastoral culture, rapidly are being transformed into sugar-cane, rice, and cotton plantations. As indicated by the data presented elsewhere in this chapter, it is here

TABLE 15

NUMBER AND PROPORTION OF THE MUNICIPIOS IN WHICH THERE WAS ONE OR MORE TRACTORS, BY DEPARTMENTS, 1960

Department	Total number of municipios	Municipios in which tractors were reported	
		Number	Per cent
Total	824	480	58
Antioquia	102	39	38
Atlántico	21	21	100
Bolívar	43	43	100
Boyacá	123	34	28
Caldas	47	24	51
Cauca	33	19	58
Córdoba	21	21	100
Cundinamarca	114	74	65
Huila	33	27	82
Magdalena	30	28	93
Meta	13	12	92
Nariño	49	27	55
Norte de Santander	35	13	37
Santander	75	31	41
Tolima	43	33	77
Valle del Cauca	42	34	81

Source: Pages 23-91 of source for Table 1.

that the mechanized system of agriculture is making the most headway. El Valle del Cauca is rivaled in this respect, however, by the neighboring department of Tolima, which includes a large portion of the broad level plains in the upper Magdalena Valley, areas that for centuries were used for a cattle economy even more rudimentary than that of El Valle del Cauca, and recently have been converted into cotton plantations. Ten of the municipios in this department had 75 or more tractors reported as being owned by the planters and farmers,

TABLE 16

Municipio and department	Number of tractors	Resident agricultural population
Palmira, Valle del Cauca	501	21,482
Espinal, Tolima	403	12,414
Candelaria, Valle del Cauca	349	10,885
El Cerrito, Valle del Cauca	313	8,261
Augustín Codazzi, Magdalena	295	6,916
Armero, Tolima	278	6,951
Guamo, Tolima	270	19,808
Aracataca, Magdalena	204	10,475
Villavicencio, Meta	190	12,289
Pradera, Valle del Cauca	182	7,986
Tulúa, Valle del Cauca	181	18,148
Calota, Cauca	150	14,236
Purificación, Tolima	149	19,581
Guacarí, Valle del Cauca	146	6,002
Jamundi, Valle del Cauca	141	14,081
Monteria, Córdoba	138	48,076
La Dorada, Caldas	138	4,037
Florida, Valle del Cauca	135	6,593
Miranda, Cauca	128	6,443
Tunja, Boyacá	128	20,889
Valledupar, Magdalena	126	32,267
Ibague, Tolima	123	31,898
Ambalema, Tolima	118	1,113
Lérida, Tolima	114	4,142
Ginebra, Valle del Cauca	99	3,818
Cucutá, Norte de Santander	98	16,853
Cíenaga, Magdalena	97	25,469
Santander, Cauca	94	19,577
Flandes, Tolima	92	3,086
Cali, Valle del Cauca	91	14,601
Buga, Valle del Cauca	86	8,663
Corinto, Cauca	85	11,916
Pasto, Nariño	81	29,416
Robles, Magdalena	79	10,140
Ortega, Tolima	78	19,528
Carmen de Corupa, Cundinamarca	78	7,942
Alvarado, Tolima	77	5,352
Piedecuesta, Santander	77	9,235
Campo Alegre, Huila	75	5,536
Corozal, Bolívar	75	17,379

Source: Departamento Administrativo Nacional Estadística, 1962, pp. 23-91.

and one municipio, Espinal, had 403, the second largest number for any municipio in the Republic. The department of Magdalena, on the northern coastal plain, has five municipios in the list given in Table 16, and the department of Cauca, which includes those substantial sections of the Cauca Valley which are not in El Valle del Cauca, has four. The remaining 10 municipios in the list of the 40 most mechanized agricultural areas are spread among 10 of the other departments, the municipios included being those containing the department capitals in the cases of Meta, Córdoba, Boyacá, Norte de Santander, and Nariño. We may expect that in the decade ending in 1970 the system of agriculture based upon the tractor and its attachments will spread very rapidly from the centers represented in the list in Table 16, and also from the surroundings of Bogotá and Barranquilla, which are not represented in it, to many more extensive areas which presently are still in pastures for a not very high grade of beef cattle. This mechanized system of farming, in turn, seems to be converting many of Colombia's affluent landowners from persons highly partial to pastoral activities to entrepreneurs with a primary interest in sugar cane, cotton, and rice.

6

Agrarian Reform

COLOMBIA is distinguished by the interest its intellectuals have long exhibited in matters pertaining to agrarian reform, the determination of its humble rural masses to secure the ownership and control of small tracts of land, and the efforts its national government has taken in endeavors designed to improve the institutionalized relationships of man to the land. None the less, neither the long series of reform measures that have been attempted nor the nature of contemporary programs are well known beyond the limits of Colombia or even by many important segments of the people in that country itself.

BACKGROUNDS OF AGRARIAN REFORM

Much of the background for contemporary agrarian reform endeavors in Colombia is given in other chapters of this book, but even so it seems appropriate to summarize here some of the most important of the developments involved. The New Kingdom of Granada was an integral part of the overseas possessions of the Spanish crown for three centuries; but nevertheless the natural history of man-land relationships in this important part of the New World has many features that distinguish it from the developments in New Spain, Peru, the La Plata area, and other parts of the far-flung patrimony of the Spanish monarchs. In spite of this, Colombia resembled the other parts of the Spanish Empire in the inheritance from the mother country of a system of social stratification consisting of only two classes, namely a small upper class made up of the members of the elite group who owned and controlled the land and mineral resources and the huge stratum at the very bottom of any social scale composed of Indians, mestizos, Negroes, mulattoes, and even whites, and mostly agricultural laborers who were either enslaved, held in encomienda, or kept in some other form of servile or semi-servile status. During the course of the sixteenth, seventeenth, and eighteenth centuries the members of the elite stratum, with their residences and seats of power in the major new Spanish garrison and administrative cities such as Bogotá, Tunja, Popayán, and Cartagena, took advantage of the good will of the Crown and the generosity of the viceroys to consolidate into immense landholdings the numerous grants they received. Also, due to the lack of any systematic form of surveying and registering titles to the land, they proceeded to incorporate into the estates they claimed other tremendous areas of the most desirable land. Indeed less than a century, following the arrival (1538) of Jiménez de Quesada in the delightful and intensively cultivated territories of the Chibchas, sufficed for the development throughout the New Kingdom of virtual chaos in property rights to the land and many other aspects of man-land relationships. In a word, an acute need for an agrarian reform arose while many of the first generation of those born in the New World were still alive.

As is well known in the beginning of the Spanish regime in America, the gifts and grants of lands to the conquistadores and other Spaniards were extremely generous. At first the only manner of securing property rights to land was by such *mercedes* by the King, his representatives, or the cabildo or council of a newly established city or town. But the conquerors were by no means content with these grants, and not withstanding the facility with which some of them secured one grant of an *estancia de ganado mayor*, or cattle ranch, after another, and this of lands that were the most fertile and best situated, the first settlers resorted to every means possible to extend the limits of their immense claims. Frequently they merely fixed their landmarks so as to include within their estates areas much greater than those specified in the grants; but there also was a wholesale issuance of deeds to land on the part of persons and officials who had no authority whatsoever to distribute crown lands. Thus the concoction of false deeds grew to be a business of sizeable proportions. As the years passed many of the property rights to the land, legal as well as illegal, were passed from hand to hand and the number of those who in good faith were holding rural real estate by titles that were either completely fraudulent or of dubious legality came to be considerable. In an attempt to correct this chaotic condition the King issued in 1591 the famous *Cédulas del Pardo* which put into effect a *composición de tierras*, or a regularization of claims to land, which in effect amounted to a genuine agrarian reform.

The exact text of the terms of this composición, in a fairly literal translation, is as follows.

All of the land that is being held without just and legal titles shall be restored to Us, so that in our hands and belonging to Us, and reserving the portions that appear to Us, or to the viceroys, judges and governors to be needed for town plots, *ejidos, propios,* pastures, and public domain for the places and Councils that are established, both with reference to their present condition and looking forward to the growth they may have, and dividing among the Indians that which is necessary for fields, plantings, and pastures, and confirming to them that which they now hold, all the other lands shall be or are free of any restrictions for Us to grant and dispose of according to Our wishes. Accordingly We command and order the Viceroys and the Presidents of the Audiencias that, at their convenience they fix the dates during which the landholders shall exhibit to them, and to the ministers of the Audiencias which they shall nominate, the titles to the lands, *estancias, chacras* and *caballerías;* and confirming the titles of those with valid deeds or just claims, the remainder shall be returned and restored to Us to dispose of according to Our pleasure.[1]

It may be, of course, that in some of the Spanish colonies the composición or agrarian reform decreed during the closing years of the sixteenth century remained merely as a dead letter. This, though, definitely was not the case in the New Kingdom of Granada in which the Cédula del Pardo sent out in 1591 created "a general state of inquietude." With respect to local events, rumors, and scares in Bogotá during the period in which the composición came to bear upon the lives of the powerful families residing in that city and others throughout the territory that is now Colombia, we have the words of the chronicler Juan Rodríguez Freile who has left us a fairly detailed account of most of the scandals that took place in the capital during the years 1539 to 1636. Very bitter indeed are his criticisms of the government of Dr. Antonio González who was governor from 1589 to 1597. Despite the professions of Rodríguez ("It is not for me to judge if he did good or evil"), among the charges he made we encounter the following: "That which he did was to extract from this Kingdom more than 200,000 pesos of gold from the composiciones of estancias and encomiendas of Indians, but this was of the royal accounts, and we do not need to deal with it."[2]

It would appear that there were few lasting effects of this first agrarian reform in those portions of the Spanish dominions that now make up the Republic of Colombia. The members of the few power-

1. *Recopilación de las Leyes de las Indias,* Libro IV, Título XII, Ley XIV.
2. Rodríguez, Freile, *El Carnero,* p. 166.

ful families continued taking for themselves those extensive portions of the best land which they desired, whereas the Indians and mestizos, that is the humble elements that made up the great mass of the population, had to retreat back into the rugged ravines and up on the steep slopes of the mountains in order to find small acreage of land which they could use for the production of the subsistence crops upon which their lives depended. In this connection, in order to avoid unnecessary repetition, permit us to refer the reader once again to the words of one of the last of the viceroys, who also was an archbishop, who provided the description of affairs as they were at the end of his stewardship in 1789 which we have quoted already on pages 193-94. Also pertinent at this place is an indication of the fact that some of the religious orders, and especially the Jesuits, were responsible for the formation and perpetuation of many of what were and what continue to be the most extensive latifundia in Colombia. Data available indicate that the Jesuits alone, prior to their expulsion in 1767, brought together in more than 100 huge haciendas a very substantial share of the best located and most fertile land in Colombia.[3] Personally I have had the privilege of observing the effects of the high degree of concentration in the ownership and control of the land in many parts of Colombia; and I have studied with intense interest the life histories of some of the most famous of the haciendas, such as that of Tena, famous barony which once was the property of Bolívar and Santander, whose 400-year history is referred to elsewhere in this volume. But of all the available facts relative to what the large estates have done to Colombian society, almost from the beginning, and continuing to the present, perhaps those given by two of the long list of reputable authorities are most deserving of emphasis. One of these, Antonio Manso, who reported upon his stewardship as President of the New Kingdom of Granada in 1727, has already been presented in translation (see pp. 60-61); and the second, one of the Colombian intellectuals who did the most to help usher in the modern era, is as follows.

One of things of which, as a reformer, I am most proud is my contribution in the Assembly of Antioquia towards the annulment of the police ordinance by virtue of which a laborer could be compelled by the authorities to repay through work for a patrón advances of money or goods the worker had received, which is the equivalent of servitude enforced by means of the law. But I am not sure that in all parts of Colombia comparable steps have been taken, and only a

3. Cf. Borda, *Historia de la Compañía de Jesús en la Nueva Granada,* II, 126-40.

short time ago haciendas in the Department of Bolívar were sold in which the price paid included the peons who had been reduced to servitude through the advancement of money and goods. In a study of the ramifications of the social vice of giving and receiving credit, one must not omit these data, which indicate that a part of the people in the class of directors [i.e. the upper or elite class] use indebtedness as a means of enslaving the ignorant.[4]

The preceding paragraph, and many others like it found in this volume, make it evident that little or no improvement in the distribution of ownership and control of the land in Colombia resulted from the acquisition of independence from Spain. The policies of the Republic in all related to this critically important matter differed little if at all from those of the monarchy it replaced. Tremendous expanses of the public domain were divided among the military chieftains to augment the latifundia established during Colonial times by the feudal concessions of the Republic. All of the region between the Cauca and the Atrato rivers, for example, fell into the hands of a few wealthy men, and in Antioquia the entire district located between the Rio Pozo and the Rio Chinchiná was the property of one person. As has been pointed out by Ramón Franco R., the virgin forest was preserved intact while the cultivated land was insufficient to support the population.[5] Moreover, in contrast with the subdivision among the soldiers who fought in the American Revolution of the huge estates confiscated from the United Empire Loyalists of New York, a reform which did much to implant family-sized farms in the northern part of the United States, in Colombia the immense haciendas confiscated from the Royalists were conserved intact. Moreover many of the extensive landholdings in what is now Colombia were possessed by men who led the revolt against Spain, so naturally there was no thought of taking over any parts of their estates, as likewise was the case in the southern part of the United States where most of the planter class including men such as George Washington and Thomas Jefferson fought and worked to the limit in the cause of independence. It is this high degree of concentration and control of the land, and the social system based upon it which is analyzed in Chapter 2, that contemporary Colombian society, or at least constantly growing segments of it, is attempting to change by means of an agrarian reform. Perhaps to an even greater degree than many of its proponents real-

4. López, *Problemas Colombianos,* pp. 100-101.
5. *Antropogeografía Colombiana,* p. 178.

ize, in order to achieve the reform envisioned almost a completely different rural social system must come into operation, with its components rooted in the laws, in customary behavior patterns, in the socio-cultural values which give meaning to the society and prescribe its acceptable modes of conduct, in the types of thinking on the part of its intellectuals, and in its economy. This is to say that the genuine agrarian reform involves revolutionary changes in the socio-economic, legal, intellectual, and technological orders.

Today throughout Latin America, and particularly in Colombia, the texts of the laws and proposed laws governing agrarian reform are replete with propositions for developing and strengthening agriculturists of the middle social class, i.e. owner-operators of family-sized farms. On this point the Colombian *Ley de Reforma Agraria Social* of 1961 (Law 135) in Article 50 is specific in indicating that such a family-sized farm, or *unidad agrícola familiar,* is one which "meets the following conditions."

> (a) that the size of the tract, in accordance with the nature of the zone, the type of soils, waters, location, relief, and possible nature of crops shall be sufficient, if utilized with a reasonable degree of efficiency, to provide to a normal family an income sufficient to cover its living expenses, to meet the payments on the purchase or improvement of the land, if this is involved, and to permit the progressive improvement of the dwelling, the farm equipment, and the general level of living;
>
> (b) that the said extension normally shall not require for its use with reasonable efficiency more labor than that of the proprietor and his family. It is understood, though, that this last regulation is not incompatible with the employment of extra labor during certain periods of the agricultural work, if the nature of the farming operations makes it necessary, nor with mutual aid through which neighbors may help one another with specific tasks.[6]

It would be difficult for anyone to specify more adequately the fundamental criteria which differentiate family-sized farms from other agricultural units. Nevertheless it is necessary to emphasize that when the day comes in which the operators of family-sized farms and the members of their families constitute the bulk of these who live from agriculture in Colombia, a fundamental change in the dominant rural social system will have taken place, a change reminiscent in many ways of the one that actually occurred in Denmark more than a cen-

6. For the complete text of this law, see Morales Benítez, *Reforma Agraria,* pp. CDVII-CDXLV.

tury ago. Based upon the analysis given in Chapter 2, one can indicate with some degree of confidence that the following will all be involved: (1) a change in the system of social stratification that will make the importance of the middle sectors of the class structure much greater than they are today; (2) a speeding up of the currents of vertical social mobility, so as to carry far more people up, and also down, the social scale; (3) a substantial reduction in the caste element; (4) a type of education and work that will add immensely to the ability of rural Colombians to adapt to new situations, i.e., a huge increase in the general level of intelligence; (5) a transformation revolutionary in the extent to which the average person engaged in farm and pastoral activities is capable of carrying on proprietary and managerial functions as well as those of the more creature-like activities of the agricultural laborer; (6) the development almost to the point of obsession on the part of the farmers of a search for improved and more efficient ways of organizing and carrying on the multifarious activities involved in farming; (7) the replacement of order-and-obey types of personal relationships in the rural districts by those of an equalitarian nature; (8) the attainment of norms and values in which manual labor is considered as honorable and dignifying; (9) the accomplishment of a huge increase in the average level of living; (10) the establishment of a situation in which the typical head of a farm family is motivated to spend every available hour, and to encourage and direct the members of his family to do likewise, in the extremely diverse activities involved in building up the farm, its buildings, and equipment, and in improving the home and its surroundings; and (11) the promotion of habits of thrift and saving on the part of the bulk of the farm families.

INDICATORS OF THE NEED FOR AGRARIAN REFORM

The changes in the nature of the socio-cultural values which make an agrarian reform necessary already are well advanced in Colombia. From an examination of the sources which it has been feasible to consult, it would seem that the distinguished intellectual Salvador Camacho Roldán was the great forerunner or herald of agrarian reform in the country he loved so passionately, just as he appears to have been the one to introduce the subject of sociology to his countrymen. Be this as it may, well before the close of the nineteenth century he not only was calling the attention of Colombia's landed gentry to the deplorable conditions of her agriculture, in the address to the inaugural session of the Colombian Agricultural Society (from which we have quoted in Chapter 5), but he was also propagating from Bogotá conclusions and generalizations of the most comprehensive and penetrating nature which he had arrived at on the basis of his own extensive travels and omnivorous reading. In one of his publications we find the prototype of the system of rural social organization he dreamed of bringing to Colombia, one demanding a drastic agrarian reform, a most cogent statement of the need for agrarian reform, described and evaluated as follows.

Among the causes of the prosperity of Anglo-Saxon America I consider the principal one to be the system adopted from the beginning for the distribution of the public lands in small allotments, which put within reach of the worker this primary element of all riches, the first condition of independence and of personal dignity among men, and the indispensable basis of political equality, without which republican forms are a fraud. This system and the institution of the Homestead Law, which established the cultivation of the land by the worker as the only way of acquiring the ownership of land and which assured its possession by the family, has given an enormous stimulus to labor of the proletarian classes; it has completely changed the conditions of ancient social organization, which placed the land in the hands of a few privileged persons; it has established imperishable bases for democracy; it has founded upon general participation the most perfect cooperation between those involved; it has cheapened the price of the means of subsistence; it has been a powerful attraction to immigrants from other countries; it has given the incentive for the construction of a vast net of railways; it has sustained the demand for domestically manufactured goods; and it has created in all parts new articles for international trade.

Indeed, what, if not the hunger to acquire the ownership of land, has attracted this enormous current of American and European migrants to populate the solitudes of the West and to found these new and powerful States in the Valley of the Mississippi? What, if not the demand created by the extremely numerous and well-to-do *farmers* of these new regions, supports and sustains New England's mills for manufacturing textiles of cotton and wool, machinery, and agricultural implements? Who, if not these four or five million small owners, collect in their harvests these hundreds of millions of loads of corn and wheat and fatten each year these forty million hogs, and care for and milk these sixteen million milk cows, the products that make up two thirds of the food of the American people and two thirds of the articles exported? And where, if not in the Mississippi Valley, among these virile cultivators of the soil, were first organized the hundreds of regiments of volunteers who, under the command of Grant, Sherman, Sheridan, and Thomas, gave the stroke of death to the slave-holding Confederacy at Mill Springs, Fort Donaldson, Vicksburg, Pittsburg Landing, Chattanooga, and Nashville? Is not the aspiration to become owner of a small piece of land [to the members of Colombia's elite, landowning class whose system of large estates and system of rural social organization he was challenging, a Midwestern farm of 160-320 acres was "a small piece of land"], to become free of the *rack-rent,* of the ever-increasing rent of the already monopolized lands of Europe, the principal thing which leads the English, Irish, and German cultivators to abandon their homes in numbers of more than half a million per year in search of security and dignity in the American prairies? Is not the competition of millions of those who sell the foodstuffs that which, by lowering the prices of these, makes life easy, cheap, and abundant in these regions?

The large mass of owners of small farms, established principally in the West, today dominates the elections in this Republic and maintains the equilibrium between the semi-feudal ideas of the large proprietors of the South, the aristocratic tastes of the wealthy owners of factories in New England, and the magnates of speculation in the central States of New York, Pennsylvania, and New Jersey.[7]

After presenting more facts relative to the effects of the family-sized farm in the United States, in an analysis that in no way can be thought to suffer in comparison with that given by the celebrated Alexander de Toqueville, author of the much cited *Democracy in America,* the perceptive Colombian author, whose instructive words we are attempting to rescue from the oblivion in which they have rested for almost a century, sought to drive home the significance of his observations for those genuinely concerned about the general welfare of the society of which he formed a distinguished part. Few more cogent paragraphs about the need for agrarian reform in Colombia and other parts of Latin America, not to mention other immense parts of the earth's surface, have been written, and we offer some of them in translation.

Thus, it is in the United States that one best can study the change that the nineteenth century is beginning to bring about in the conditions of the collective life of the people. The ancient world was the kingdom of privilege, of the shameful exploitation of the multitudes in favor of the few; of the luxury of the aristocrats amidst the destitution and misery of the masses. In the French Revolution there arose, alongside the nobility and the clergy, the Third Estate, into whose composition entered the manufacturers, the merchants, those in the liberal professions, and the scholars and writers; at the present time the Fourth Estate is already surging forward in the form of the

7. Camacho Roldán, *Notas de Viaje,* pp. 677-79.

body of artisans and laborers who have received the right to vote in elections. In the United States, in 1880, of nine million of those who cultivated the soil, nearly five million were landowners and barely four million were agricultural wage hands. In this shines forth, therefore, the aurora of the redemption of the oppressed. Those who were previously slaves hitched to the ball and chain, later serfs of the glebe, and still later sharecroppers, have already begun to be the owners of the land which they water with the sweat of their brows. And this transformation is not as a result of the blood of martyrs, nor by means of a violent convulsion of the social structure with a promise of order and peace, but through the slow and sure action, peaceful but victorious, of the best type of human social organization.

Of all the grandeurs that I had the opportunity to see during my rapid trip through the heart of that country, none appeared to me so great as this social fact, because the independence, the liberty, and the equality of men does not consist in mere words written as a promise in the political constitutions, but in true and tangible facts which place men on the road to redemption. How can anyone consider as a *free man* the one who for his subsistence and that of his family is dependent upon the will of a landlord? Can there ever be equality between a wage hand and his patrón? More fearful than the tyranny of men is the tyranny of things, and this result of the functioning of an institution suffices for the understanding of the difference which should exist between peoples who have their historical point of departure in the feudal control of the land and those who have sought to establish themselves by means of an equitable distribution of this primary basis of production in proportion to its occupants' capacity to work. . . .

Moreover, one cannot deny that the concentration of the ownership of the land in a few hands is an instrument for concentrating wealth among the smallest number of producers; this leads to the development of luxury, of artificial pleasures, and of vices among the few and the degradation of the others, all of which results in the creation of useless riches, since they are not employed in the satisfaction of true necessities. As between better production and better distribution of the riches, the moralist and even the economist always favor the latter. For my own part, in summary, I believe the principal problem of modern societies consists in seeking, through natural means, the elimination of unjust institutions and better distribution among the producers of the values created by production.[8]

During the years in which the ideas germinated in the keen mind of Salvador Camacho Roldán were permeating the clubs and coffee shops frequented by the socially elite of Colombian society, the ideal of a rural social system based on family-sized farms was gaining

8. *Ibid.*, 680-83.

strength[9] and the humble rural masses of the country were beginning to become aware of their rights under the constitution. Above all they began to become aware that they were free to take possession of unoccupied portions of the public domain and, through hard work at the tasks of clearing and cultivating the land, gain property rights to the small plots they were occupying. Especially in Antioquia and Caldas, with small farms devoted to coffee culture, such spontaneous colonization activities greatly augmented the number and importance of owner-operators and added tremendously to the productivity, particularly that for commercial purposes, of Colombia's agriculture.[10] But these important developments took place in parts of the Republic in which the aborigines had been decimated early in the colonial period, so that the lands involved were entirely vacant and unoccupied. In many other parts of the nation the lands were claimed and used, or, even though covered only by virgin forests, figured as parts of the domains held legally or illegally by the powerful landowning families. Moreover, as generally was the case throughout Latin America, the lack of any systematic procedures for the surveying and deeding of the land being transferred from public to private ownership made it impossible for either the settler or the government to determine which areas were part of the public domain and which had previously been alienated. Confronted with this chaotic condition, which has been discussed at some length in Chapter 4, and propelled by a rapidly increasing rural population, numerous families of lower-class status formed the habit of entering upon and taking possession of any unoccupied territory, irrespective of whether it belonged to the government or was claimed as private property, as the sites on which to build their modest homes and plant the subsistence crops on which they lived. Thus very rapidly, especially during the first decades of the twentieth century, there was the development of the so-called colono problem, or the invasion of the haciendas by the members of the lower social class. With the invasions and subsequently the expulsions by the large landowners and their allies, especially the officials of the local governmental units, came the resort to legal measures that have been described in Chapter 3. This was nothing more or less than a head-on collision between the two greatest forces in the na-

9. Perhaps no better account of the vicissitudes of the kaleidoscope of Colombia's history during Camacho Roldán's lifetime is to be found than the biography of his father written by Phanor J. Eder. See his *El Fundador*.

10. Cf. Franco R., pp. 178-79, *passim;* and Parsons, *Antioqueño Colonization in Western Colombia,* pp. 67-101.

tion. The powerful families who long had controlled the land, the financial resources, the government, and all other aspects of the society were colliding with the rapidly increasing masses.

With the awakening to the facts that the nation needed a drastic change in its procedures for surveying and conveying titles to the land and in making access to public lands more available to the campesinos came the upsurge of a tremendous wave of discontent and agitation during the years 1930-36. As early as 1926 there were suits before the supreme court of Colombia between campesinos and large landowners over the rights to the portions of the haciendas that had been occupied by the colonos or squatters. On the 26th of May, 1934, this high court handed down a decision which held that in all having to do with the property rights to land which the settlers claimed belonged to the public domain and their adversaries maintained was privately owned, the proof that the land in question had actually been alienated from the dominion of the state should consist solely of "the original deed which demonstrates precisely the exact manner" in which the rights had been transferred.[11] The effects of this, as indicated explicitly in the quotation from Dr. Guillermo Amaya Ramírez given in Chapter 3, were times of tumult in the countryside.

The dimensions of the problem of monopolization of the land, the recognition of which played an important role in bringing about a widespread awareness of the need for substantial agrarian reform in Colombia, were brought out in the course of the investigations launched by the Ministerio Público. These showed, for example, that in 1933 "a surprisingly large area of the public domain has illegally been appropriated by individuals, who, with no legitimate papers have usurped it from the dominions of the state, and this has made it necessary for the Government to authorize the Ministerio Público to initiate suits for surveys and proof of ownership in various regions of the country. In the departments of Cundinamarca and Tolima alone . . . the authorizations for such suits against those illegally holding parts of the patrimony of the state involves areas of approximately five hundred thousand (500,000) hectares.[12]

The degree to which the attention of many of the higher governmental officials was being called to the necessity of substantial efforts

11. Cf. Carvajalino, "Informe del Jefe de la Sección de Tierras," in Restrepo, *Memoria del Ministro de Agricultura y Comercio*, II, 117.

12. Francisco José Chaux, "Exposiciones de Motivos del Proyecto de Ley 'Sobre Posesión de Tierras,'" in Martínez E., compiler, *Régimen de Tierras en Colombia*, I, 73.

to better the lives of the campesinos also is evident from other of the words of the same authority.

> In many parts of the country, and especially in Cundinamarca, Tolima, Boyacá, and Magdalena, the interference of land titles has brought about the formation of huge latifundia in which are found a mass of laborers subjected to the despotism of an economy of minimum production of things immediately consumable and with no margin of saving, persons who lack rights to the soil which nourishes them, who never secure permanent homes for their families, and who instead of being factors for the creation of riches are foci of social unrest. If for a long time these masses have remained quiet, often submitted to the ignominious regimes of work, condemned to eternal indigence, the increase of their numbers and the awakening of their collective conscience have now torn them from that submission and have inspired them to an anguished and urgent demand for land. This contributes in no small measure to the grave situation of misery which has precipitated the present crisis, for it should not be forgotten that their only means of subsistence is the cultivation of the soil.[13]

Amid this chaotic condition in the relationships between man and the land and the general state of unrest in the countryside, Alfonso López was elected as president of Colombia with a program of action which many considered as extremely radical. Be this as it may, López was convinced that substantial changes in the welfare of the campesinos were necessary, and he believed that much of this could be accomplished by means of a law that would bring order into the possession and ownership of the land. His objectives in this aspect of his administration are well stated in his 1935 presidential message to the congress:

> Technically, then, we are faced with the juridical alternatives of turning the nation to a socialist orientation or of revalidating the deeds to private property by purifying them of their imperfections. The Government has chosen the second course. The project of the land law has no purposes other than to strengthen property rights, organizing them on the basis of principles of justice, and of resolving the conflicts which have grown out of the vagueness of existing titles. . . .
>
> Some landowners when confronted with the agitation, often justified, sometimes unjust, but understandable, have solicited from the state armed forces of public order to clear the title to the property or even the land itself from the dangerous ideas. The law provides for this to be given in accordance with the decisions of the judges and makes the alcalde the agent of reaction. The eviction notice should

13. *Ibid.*, pp. 53-54.

be followed by the machine gun to prevent resistance. My Government serves notice that this is not its criteria, neither with respect to the evicted campesino nor with respect to the squatter who has invaded uncultivated lands supposing them to be in the public domain [. . .]. But the present administration does not wish to prolong an intermediate condition that would be harmful to the national economy. Property should be guaranteed in its use—not in its abuse—so that it will fulfill its social and economic function. In a country such as ours landownership should be acquired by two titles, whose provisions and limits should be established by law: by labor and by public deeds, but without the latter giving endless right to the possession of undeveloped lands. The government wants the law to define how, when, and for what reasons one is a landowner, so as to prevent property being held by usurpers and so as to establish the validity of the titles of the large landowner who is putting his holdings to use and also to clarify those of the colono who, with tremendous energy, wrests from the jungle a plot of land on which to build his home and raise a family.[14]

On the basis of the materials presented above anyone should be able to determine the high degree to which Colombian society has exhibited all of the specific indicators of the need of agrarian reform such as: (1) a high degree of concentration in the ownership and control of the land; (2) latifundismo, i.e., huge extensions of land maintained in idleness; (3) a high proportion of wage hands, peons, and other laborers in the agricultural population; (4) low productivity per worker; (5) low average levels and standards of living; and (6) a system of social stratification dominated by the two-class system, or a small number of elite families at the apex of the socio-economic scale and a huge mass of humble rural people at the very bottom of the range living amid conditions that should hardly be the lot of human beings.[15] Moreover, as indicated in Chapter 3, on the basis of the data gathered in Colombia's first agricultural census taken in 1960, an estimated two-thirds of all the farm families in Colombia are headed by persons who fall in the farm laborer category. Such a percentage alone is an indicator of acute need for substantial agrarian reform.

OBJECTIVES AND METHODS OF AGRARIAN REFORM

In the references above to the proposals of President Alfonso López made during this first term as head of Colombia's government, a beginning was made in the discussion of matters relating to the objec-

14. This part of the Message is reproduced, *ibid.*, pp. 13-18.
15. For a fuller discussion of the principal indicators of the need for agrarian reform, see Smith, *Agrarian Reform in Latin America*, pp. 33-43.

tives and methods of agrarian reform. In 1935, in spite of the fact that the ideas sown by Salvador Camacho Roldán were still in circulation, it was commonly supposed in Colombia that a general law dealing with the ownership and control of the land would put an end to most of the problems arising from the illegal monopolization of lands belonging in the public domain, those growing out of the invasions of the haciendas, the lack of land for the vast majority of the campesinos, and many other difficulties of rural life in that country. With the passage and approval of the famous Law 200 of 1936 this method of attempting to better the relationships between man and the land went into effect, and with all impartiality and objectivity one must admit that the results of this legislation were highly beneficial. Little by little the general state of unrest in the countryside began to calm down and it may be that a violent and bloody revolution was avoided. Many of the "social problems," or the so-called problem of colonos, were reduced. In a word, during the first term of President Alfonso López (1934-38) and that of his successor, Eduardo Santos (1938-42) the country was becoming pacified and considerable advances were made in the life and labor of the rural population. These were years in which many haciendas were subdivided, some by the owners themselves and others by various banks and the Ministry of Economy. The organization of the Caja de Crédito Agrario, or Agricultural Credit Corporation, and its work represented an important step in the search for ways and means of improving the general welfare of the rural population.

In spite, though, of the progress in improving rural life which it brought about, the famous Law 200 also created some serious difficulties of which the following deserve special mention: (1) although the law specified that only the economic use of the land was a sufficient basis for establishing the legal presumption that "the lands held by individuals actually are private property and not a part of the public domain," the criteria of such economic use were not defined sufficiently and the judgment was left to the courts; (2) those claiming ownership rights were given a period of ten years in which to demonstrate that they were making economic use of the land; and (3) the doctrines embraced in Law 200 actually came to be another philosophy of ownership which soon came into serious competition and conflict with the traditional system of deeds or titles.[16]

16. On this point, see Smith, "Conflicto de Teorías sobre la Propiedad de la Tierra en Colombia," and "Observations on Land Tenure in Colombia."

With the re-election of Alfonso López as president (1942-45), agrarian reform was given another important impetus. On the basis of the experience they had already obtained, Colombia's leaders were prepared to attempt more advanced measures. The president and his brother, Miguel López Pumarejo, had become convinced that their country never would enjoy a stable and prosperous condition until it had in its rural districts a large and powerful class made up of the owner-operators of family-sized farms, that is of agricultural establishments ranging in size from about 50 to 200 or 300 hectares. I know well the purposes and endeavors of the program of colonization and subdivision of haciendas, or *colonización y parcelación,* undertaken during the period, based upon three years of experience, beginning in 1943, when I served as *asesor técnico* on matters related to these aspects of agrarian reform. During these years the responsibilities and activities of those in the administration constituted no "bed of roses." As is well known, the president was confronted with opposition so strong, on the part of some of the chieftains within his own party as well as from those in the opposition party, that finally in 1945 he resigned the office, only a couple of years before the internal conflict entered into the stage of a genuine and bloody civil war and literal chaos. The general situation with respect to agrarian reform, immediately prior to the rapid degeneration of all that has to do with the security of life and property following the López resignation, is described in the memorandum I prepared immediately before the termination of my work as advisor to the Colombian government. This memorandum, submitted in August, 1944, to Dr. Miguel López Pumarejo, director of the Caja Agraria and to Dr. Justo Díaz Rodríguez, director of the Departamento de Tierras, includes the following paragraphs.

1. *Progress will be slow.* Don't expect too much too soon. I am convinced that at least 25 years jammed full of setbacks, disappointments, and failures or partial failures will have to elapse before Colombia can acquire the experience, train the personnel, and gain sufficient public support for providing the financial assistance necessary for a substantial colonization program. . . .

2. *To strengthen and increase the middle class of agriculturists is the great objective for such colonization efforts.* Any additional efforts to establish colonists on holdings of from 2 to 10 hectares should be heartily discouraged. . . .

3. *Sources of recruits for the middle class.* Colonists with a reasonable chance of becoming middle class farmers may be secured from

two sources. (a) A few of the *campesino* class who have demonstrated the most intelligence, initiative, and industry, successfully may be aided to move up one rung higher on the agricultural ladder. If even a few can make the transition it will serve as a great stimulus to the others. . . . (b) Unless Colombia urbanizes and industrializes very rapidly there will not be room in the upper class for the numerous children which its members are begetting. There seems little reason to predict any widespread adoption, on their part, of the practice of limiting the size of the family. Therefore, a considerable part of the children of present-day, upper-class families probably will have to accept middle-class status. They could contribute greatly to the formation of a genuine class of farmers in Colombia.

4. *Elements involved in the status of a middle class farmer.* The development of a farmer involves a great deal more than taking a man and giving him or selling him 25, 50, or 100 hectares of land. In the personality of the farmer are combined the execution of all three of the basic economic functions, namely, those of the capitalist or entrepreneur, the manager, and the laborer. The farmer's income comes in part as a return to the capital which he has risked in agricultural enterprises, in part as a reward for his managerial activities, and in part as a wage for his labor. In a society where these functions are not commonly combined in one individual it may be very difficult to get them all performed by one person. The *campesino* can perform the labor function with no difficulty, but the most careful selection will be necessary in order to secure the few who can successfully perform the functions of manager and capitalist. The children of the upper class, on the other hand, may have all the necessary habits, skills, and attitudes of the capitalist, and be able to acquire those of the manager, but for them to accept the third indispensable role of the farmer, that of the laborer, may be practically impossible. However, by radical changes in the system of farming and the nature of the farm tasks, by substituting the use of draft animals, the wagon, the plow, and other small farm implements, and even tractors, a much greater part of the necessary labor on the farm may be made socially acceptable.[17]

The years 1947-58 were among the most difficult and bloody periods in the entire history of Colombia as a nation. Fighting within the pueblos, conflicts between pueblos, regional battles, all figured in a wave of violence and civil war which affected nearly all parts of the republic.[18] For this reason it is not strange that matters relating to

17. In addition to the publication of the Spanish version of this memorandum in *El Tiempo* and other Colombian newspapers during August, 1944, the Spanish text is available in Smith, *Sociología Rural*, pp. 83-87; and the English text in Smith, "Colonization and Settlement in Colombia."

18. The most substantial work dealing with this epoch of great political and administrative instability is Guzmán Campos, Fals-Borda, and Umaña Luna, *La Violencia en Colombia.*

agrarian reform were more or less paralyzed during this difficult period. Nevertheless, during the years in which "la violencia" more properly might have been designated as a civil war a few important studies were made of some of the problems of development, with some sections closely related to ways and means of improving the life and labor of the rural population.[19] With the formation of the Government of National Union and the selection of Alberto Lleras Carmago as president in 1958, a great impetus was given to a genuine agrarian reform as a measure for recovery and development. At this time all sectors of the population were enthused with the idea of achieving substantial changes in the relationships of man to the land such as improving the system of land tenure, achieving a better distribution of the ownership and control of the land, improving the system of agriculture, and carrying on a substantial program of community development. Various projects were debated at length in the national congress, in the universities, in the newspapers in all parts of the republic, over the radio, and above all in the small, daily gatherings in the coffee shops, the clubs, the bars, and even in family circles. As a result when in December, 1961, Law 135 (*Sobre Reforma Agraria Social*) was signed and became official it represented, to an exceptional degree, the consensus of thinking of all sectors of public opinion.

The objectives of this legislation are very clear, and the best way to express them seems to be to present in translation the six propositions given in Chapter I of the Law.

> *First.* To reform the agrarian social structure through procedures designed to eliminate and prevent the inequitable concentration of property in land or its subdivision into uneconomic units; to reconstitute adequate units of cultivation in the zones of minifundia and to provide lands to those who lack them, with preference being given to those who will utilize them directly through the use of their own personal labor.
>
> *Second.* To promote the adequate economic use of unused or deficiently used lands, by means of programs designed to secure their well-balanced distribution and rational utilization.
>
> *Third.* To increase the total volume of agricultural and livestock products in harmony with the development of other sectors of the economy; to increase the productivity of the farms by the application of appropriate techniques; and to endeavor to have the lands used in the way that is best suited to their locations and characteristics.

19. Especially deserving of mention in this connection are the following: Currie, *et al.*; Fals-Borda, *El Hombre y la Tierra en Boyacá;* and Lebret, *et al., Estudio sobre las Condiciones del Desarrollo en Colombia.*

Fourth. To create the conditions under which the small tenants and sharecroppers shall enjoy greater guarantees, and they as well as the wage hands shall have less difficult access to landownership.

Fifth. To elevate the level of living of the rural population, as a consequence of the measures already indicated and also through the coordination and promotion of services related to technical assistance, agricultural credit, housing, the organization of markets, health and social security, the storage and preservation of products, and the promotion of cooperatives.

Sixth. To insure the conservation, defense, improvement, and adequate utilization of the natural resources.

In order to put into effect the objectives of its agrarian reform law, the government of Colombia organized the Instituto Colombiano de la Reforma Agraria (INCORA); and this Institute, in turn, has developed its program of action along the following lines.[20]

The Administration of the Public Domain.—Because of the long continued state of chaos in all having to do with unalienated public lands, there are many possibilities for bringing about substantial improvements in rural life in Colombia merely by developing and putting into effect adequate measures for the adjudication, surveying, giving titles to, and even determining which lands still belong to the public domain. It would seem that the number of adjudications made is on the increase, although the total area involved appears to be less than was the case a few years ago. This probably indicates better control of the illegal usurpation of public lands. Nevertheless, there seems to be a general obliviousness to the great need which Colombia has for a systematic plan for the survey and alienation of the public domain and for distributing among actual settlers the huge areas presently being held in ways that are contrary to the provisions of Law 200 of 1936. Today the necessity of a general ordinance that will institute system and order into the occupation and survey of these public lands seems to be just as great as it was in 1944, when the project for such a law was presented to the Congress, before the civil war and violence put a halt to parliamentary procedures, or in 1958, after the Congress was reconstituted, when it was presented for the second time.[21]

Extinction of Private Claims to Ownership.—This part of the program has to do with carrying through some of the principal provisions of Law 200 of 1936. On the basis of its survey of the holdings

20. For another general view of the backgrounds and program of agrarian reform in Colombia, see Hirschman, *Journeys Toward Progress,* Chap. II.

21. For the text of the proposed law, see Chapter 4.

of more than 2,000 hectares in size, the Institute calculated that the number of such large holdings came to 1,238; and from information supplied by the proprietors of the same the officials of the Institute found that places of this size included a total of 7,408,908 hectares. However, of the huge expanses of territory included within the claims of these large landowners only "2,840,347 hectares were cultivated and there were 4,568,561 hectares without any use whatsoever."[22] In 1961 and 1962 the Institute initiated 108 suits for the extinctions of claims to land covering an area of 1,128,735 hectares, but the high proportion (62 per cent) of land "in a condition of economic abandonment . . . is sufficiently indicative of the urgency that exists for the application with full force of the rules for the extinction of private claims, and this is even more the case if one considers that actually these figures suffer from understatements of amounts of unused land, since it is natural to presume that in many cases the proprietors have over-stated the quantities actually being used."[23]

Subdivision Programs.—By means of its subdivision activities the Institute is attempting to comply with its obligation to establish family-sized farms for the landless campesinos. By the end of 1962 in this line of work there had been approved "nine subdivision projects, in the departments of Bolívar, Córdoba, Norte de Santander, Tolima (in three locations), El Valle, Nariño, and Atlántico. These projects involve plans for the subdivision of 200,000 hectares and the establishment on farms of 15,000 agricultural families."[24]

Colonization Programs.—In its activities the Institute is giving preference to subdivision projects and not to the very costly official colonization projects. Nevertheless the process of undirected or spontaneous settlement or colonization is taking place on such a large scale that it commands the attention of those charged with the administration of the agrarian reform program. "As yet exact data are lacking, but it is estimated that presently there are between 80,000 and 100,-000 families engaged in spontaneous colonization activities in various parts of the country. But unfortunately the economic debility of these campesinos obliges them, after they 'have felled the forest and begun the raising of crops, to sell their improvements to other persons possessed of greater resources.' "[25] This process of spontaneous coloniza-

22. Peñalosa Camargo, *et al.*, p. 41.
23. *Ibid.*
24. *Ibid.*, p. 9.
25. *Ibid.*, p. 43.

Small, scattered farmsteads on one of the earliest private colonization projects. (Photo by the author.)

tion has been going on in Colombia for a long while, and measures to correct its deficiencies are still being awaited.

In conclusion, it should be indicated that the current program of agrarian reform in Colombia is new and surely with the passage of time the methods used will be amplified and improved. The day may come in which the nation will be prepared to use a strong and graduated tax upon the land so as to put an end to the problem of latifundismo (or that of huge expanses of land maintained in idleness), to terminate the situation in which the ownership of land is an asylum for capital, and to obtain the funds that are essential for realistic programs of community development. In the years to come Colombia may decide to limit the amount of land that may be owned by one person or by one family; it even is possible that in the future we may be able to observe in that country adequate systems of elementary education and the training in secondary schools of youths who are interested in farming, substantial efforts to prepare farmers to exercise the managerial functions, and thoroughgoing endeavors to improve the methods used in extracting products from the soil. In any case the activities of Colombia in all that has to do with agrarian reform between now and 1975 should be very interesting to observe.

7

Patterns of Settlement

THERE ARE three principal ways or modes of arranging the agricultural population on the land, namely, the true agricultural village, single farmsteads, and an intermediate type which may be called the line village.[1] The particular form of settlement in use in any given rural society is one of the most powerful of all the determinants which influence the relations of man to man. The first of the three, the genuine agricultural village, is the type in which the dwellings of the cultivators are grouped together in a cluster apart from the arable lands. In order to cultivate the soil and care for the crops the agriculturists must commute daily to their fields. This pattern of settlement is the one which is most prevalent in the world today and the one which has conditioned the behavior of the bulk of the world's cultivators ever since recorded history began. The second type, typified by single, scattered, or isolated farmsteads, is one in which the homes of the farmers are scattered about over the landscape, each on the particular tract of land cultivated by the family. This form of settlement is dominant in the United States, and is looked upon generally by our population as the "natural" arrangement. The third, the line village, resembles the true village in that there is a grouping of the homes of the cultivators, usually achieved by a system of surveying the land which makes the length of the holdings large in comparison with their width. It differs from the true village in that each farm family lives on the tract of land that it cultivates. This third type of settlement combines most of the social advantages and the efficiency in transportation and communication which characterize the village pattern with the economies in farm management which are the principal advantage of the single-farmstead form of settlement. It reaches its own maximum efficiency in well-planned communities such as the Jews recently have established in Israel, settlements in which the basic line of departure is a circular street enclosing a central park or plaza. Around this are the homes of the farmers, each at the narrow front of

1. Cf. Smith, *The Sociology of Rural Life,* pp. 201-16.

a wedge-shaped holding which runs back from the core of the settlement. From the air such a settlement resembles a huge wheel on which the nucleus of houses makes up the hub and the dividing lines between the separate holdings are the spokes.[2]

Most large countries know all three of these types of settlement, and Colombia is no exception to the rule. However, in spite of the fact that the agricultural village was in use by the large sedentary Indian population which occupied most of the presently inhabited por-

Minifundia and scattered-farmstead settlement pattern, department of Nariño. (Courtesy of L. Eduardo Montero.)

tion of Colombia at the time the Spaniards arrived, and although the Spaniards themselves in the mother country were mostly settled in the village manner, the agricultural village is not the predominant form in which the population of Colombia is arranged on the land. One who has been accustomed to thinking of Spanish America as a land of agricultural villages (familiarity with the Mexican scene is probably largely responsible for this idea) is rudely shocked when he visits Colombia and observes the great extent to which the agricultural population is scattered over the land on tiny single farmsteads.

2. For an excellent aerial view of one of these settlements, see *ibid.*, p. 215.

CONTEMPORARY PATTERNS

In present-day Colombia, scattered farmsteads are by far the most prevalent manner of arranging the agricultural population on the land; village settlements are a poor second; and line villages are found only in a few scattered localities. In sketching the facts relative to the importance and distribution of each of these types, it is economical of time and space to give the details about the villages and line villages, since the great bulk of the country is occupied by scattered farmsteads.

Village Settlements.—Only a few remnants of the once dominant village manner of settlement survive in Colombia. One group of these are the workers' villages which are present on the large sugar plantations in the Cauca Valley and on the northern coastal plains. As is generally the case in sugar plantations throughout the world, the cottages or huts of those who do the manual labor in the production and processing of the sugar cane are grouped together in a village or hamlet in close proximity to the sugar mill. Since the cultivators live apart from the land on which they work, these settlements are of the village type,[3] although the other man-land relationships make them vastly different from village communities composed of freeholders. They are not very numerous, and play a relatively unimportant part in the social and economic affairs of the rural masses.

A few of the largest coffee fincas still retain the nucleated villages as locations for the humble dwellings of their campesinos, a pattern which seems to have been much more general before the abolition of slavery. But today in Colombia, coffee farming as a rule is not on a scale that permits the workers' villages or hamlets to attain any considerable size. Therefore one finds comparatively few coffee fincas which even remotely resemble the large coffee fazendas in Brazil on which the "colonies" for the workers are such prominent features. But that such estates were once fairly prevalent is indicated by the following description and generalization by Lieutenant Richard Bache who visited Colombia during the closing years of the struggle for independence:

> Estanques is a fine hacienda, owned by some gentlemen of Bogotá. It is situated in a narrow valley, traversed by a creek, which is so

3. Says one observer of La Manuelita, noted sugar plantation near Cali: "Immediately without the wall surrounding the house is the *peon* village consisting of some fifty-odd houses of uniform size and appearance, and the sugar-factory." Miller, *In the Wilds of South America,* p. 15.

remarkably serpentine that we crossed it twenty or thirty times in the course of an hour. The coffee and cacao plants are protected by majestic shade-trees, which give to the cultivated part the appearance of a venerable forest. . . .

The village consists of the mansion-house, at present occupied by the overseer, and the huts of the slaves, who are almost all females; the men, probably, having joined the army. It also contains a large church, but has no resident priest; the service being occasionally performed by one from a neighbouring town. . . .

This distinction [i.e., "sociable animals"] is possessed by the Colombians, in an eminent degree. High and low, rich and poor, are alike unable to dispense with society. For this reason, the whole population is collected into towns and villages. In passing from one to another, you invariably cross a desert, and step at once from the haunts of wild beasts, to those of men.[4]

In some of the more out-of-the-way portions of Colombia are to be found genuine village communities of small freeholders or squatters. I have visited a few of these in various sections of the country. They are not uncommon in parts of Magdalena, especially in the isolated tracts of coastal plain at the base of the Santa Marta Mountains near the little port of Rio Hacha. One of those which was visited is called Metita. Among the notes made on this occasion are the following: "Rio Hacha, February 10, 1944. We did not hurry about arising because the car was not due until 8:00 A.M. We were at breakfast when the chauffeur reported and placed himself at our orders. He then went to get his breakfast, while we completed ours.

"We bought some canned sausages, bread, and mineral water because we were assured that we could get nothing at Metita. At Kilometer 18 we turned off on a cleared strip which led to the trail called El Camino Real and followed it to Metita. This is a collection of some 60 or 70 wattle-and-daub, thatched-roofed huts, collected together with no semblance of a plan. In them live about 70 families of colored colonos who have rozas in the surrounding area. None of them as yet have title to their little plots of ground, but they were interested and García (Dr. Luis Roberto of the Departamento de Tierras, Ministerio de la Economía Nacional) wrote out a form for them to use in requesting that a commission be sent to make the adjudications.

"They grow corn, pasture, bananas, yuca, etc. Cane and rice are cultivated to some extent, but they do not do well on account of the lack of water for irrigation purposes. No oranges or pineapples

4. *Notes on Colombia Taken in the Years 1822-3.* . . , pp. 189, 191, and 193.

have been planted. Cotton grows wild, as we could easily observe, for it was blowing away because no one was taking the trouble to gather it. Sesame is also said to grow wild hereabouts."

Later on about 12 other similar settlements were visited, and the conclusion was reached that there must be 40 or 50 of them in the area. Notes taken at the time indicate that "all are composed of the wattle-and-daub, thatched-roofed huts of colonos who make their rozas in the surrounding areas. A mud plaster and coat of whitewash makes some of these huts into fairly presentable places. The floors, if any, are of the very crudest tile. These little centers are almost entirely lacking the commercial function—one cannot buy anything, not even a drink of beer, in one of them. This is a sure sign that commerce is nil."

Throughout the northern part of El Valle del Cauca, in the section to the south of Cartago, the village manner of arranging the population on the land has retained considerable importance. However, the actual number of communities involved is not very large; and even here not a few of the cultivators have their houses in the open country amid the fields.

The village form of settlement has persisted to the greatest extent in the southern portions of Colombia, especially in the high mountain valleys of the departamento of Nariño. It is here that the Indian elements in the population have retained the largest proportions of their aboriginal culture, including the village manner of arranging the population on the land. The numerous Indian village communities or resguardos which were established when the encomienda system was abolished, in order that the natives might have a better chance of survival, have held their own in Nariño to a greater extent than anywhere else in Colombia. According to the conclusions of Sergio Elias Ortíz,[5] in all of Colombia it is in Nariño where "the Indians form an ethnic and racial body uncontaminated to any appreciable degree and still subjected to the old Spanish colonial systems in all aspects of life." This authority, one of the greatest in Colombia, also identifies 89 separate and distinct resguardos existing in the departamento in 1935, gives the municipios in which they are located, and the number of hectares belonging to each of them.

In the course of a field trip in February, 1944, I observed that most of these communities retain the village form of settlement. Since more than a dozen of the resguardos or reservations literally have the capi-

5. *Las Comunidades Indígenas de Jamondino y Males.*

tal city of Pasto hemmed in on all sides, it is not difficult to secure some of the most essential facts. The very first day we were in the departamento two of them were visited, at which time the following observations were recorded.

"In Catumbuco there are about 450 men over 21 years of age. The community owns 240 pieces of land, totaling 40 hectares, so that the average size of the plots is only a fraction of an acre. Some of the parcels are allotted to widows. These lands have not been subdivided legally, but they have been distributed by the Cabildo of the Indigenes, and these rights are inherited. If a man dies without heirs his lands revert to the community and are reassigned.

"These pieces are far too small to provide a livelihood to the families, and the Indians must seek work in Pasto or on the haciendas of the area. On the latter they obligate themselves to work for two or three days per week and in return they receive the use of a small piece of land.

"Pau de Aco has 80 families and 52 houses. One of the men could count all of the latter from where we stood conversing with him."

A few days afterwards, in connection with a trip to La Unión, a stop was made at Buesaco, "a small pueblo built along a divide and hemmed in closely on both sides by the lands of a large resguardo. Two hundred families of Indians possess 2,000 hectares of ground in the resguardo. The Indians live in Buesaco, and their plots are redistributed at intervals."

Visits were made to a number of other resguardos in Nariño, including Guachucal, Colima, and Cumbal. Interestingly enough the latter is one in which the Indians live dispersed over the land. Notes taken at the time of the visit include the following: "In Cumbal there is one resguardo and also a large (1,500 hectares) *ejido*. This lies just outside the village and is filled with cattle and sheep. This, too, is in dispute. (Disagreements over the rights in the ejidos were the general rule at the time of our visits.) The Indians say it is theirs; the whites contend that it belongs to the entire community. At present all are making use of it. The resguardo includes some 7,000 indigenes. They say there are 4,000 hectares in the reservation, but this figure is open to suspicion. The indigenes live on their parcels, where they grow wheat, potatoes, and beans. All work is by hand. Each family is said to possess four or five head of cattle, and a few have horses. All the land is in parcels, but there is one hacienda outside the resguardo owned communally by some 60 persons.

"Some of the indigenes work on the haciendas at 40 centavos per day, seco.

"They have an 'escritura' from the king, dated 1758. They decidedly do not want to have the resguardo legally subdivided. Some whites have bought lands from the Indians, but these transactions have never been authorized by the Cabildo. Probably there are as many as 200 cases of this, most of them taking place prior to 1889 and still in dispute. Frequently the defrauding of one heir by another is said to be involved."

Before closing the discussion of the village form of settlement, the rôle of the larger towns and cities as residential centers for those who live from agriculture should be mentioned. Not a few of the upper-class, landowning families have at least two dwellings at their disposal. One of them is in a town or city of some consequence, and the other is on the hacienda. Bogotá itself is the seat of the town houses of large landholders whose estates lie in far distant sections of the Republic; and each of the state capital numbers among its leading citizens hacendados whose lands lie in all parts of the departamento. Some of those upper-class families spend most of their time in the city, and others divide their time more equally between the home on the land and that in the town. But in any case even the largest towns and cities are important as residential centers for families who live from their agricultural enterprises.[6]

The Line Village.—The arrangement whereby farmers reside on their lands and at the same time enjoy the social and economic advantages of village life is found only to a limited extent in Colombia.

6. This state of affairs has been commented upon by a large share of the travelers who have reported upon social relationships in Colombia. For example, the British officer, Colonel J. P. Hamilton (II, 161), wrote as follows: "The population of Bouga, at this time, was computed at between 5000 and 6000 persons; before the civil war it was much more numerous. The canton contains 20,000 souls. Most of the best houses in the town belong to gentlemen who have haciendas in the neighborhood, where they reside for nine months in the year, and the other three at their town residences, following the example of our rich people in England. Christmas is the time when they come to Bouga to enjoy the festivities of the carnival." A young American officer, Lieutenant Richard Bache, who wrote at approximately the same time, generalized as follows: "The same fondness for society, induces the wealthy planter to take up his residence in a city, where, surrounded by numerous servants, lost to productive labour, he follows the bent of his inclinations, to the entire neglect of his own interests, as well as those of his dependents. His plantation, in the meantime, left at the disposal of ignorant, negligent, and dishonest overseers, is but half cultivated; and thus, while undermining his own fortune, he assists in the impoverishment of his country." P. 192. And among the first notes entered

In spite of the fact that the line village form of settlement is ideally adapted to landscapes in which steep escarpments are plentiful and those in which the dependence upon water transportation places a premium upon river frontages, settlements of this type are rarely found in the Republic. But they are not entirely lacking.

It would be difficult to find more perfect examples of the line village than are to be observed along some of the water courses in the central portion of the Magdalena Valley. The flight from Barranquilla to Bogotá, which passes directly over a number of such settlements in the western portions of Magdalena and Santander, gives one an excellent view of an area in which this manner of arranging the farm population on the land has been employed. The long, narrow, ribbon-like holdings, each with the dwelling at the front near the stream in close proximity to houses on the right and the left, are fully as impressive as those which are so characteristic of the St. Lawrence Valley in Canada and the Bayou sections of Louisiana.[7] But they do not cover an extensive area, and few of their counterparts were observed in the other sections of Colombia which I was privileged to visit. However, R. B. Cunninghame Graham has described such settlements along the Sinú River in Bolívar where in some places for mile after mile the straggling settlements form a street on each side of the stream.[8] And Holton commented upon the settlement pattern at Margarita, above Mompos on the Magdalena: "There is no clump of houses, but a long street of many miles, with houses on the west side of it fronting the river, and buried in oranges trees. In the middle of this long succession of ruralities stands the church."[9]

Near Chocontá in Cundinamarca, I observed another example of the line village settlement. It is one in which the homes are strung

---

in my Journal when I began study trips into various sections of the country was the following: "Dr. García explains that in this part of Boyacá almost all the country people of the middle and upper classes have both the house on the land, where the man spends most of his time, and one in the village or town, where the family resides." For reports of similar phenomena in other parts of the *tierra fría* see Ancízar, *Peregrinación de Alpha,* pp. 145-46, *passim.*

7. One of these is probably the settlement mentioned by Steuart, *Bogotá in 1836-7,* p. 71. "We wandered along a small canal or arm of the river for full two miles, through fine cocoa plantations; and the little huts of the possessors, which were scattered thickly along its banks, were the neatest of any I had yet seen."

8. *Cartagena and the Banks of the Sinú,* p. 9.

9. Holton, *New Granada,* p. 64.

along the stream in the valley bottom and the long, narrow plots cut across one side of the valley at right angles and extend far up the steep hillside.

A few notes describing a scene in the southern part of Norte de Santander, on the road to Pamplona, refer to a modified type of the line village such as is fairly prevalent in the deep valleys or canyons in many parts of the country. "After crossing the windswept and bitterly cold páramo of Almorzadero in the early morning we descended to Chitagá for a breakfast of onion soup, arepa, eggs and coffee. From here we followed the river for a while, then crossed it, and began to wind along the sides of some of the most razor-backed divides that I have ever seen. The slopes seem to be at least 45 degrees and most of them are planted with wheat and barley. Many of the habitations resemble a beaded string running along in the bottom, but others are perched in what would appear to be dangerous positions on the side of the mountain. This takes the prize for mountain or hillside agriculture over anything I have seen in Europe or Mexico. The land is not terraced as in Peru, and many of the plots seem to be as steep as loose dirt will lie."

Examples of line village settlements also were observed in other parts of Colombia in quite different situations. Thus in some valleys, such as those around Ubaté in Cundinamarca, the small holdings and the continuous line of farm houses produce a very compact form of the line village arrangement. Another small area of line village settlements is found in the cacao producing section along the Cauca river between Cali and Puerto Tejada. This was visited on November 11, 1943, when the following notes were taken. "We passed down the road through what comes the nearest to being a real line village type of settlement that we have seen so far in Colombia. This is because the small plots of from one to ten fanegadas have been sold to small proprietors. Here they plant an intermingled lot of bananas, coffee, and cacao, with possibly a little maize and yuca. There is not much of the latter, however. The result of having all these small tracts fronting on the road is a line village arrangement, although some of the workers we encountered in the groves, owners of the land, lived in the villages or pueblos."

Single Farmsteads.—By far the most prevalent type of settlement in Colombia is that of the single or scattered farmsteads. Literally hundreds of thousands of these, most of them so small that they deservedly have been given the name of minifundia, are scattered in a

Small, single farmsteads and some aspects of rudimentary plow culture in the uplands of Colombia. (Photos by U. S. Department of Agriculture.)

crazy-quilt pattern over great expanses on the slopes of the Cordilleras, the high mountain valleys, and in much of the lowlands as well. Nothing made a greater impression upon me during my first long trip through the tierras frias north of Bogotá than "the extent to which plots of all shapes cover the sides of the mountains, themselves extremely irregular, fields of a crazy-quilt pattern." And a similar impression continued to force itself into my consciousness in nearly all other sections of the country. Whether it was in the densely populated mountain valleys or the more sparsely inhabited mountain tops of Antioquia and Caldas, along the knife-like divides of the Central Cordillera in Tolima and El Valle, on the steep eastern slope of the eastern range in Cundinamarca or Boyacá, or in the extensive valleys of the Cauca and the Magdalena, the bulk of the agriculturists were found to have their homes scattered about in the fields, quite apart from one another. As section after section of the country was visited, it soon became evident that it was the village and line village settlements that were the exceptions, while scattered farmsteads were the prevailing mode of arranging the population on the land in Colombia. During the course of almost a year and one half spent visiting and working in nearly all sections of the country, I observed thousands of neighborhoods and communities comparable in settlement patterns to the description of La Vega, Cauca, given by one observant natural scientist: "La Vega means 'fertile plain,' and the surrounding country fully justifies the name. Far as the eye could see the gently sloping mountainsides had been divided into a network of small, irregular plots by rows of high, thick hedges. Wheat, corn, cabbage, and rice flourished under the cultivating hand of the Indian; there were also small flocks of sheep, and occasionally a few head of cattle. Small mud-walled huts, singly and in clusters, dotted the maze of green landscape, and over all breathed an air of quiet and contentment."[10]

The case of Tabio, a municipio in which two colleagues and I conducted a detailed social survey, serves to exemplify with concrete data the nature of settlement patterns in Colombia. This municipio, located in one of the small coves that leads off from the Savanna of Bogotá, about 30 miles from the national capital, probably is fairly representative of the average situation in Colombia. The details of the settlement patterns in this municipio are given in the following quotation.

10. Miller, p. 77.

The arrangement of the population on the land in Tabio represents a great departure from the village patterns of settlement which the Spaniards used in Europe, those which they found among the Indians who inhabited the Savanna of Bogotá, and those which they used in all their colonies from New Mexico to Chile. Today, in Tabio and throughout the Savanna, the form of settlement is that of the scattered farmsteads or isolated farms. There remain only a few survivals of the nucleated patterns which once existed. The data gathered in the survey bring this out clearly. Of the 240 farm operators for which the records were sufficiently complete to allow analysis of this feature, only 26, or 11 percent, resided within the village center.

Typical single-family dwelling on the Savanna of Bogotá. (Photo by the author.)

In the open country lived 13 operators of *haciendas* (over 50 fanegadas), 119 operators of fincas (5 to 50 fanegadas), and 87 operators of *parcelas* (less than 5 fanegadas). Furthermore, the process of dividing and redividing the former estates of the original encomenderos among their numerous descendents has gone on without any well-defined rules and regulations until now the small plots have become subdivided in a haphazard manner that makes the isolation of one farm family from another about as great as is physically possible with holdings of the prevailing size.

Nor do the farm laborers live in the village center. In Tabio, as is so generally the case throughout Colombia, the permanent laborers on the haciendas and fincas either own or rent a small piece of ground on the outskirts of the larger farms. The slopes of the mountains surrounding the valley bottoms, whose more fertile soils are monopolized by the *hacendados* for their pastures, are the areas most frequently given over to the laborers as small holdings or as *estancias*. Here they live widely separated from one another, from the *casa grande* of the estate on which they work, and from the religious and market center which forms the seat of the municipio. With proper planning, the holdings of these laboring classes could have been laid off in a line village arrangement, similar to those which border the Louisiana sugar plantations, with great social and economic benefits to the workers and to society in general. Only 5 of the 187 families of farm laborers lived in the village center.

Finally, the practice of having a home in town, to which to resort on Sundays and holidays, as well as the residence on the land, is not very prevalent in the municipio of Tabio. Only six families, five of

Some better type of homes and statue of the Virgin in a fork of the road on the Savanna of Bogotá. (Photo by the author.)

the farm operators, and one of the laborers, had such a secondary residence in the pueblo of Tabio. Thus the scattered-farmstead mode of arranging the population on the land is fully as characteristic of this municipio as it is of the typical rural community in the United States.[11]

SETTLEMENT PATTERNS IN COLONIAL TIMES

In the period of the conquest and the beginning of the colonial epoch all of the factors seemed to have favored village settlements. The nucleated patterns were the ones with which the Spaniards were familiar in the Iberian Peninsula and, consequently, the types they regarded as "natural." It seems, too, that the Chibchas were

11. Smith, Díaz, and García, *Tabio*, pp. 23-24.

settled in the village manner when Jimenez de Quesada and his colonists arrived on the Savanna of Bogotá. Furthermore, from the time of Queen Isabella the crown ordered that the Indians living dispersedly should be gathered together within villages, "reductions" or "congregations," each with its church, school, and local government.[12] In addition there can be no doubt that all the early Spanish settlements were established in the village form.

Each village nucleus was oriented about the square or plaza on which fronted the church, the cabildo, and the prison. Often in the center of the square stood the *arbol de justicia,* the pillar of wood or stone which served as a symbol of justicial authority and marked the spot where executions and other sentences were carried out. Each Spanish *vecino* (citizen or settler) was assigned a town lot or *solar* on which to build his home, a garden plot just outside the town limits, and one or more tracts of arable land (caballería or *peonía*) in the surrounding territory. In addition he enjoyed the privilege of pasturing livestock in the adjacent communal ejidos. Additional details of the early settlements are given in the foregoing chapters but for the moment it is important to emphasize that the village nature of the early Spanish settlements is clear and unmistakable.

It should be stressed that the first pueblos built by the Spaniards, in contrast with those of the Indians which they found thickly spread over the landscape when they arrived in the Andean highlands, were conceived of as administrative and residential centers. In them the Spanish overlords built their own homes, public buildings, churches, and convents, and in them they expected to live in comfort and plenty on the tribute they exacted from the Indians whom they received in repartimiento or encomienda.[13]

12. Cf. Haring, *The Spanish Empire in America,* p. 70. However, some indications are that scattered farmsteads may have been used to a considerable extent by the Chibchas, see Fals-Borda, *El Hombre y la Tierra en Boyacá,* pp. 44-50.

13. The distinction between these two ways of securing vassalage over the Indians, at least as the practice went in Nueva Granada, is excellently set forth in the following quotation from Pedro de Aguado, an intelligent friar who took pains to set down his sixteenth-century experiences for the benefit of succeeding generations: "It has been the usual practice in the Indies for any Captain who has gone or who comes to discover new lands, with Royal authority or without it, after having discovered some rich province and pacified the natives of it and established his pueblo, in order that those who have participated in the work with him may better sustain themselves and remain in the country and keep it in peace, to assign each one a certain quantity of Indians such as seem sufficient to provide him with a comfortable living in

Consider the description of Tunja in 1610, only 61 years after it was established by Capitan Gonzalo Suárez Rendón upon commission by Jimenez de Quesada. At the opening of the seventeenth century this important center boasted the central plaza, two smaller ones, and seven streets. In drawing up the original plan the town had been laid off into squares measuring 150 paces on each side. Each of these squares or blocks was divided into four solares, and one of them had been assigned to each of the original settlers; others were given to newcomers as they arrived. Each of the solares was enclosed with mud walls. At this time there were within the city a total of 313 houses, of which 88 were of two stories covered with tile, 163 of one story with tile roofs, and 60 of one story and covered only with thatch. There were also many vacant solares in the town. Facing on the central plaza were the principal church, the town house or cabildo, and the offices of the *escribano* or clerk. The cabildo was of two stories, "moderate and short," and beside it stood the jail.

---

accordance with the quality of the land and also of the person; and sometimes these assignments are by persons, saying 'I give and assign to you so many married Indians, including their women and children'; and other times they are by houses and huts, assigning them so many residences, and it is understood that they must be inhabited, because there are in some places Indians who have two and three houses, and all of them with one owner, and these count only as one; on other occasions they are given by chieftains and rulers, naming the chief or master of a given place with all his subjects and vassals; and sometimes by limits, or the Indians between one place and another, or those in a certain valley. That which the Captain does, if he lacks the Royal power to give in encomienda, is called merely repartimiento and *apuntamiento* of that which he assigns to each one, but it has no more force than the wishes of the King or of the person whom the King has commissioned to give encomiendas of Indians, and because this first division of the Indians has been called repartimiento, there has remained and remains the name repartimiento for that village or group of Indians which has fallen to each colonist, and thus ordinarily the Indians that each Spaniard has in his charge are called the repartimiento of John Doe. This first repartimiento or apuntamiento, made generally of the natives of a newly discovered and colonized province, is carried to the President or the Governor, who are those to whom the King usually gives power to grant in encomienda, and these superiors, if they see that the apuntamiento or repartimiento made by the Captain is without injury or prejudice to the other Spaniards who were with him, will confirm it, giving in encomienda the Indians to those to whom they had been assigned and appointed, and taking some away in other cases, as appears to be the just thing to do." *Primera Parte de la Recopilación Historial Resolutoria de Sancta Marta y Nuevo Reino de Granada de las Indias del Mar Océano,* Tomo Primero, Madrid: Espasa-Calpe, S. A., 1930, pp. 56-57.

The walls of most of the buildings were made of a mixture of mud and stone, but some of the portals presented a good appearance and a few of the archways were of stone.[14]

Even at this early date a population of demoralized Indians and half-breeds was mushrooming in the area immediately adjacent to the city, as is evidenced by the following quotation: "The city has four suburbs in which there are 19 one-story houses roofed with tile and 77 covered with thatch, which are called *bohios*, the homes of Ladino Indians and other poor people."[15]

At the time the report was prepared, the city contained about 300 Spanish citizens or vecinos. This number included a total of 73 encomenderos, of whom 55 were holding the Indians in encomienda for the "first life" and the remainder were already going on the "second life." Most of the encomenderos were married men with families, but several of them were minors, the children of other encomenderos. Such was the case with Diego Holguin Maldonado, who had one pueblo of Indians although he was only six years of age, and his father enjoyed three pueblos in his right; and also with Félix de Bintron Hoxica, who was only 10 years of age. Both of these young encomenderos were already engaged to be married.

Among them the encomenderos of Tunja held 152 pueblos of Indians, and the King himself had 9 more in the province. Together these 161 pueblos contained, it was estimated, about 20,000 Indians. Most of the encomenderos had only one or two pueblos, but not a few of them had three, several had five apiece, and one had ten. Except for the King, Fernando de Oruña who had been absent for over 13 years, Juan de Fuente who had been in Spain for 10 years, Juan de Noboa Sotela who had been there for two years, and Francisco de Noboa who held other encomiendas in the jurisdiction of Bogotá and lived in that city, all of the encomenderos made their homes in Tunja.

The account makes it perfectly clear that the encomenderos depended upon Indian labor for the cultivation of their haciendas and estancias and that these were separate and distinct from the lands used by the Indians themselves in order to support themselves and to pay the tribute levied by the encomenderos.

14. "Descripción de la Ciudad de Tunja, Sacada de las Informaciones Hechas por la Justicia de Aquella Ciudad en 30 de Mayo de 1610 Años," reproduced in Luis Torres de Mendoza, *Colección de Documentos Inéditos,* IX, 393-448.
15. *Ibid.,* p. 407.

The encomenderos occupy the Indians of the repartimientos in the work of their haciendas by permission of the Real Audiencia, whose *visitadores* have ordered and commanded that they must be paid for their services every year, and this is done and has always been done.

According to the quality and value of each encomienda, the encomendero maintains priests for the Indians, arms, servants, and horses, although there are some whose haciendas and encomiendas are so tenuous that they and their families of wife and children cannot sustain themselves with them. . . .

The tribute that the Indians pay to their encomenderos is generally in cotton blankets [mantas], which at the most are valued at 4 pesos of gold *corriente,* and in addition to this they pay the royal tribute, which is one for every five; thus if they give five mantas to the encomendero, they give another for Your Majesty, and an additional *tomin* towards the salary of the corregidor of the *partido,* and all of this is paid also by the Indians who wander away from their pueblos; but some of them pay very poorly, and there are many delinquents.[16]

It is evident from the report that even at this time powerful forces were tending to break down the village pattern of settlement and to spread the population who lived from agriculture about on the land. If this were the case in Tunja, at that time second only to Bogotá as an administrative center, no doubt it was even more apparent in the centers of lesser importance. Therefore it is significant that our informant wrote as follows. "All of the enterprises and undertakings of the citizens of this city have been on the decline for many years; therefore, except for a few great encomenderos and some rich merchants the citizens sustain themselves with much difficulty in notoriously straitened circumstances and well known misery, so much so that almost the entire year they remain in the country on their haciendas and estancias, because they are not able to sustain themselves in an ordinary manner in the city, except those who have great haciendas, and even they stay on them much of the time."[17]

Our unknown author went into an elaborate analysis of the causes for the hard times that had come upon the city and province, and among the points he emphasized were the following: the decrease of the Indian population, and the large increase in the number of Spaniards "from those who are born every day, and from those who newly come from Spain"; the high price of European goods; restrictions upon the circulation of gold; the increased costs of hiring

16. *Ibid.,* pp. 417-18.
17. *Ibid.,* pp. 422-23.

Indians, which caused them to be used too hard with consequent disadvantages for all; the "composición de las tierras," or the scrutiny of land titles, which had been discontinued after its evil effects became apparent; and "the host of ministers of justice who have been posted or stationed (*añadido*) in the Indian pueblos, who might be called *encomenderos añadidos*, because they help themselves to the Indians, making them work in their fields and pastures, the manufacture of mantas, and other enterprises without payment, in addition to the fact that these miserable people must pay the salaries of the corregidores, each Indian contributing a little."[18]

Santa Maria de Leiva is one of the few settlements which the Spaniards established in the midst of the Indian pueblos for which we have an early, informing description. It was founded in 1572 by the President of the Real Audiencia de Santa Fé, don Andres Diez Venero de Leiva, in order to rehabilitate the 64 survivors of Quesada's expedition to the Llanos in search of El Dorado.[19]

From a *Relación*[20] published 35 years later we learn many of the more significant features about the social, economic, and political life and standing of the community. The account opens with the statement that the villa, inhabited by Spaniards, is situated four leagues from the city of Tunja. It was established on the plain, at the foot of the mountain range, from which flowed a stream that moved six flour mills, a quarter of a league from the center, each possessed of a single wheel and grinding an average of ten fanegas of wheat per day. The main crops grown were wheat, barley, and chick-peas, but the area was also suitable for fruits such as peaches, figs, and pomegranates. One league from the town was the forest from which wood for construction and fuel was obtained. Apparently the rights to this were communal.

At the time our unknown observer prepared his report there were 150 farms (*estancias de labranza y crianza*) in the community, and both sheep and goats were reported to do well. Unlike the important centers of Bogotá and Tunja, Leiva was the residence of not a single encomendero. "Its inhabitants are for the most part farmers [labradores] and they perform their cultivations with *mitayo* Indian day laborers [jornaleros]; the Indian pueblos lying within the juris-

18. *Ibid.*, p. 424.
19. Rosales, *Histórias y Paisajes*, p. 152.
20. Reproduced in Torres de Mendoza, IX, 448-51.

diction of this villa belong to encomenderos who serve in the city of Tunja."

Since this settlement was a new one, merely one small nodule of Spanish settlement set down among the Indian pueblos which were dotted along the western slope of the Eastern Cordillera when the white man first came, it is not surprising that it was laid out in rectangular form oriented about the central square or plaza. The report which the King received from our anonymous writer indicates that the plaza was a good one, and that the village contained 80 dwellings. The latter were all of molded adobe construction, and except for six that boasted tiled roofs, all were covered with thatch. On one side of the plaza were eight buildings devoted to trade or official purposes. These were, of course, more ostentatious than the other buildings, all having tiled roofs and each being adorned in front with the characteristic arched gateway or portal of stone. The buildings of the cabildo, however, were said to be low and roofed merely with thatch.

At the time of our report Leiva was subject to the corregidor of Tunja and to the Real Audiencia of Santa Fé (Bogotá). Resident in Leiva was a lieutenant of the corregidor, two *alcaldes ordinarios* named by the cabildo at Tunja, and two *alguaciles* named by the *alguacil mayor* of Tunja. None of these positions was salaried, but they were entitled to certain fees from the royal revenues. The village itself owned no land except one large stone pit from which mill stones were secured. Two pesos per stone was the price, and business had been so poor that for six years the pit had been rented for 500 *pesos de oro* of 13 *quilates*.

As yet no privilege whatsoever had been bestowed upon the community. It enjoyed no distinction of rank, and it possessed no coat of arms, that of the King only being displayed in the buildings of the cabildo on the plaza.

The village contained a parochial church with a regular priest; and two other clergymen served two chapels that had been built and endowed by deceased benefactors. It was reported that the revenues available to each of the latter were on the decrease due to the fact that the possessions with which they had been established were of little value. In addition the village then, as now, contained a convent of Augustin friars, consisting at that time of a prior, one other sacerdote, and two assistants. At the time of the report they were just in the process of erecting the building for the nunnery of

Santa Barbara which figures so prominently in all later accounts of Leiva. Two leagues from the village and four from Tunja was another convent of Augustin friars. It belonged to the order of barefooted, recollect Augustins, devoted to Nuestra Señora de Candelaria, and contained the prior, two priests, and ten lay brothers. Although located in a delightful valley beside a river, this convent had no fixed income from property but depended upon offerings from the residents of Tunja, Leiva, and "the inhabitants of the surrounding territories, living on their estancias and repartimientos, and those who came to visit the church and say their novenas in it."

When our observer was visiting the village a hospital was in the process of construction. Already built were the walls for a fine edifice. It has been provided for in the will of the deceased Licenciado Caraça, who had been a resident of the community. This benefactor had left an estancia which was sold for 1,570 pesos de oro of 20 quilates; in addition this hospital was entitled to a part of the tithes collected in the villa.

THE TRANSITION TO SCATTERED FARMSTEADS

As yet the historians have given us no clear analysis of the process by which the Colombian settlement pattern was transformed from one in which the village form predominated to a type in which scattered or single farmsteads are the general rule. That the process began very early there can be no doubt, and that it is now almost complete also should be equally clear. A perusal of the writings left by the priests and others who lived and worked in New Granada during colonial times helps one to gain some understanding of the changes that took place and the factors which brought them about. Among the developments which had much to do with the transition are the following: (1) many of the Indians quickly got out of hand; (2) the marginal position of the mestizos facilitated their dispersion; (3) strong economic forces attracted the Spaniards away from the administrative centers, in which they were obliged to maintain occupied houses, and out onto their fincas and haciendas; and (4) the wars for independence, with both armies living off the land and the unwilling citizenry impressed into service, caused thousands of persons to flee the settlements and establish themselves in the most remote mountain fastnesses.

That many of the Indians quickly got out of hand there can be no doubt. They soon learned that when any white men appeared with a long scroll in their hands and began to mumble in the unintelligible tongue, it was time for them to take to the woods or retreat to the mountain fastnesses. Hence from the very beginning the contact with Spaniards tended to break up the Indian villages and to scatter at least a part of the natives throughout the coves, hidden valleys, inaccessible slopes, and other mountain retreats.

Probably even more important was what happened to the large numbers of mestizos who were not long in making their appearance. A few of these succeeded in attaining the status of whites in the Spanish settlements, but the lot of the masses certainly was less

Village trade and service center surrounded by small, scattered farmsteads. (Courtesy of the Office of Foreign Agricultural Relations, U. S. Department of Agriculture.)

fortunate. No doubt the accretions of uprooted humanity which formed on the outskirts of Tunja and the other cities were composed largely of this element. But thousands of them must have gone pretty much their own way, subject to few restraints and possessing few ties either with the Indian pueblos or the Spanish parishes.

But the extent to which the Spaniards themselves and their children were drawn out onto the land is probably the most important of all the developments. It would seem that economic forces such as those referred to above in the case of Tunja, were the all important stimuli which brought this about. Such forces must have been strong enough to offset and even to modify the wishes of the church and to bring the settlers to offer almost open defiance to the law.

Consider, for example, some of the provisions in the Laws of the Indies which were in force when most of the important developments in Colombia took place. Libro VI, Título IX of the compilation contains such enactments as the following: Ley IX (March 4, 1534) ordering that each encomendero should build a house of stone in the place designated by the Governor; Ley X (March 31, 1583) obliging the encomenderos to have *inhabited* houses in the cities which were the *cabezas* of their encomiendas; and Ley XIV (April 24, 1550) forbidding the encomenderos, their wives, parents, children, relatives, servants, guests, mestizos, mulattoes and Negroes, whether slave or free, from residing in the Indian pueblos.

Were other evidence lacking such orders would seem to be rather conclusive, but fortunately one scholarly priest, Basilio Vicente de Oviedo, included in the summary statement of the pros and cons of each of the parishes in New Granada,[21] which he prepared in 1763 for the guidance of his fellow clergymen, a note which is highly informative. This authority repeatedly pointed out that settlements of Indians were designated as pueblos while those of the Spaniards were called *parroquias*.[22] In the note to which reference has been made he commences by saying that for the last 130 years everything Indian in the pueblos has been on the decrease, while everything relative to the whites had been on the increase. To explain this he referred to the difficulties which the colonists once had encountered in administering the affairs of their estates and at the same time performing their duties in the parroquias. As a result the Viceroy Fernando de Ugarte in 1622 had ordered that one half of the parochial rights should be transferred to the priests in the Indian pueblos (the *doctrineros de indios*). Among other things the doctrineros were authorized to perform the marriage ceremony for those who were *agregados* of the pueblo; and it also was specified that the obligatory annual communion might be taken by the agregados in the pueblos. For this reason says Oviedo, they came to be called "vecinos of the city of Tunja, and agregados of the pueblo of Tequia, of Chita, of Soata, of Sativa, etc." This same practice was later confirmed on various other occasions in Bogotá.[23]

As to the results the learned priest is very specific. The Spanish vecinos, now agregados of the pueblos, "through matrimony or in

21. *Cualidades y Riquezas del Nuevo Reino de Granada,* pp. 116-18.
22. *Ibid.,* pp. 52, 76-77, *passim.*
23. *Ibid.,* p. 117.

another way which it is not important for us to name have been multiplying the mestizos and calling them Spaniards or whites, and the Indians in the pueblos have been diminishing . . ." He notes that in Tunja and Velez there had been reported a great increase in the Spanish population and a large decrease in the number of Indians and emphasizes once more that many are called Spaniards who in reality are only Indians. Then he gives an example to make sure that there can be no confusing his meaning.

> If some donkeys are placed in a pasture where there are many horses, if the donkeys are not castrated the burros will prevail and the mules will multiply; and thus having the advantage in the pueblos the white burros have multiplied the mestizo mules and the Indian horses and mares have been decreasing.
> I will give an example to show it clearly. In the jurisdiction of what today is the villa of San Gil, there once were three pueblos containing 1,000 Indians, namely, Guane, Chanchon, and Charala and Oiba. Today in all these pueblos are only 200 Indians, and of those they call Spaniards (which includes everything, Spaniards, mestizos, *cuaterones* and *cholos*) there are more than 10,000, and in truth there have come from Spain to settle not even 200 Spaniards.[24]

Other of the early documents give more details of what was taking place. Thus in 1776 one of the Viceroys, Manuel de Guirior, called attention in the report prepared for his successor to the haphazard manner in which the white population was dispersed over the territory and made suggestions as to how the situation might be improved. After indicating that the government had a responsibility for the increase of the population and the manner in which it was arranged on the land, the Viceroy indicated that population was growing by natural increase and by the immigration of Europeans. Next he pointed out that it lacked the good order necessary for its enlightenment and that the trouble was of long standing. It had persisted since the conquest of the Nuevo Reino. Then he gave the causes as they appeared to him and asserted: ". . . few are the settlements of the Spaniards (including in this category all those who are not Indians), and the larger part of the people of middle class live dispersed in the fields, in the neighborhood of and within the pueblos of the Indians, making use of the resguardos of the latter and of some small piece of ground which enables them to live miserably, not being able to observe the laws which prescribe their

24. *Ibid.*, pp. 117-18.

separation [from the Indians], nor to avoid the damage caused by consorting with them. . . ."[25]

Even more explicit is the notable report of another of the Viceroys, the Archbishop of Córdova. His descriptions are so detailed and informing that one can hardly do better than to present them at considerable length:

> One sees the most fertile valleys, whose abundance pleads for the hand of man, more to harvest than to labor; and nevertheless they are found to be empty without a single inhabitant, at the same time that the rough, sterile mountainsides are peopled by criminals and fugitives, persons who have fled society to live without law or religion. It is sufficient to delineate a small map of the population of the Kingdom in order to appreciate the confusion and disorder in which these men of the mountains live, electing of their own choice and without the intervention of the Government nor of the local judges their places of retreat, the more remote from the pueblo and its church the more pleasing to them. Except for the few cities of the first class which hardly merit second class rating from the mere appearance of their unhappy buildings or third class rating of pure name from the memory of their ruins and remains; except also for some Parishes which recently have been established on better lines, all the other population centers are merely small collections of miserable *ranchos, chozas,* and *bujíos,* which constitute only the twentieth part of the inhabitants attributed to the respective places. This comes from the old and deep-seated liberty of fleeing from one to the other to live at their expense without fear of apprehension in their infamous and vile undertakings. Men designated as fairly well off are those who from the lack of measures designed to prevent the concentration of land in the hands of a single person, have succeeded in acquiring at exorbitant prices immense holdings in which they regularly hold as serfs the less well-to-do. The former preserve more firmly their possessions through the income which they receive from their broad domains; but the latter, who make up the great majority of the free inhabitants, constitute strictly speaking a migratory, floating population who, forced by the tyranny of the land owners, move about with the facility conceded to them by the small amount of their household goods, the slight value of their huts, and the lack of love for the fonts in which they were baptized. They have the same in the place they die as in the one in which they were born, and in any place they find the same as they left. They eat little with considerable grossness, but they are not so temperate in drinking. They are always ready and willing for games, dances, and functions, inclined to laziness, to which the fertility of the land contributes, a little work sufficing to supply their few necessities. Their children, educated in this school, go on imitating faithfully their parents; they continue

25. Posada and Ibáñez, *Relaciones de Mando,* pp. 149-50.

propagating always the same thoughts and the same conduct and rusticity, and in spite of the general increase in population, they only increase the number of such useless vassals, who with great strides are precipitating themselves in the same barbarity as the first inhabitants.[26]

The testimony of others who wrote at that time is similar. Thus after describing the classes and castes of Nueva Granada, Padre Joaquín de Finestrad, writing in 1783, asserted that their number was infinite and that it would be impossible for such a large population to subsist if they were permitted to continue their vagabond ways. "As a rule they live in the woods and caves; they lead a wild, lazy life, moved by unbridled brutal passions, exposed to robbery, rape, and other abominable excesses which can never be useful to the Prince or the Republic."[27]

This same padre was greatly concerned about the "revolt of the Comuneros" which occurred in 1781; and to his interest in bringing about reforms that would improve social conditions in the New Kingdom and prevent a repetition of the disorder we are indebted for one of the most informing accounts of conditions there during the eighteenth century. It is readily apparent from the projects for reform which he thought it necessary and desirable to undertake that the Indians and mestizos had gotten rather completely out of hand, and that among other things the bulk of the population was scattered about on the land. Second only to the selection of good officials was his proposal that the population should be gathered together into villages. His own words are as follows. "To reduce to society all the people who live spread about in the woods and ravines, obligating them to build a house in the place of their domicile in which they should lead a civil life. Those that do not have a hacienda at a great distance may go out each morning to work in the fields and for no reason should they spend the night away from home. Those who have haciendas which are distant, a day's journey, may spend the entire week working in their pastures and fields, returning to their homes on Saturdays."[28] Where there were many haciendas at a distance he recommended that a sub-parish be estab-

26. Translation of the "Relación" made by the Arzobispo Obisbo de Córdoba who served as Viceroy from about 1769 to 1789 when he transmitted the authority to his successor. The "Relación" has been reproduced in *ibid.*, pp. 237-39.

27. "El Vasallo Instruido," p. 104.

28. *Ibid.*, p. 123.

lished, which should eventually be developed into a new community.

Another indication of the extent to which the population was dispersed over the landscape, hidden away in the valleys and coves, and buried in the jungles, is found in the claims of Antonio de la Torre Miranda, one time lieutenant colonel of infantry. Rather dictatorial powers were conferred upon this officer by an order dated at Cartagena on August 12, 1774, and signed by Juan Pimenta. Because "the dispersion of the citizens which occupy the terrain of the Isle of Varu, scattered about on various haciendas, or estancias and *rancherias,* isolates from society to the utmost degree those inhabitants who lack spiritual care and the administration of justice, living in ignorance of the Doctrine and delivered over to vices," Antonio de la Torre was charged with the responsibility of bringing them together and establishing them for "subsistence in peace or in war. . . ." After his return to Spain, de la Torre claimed that he had brought together "41,133 souls, to unite them in 43 villages which I founded, adding 22 parishes to that Bishopric." He relates that in order to establish these settlements he brought out "at the cost of an immense amount of work . . . the descendants of deserters from the Army and the Navy, of the many vagabonds who without license or occupation went to those dominions, of the Negroes, of slaves who had run away or fled from their masters, and of others who having murdered someone or committed other crimes had sought shelter from excesses by scattering about to free themselves, some from punishment and others from servitude, there being among them many Indian men and women who mixed with mestizos, Negroes, and mulattoes propagated an infinity of castes. . . ." All of these he established in their new parishes and settlements, where they engaged in agriculture and the fabrication of cloth from cotton and other fibers. Lands were given them for their plantings and for pastures, and, if Torre's account may be trusted, by 1794 they were living together in settlements of the village type under rather idyllic conditions.[29]

And finally, from the *Relación*[30] which Pedro Mendinueta gave of his stewardship upon relinquishing the post of Viceroy to his successor in 1803, we gain important information concerning the general

---

29. *Noticia Individual de las Poblaciones Nuevas Fundadas en la Provincia de Cartagena.* . . . Finestrad confirms the account, but he gives the number of pueblos as 23, varying in size from 500 to 1,000 inhabitants, *op. cit.,* p. 109.

30. Reproduced in Posada and Ibáñez.

rules by which the settlement of the country had been proceeding. He indicated that inasmuch as all the old pueblos possessed extended territories so that "the abundancy of land was sufficient for all" the settlers spread out in their houses "although they also had them in the *parroquia* or *poblado*." He indicated that this made it difficult, on account of the distance, for the priest and the judge to attend to them or to secure their assistance. For this reason "when the number of *colonos* or small *hacendados* is considered sufficient to maintain a priest, they then request the establishment of a parish, and when granted, they build their church, and little by little they continue to improve their settlement with their own resources."[31]

Unlike some of his predecessors, Mendinueta did not think it necessary for the government to undertake large scale settlement projects in which the vagabond population would be gathered together forcibly into organized communities. However he did recognize the necessity in special cases of "accelerating the formation of villages, either to assemble the dispersed inhabitants, to destroy some prejudical *canchera* [an Americanism used to designate the refuge and hiding place of vicious persons, fugitives from justice . . .], to facilitate communication, or maintain a road. . . ."[32]

These excerpts from those in best position to know and to report should make it evident that to a considerable extent the village pattern of settlement had given way to dispersed form even before the outbreak of the wars for independence. But undoubtedly this tendency was greatly strengthened and accelerated during the decades of struggle between the patriots and the forces of the King. For many years the sweep of armies across the country made for such great insecurity of life and property that thousands fled the settlements and established themselves with their families, livestock and other possessions in the most out-of-the-way mountain recesses. During these uncertain times the coming of friendly armies was to be dreaded almost as much as the presence of the enemy, for both of them lived off the land. But whatever the reason for fleeing the settlements, once farms and pastures had been developed elsewhere not all of the inhabitants were content to return to the villages upon the cessation of hostilities. No doubt the Indians and mestizos, many of whom probably got almost entirely away from feudalistic controls, were especially reluctant to return.

31. *Ibid.*, p. 460.
32. *Ibid.*

Fortunately not a few American and European travelers visited Colombia during the struggles or shortly after independence was gained, and from their accounts one may gain a fairly accurate idea of what was going on. Thus Colonel (later General) William Duane, who visited Colombia in the years 1822 and 1823, repeatedly referred to the fact that the inhabitants of the thickly populated districts had deserted their homes for the mountain fastnesses. To quote his own words: "In the rich countries the whole population moved *en masse*, with their cattle, to some of the remote valleys out of the reach of the pillage or the march of the armies; and out of reach too of the military conscription . . . it was a frequent apology that exaction was as common with the troops of the republic, as with the *Godas*."[33] And again, in referring to his conversations with Father Rincon with whom he enjoyed a visit at Paipa, Duane wrote: ". . . he thought that the population of Colombia would augment even more rapidly than the United States; and that many thousands of the former population, supposed to be killed, were now settled in remote valleys, from which they would not return. . . ."[34]

The comments of other travelers are similar, and some of the reflections included reflect a healthy skepticism about the possibility of things returning to "normal" with the establishment of peace. Thus the following quotation from a French visitor indicates that processes had been set in operation that were bringing about radical changes in social organization.

> If the dispersion of the inhabitants caused by the fear inspired by the passage of troops, is favourable to the clearing of new lands and the increase of the population which is always on the decline in towns; on the other hand, as the markets are not held in consequence of the destruction of the villages, no one sows more than is sufficient for the maintenance of his family; this is very little: the church even offers but a small attraction, as the ecclesiastics no longer mount the pulpit except to preach contribution and taxation; men consequently accustom themselves to live isolated, and visit each other but seldom;

33. *A Visit to Colombia*, p. 251. A British visitor, Colonel J. P. Hamilton, who was in Colombia at about the same time gives us the following account of one of his own observations. "In passing by the goal at Tocaima, I was surprised to see it full of young men; and on my remarking to the commandant that I supposed there were many robberies in the neighbourhood, he replied 'Oh no, the people were honest and quiet; that these prisoners were only young *volunteers*, from the province of Neyva, going to join a newly raised regiment at Bogotá, and that these volunteers were confined for the night, to prevent their running away.'" I, 279.

34. P. 423. See also pp. 253, 328, and 609 ff.

and when intercourse is interrupted amongst a people, commerce, agriculture, and industry become extinct; ignorance spreads itself in all directions, and excesses of every kind are the consequence."[35]

And a second extract from the same source indicates that the revolution was a powerful factor indeed in the disruption of the village settlements, even though they were not conveniently located with respect to the arteries of communication.

> The next day we experienced considerable difficulty in climbing up a very high mountain, which the rains, that had fallen for some days, had rendered extremely slippery. It was very late before I arrived at Pedregal, an Indian village; all the inhabitants with the exception of the curate had fled. I have already observed that, since the breaking out of the war, hospitality had become a scourge from which the people saved themselves by taking up their abode in inaccessible places; thus a few years of contention have destroyed the work of three centuries. The Indians grown familiar to the yoke, threw it off, and returning to the woods, resumed their former barbarous manners.[36]

The accounts left by some foreign members of the Colombian forces are revealing on the points in which we are interested. For example, we are informed that at Santa Marta the commander of the patriot army which had landed intending to live off the land "was by no means prepared for the kind of hostility he encountered. . . . On entering Guimaro, not a living creature was to be seen, for not only had the inhabitants fled to the woods, (*al monte,*) but they had carried off with them all their domestic animals, and every moveable article of their household furniture."[37]

The English officer who has left us the account states that General Careño, proceeded in a few days to Peñon, "another considerable village on the banks of the river; but it was just the same—the inhabitants were all *al monte.*" Then he adds that it is:

> . . . no great inconvenience for a family in the warm climate of South America to make this little change in their residence; for they are not encumbered with a superfluity of household goods and in the dry season the hammock will hang as commodiously between two trees in the wood, as from the rafters of the house in the village: the pigs and poultry, likewise, are so domesticated, that they comply without scruple with the migratory fancies of the family; and the

35. Mollien, *Travels in the Republic of Colombia in the Years 1822 and 1823,* pp. 259-60.
36. *Ibid.,* pp. 264-65. See also, Hamilton, II, 10-11.
37. An Officer, *The Present State of Colombia,* p. 66.

plantain walk is generally some distance from the town, so that they can come, in the course of the night, and help themselves to what they want. They make, therefore, these temporary changes of abode on much more trivial occasions than when they expect to have their throats cut by the invading enemy: often, during the war, I have known the whole male population of a district resort to this expedient to avoid the arbitrary conscriptions by which the ranks of the army were at that time filled.[38]

38. *Ibid.*, pp. 69-70.

8

Community and Community Development

THE LOCALITY groups which are designated as communities and neighborhoods are other features of Colombia's social structure that deserve careful, analytical study. In a very real sense these particular social groupings are the cells out of which the principal anatomical parts of society are formed. This is because men in their relationships with one another almost always are limited, to an overwhelming degree, to a highly restricted area of the earth's surface, no more in most cases for most of the time than a few square miles of territory. This remains true even in the nuclear age after a few astronauts have been thrust into outer space. Because area and distance per se are highly limiting factors, during the second half of the twentieth century as in all of the epochs that preceded our period, men divide the surface of their planet into small areas of common living, contact and association, and conscious or unconscious interdependence and assistance. Expressed in other terms, in Colombia, in the remainder of South America, and on all of the other continents, wherever people are to be found one also may observe various locality groupings. In each case within the small area involved the lives and activities of the inhabitants are intertwined and interdependent to such an extent that they literally are all "in the same boat," and not infrequently they have developed an awareness of that basic fact. When this is the case, efforts to promote the well-being of the group are greatly facilitated. But irrespective of the existence or nonexistence of such awareness, and regardless of the personal affinities, or of the animosities, among any two or more of the persons or of the families involved, nearly all of a general nature that has a bearing upon the welfare of the one also acts for better or worse upon the others who by design or accident are living in the same locality.

The particular kind of human groupings under consideration, ones in which area as such or territorial proximity constitutes a major factor in the cohesion, interdependence, and solidarity of those who together are in a particular "boat," are known as locality groups.

This category includes social bodies of great variety, the utmost difference in size or membership, and of radically differing complexity; but to date, as is discussed in some detail below, the ingenuity of sociologists and other social scientists has identified and described only two major types or kinds, namely those called neighborhoods and those designated as communities. Even if the family or household, which obviously also is a locality group, is added at the one end of the range, and the state, a social grouping in which territory is of the utmost significance, is included at the other, there still remains a vast range of locality groupings for which we have only two terms, neighborhood and community, available for classificatory and other analytical purposes. In Colombia the range between the smallest neighborhood and the largest metropolitan community includes everything from a small cluster of families of fisherfolk on the banks of the Magdalena or some other stream, or a few households of kinfolk occupying one of the coves of the Andes, to the great city of Bogotá plus the large zone which surrounds and is tributary to it. This second part of the metropolitan community includes all of the territory in which the life and labor of those living in smaller cities, towns, and villages and on the haciendas and subsistence tracts in the open country, already are bound up with that of those who live in the metropolis itself. In this greatest of Colombia's communities, the central city itself or the nucleus of the metropolitan community contains more than 1,500,000 people and the outlying sections of the huge locality group probably contain at least that many more.

Throughout the strictly rural parts of Colombia one may observe, in addition to tens of thousands of neighborhoods of one kind or another, several more thousands of locality groupings whose nuclei are formed by mere hamlets or by villages of various sizes. The latter definitely are not characterized by frequent, intimate, and face-to-face contacts on the part of their members; hence they may not properly be classified as primary groups or neighborhoods. Nevertheless they are far too small, too lacking in self-sufficiency, too dependent upon larger centers, and so on, for them to qualify as communities of any size. At best they are partial, incomplete, or sub-communities. However, we lack the precise observations, the classifications, and the designations needed in order to deal adequately with this important facet of Colombia's social structure or organization. This matter will be discussed in greater detail below, but before turning to that it is well to consider briefly and specifically the nature of the concepts that we do have, namely, those of the neighborhood and of the community.

THE NATURE OF THE NEIGHBORHOOD AND THE COMMUNITY

The difficulties of vocabulary pose perplexing problems for all who attempt to communicate precisely upon the subject of locality groups such as neighborhoods and communities. Sociologists, social workers, and other social scientists, not to mention the journalists, and other writers of various kinds, make use of these terms to designate an extremely varied set of phenomena; and it is difficult to detect any genuine correspondence between the concepts as they are employed by any two or more of them. For this reason it is of the utmost importance that the precise senses in which these terms are being used should be given by anyone who makes any substantial use of them. Before this is done, though, it seems essential first to state as explicitly as possible my understanding of the role of sociology in all that has to do with the community and the process of community development.

The scientific study of the community as a locality group is an important and integral part of the discipline of sociology, or that branch of science which deals primarily with the collective aspects of human behavior. Historically, and for very specific reasons, this has been especially true of that part of the social science involved which is properly denoted as the sociology of rural life, or, as many choose to call it, rural sociology. But it also is important in the other part of the large dichotomy, or the sociology of urban life. As a matter of fact to a highly significant extent the emergence, growth, and development of rural sociology as a scientific discipline accomplished the specific studies of rural communities in various parts of the United States.[1] Moreover, one trail-blazing endeavor of Charles J. Galpin[2] not only produced a pragmatic and enduring definition of the rural community but served as a major stimulus to Dr. Robert E. Park for the studies of urban ecology which he launched and directed at the University of Chicago.[3] Furthermore in Colombia

1. For an account of these pioneering efforts, and an effort to assay the importance of each, see Smith, *Rural Sociology: A Trend Report.*

2. *The Social Anatomy of an Agricultural Community.*

3. The information relative to the latter part of the statement was given directly to me by Dr. Park in conversations at Baton Rouge, Louisiana, in the 1940's.

specifically, as is also true in many other of the so-called under-developed countries, the studies of particular communities and sub-communities, including especially those of Tabio and Saucio,[4] have played major roles in awakening and promoting interest in modern, empirical sociology. This is the type of work, in turn, that has most to offer those in charge of community development projects, now an important feature of developmental activities in Colombia.

No branch of science can or should have the responsibility of inducing, promoting, guiding, and directing community development activities in Colombia or any other country. But in spite of this, it is fair to say that sociology is the particular science that is most deeply involved in all having to do with community development. In this area sociology seems to be related to community development programs in about the same way that physiology is to medicine, anatomy is to surgery, economics is to banking and commerce, chemistry is to papermaking, mathematics is to space travel, geology is to the extraction of petroleum, and chemistry is to farming. In a word sociology is the scientific discipline that is largely responsible for the study of the community in its structural and dynamic aspects. Therefore, anyone or any agency is ill-advised if it attempts substantial programs designed to change this basic locality group without first becoming informed about the systematized knowledge about community structures and processes that sociologists have developed.

It also is necessary to take cognizance of two very different senses in which the term "community study" is used before we turn more specifically to an indication of the nature and definition of the community and neighborhood. One of these, the one we are concerned with primarily in the pages that follow, has to do with the specific nature of the locality group that properly may be classified as a community. In such community study one endeavors to isolate, analyze, and describe community phenomena as such, and he is not necessarily highly concerned with the varieties of social, cultural, and institutional phenomena which may be found in any particular locality group. The second, which it would be better to designate as "the study of society in miniature" than as community study, is focused upon the observation and description of the entire pattern of

4. Cf. Smith, Díaz, and García, Tabio, (Tabio: un Estudio de la Organización Social Rural, Bogotá: Ministerio de Economia, 1944); and Fals-Borda, Peasant Society in the Colombian Andes, (Campesinos de los Andes, Bogotá: Editorial Iqueima, 1961).

social and cultural phenomena as these occur in any specific small segment of a society. In the "community studies" of the second type, as a general rule one could strike out the term community every place it occurs and substitute another, such as locality, village, hamlet, district, settlement, even the proper name of the place being studied, or indeed any other designation for one small segment of territory, without in any way affecting the nature of the study or of the findings. Indeed not infrequently in the reports published under the general heading of community studies, one will discover that the authors did not even take the trouble to ascertain whether or not the locality they were investigating actually qualified as a community. This does not necessarily destroy the value of their observations and analyses, but it does raise an important question about the propriety of including the term community as the key word in the designation of their investigations. However, not infrequently, or so one is almost compelled to think by the flood of poorly prepared publications that come to his attention, the so-called community study not only fails to contain any analysis that is specific to community as such; but often seems to consist merely of lengthy cataloging of the most superfical type of a heterogeneous set of specific items or traits. In the lists presented one generally encounters a few features, which probably would be of some significance if properly observed, described, and interpreted. And there is the chance that the set will be of some value to a scientist who is interested in the geographical distribution of various cultural and social phenomena. Nevertheless, for the most part the items that might be of significance are indiscriminately mixed with dozens or hundreds of others which neither the studies themselves, nor the knowledge possessed by others give any reason for supposing to be of any particular importance. Some of the catalogs are little less than ludicrous. In brief a publication dealing with social and cultural affairs in a small locality is not necessarily of significance merely because it has been labeled as a "community study."

Familiarity with the concept of rural community as developed by Dr. Charles J. Galpin is the basic starting point for all endeavors to get an adequate idea of the nature of the community in Colombia. This is because Colombia, like Walworth County, Wisconsin, site of Galpin's classic study, is basically a land of scattered farmsteads. In Colombia, as in the greater part of the United States, the rural community seems to consist of the same two parts identified and described by Galpin; namely: (1) a village nucleus, which is essentially a market and service center; and (2) a surrounding zone of open country, dotted with dwellings, whose inhabitants are dependent upon the village for trade, financial, social, religious, recreational, and other services. With this concept as a starting point, I sketch the following propositions related to an understanding of the nature and function of the rural community.

First, it is one of the "natural areas" with which the sociologist deals. Each such community has a definite physical expression; it is one small and definite segment of the earth's surface. It has definite boundaries and these are indelibly etched in the minds of the local inhabitants, even if they rarely figure on the geographer's maps along with the streams, divides, and other so-called natural phenomena. These community limits determine effectively the area of social participation, mutual awareness and common concern, and collective action of many types. Hence one should think of the community as a specific part of state, national, and world territory in which all of the residents realize that they are "in the same boat" and in which they are impelled to efforts making for the welfare of the group that are over and above those produced by family, kinship, and neighborhood ties and obligations.

Second, the rural community is also an area of interaction, a locality group. As such it has all of the essential features of any social group, such as plurality of persons, social interaction between the members, and social cohesion or social solidarity. But it also differs fundamentally from other locality groupings, and particularly the neighborhood which is the only other category that has received much attention and study. Even a rural community may encompass hundreds of families and dozens of neighborhoods. Moreover, whereas the neighborhood, along with the family, is a classic example of the primary group, i.e. one characterized by frequent, intimate, face-to-face contacts and one primarily responsible for the formation of human personalities, the community generally includes persons and families who are completely unknown to one another. Indeed, some of the families and neighborhoods who together make up a community may even be openly hostile to one another. Many rural communities consist largely of clusters of neighborhoods, but the group as a whole may be highly diverse in its ethnic and other social characteristics and numbers of its members may be exceedingly individualistic in many of their activities. Actually those comprising the membership of a given community may have very little in common with one another except the fact that they all reside in one small and specific fragment of territory, they all are dependent upon its institutions and agencies for the satisfaction of their basic needs, and most significantly of all, they share for better or worse in the vicissitudes of the locality's existence.

Village trade and service center surrounded by tiny farmsteads on the eastern slope of the Eastern Cordillera. (Photo by the author.)

Third, wherever the village type of settlement prevails, i.e. in those societies in which the farmers' dwellings are clustered together into villages, as is the case in Mexico, most of Spain, and almost all of India and China, the limits of the community's boundaries are obvious to anyone. It is easy to discover where the lands tributary to one village end and those of another begin and easy to determine the relationship of the community to various subdivisions of the province or state. But in Colombia, as in Brazil, the United States, and Canada, in which the homesteads are dispersed throughout the open country, with each farm family ordinarily having its dwelling in close proximity to its plantings, the boundaries of the rural community are not readily apparent. The careful observer can note the paths that connect the houses with one another, the trails that lead from these paths into larger ways, and the manner in which these are linked with those deserving to be called roads and highways; and if perceptive enough, he may arrive at the conclusion that the system or network of these paths, trails and roads which spreads out from a given population center is an objective indicator of the territory which is tributary to that village or town. But, especially in zones influenced by modern highways, such a manner of determining the limits of the open-country part of a given community may be difficult or impossible to use. In such cases there is a strong likelihood that the limits of the political subdivisions, those of tax districts, and other significant boundaries will cut directly across the actual communities and other "natural areas." The more advanced the entire process of social differentiation, of course, the more likely this is to be the case. As early as 1943, for example, in our study of the municipio of Tabio, some 45 kilometers to the north of Bogotá, we found a decided lack of correspondence between the boundaries of the administrative subdivision, or the county-like municipio, and the actual community of Tabio. Families living in the northern part of this municipio already still were largely dependent upon the small village of Tabio for religious, educational, and political purposes; but for marketing and other economic activities they were resorting to Zipaquirá, a small city which is the seat of a neighboring municipio.[5] Were another study made of this important matter, it probably would be seen that there is an increasing tendency for Colombian rural society to differentiate, for ever greater differences between the boundaries of the municipios and those of the actual rural, rurban, and urban communities to develop. Nevertheless, as will be stressed below, at the level of integration that may correspond with the smallest of the administrative subdivisions, the possibility that many of the rural municipios which are fairly remote from urban centers of any considerable size will develop into genuine rural communities is one of the chief opportunities for any substantial strengthening of community units in Colombia.

Fourth, and finally, MacIver's statement that "any circle of people who live together, who belong together, so that they share, not this or that particular interest, but a whole set of interests wide enough

5. Smith, Díaz, and García, *Tabio*, pp. 36-37.

and complete enough to include their lives is a community,"[6] adequately sets forth the other basic features of the community. To meet such criteria, even the smallest community, which we designate as the *rural* community, must contain all of the basic institutions which are essential in order to provide for the domestic, economic, educational, governmental, administrative, religious, recreational, health, and welfare needs of its members.

The Camino de Herradura (paved mule trail) which leads over the crest of the Andes from the eastern slope to Bogotá. (Photo by the author.)

The Paucity of Conceptual Tools for the Study of Locality Groups

Before proceeding with an analysis of Colombia's communities, it seems advisable to explore a bit more in detail the paucity of sociological terms and concepts that are presently available for use in taking stock of the locality groups present in that nation or in any other part of the earth. As indicated above the groupings involved range all the way from a very small cluster of families closely integrated into a little primary group or neighborhood, at the one end of the scale, to the great metropolitan community such as that centering in Bogotá,

6. MacIver, *Society*, pp. 9-10; see also the same author's earlier study, *Community*, Chapter 11.

or those having as their central cores other great cities such as Cali, Medellín, or Barranquilla, at the other. As indicated above, however, to date we have only two basic concepts, namely those of the neighborhood and the community, to apply to all of the X's in the huge range of human association that is involved.

Only slightly larger and more complex than the neighborhood, is the locality whose inhabitants are enmeshed in a web of life centering in a very small hamlet that has arisen at a landing, along a river, or at the intersection of two or more trails or roads. As compared with the genuine neighborhood, whose members are in intimate, daily, and face-to-face contact with one another,[7] its inhabitants are more diverse in their characteristics, its people in less frequent and intimate contact with one another, and its families more involved in larger and less exclusive circles of association. On the other hand, it definitely does not meet the criteria for classification as a community. The institutions and services provided by the hamlet and its tributary zone of influence are much too limited in variety and too restricted in number, those living in locality are far too greatly attached to and dependent upon other larger and more distant population centers for the satisfaction of a large proportion of their social, economic, religious, educational, and recreational needs for it to be considered even as a partial, incomplete or sub-rural community. It can only be regarded as X_3 in a series in which the rural family itself is X_1, the neighborhood X_2, and the great metropolitan community X_n in what eventually may be an adequate identification and description of the basic locality groups.[8]

To a certain extent a judicious use of modifiers is helpful in a preliminary consideration of other entities in the series. In this connection, of course, the terms *rural* community and *urban* community immediately come to mind, and to those well acquainted with an ample range of sociological theory the designation *rurban* community also may be recalled. If we merely call attention to the locality groups which are larger, more complex, and more complete than the X_3 entities mentioned above, or various kinds of *semi, incomplete,* or *partial* communities, it is likely that at least the X_4, X_5, and X_6 eventually will be required to take care of the corresponding varieties of

7. Cf. Cooley, *Social Organization,* p. 23.
8. For an earlier endeavor to deal with some of the problems inherent in such a classification of locality groups, see Smith, *La Sociología y el Proceso de Desarrollo de la Comunidad,* pp. 17-19.

sociological realities. If this is the case, then X_7, X_8, and X_9 could be used for *rural communities, rurban communities,* and *urban communities,* respectively. In order to distinguish these three important classes or types of communities from one another, I propose the following. The *rural community* category should include all of the locality groups that are large enough and complete enough to qualify as communities, in which the population, trade, and service center which forms the nucleus of such a societal cell definitely is directly dependent in all essential respects upon the trade and patronage of the farmers and collectors who live beyond the village limits in the surrounding territory. Thus agricultural and collecting activities are the dominating economic bases of the rural community. The *rurban community* class or type should include all those locality groups that qualify as communities, in which the economic activities performed by the nucleus are approximately equal in importance to those of the farmers and collectors who live in the open-country part of the entity. This is to say that in the rurban community activities connected with trade and commerce, transportation and communication, manufacturing and processing, professional services, repair and service agencies, and so on, are about in balance with farming, stock raising, fishing, hunting, and other collecting enterprises, in providing the economic basis upon which the inhabitants depend. Finally, for the purposes of the present exposition, the *urban community* category should include all of integrated locality groupings (and not merely the portions which are located within the corporate limits or "build-up" area of a given city) in which the farmers and villagers who live in the districts surrounding an urban center have their social and economic life heavily intertwined with that of the people who live within the center itself. In the urban community, however, agricultural interests definitely do not dominate life and labor of the people involved, as is the case in the rural community, nor is there an approximate equilibrium between the two large segments of the locality group, as is true in what we are designating as the rurban community. Rather the needs, wishes, and basic objectives of the agricultural and collecting parts of the population who live in the zone tributary to any substantial urban center definitely play secondary roles, if indeed they play any significant roles at all, in the determination of the policies and activities of the urban community. As a general rule those farmers whose lives are unextricably enmeshed in the societal fabric of a sizeable urban community are limited in their personal relationships with persons who live in the city itself to contacts with those who manage certain mercantile establishments, with those who operate some particular service agencies, with the people who direct the activities of specific social institutions, and so on. In brief in most urban communities throughout the world, the farmers who live and work in the peripheral parts of the locality group are able to do little or nothing to influence directly and appreciably their community's services and agencies. As will be stressed below, however, in Colombia and other Spanish American countries (in which the small group of large landowners who hold and wield most of the economic, political, and military power of the nation traditionally have been and continue to be residents of the exclusive residential areas within the city) the exceptions to this rule are general insofar as the large landowners themselves are concerned. With respect to their retainers, though, and to those segments of the humble mass of the agriculturists who are not directly dependent upon the proprietors of the large estates, the degree to which the campesinos who are encompassed within the social and economic web of an urban community are complete nonentities in the affairs of the large locality group of which they form a part is even more pronounced than generally is the case.

For the part of the scale or series, or the X's which fall in the range above X_9 or any other symbol selected to designate the urban community, the analysis, concepts, and names available are even more incomplete and unsatisfactory than they are for the portions already touched upon. One could, of course, use such modifiers as small, medium, large, and great or huge urban communities, and metropolitan community and megalopolis also are available. But an agglomeration with a built up area containing 100,000 or 200,000 inhabitants, that might very well be the nucleus of a "large" urban community in one location, might be merely one of the satellites or "bedroom" towns of the city in question if were situated in close physical proximity to a great metropolis such as London, Paris, Buenos Aires, New York, or Rio de Janeiro. Likewise Bogotá and its tributary territory certainly constitute a metropolitan community that is vastly different in size, complexity, and structure than Cali or Barranquilla, although both of the latter undoubtedly also qualify for the general designation. In brief, when the appropriate analysis has been made and published, it probably will be readily apparent that there are at least five or six additional X's beyond that representing the urban community, in the series of locality groups which has the household on a single farmstead as X_1 at the one end and the huge metropolitan community as X_n at the other end of the schema.

NEIGHBORHOODS

As the next group beyond the family that is of sociological significance, the neighborhood has been and continues to be one of the more important units in Colombia's social structure. This is especially true in the extensive rural sections of the country, but it also has validity for many parts of the cities and their surrounding rings of suburban slums. In fact the mutual-aid characteristic of the small clusters of the transplanted campesinos appears to be one of the principal factors which enables them to survive amid the rudimentary, congested, promiscuous, and generally sub-human conditions in which they live.[9] Most study of the Colombian neighborhood remains to be done, and the inventory, if ever it is made adequately, should reveal a rich variety of small, intimate, face-to-face locality groups in that highly segmented society. There probably are many interesting and closely knit groupings in the extensive, tumbled masses of rugged, mountainous terrain which form parts of the three great chains of Cordillera on whose slopes and in whose valleys the overwhelming part of all Colombians have their domiciles. But many other kinds probably will appear when we know more about the structure of society and the stage of social differentiation that prevail on the broad coastal plains of the north, on the huge expanses of grasslands to the east of the Andes, and in the inhabited portions of the large valleys of the Magdalena and the Cauca rivers. Still others, many of them probably harking back to a time when the neighborhood and the community were almost one and the same thing (so small was the group involved, so little advanced the processes of division of labor and specialization, and so slightly in contact the members of one small locality group with those of any other), are likely to become apparent as the empirically oriented sociologist tackles the job of observing, analyzing, and describing the basic components of the social structure of the inhabitants of the far-flung, hot, humid, lowland jungles which comprise a high proportion of the national territory.

It seems almost certain that in many of the sparsely populated sections, the obstacles to human occupance, and the difficulties of transportation and communication alone are sufficient to keep the popula-

9. See, for example, Zabala C., *Estudio Social sobre un Barrio de Invasión*, *passim.*

tion nuclei small, the families in any one particular settlement largely restricted to contacts with others in close territorial proximity, and the handful of settlers in any one locality highly dependent upon one another. At most the area involved, the range of activities, and the nature and variety of contact and associations with persons living more than a few miles from their homes, and especially with people residing in population centers of any size, must be extremely limited.

If one considers rural Colombia as a whole, it seems evident that neither now, or in the past, have the masses of the campesinos been in position to develop any large, highly differentiated, and well-integrated locality groups of their own. Except in the now rapidly expanding zones of influence of the major cities, and especially along the new highways that have been built to link them with one another, the humble rural folk remain largely in the neighborhood stage of rural social organization. In sharp contrast with this, of course, are the locality-group attachments of the well-to-do families who own or otherwise control a large part of all of Colombia's most fertile and best-located land. Their homes and bases of operations always have been, of course, in Bogotá and the other principal cities. Their relationships, even those with the families of retainers who live and work on their haciendas, are of the "touch-and-go" variety; they never form any integral part of the communities in which their holdings are located, and, of course, they play little or no role in fostering expanded social horizons on the part of the campesinos. Even less do they exercise any influence upon the locality groupings of the rural families who live beyond the limits of their properties. In other words, there long have been important factors which have worked to maintain the social significance of the neighborhood; and it only is in recent years that a genuine trend of "community development" for the people as a whole has gotten underway.

Although little attention has been given by sociologists and other social scientists to Colombia's neighborhoods, at least two significant soundings and one thorough and complete sociological analysis have been made. All of these, though, were done in areas that are in fairly close proximity to and contact with major urban centers and in locations in which the systems of communication and transportation are among the best in the nation. That even in these situations the neighborhood continues to play a significant social role is strong evidence of its still greater importance in the more remote and isolated parts of the society.

The first of these soundings was in connection with our own survey of Tabio, a municipio some 45 kilometers to the north of Bogotá, which in the 1960's is finding its entire social and economic existence being reshaped as it becomes merely one small segment of the middle portion of the wide zone that now makes up the outlying part of the Bogotá metropolitan community. Even in 1944, when the study was published, however, it is likely that the neighborhood groups in Tabio encompassed the lives of the campesinos of the municipio to a far less degree than typically was the case throughout Colombia.

Be this as it may, at that time, on the basis of a painstaking house-to-house survey of the entire municipio, plus intensive study of all the statistical materials available in governmental and ecclesiastical agencies, we were able to report:

> Some of the outlying *veredas* also could be classified as neighborhoods, for there is a network of intimate social relationships between the families who live in Río Frío Oriental, and also among those who reside in Río Frío Occidental. For example, the families of these neighborhoods lend one another farm implements, aid each other in cases of sickness and death, and generally practice a system of mutual aid. In fact, the case is not rare in which the adults of a family going elsewhere in search of temporary employment leave their small children with a neighbor for the months they are away. Elsewhere in the municipio the neighborhood groupings are less well defined, but they are present nevertheless.[10]

The second of the soundings, one more highly focused upon neighborhoods as such and more intensive, is that published in 1958 that describes the nature of the locality groups, housing, and related matters, in a well-located district in the famed Cauca Valley.[11] It was done under the auspices of the Inter-American Housing and Planning Center, with headquarters in Bogotá, and directly under the guidance and supervision of Colombia's best trained and most accomplished sociologist, Orlando Fals-Borda. I had the pleasure of visiting the project, discussing the work with the directors and the field workers, and interviewing the heads of households in about ten of the families included. As in the case of the study of Saucio, discussed next, there was no lack of sound theoretical orientation and methodological competency on the part of those responsible for the study of Chambimbal. They understood the exact nature of the neighborhood concept, they were keenly aware of the difference between a neigh-

10. Smith, Díaz, and García, *Tabio*, p. 47.
11. Vautier and Fals-Borda, *La Vereda de Chambimbal.*

borhood and a community, and they took care to make the observations needed in order to delimit and to classify properly the territorial unit they were investigating. All of this is in healthy contrast to the lack of adequate preparation on the part of so many of those who are carrying on community studies throughout the world. Moreover, it is interesting to note, the authors of the report were conscious of the paucity of meaningful sociological terms available for dealing with the plentitude of varieties of actual locality groups, and they introduced a distinction between the larger neighborhood (*vecindario mayor*) and the smaller neighborhood (*vecindario menor*). This indicates that I am not alone in realizing the need for additional and more definite concepts to apply to those genuine locality groupings that are too large and too diverse to qualify as neighborhoods, while at the same time that they definitely are not entitled to be denoted as communities.

The reality and nature of the neighborhood groupings observed and described, however, even in a location only a few miles from the important little city of Buga and definitely within the zone embraced in the metropolitan community of Cali, makes this study of particular significance. Therefore it is desirable to give in a rather literal translation a few of the paragraphs in which Vautier and Fals-Borda dealt specifically with the locality-group structure in the area they were studying. Thus they indicate, first of all, that the "rural neighborhood of Chambimbal is located in the Municipio of Buga, departamento of El Valle del Cauca, in Colombia, from whose *cabecera* (head town or seat) it is separated by a distance of five kilometers. As a political and administrative entity called a *vereda* in Colombia, which is a subdivision of a municipio and is in charge of a commissioner, it is delimited as follows. . . ."[12]

However, the larger neighborhood which corresponds to the administrative subdivision studied, itself is a cluster of three genuine locality groups of the primary type, or as stated in the report itself:

> Chambimbal has three rural neighborhoods of the primary type which function in a manner very similar to others that have been studied in Colombia and some other American countries. They are based upon the frequent, intimate contacts between their members, who have common activities, and practice mutual aid which produce social bonds that identify and perpetuate the group in time and space.

12. *Ibid.*, p. 7.

Outstanding among these bonds are: the physical proximity of the dwellings to one another and dependence upon the road for going to and from work in the fields and for getting to and from the city (Buga), which produces social contacts; the use of the place name, because the inhabitants identify themselves as belonging to "the vereda of Chambimbal"; kinship ties, because many of the local families are related to one another; religion, because they are Catholics and they participate together in religious activities; political affiliations, because they all belong to the same political party; recreational interests and participation, because they have [sports'] fields, taverns, and kiosks in the vereda to which they resort in their spare time; the rural schools located in the district which they attend; and a certain degree of mutual aid manifested in the loan of tools and implements.

Actually the larger neighborhood functions only as a political-administrative group, with its place name of Chambimbal, and it really is composed of three smaller neighborhoods which are separated from one another by haciendas. The inhabitants identify these smaller neighborhoods as *"caseríos,"* named after the lanes on which they are located as Balanta, Chambimbal (of the South), and Cauca.

There are few relationships between the smaller neighborhoods. Distance is a factor in this, since the neighborhoods are separated from one another by the haciendas. There is some rivalry between the three, expressed by the desires of each one to enjoy certain material advantages such as water and light. Nevertheless the prevalent attitude among them is that of indifference to one another. There is some recognition of racial differences between these neighborhoods, for those of the southern lane say that the people of Balanta are Negroes.

The larger neighborhood of Chambimbal, the "vereda" or *corregimiento,* with its three smaller nuclei, forms an integral part of the Buga community, to which also belong other "veredas" and parts of adjacent municipios. Buga exercises an attraction that is primarily economic, recreational, and religious, although it is beginning to provide educational and credit institutions.[13]

The third of the genuine sociological studies of Colombian neighborhoods is by far the most thoroughgoing and complete of the three. It was done by Dr. Orlando Fals-Borda, co-author of the Chambimbal report, over a period of years in which he came to know personally all of the families in the neighborhood. It was not primarily a study in community or neighborhood delineation, although this indispensable feature of an adequate investigation was done with care. Indeed it stands as a model not merely of the delineation of the locality group, but also as a piece of sociological research in depth dealing with society in miniature.

13. *Ibid.,* p. 20.

The methodology employed by Fals-Borda in his painstaking study of the neighborhood of Saucio[14] deserves special comment. In addition to a detailed schedule of questions which he personally used in his interviews with members of all the families, aids to observation employed included aerial photographs of the area and detailed base maps of the locality and its adjacent territory. These base maps provided information on the exact location of each of the dwellings, and those of the stores and the school. They also showed the routes of the highway and the railroad, as well as all of the trails and footpaths, the rivers and creeks, and the contour lines indicative of variations in altitudes.

The first step was to determine the limits of the Chocontá community, within which the neighborhood of Saucio is located, and to whose small urban nucleus the campesinos of the area go for market and church purposes. Next, the young sociologist sought to determine the extent to which the people in the locality identified themselves with the place name of Saucio. Then he attempted to identify the "kinship" area, which proved to be somewhat larger than the "self-identification" neighborhood; and finally he mapped the area of influence of each of the stores and that of the school.

On the basis of the thorough investigation he had made, Fals-Borda concluded that "the sociological, or 'real' boundaries do not follow the lines set up for the legal district or township—also called the 'vereda' of Saucio. . . ." Rather it includes not only this legal or administrative district, but "also portions of two neighboring 'legal veredas,' called Vera Cruz and Cruces."[15] The neighborhood in 1951 embraced an area of about five square miles and 77 dwellings or households.

In no sense of the word are the three soundings that have been taken of the neighborhoods in Colombia a representative sample of the small locality groups of that nation. All of them were made in locations that are much more influenced by the proximity of large, thriving metropolitan cities than is true of Colombian rural territory generally. But in a certain sense the findings of the three studies are of even greater significance than they otherwise would be precisely on that account; for they demonstrate that the small, intimate, primary groups persist to a very high degree even in the portions of the Republic that have been most influenced by contact with twentieth-

14. See Fals-Borda, *Peasant Life in the Colombian Andes,* Chapter 3, entitled, "The Morphology of a Neighborhood."
15. *Ibid.,* p. 47.

century developments. They show that such little locality groupings are a factor to be reckoned with in community development programs and all other features of realistic social planning, from that connected with the organization of such entities as schools and cooperatives to that having to do with programs of agricultural and industrial development.

As transportation and communication systems improve, however, it is likely that the vitality of Colombian neighborhoods will decrease even more rapidly than has been the case in the United States and Canada. This is because the factor that has done most to preserve small, intimate primary-group localities or neighborhoods in the latter, namely the small open-country church and its associated cemetery, is practically lacking in Colombia. In other words the highly important religious groupings which have tended to preserve small neighborhoods in the rural portions of America north of Mexico, have exerted their influence in exactly the opposite direction in Colombia, where definitely they help promote the strength of rural and rurban communities.

VARIETIES OF COMMUNITIES

Other than the study of the rural community, which has been one of the principal features in the development of the sociology of rural life in the United States, it is fair to say that comprehensive analysis of the community as such is lacking. This is to indicate that social cytology is in a very undeveloped stage, both theoretically and functionally. It is not to be interpreted as indicating, however, that much highly important analysis has not been made of certain large central cities, or the nuclei of important communities, such as Chicago or Los Angeles; nor is it a contention that competent analysis has not been made of the little urban places which constitute the centers of smaller communities, such as Muncie, Indiana ("Middletown"). It is intended, though to stress the fact that investigations of the total community (of the entire web of social relationships which constitutes the large locality group as such), be it rurban, urban, or metropolitan, is still a thing of the future. Since this is the case in the United States, Europe, Japan, and India, it is not strange that it also is true in Colombia. In the latter, specifically, the studies of complete locality groupings have been limited so far to those of rural neighborhoods and sub-communities; and sociological analyses of complete communities, even those of the rural type, have not yet been undertaken. Therefore, what is said in this section necessarily must be considered as preliminary and tentative. It consists largely of ideas and hypotheses that are based for the most part upon personal observation of the area involved over a quarter of a century.

The Metropolitan Community.—From the earliest decades of the conquest until the present, the capital, Bogotá, has maintained its hegemony over most of the entire area presently embraced within the limits of the Republic of Colombia. This preponderant influence, though, long was largely confined to administrative and ecclesiastical matters and was limited to the intermingling of the interests of the dominant families of Spanish origin and their patroonships over the Indians and mestizos in the rural areas. Moreover, even these overlords operated largely out of secondary centers such as Tunja, Pamplona, Cartagena, Popayán, and Pasto, wherein most of the aristocratic families had the seats of their power. Today Bogotá retains the governmental and administrative hegemony of the entire nation, as seat of the presidency, as location of the legislative and chief judicial branches of the government, as the main residence of many upper-class families whose ancestral estates are located in all parts of the nation, and as the arena of operations of the vast majority of those who make up the bureaucracy. Thanks to the constitutional provisions whereby the President appoints all of the governors of the departments and the latter name the alcaldes of the municipios (or counties), the power and influence of the Ministries seated in Bogotá reach frequently, quickly, and forcefully into every segment of national territory. Nowadays, perhaps, the traditional preponderance of the capital in ecclesiastical matters may be less than it once was, as indeed is true of church influences in social, economic, political, and administrative affairs generally. Even if this is the case it probably is far more than offset by other new and potent forces which now are in operation, that is from the standpoint of the extent to which Colombia is one vast metropolitan community having Bogotá as its nucleus. The forces include: (1) the use of the airplane to place copies of the capital's newspapers in the hands of readers throughout the Republic the day they are published; (2) the great reliance upon official banks, credit agencies, and national appropriations for operating capital by those who control the large agricultural enterprises, the business firms, and the industrial plants; (3) the rapid development of Bogotá as a genuine hub of the transportation system by the building of a network of highways, the extension of the railroad lines, and the mushrooming of international and national air services operating through and out of the great airport of El Dorado on the Savanna of Bogotá; and (4) the ever-increasing variety and frequency of the circulation of officials and employees of the central governmental agencies throughout the cities, towns, and villages which dot the national territory.

It would be unwise, however, to make the assumption that Bogotá, through intensive study and analysis of pertinent data, would be found to be the only city in Colombia entitled to be designated as the nucleus of an important metropolitan community. The preliminary observations and analyses made to date would indicate that at least Cali, Medellín, and Barranquilla are the hubs of genuine networks of community interrelationships, and that the central city of each plus the extensive zone over which it exercises a preponderant influence also is a genuine metropolitan community. It is true that the political-administrative functions of each, even within the parts of their tributary zones made up of the area of the departments of which they are the capitals, fade into insignificance in comparison with those of Bogotá. But in commercial matters, and especially the extent to which they are the wholesale and distributing centers for extensive surrounding areas, these cities compare favorably with the national capital. Likewise they are the seats of operations for affluent landowning families who own and control the haciendas and plantations within a radius of many miles in all directions from each of the flourishing cities indicated.

Before many more decades have passed one may confidently expect that some of these aspects of Colombia's community structure will have been studied. Then in the case of Cali, for example, we shall know the extent to which Buenaventura and the entire area surrounding that important Pacific port are involved in the warp and woof of the Cali metropolitan community; we shall be able to ascertain the extent to which Popayán is within the zone preponderantly influenced by the same important center, and indeed we shall learn how much further to the South the actual limit of the great community extends; we shall have had demonstrated clearly whether or not the crest of the Central Cordillera forms a line for many miles which separates the metropolitan community of Cali from that of Bogotá; and we shall have information as to whether or not the metropolitan communities of Cali and Medellín share a common boundary, if so the location and extent of the line separating them, if not the nature and form of the interstitial zone between the two, and how the smaller urban center of Manizales and its peripheral area of influence fit into the general picture.

Urban Communities.—Perhaps the Colombian communities actually entitled to the designation of metropolitan are limited to the four mentioned above, Bogotá, Cali, Medellín, and Barranquilla. Certainly all of them qualify for inclusion in the category of the largest and most important of the locality groups in the nation. There are several others, however, such as Cartagena, Bucaramanga, and perhaps even Cucutá and Manizales, which might be considered as having nuclei that are large enough, sufficiently diverse, and with peripheries extending beyond the departments of which they serve as capitals to a degree high enough to justify placing them in the metropolitan group. It is more likely, though, that they presently most properly belong in the urban-community class, although with a modifier of "large" added to distinguish them from other significant locality groups definitely entitled to a place in the category under consideration, but formed of population centers and their tributary areas that are much smaller and less dilated than the communities named above. In the case of Cartagena, for example, we definitely are dealing with an urban community whose periphery extends to the south far beyond the limits of the department of Bolívar, of which the city itself is the capital, to compete with Medellín for hegemony in commerce, trade, and transportation matters over Montería and the agricultural and pastoral areas of the Sinú Valley and other parts of the department of Córdoba. But as in the case of the other great webs of social and economic ties and relationships, we neither know the boundaries of these community interests and bonds nor the exact features of which they are composed. Bucaramanga, Cucutá, and Manizales, on the other hand, probably have the degree to which their realms of community influence extends into adjacent parts of departments neighboring upon the ones of which they are the capitals more than offset, from the standpoint of qualifying as metropolitan communities, by strong rival urban communities within their own departments. In the case of Bucaramanga the river port of Barrancabermeja definitely enjoys some advantages as the commercial and distribution center for much of the department of Santander; Cucutá by no means is able to take over all of the zones of influence traditionally tied in with Pamplona and Ocaña; and Manizales must share the territory which might form part of its tributary zone with thriving little cities such as Pereira and Armenia. The actual mapping of the limits of all these urban communities, irrespective of whether some of them may be thought of as metropolitan, or large, as the case may be, though, as well as a determination of the exact nature of the principal community ties involved, all is still to be done by the new generation of pragmatically oriented sociologists. The same is true of the urban communities whose nuclei serve as capitals of other departments, including Pasto, Popayán, Neiva, Ibague, Villavicencio, Tunja, Montería, and Santa Marta; and dozens of other smaller urban communities scattered throughout national territory.

Rurban Communities.—The tasks of identifying, mapping and properly classifying the few metropolitan communities, approximately a dozen "large" urban communities, and perhaps as many as 100 other genuine urban communities are fairly substantial. But these tasks, large as they are, are relatively small in comparison with those of a proper sociological inventory of Colombia's rurban communities, or those locality groups in which agricultural and pastoral activities are approximately in balance with the strictly urban functions such as trade and commerce, communications and transportation, manufacturing and processing, and so on. The number of such communities may run into the hundreds, and adequate criteria and carefully made observations will have to be made before one may be sure that a given community actually belongs in the rurban category as such and not in the urban class which is located above it in the scale or in the very numerous group of rural communities, which make up the class below it in size, complexity, and importance. Offhand there is some reason to suppose that many seats of municipios, particularly those that have developed the commercial function to the extent that they are drawing considerable trade from neighboring municipios, make up the bulk of the rurban communities. Probably an important feature for helping to distinguish the rurban from the rural community is the relative importance of the weekly market as opposed to the stores and shops of established merchants. The traditional open-air, weekly market held in the central plaza and accompanied by a scarcity of established retail outlets is a strong indicator that the village is the nucleus of a rural community. On the other hand the presence of many general stores, food stores, drygoods stores, and other specialized businesses, and the relegation of the weekly market to a secondary role, frequently to a location other than the central plaza, denotes more of a balance between agricultural and nonagricultural interests and activities within the community and the attainment of rurban status by the locality group taken as a whole. In line with this thinking, the criteria for meriting classification in the rurban category are present in many or most of the cases in which the population of the little urb which forms the nucleus of the community has reached 2,500 or 3,000 and constitutes at least about 35 to 40 per cent of all the people in the municipio in which it is located.

The Rural Community.—Traditionally the mass of Colombia's population has always consisted of the campesino element, that is of humble people who tilled the land and cared for the herds, generally as retainers of the privileged upper-class landowners who operated out of a few important urban centers, although in considerable numbers as owners or renters of, or squatters upon, small subsistence tracts. This is to say that they not only have lived in strictly rural communities, but for the last 150 years their scattered settlement patterns have been the general rule in the open-country or at least non-village parts of such communities. Only in the second half of the twentieth century, as droves of up-rooted campesinos swell the numbers of the miserable proletariat in the cities, is the numerical superiority of the members of the rural communities being challenged.

Structurally, the type of rural community identified and described by C. J. Galpin, working in Walworth County, Wisconsin, at about the time of the outbreak of the First World War, is the predominant one. In other words, the typical rural community in Colombia consists of two parts: (1) a small market, trade, religious, ceremonial, and administrative center; and (2) a tributary zone of open country whose inhabitants can reach the village or town on market days and Sundays, generally on foot, and return to their dwellings before nightfall. Each community probably consists of a cluster of smaller locality groups, neighborhoods and sub-communities, although the lack of open-country churches and plants for processing farm products (cheese factories, cotton gins, and so forth) does not foster the preservation of tiny locality groupings within the rural community to the extent that their presence does in parts of the United States. The second structural type of rural community is practically non-existent in Colombia. That is the one made up of a true agricultural village, which is primarily a residential center for those who till the land, plus the surrounding zone of arable and pasture lands, to

The weekly open-air market is a principal integrating factor in the Colombian rural community. (Photos by the author.)

The parking lot is an indispensable adjunct to the weekly market. (Photo by the author.)

Those of all ages who live on farms take something to the weekly market. Here one boy has a rooster, the other a load of wood. (Photos by the author.)

As the market ends, campesinos head for their homes in the surrounding area.
(Photos by the author.)

which the villagers commute daily for work on their badly fragmented holdings. Indeed the sharp contrast in the structural type of rural community that prevails is one of the important social and cultural forms which distinguishes the texture of Colombian rural society from that of the mother country, Spain, on the one hand, and such Latin American countries as Mexico, on the other. In this respect the rural community in Colombia resembles that in the United States.

As has been indicated above, we know comparatively little about the sociology of the Colombian rural community. It is likely that the vast majority of all seats of municipios in Colombia are the nuclei of corresponding rural communities; it is probable that in a large portion of those in which the areas of the municipios are small enough to permit sufficient contact between the families in the outlying districts and the center, given the rudimentary systems of transportation that prevail, there is a substantial tendency for municipio and community limits to coincide. The strength of this tendency is a matter calling for sociological research. In a few cases, such as that of Guaduas in Cundinamarca, the 1951 census indicated there were two "urban" centers, that of Guaduas the administrative center, with 2,466 inhabitants, and that of Puerto Bogotá, with 1,516. According to the line of thought developed here, these data indicate that there are at least two communities in that municipio, the larger of which might even qualify as rurban.

Finally, in closing this brief discussion of the varieties of communities in Colombia, perhaps it is well to indicate the two things which are essential if a genuine understanding of the Colombian communities is to be secured. The first of these is a careful study of selected locality groups by dozens of graduate students from Colombia and other countries who are gaining experience in research connected with theses or dissertations. The second calls for substantial improvements in the ways in which Colombian census materials are tabulated and published. Two chief innovations are long over due. (In this connection the practices followed by Mexico and Peru might well be considered.) One of these is to subdivide the municipio, for statistical purposes, into a number of smaller and more homogeneous sections, for which information at least on the total number of inhabitants would be published. The other is to identify all population centers, villages, hamlets, and so on, irrespective of whether or not they have any administrative function, and to publish at least the total number of inhabitants in each of them.

COMMUNITY DEVELOPMENT

As indicated above, there is much confusion in Colombia and elsewhere as to the meanings of such terms as community and community study; but even so the multiplicity of vaguely conceived and imprecisely expressed ideas relating to those two concepts is dwarfed by the chaotic condition of all that has to do with the expression "community development" or the equally ambiguous "community organization." In Colombia alone community development may denote anything from the organization of rural educational institutions, as expressed by those promoting various programs of *acción comunal*, to measures designed to locate, delineate, and analyze specific locality groups with a view to strengthening the functions and increasing the cohesion of the communities involved, as generally is the case when professional sociologists are involved. Most frequently, though, is probably a line of departure which assumes that community development consists of organizing welfare activities or local self-help activities which seem to be the points of departure of the social workers and anthropologists, respectively. All of these activities are badly needed in a rural society, such as that in Colombia, in which the two-class system of social stratification has prevailed for centuries, in which the mass of the rural people are either agricultural laborers or at most the owners or renters of very small plots of relatively poor land, in which hoe culture and the still more primitive system of felling and burning are the principal ways of getting products from the soil, and in which the smallest subdivision of government is really an administrative division of the national government and not a unit that by any stretch of the imagination is entitled to be called an entity for local self-government. But it hardly improves the situation intellectually and scientifically to designate everything designed to accomplish changes as "community development." In this section this expression is intended to denote the process of increasing the role and functions, the strength and vitality, and the greater adequacy in general of locality groups properly classified as communities, be they rural, rurban, urban, or metropolitan. In this connection five sub-topics are discussed, in turn: (1) locating and identifying the community and its limits or boundaries; (2) community organization measures; (3) the construction of community score cards; (4) the causes of the backwardness of specific communities; and (5) the need in modern societies for adjusting community limits and the boundaries of local governmental units so that the two will coincide.

Locating and Identifying the Community.—It would seem to be axiomatic that before a specific community can be developed, precise information is needed about the community itself, its principal features, and the locations of the boundaries that separate it from other community groupings. This type of work has indeed been a major interest of those interested in the sociology of rural life from about 1910 until the present. As indicated above, it figured prominently in the pioneering work of Fals-Borda and his associates in Colombia. Nevertheless, it must be stressed that such work, further refined so that it would be clear in each case whether the level of social integration at which the work was being done was that of the rural community, the rurban community, the urban community, or the metropolitan community, respectively, must be the first step in all well-planned programs of community development.

Community Organization Measures.—In Colombia, where everything related to genuine community organization is still to be done, some endeavors to organize a small council to take stock of community needs and to propose specific community actions undoubtedly are the first steps to be taken. Such a council will be useless, of course, unless it is composed of respected representatives of all the principal interests in the locality, such as the leadership of the religious, educational, mercantile, and agricultural interests. But it must also include persons who can be considered knowledgeable and who will speak for things of concern to those in the various smaller locality groups of which the community is made up (neighborhoods, sub-communities, and in case of the higher levels of integration, the rural communities). Similarly, it must be evident to all that the community council should include some members who are from the campesino and other portions of the humble class, and not exclusively those who are members of or retainers of the families that traditionally have owned the haciendas and largely controlled affairs in the locality. Merely the organization of an effective community council in many parts of Colombia may prove to be so great a hurdle as to preclude any realistic programs of community development. This will be true even at the rural community level where the limits of the municipio may define fairly well those of the community; it will be even more difficult, or impossible, at the rurban stage in which there still is little or no recognition of the ways in which the well-being of a small city is increasingly becoming interlinked with that of those who live in adjacent municipios; and it remains to be seen if through a council, or in any other concrete way, the larger urban and the metropolitan centers will make any endeavors to promote the welfare of the smaller communities, the sub-communities, the neighborhoods, and the single families who make up the huge segments of the actual communities which lie beyond the city's limits.

Community Score Cards.—It is a curious fact that, in the development of scientific techniques, sociologists (or those assertedly concerned primarily with group, collective, and institutional phenomena) have rivaled psychologists (or those admittedly chiefly preoccupied with individual behavior as such) in the extent to which they have developed and tested various scales and other devices for the measurement of the features, or characteristics, or traits of specific persons. Alongside the substantial accomplishments in this rather psychological endeavor, however, stands an almost complete failure to develop the appropriate tests and scales for studying social groups, social classes, social institutions, social processes, social change, and other pivotal features of any social system. Hence we know or have the scientific paraphernalia needed to ascertain considerable about the personality of Mr. A. or Mrs. B.; whereas we neither know nor have we perfected the tools that are needed to analyze the "personality" of a city or village, of a school or a religious congregation, of a community or neighborhood, and so on. There is no reason why such obvious next steps in the development of sociological methodology might not be taken in Colombia, either by some of the new generation of pragmatic sociologists or by their fellows from elsewhere who are interested in understanding Colombian society.

The need for such a tool is patent. It is almost an indispensable piece of intellectual equipment for anyone who would seek to determine the nature and degree of change involved in community development programs. Only by a measurement of the situation at a given time, followed by a repetition of the "test" at a subsequent date and a careful comparison of the results of the two is it possible to determine with any degree of accuracy the type and magnitude of the changes actually taking place.

Theoretically, the construction and standardization of a scale or scales (any kind of a score card) are fairly simple undertakings. Indeed the perfection of a community score card should be far less complex and difficult than the jobs, already completed with a fair degree of success, such as devising ways to measure attitudes, developing social status scales, determining indicators of levels and standards of living, and perfecting personality scales. Perhaps the most difficult part of the entire process consists of establishing a few basic and appropriate assumptions relative to the values which prevail during the second half of the twentieth century which must be made before anyone can undertake the actual work of making the score card itself.

Were I to undertake the construction and standardization of a community score card, especially one for use in Colombia, I would start with a device designed to evaluate the rural community since it is the smallest of the community groupings, is less complex than the larger units, and is the one which encompasses the lives of the majority of the Colombian population. Moreover, among the basic assumptions I would have in mind in designing the exact information to be secured as the basis for arriving at the scores for various communities, the three following ones would have prominent places.

First, in order for a rural community to be considered as a strong or highly developed locality group, all of its members must have had their human capacities and abilities developed to levels that fairly approximate their potentialities. In a rural and agricultural setting this favorable condition is most nearly attained when each person who gains a livelihood from farming and stock-raising activities is able to perform in a skillful manner all three of the basic economic functions, namely those of the entrepreneur who accumulates and invests money in agricultural enterprises, those of the manager of such enterprises, and those of the worker who actually performs the tasks or manual labor on the farm. A few words of elaboration relative to each of these three functions may help in understanding better how they exercise decisive influences in the development of the human personality.

Although we do not yet know why it was that mankind alone hit upon and perfected the means of transmitting knowledge of rudimentary tools and implements from one generation to another, so that children could build upon the knowledge possessed by their parents, we can be certain that the building of culture originated in this simple manner; and we also are well aware that dexterity in the use of tools, implements, and machines continues to be a major distinction between human beings and other members of the animal kingdom. Likewise mankind alone, except for some of the social insects, has the ability to maintain, discipline, train, harness, pack, hitch, or otherwise guide and direct other animals in ways designed to ease his burdens, share his labor, and provide many of the things such as milk, eggs, meat, and butter, which form basic ingredients in his diet. Mastery of tools, implements, and machines and great skill in the care and management of livestock are essential in the efficient performance of the essential labor function of an agricultural mode of existence. In a well-developed rural community the bulk of the adults are well-equipped to do all the essential tasks on the farm, and the children acquire such training almost from the day they are able to walk. In such a community a host of factors such as crude and outmoded tools and equipment, servitude to established work routines, overpopulation, and underemployment do not result in the needless and senseless expenditure of labor in the productive process. In Colombia, as is evident from some of the other chapters in this volume, great strides could be taken in community development merely by local, regional, and national programs designed to improve the hand implements through which much of the farming is done, to substitute animal power for manpower in the agricultural processes, and to promote the mechanization of agriculture along lines directly beneficial to those who cultivate small acreages of land.

The original nature of man also enables the average human being, including the children born to the typical Colombian campesinos, to acquire a vast range of managerial skills and aptitudes. If given a chance by the institutional framework within the rural community, these peculiarly human abilities can become the central features of the mass of those who inhabit the rural areas of Colombia. In the strong or well-developed rural community, they are being exercised to a high degree by the heads of almost all the farm families and children in these families are growing up expecting to perform them as a matter of course.

In addition to his ability as a worker, and his potentiality as a manager or farm operator, the typical Colombian campesino, given the proper rearing and training during his formative years, is capable of developing habits of thrift, saving, and investment. He, too, can postpone the pleasures of immediate consumption in the hope of enjoying even greater satisfactions later on, and he can acquire all of the other features that lead to the accumulation and exercise of property rights to land and farming equipment. In tens of thousands of well-developed rural communities throughout the world, all of the farmers are highly inculcated with attitudes and habits of thrift, saving, and entrepreneurship, while at the same time they are occupied day and night with the problems of farm management with only themselves to do all of the manual tasks required in their enterprises. Eventually the same may be true in Colombia. If this is to be so, however, substantial and realistic programs of community development must become a central part of all development activities. Irrespective of whether or not such programs are actually perfected and put into effect, specific items which help to gauge the extent to which this is the case must form a part of the community score card of which we are writing.

Other components of the scoring device or community test proposed should be derived from the second of the three basic assumptions mentioned above as underlying the actual work of developing the instrument. This assumption is that in a strong or well developed rural community the families directly dependent upon agriculture are enjoying levels and standards of living that are high relative to the resources and potentialities of the area in which they live and work. This is, of course, highly interrelated with the factors mentioned specifically in connection with the first assumption. In addition to those, however, certain others deserve specific mention. These include a population that is not excessively large in comparison with "the carrying capacity," if a phrase may be borrowed from animal industry terminology, of the community's area, combinations of the factors of production in ways which make generous inputs of capital and management and tend to be parsimonious with labor, freedoms and intellectual stimulations which expand the wants and aspirations of the farm people, and abundant technical and scientific information readily available to each farmer and the members of his family.

The third and final assumption to be mentioned at this place which is highly relevant as a basis for helping to determine the specific items that should be selected for use on a community score card has to do with the community's institutions and agencies. Briefly this assumption holds that a rural community is strong when its local institutions are organized and functioning in a way that provides the fullest satisfactions for the fundamental needs of those who form part of the locality group, insures that the members of the oncoming generation will develop full and well-rounded personalities, and has effectively in operation all of the agencies required to provide adequately for the care and welfare of all those who for any reason are unable to look out for themselves. In addition to the specific items mentioned in connection with the two preceding assumptions, in

Workers from the Candelaria Health Center, a rural project of the faculty of medicine of the University of El Valle, make home visits to encourage pregnant women to attend the center's prenatal clinic. (Courtesy of the Rockefeller Foundation.)

order to satisfy such a criterion, the rural community must be characterized by strong family organization which makes this basic kinship unit function effectively both as an educational and as a welfare agency. Furthermore, it must have a school system and a set of welfare services that will compare favorably with those in the strongest rural communities throughout the world.

Causes of Arrested Community Development.—Sociologists, and particularly those who have given the attention deserved to those institutions that govern man's relationship to the land, are able to identify and measure to some extent the forces which are responsible for the comparative lack of community development in Colombia and many other countries. By so doing they can contribute greatly to more realistic efforts on the part of those who are charged with the responsibility for framing and administering programs of community development or for overcoming the barriers to the rise of strong, virile, and adequate community groupings in any particular country. As is the case with most social and economic matters, the factors responsible for arrested community development are many and complex, and many of them are closely interrelated in the causative patterns that are responsible for the comparative weakness of the community units in Colombia, Brazil, the United States, or almost any other part of the world. Nevertheless, certain of these factors are so closely associated or correlated with the prevalence of weak and debile community groupings that one must be fairly sure that they are indispensable elements in the complex of determinants which produces community atrophy or retardation. Almost without exception they will be found as central elements in the social system that prevails in areas in which the communities are weak and poorly developed; and wherever they have been allowed to play any considerable role in social and economic affairs, community organization is almost sure to be found in a condition of considerable backwardness.

Most of the factors primarily involved in retarded community development are dealt with in some detail in other chapters of this volume. To some extent they overlap, and of course they all are related to the cultural heritage received from Spain. This, the mother society, was one in which most important matters had been concentrated at the Court for so long that, at the time of the conquest, the once important roles played by the various pueblos had dwindled away almost to the vanishing point. But not all of the reasons for the atrophied condition of the modern Colombian community should be attributed to defects in the social patterns that were transplanted from the Old World. Many of them are inherent in the manner in which social institutions developed in the New. Among the latter, first in order as it usually is first in importance, is the high degree of concentration of the ownership and control of the land and its corollary, the all-important fact that the masses of the population were reduced to and maintained in the status of mere agricultural laborers. Where a favored few own and control the bulk of the best located and most fertile land, as is true in much of Colombia, in many other parts of Latin America, and in some sections of the United States, the bulk of the population is debased to positions at the very bottom of the social and economic scale. As is indicated in Chapters 2 and 3, this means that they are deprived of all opportunities of acquiring and exercising the managerial and proprietorial functions, and at best they can receive no larger share of the product than the rewards attributed to their poorly utilized toil. Even more important, it also means they are unable to transmit to their children any attitudes, aptitudes, habits and skills other than the ones involved in the routinary performance, under the watchful eye of some driver or overseer, of a few kinds of manual labor. It is true that in some cases the lordly masters of the huge landed estates, from humanistic or other motives, may seek to provide for the welfare and development of their laborers; but such cases are not common, and they rarely are passed on from one generation of landlords to another. As a general rule the concentration in a few hands of the ownership and control of the land means that the bulk of those who live in the rural communities is reduced to a level of mere creature existence, so that anything remotely resembling a strong and vigorous community organization and life is absolutely impossible.

Closely related to the concentration in the ownership and control of the land, in the syndrome of causes responsible for the ills of Colombia's communities, is the lack of control by the people who make up the community itself of the basic forces on which their well-being is dependent. The system of large estates is part and parcel of this lack of control, and such a situation is gravely accentuated wherever, as in Colombia, most of the large landowners are absentees. In Colombia, much of the land is owned by a few powerful families whose major residences are in the principal cities. As is indicated in various places in this book, the heads of these families visit their estates only on rare occasions. Although they secure the bulk of all that is produced within the community, over and above that which must go to meet the bare creature needs of the workers and their families, they contribute very little to the support of churches, schools, and other community institutions and agencies. Moreover, at the provincial and national levels they exercise rigid controls over what may or may not be done by the communities and other locality groups. This is possible because wherever the ownership of the land is concentrated in the hands of a few large landowners, that small group has a stranglehold upon the political and administrative machinery of the nation. In Colombia they have always seen to it that there are national prohibitions which prevent the people in the local administrative districts (or municipios) from levying any significant tax upon the land and other real estate; and, as in other parts of Latin America, this means that those living in the rural communities lack any effective means whereby significant proportions of the energy expended annually and products taken from the local farms and industries can be pooled for the use of schools, the safeguarding of life and property, the building of roads, trails, and bridges, the provision of health and welfare services, and so on. As is stressed in Chapter 2 the ownership of land tends to become an asylum for capital, economic pressures do not insure its use, and the workers and their families suffer acutely from poverty, ignorance, misery, ill health, and malnutrition. Even the church languishes in communities whose lands are held by a few absentee owners.

The lack of schools and the absence of various other educational institutions, irrespective of the cause, are certainly among the factors responsible for keeping many communities in an undeveloped stage. As has been indicated above, well-organized schools and other educational agencies rarely are found in areas in which the rural social system has the large landed estate as its central core, but adequate facilities for instruction are lacking in many other communities as well. However, whatever may be the cause, unless it has excellent educational institutions freely available to all of the children and in which the members of the new generation may acquire the fundamental elements of a general education and considerable training and drill in vocational subjects, no community can reach a very high stage of development. Also essential for the fullest accomplishments of those who make up the rural community is a rich set of extension services, library facilities, visual aids, and various other means to assist the adult members of the group in their efforts to make use of current knowledge of technical agriculture, homemaking, and community life.

Another of the principal causes of atrophied community organization in many parts of the world, including much of Colombia, is the wasteful, ineffective, and inefficient ways in which large proportions of the farmers are attempting to wrest a living from the soil. This matter is analyzed at length in Chapter 5. Late in the 1960's, as mankind is well within the portals of the nuclear age, one who seriously considers the matter can hardly keep from being appalled by the fact that at least 50 per cent of all the world's farmers, and also at least one-half of all those in Colombia, are relying upon systems of agriculture that are more rudimentary and primitive than those the Egyptians were using at the dawn of history. This is to say that the bulk of the agriculturists continue to be dependent upon the ax and fire, the hoe, or the most rudimentary variety of plow culture, in their efforts to gain a livelihood. Labor, the very life blood of human societies, is being wasted with abandon, and capital and management employed most parsimoniously in the production process. As a result the annual production per man is very low, and under such circumstances the members of the rural community (in which the bulk of the people of Colombia and also those of the world still have their being) can never produce enough to enable them to attain anything except a very low level of living. In many cases, too, the amounts available to those who live and work in the community are drastically reduced because of the shares that go to the absentee landlords who own and control the land on which they work. It is for this reason that efforts to improve the system of agriculture, along with those for effecting a redistribution of the rights to the land and the tremendous essential for the building of an adequate educational system, and the whole process of community development itself, are indispensable features of any realistic program of agrarian reform in Colombia or almost any other part of the world. Happily, though, as has been shown by the studies of the diffusion of culture in general and those of the adoption of agricultural practices in particular, if given a genuine opportunity farmers are avid for the chance to possess the soil on which they work, to acquire the managerial skills needed for its proper use, and to learn the ways by which they can better prepare the soil, control the weeds and pests, ease the burdens of transportation, and otherwise improve the systems of agriculture upon which they are dependent.[16]

Finally, many Colombian communities remain in a weak and amorphous condition largely because the area in which they are located is seriously overpopulated; with the existing knowledge of natural resources and how they may be used, there simply are more people on the land than it can maintain at anything resembling a satisfactory level of living. In other words, in such communities, and despite the fact that human toil is wasted with abandon, there still remains much unemployment and underemployment on the part of the rural workers. As a matter of fact, some of the most extreme cases of this that I have observed in any parts of the Americas are located in the badly eroded, highland sections of Cundinamarca and Boyacá.

Lack of Correspondence Between Community Boundaries and Those of Administrative Districts.—Generally in Colombia, as also almost universally is the case in such countries as the United States and Brazil, the limits of the community unit do not correspond with those of the municipio, *corregimiento* or any other administrative subdivision of the department or state. Moreover the Colombian municipio is an extremely debile unit of government. These facts mean that the community as such cannot make use of the power to tax in order to secure the funds it needs in order to develop and maintain most of the essential services. In the second half of the twentieth century, though, the exigencies of modern life demand that the people of each community be able to organize and carry on extensive activities in the fields of education, the protection of life and property, health, local roads and bridges, and so forth. However, in Colombia such endeavors are practically doomed to failure because purely voluntary ways of cooperation have proved entirely inadequate to cope with the problems involved; and if funds for all of them must come from the national capital, the bales of administrative red tape, the conflicts and machinations within the bureaucracy, the competing demands of national and departmental agencies for the available funds, and so on, almost invariably preclude the development and maintenance of adequate facilities in the local community units. In the densely populated highland portions of Colom-

16. The one thoroughgoing study of these matters in Colombia is Fals-Borda, *Facts and Theory of Sociocultural Change in a Rural Social System.*

bia, the municipios are of a size that would permit many of them to be developed into genuine rural or rurban community groupings. Endeavors along these lines, and especially those which would allow the municipio itself to levy a substantial tax upon the land within its limits, could do much to bring about a state of affairs in which community limits would correspond with those of the administrative districts. In effect this would allow the community itself to make use of the power to tax, and this factor alone could unleash powerful forces making for community development. As a matter of fact, the talk about acción comunal, and the levying by the national government of a tax of 5 per mil upon real estate, with the proceeds being left in the localities for municipio purposes, definitely are steps toward a realistic program of community development in Colombia.

9

Social Stratification and the Class Structure

EXCEPT for a general understanding of some of the more prominent features of the class system, such as can be gained through
casual observation by a perceptive observer, comparatively little is
known about the social stratification and class structure of Colombian
society. Only a few Colombians and social scientists from elsewhere
who have worked in Colombia have been properly equipped (with
the scientific attitude, a basic frame of reference, and the methodology) to study such phenomena, and those who have had the necessary qualifications have concentrated for the most part upon other
fields of endeavor. On the other hand a considerable number of intellectuals have not hesitated to make pronouncements about social
stratification in general, the ways the classes are made up, the absolute and relative importance of each of them, and so on. Therefore,
one must exercise considerable caution in evaluating the various
statements he may find in print relative to the upper classes and the
roles of their members in Colombian society, the middle social classes
and their composition and relative importance, and the characteristics
and status of those in the lower social layers.

These introductory remarks are not intended to express full approval of the manner in which this important subject was handled in
what might well have been a fundamental contribution to our understanding of Colombia's system of social stratification and class structure. The reference here is to a work[1] on which large sums of money
were expended and which was done directly under the auspices of
the Comité Nacional de Planeación, or National Planning Committee,
of the Office of the Presidency, so that presumably those responsible
for it had ready access to all available sources of information in the
Republic. Therefore, if even such an endeavor failed to supply any
comprehensive information about Colombia's class structure, one
probably should be somewhat charitable with the modest accomplishments of a few sociologists who have tried to ascertain some of the

1. See Lebret *et al.*, chap. III.

more essential facts about the system of social stratification in the society under consideration.

It is true that the basic generalization that was taken as the point of departure is largely accurate. This consists of the flat statement that "up until the present time there has been no serious study of social stratification in the country."[2] Certainly this represents a rather cavalier dismissal of a host of those who included treatments of caste and class in the serious works, largely in a historical vein, which they produced from the colonial period until the present; and it likewise failed to take cognizance of two endeavors in which detailed schedules of questions and intensive personal interviews were used in an effort to take stock of the class system in two specific parts of Colombia.[3] Nevertheless, the most serious questions relative to the study under consideration are those having to do with the procedures used in the investigation itself. To begin with, the data used were limited to those on type of worker (employers, independent workers, employees, laborers, etc.) in the active labor force as given by the 1951 census of population. On the basis of these, and apparently these alone, the rural population of Colombia was divided into the four following "categories of social classes": (1) the *Burguesia*, "which does not include more than 1 or 2 per cent of the population"; (2) the *Clase Media*, "which may be estimated at 15 to 20 per cent"; (3) the *Clase Popular*, which "is the most numerous, in general 75 per cent and running as high as 85 per cent"; and (4) the *Clase Indigente*, including some day laborers, unemployed laborers, and beggars, but for whom no estimate of relative importance was given. Similarly, the urban population, admittedly more diverse than the rural, on the basis of labor-force data for the three cities of Barranquilla, Medellín, and Popayán, only, was separated into "the higher *burguesia* of around 2.7 per cent, the *clases medias* with about 12.5 per cent, the *clases populares* totaling some 77 per cent, and the *sub-proletariado* of about 7 per cent."[4] It is

2. *Ibid.*, p. 35. The footnote accompanying this assertion mentions, without giving the facts of publication, an article in *Ciencias Sociales* (which is published by the Pan American Union), Vol. IV, No. 19, and a brochure published by the Banco de la Republica, and these apparently represent the sum total of the materials considered to be pertinent to the subject.

3. Cf. Fals-Borda, *Peasant Life in the Colombian Andes*, chap. 10; and Smith, Díaz, and García, *Tabio*, pp. 48-53, or *Tabio: Un Estudio de la Organización Social Rural*, Bogotá: Editorial Minerva, Ltda., 1944, pp. 68-77.

4. Lebret *et al.*, pp. 36-37.

difficult to understand how the mere use of labor force statistics and the injection of value-laden terms, such as bourgeois, does very much to correct the deficiency of serious study of social stratification to which the study called attention. As a matter of fact, the use of a term which historically signifies an urban person of intermediate social status to denote a category of the rural population which includes large landed proprietors, non-resident as well as resident, seems particularly ill-advised. However, there seems to be little likelihood that this terminology will be copied by Colombians or others who seek to determine and describe the class system of Colombia.

Subsequent to the work of Lebret and his associates only one substantial attempt to analyze social stratification in Colombia has come to my attention. This is the rather ambitious endeavor by Whiteford to study the social classes of Popayán, as these are reflected against a background of the class structure of Querétaro, Mexico.[5] The methodology employed is described as "the usual anthropological techniques of interviewing and participant observation." No attempt was made to present quantitative materials of any type; but numerous others assisted the author in the collection of data, including Roberto Pineda Giraldo and his wife Virginia Gutiérrez de Pineda who are well-trained and highly competent anthropologists. In a summary diagram, which is reproduced in this chapter, the author presents, in graphic form, his own estimates of the importance of the upper-upper, lower-upper, upper-middle, lower-middle, upper-lower, and lower-lower classes, respectively; but any attempt of another person to reduce these to percentages probably would prove futile. More important than these, however, are his perceptive observations, interspersed throughout the volume, on the nature of the several classes.

Despite the lack of empirical study though, just as is the case in most Latin American countries, society in Colombia is highly stratified. The differences between the social status of the small upper crust and that of the great mass of the population are tremendous. The former enjoy wealth and income, political power and prestige, educational training, culture, leisure, and positions of honor to a high degree. Since the caste element is also strong (a position at the apex of the social pyramid comes largely as a birthright and not through the exceptional abilities and efforts of the individual), there is little reason for any member of the elite to question his own right to

5. *Two Cities of Latin America.*

generous portions of the better things of life. A wide chasm separates these favored few from the great masses of the population who occupy the lower positions in society. Undernourished, ill-clad, poorly housed, disease ridden, often dissipated, frequently illiterate and largely abandoned to their misery, these masses amount to little in the economic, social, cultural, and religious life of the country. Even though social relationships were greatly scambled by the wars for independence, it is only in recent decades that what may be considered as a genuine middle class has begun to emerge in the larger cities and in some of the frontier zones.

Factors in the Traditional Pattern of Social Stratification

The factors involved in the traditional differentiation of the population of Colombia into the two readily distinguishable classes, the *terratenientes* and the *campesinos,* are two: ownership of land and race. These have been inextricably bound together ever since the conquest set in operation the forces which have brought about the present situation. Some of the old families who make up the elite of Colombian society trace their origin to one of the white conquistadores who helped seize control of this part of the New World. By right of conquest this handful of Spaniards set themselves up in their own new administrative centers as a ruling oligarchy, exacted a heavy tribute from the Indians who were portioned out in encomienda as virtual serfs, rapidly took over the best lands as private possessions on which to pasture their horses and cattle, exploited the mines with Indian laborers impressed through the institution of the mita and Negro slaves imported from Africa, and established monopolies of trade. By the time the encomienda system was abolished, more or less at the expiration of the "two lives" for which the Indians were commonly assigned, some of the conquerors had already established legal title to much of the most desirable land. As a result most of the aborigines had no choice except to work for the owners of the large estates on the owners' terms or to flee into the most out-of-the-way and inaccessible retreats of the Andean fastnesses. Something similar seems to have taken place with those who resided in the occasional settlements of white small farmers which were established in some parts of the country.

The ease and rapidity with which the conquerors gained for themselves and their descendants an impregnable position at the top of the social heap was greatly facilitated by the fact that the Indians had already developed settled habits, agriculture, and nucleated settlements. Since the Spaniards possessed the firearms which the natives lacked, the aborigines were easily reduced to the servile or semiservile class of laborers. Some were parceled out among the conquerors in encomiendas, and some were forced to perform the even more decimating work in the mines. But in any case they were generally subject to the slightest whim of the master class.

Since very few Spanish women entered the colonies, a few decades were sufficient to give rise to a vast number of mestizos, persons with white fathers and Indian mothers.[6] Under these circumstances, and since immigrants avoid the areas in which a handful of landlords wring a luxurious living from the blood, sweat, and tears of the enslaved masses, the increase of the white population was slow. As a result society quickly became differentiated into a small group of aristocrats at the apex of the social pyramid and the great servile masses at the base, with persons of anything resembling a middleclass status conspicuous by their absence. A few generations of forced labor and the lower classes were stripped of all possibility of bettering their own position, while the wealth of the masters enabled them to institutionalize their positions through the positions of *mayorasgos* and titles of nobility.

As a result Colombian society early became sharply differentiated into a two-class system. At the top was a small, wealthy, highly intelligent, landowning, white, aristocratic elite for whom nothing in this world was considered too good; and far below in the social scale was the mass of the population, humble, poverty-stricken,

6. In rare instances the half-breed children of the conquerors succeeded in gaining acceptance as members of the upper classes, but probably very few of the numerous offspring of the *conquistadores* were as fortunate as Diego de Alcalá, one of the mestizo sons of Juan de Alcalá who accompanied Quesada from Santa Marta to the Savanna of Bogotá. It seems that Juan had four illegitimate children by an Indian woman of Bogotá, and that they were reared in his home. Two of the children, both girls, died in their youth, and the two boys were left in dire poverty when their father was killed in an expedition while fighting the Muzos. As early as 1559, less than a quarter of a century after the conquest, Diego was seeking to establish that he was his father's heir and entitled to share in the privileges of the conquering race. His claims were finally confirmed by The Real Audiencia, but not until 1585, long after his father's encomienda had passed into other hands. At that time he was judged to be entitled to the protection of the king and named as a solicitor. Nothing is said of his brother whose lot no doubt was similar to that of thousands of other half-breeds who failed to attain the privileged status of the conquering whites. Cf. Raimundo Rivas, *Los Fundadores de Bogotá,* pp. 43-44.

disease-ridden, uneducated, colored or mixed-blooded campesinos. As the cities have grown, especially during recent decades, hundreds of thousands of the latter have flocked into the centers and the bands of misery that surround them. This migration, though, has done little or nothing to change the class system; it has merely transferred a part of them into a degraded urban proletariat who rank at the extreme bottom of the social scale. Now and then, however, one may encounter a former campesino whose position as a chauffeur, a mechanic, a mason, and so forth is enabling him to gain a status near the upper reaches of the lower-class category; and occasionally one is found whose efforts to gain a formal education may eventually enable him to rise into the middle class. Hence it is not impossible that during the years ahead substantial numbers of the former campesinos may join the foreigners and their descendants and the less fortunate part of the offspring of those of high estate in swelling the numbers of a growing middle class. Adequate study of this process, nevertheless, is still a thing of the future.

The Concept of Social Class

The term social class as it is used in the following pages has a very specific meaning. In the first place it denotes a number of persons in a given society whose economic, occupational, and sociopolitical levels and interests are closely similar. In the second place these individuals must recognize that they have a social and economic status similar to that of their fellows; they must be conscious of the fact that the fortunes of all those on their level are inextricably bound together, and thereby be impelled to make a common front with those on a comparable social level. The second part of this definition is intended to indicate that there is no social class, irrespective of similarities in levels of living, felt needs, and ambitions, unless a "consciousness of kind," a group solidarity, also has been established.

In order to arrive at such a concept of social class one must be cognizant of the fact that all societies are divided into various economic levels, occupational layers, and degrees of social prestige and political power and influence. The varying amount of wealth and income enjoyed or received by different people is closely related to the occupations they follow. It also is closely associated with the amount of respect they command from their fellows and the extent to which they are privileged to exercise power and authority in political and other social affairs. But the three scales are not perfectly correlated. A few occupations, such as those of clergyman or college professor, carry considerable social prestige and influence, even though the monetary rewards generally are rather meager; an old aristocracy may maintain its position at the top of the heap for several generations after the bulk of its wealth and income has disappeared; and it may take a long while for the newly rich family to be accepted into the "four hundred" or its equivalent in any given society.

As indicated above, "the consciousness of kind" is another indispensable characteristic that must be present before any given group of people may legitimately be designated as a social class. (In discussing this matter use will be made of three categories, upper, middle, and lower classes, although it is recognized that for many purposes it is better to carry the classification to finer degrees of precision.) Such a consciousness of kind is intimately linked with the three basic economic functions, namely those of the one who has and invests capital, those of the manager, and those of the laborer. As a general rule upper-class status is compatible only with the first of these, and in extreme cases even that function is denied to the drones who may have a strangle hold on the wealth and income of a society. Under exceptional circumstances, such as those that prevail in new countries which are dominated by a middle-class mentality (as has been true generally in the United States and Canada), the entrepreneurial and managerial functions may be exercised by members of the elite without serious loss of face and status in the select circles. At the other extreme, manual labor, toil with the hands, is the indelible mark of the lower classes, and the one which creates among their members the recognition of common interests and the bond of unity.

Most interesting of all is the social solidarity of the middle classes. It results from the exercise of all three of the basic economic functions. Access to or membership in the middle classes, or the mentality possessed by their members, demands that the rôle of the investor be assumed. But the capital involved is in small amounts and usually results from thrift and saving. Unlike the wealth of the upper classes it will not support any elaborate ostentation or any great display of conspicuous consumption. It is merely one of the less important sources of the income from which the middle-class family derives its support. In addition to performing the rôle of the investor on a limited scale, the middle class is also the managerial group par excellence. Not a little of the responsibility for the planning and the bulk of the execution of the details in all economic activities are in the hands of its members. Self-employment in the professions and in small businesses is highly important for them and their children. Generally the operators of family-sized farms are the backbone of such a class. But neither the fact that they are investors of capital nor their managerial responsibilities bring persons of the middle class to neglect and depreciate the skills involved in working with their

The gateway to a pastoral estate of modest proportions in the Cauca Valley. (Photo by the author.)

hands. As a class they do not think of manual labor as bemeaning; nor do they tolerate the gross waste of time and money that would be required to maintain a number of lackeys at their beck and call in order that they might never have to soil their hands or "lower" themselves by some act involving manual labor. The person of middle-class status feels a strong bond in common with others who carefully guard the small investments they have built up, assume individual responsibility and self direction in most of their occupational activities, and esteem the dignity of human labor.

Class differences almost always become associated with the caste element although there is no indivisible link between the two. To the extent that free social circulation between the layers, to the degree that rising or falling from one stratum to another, is hindered by factors not directly related to the capacities of the individual members and the energies exerted by them, the class system partakes of caste characteristics. When through conquest, an old system of slavery, or any other means, readily distinguishable physical features, such as the color of the skin, come to be associated with class membership the caste features are likely to become especially strong and extremely difficult to eradicate. This creates no particular problem

Middle-class Colombian coffee farmer and his wife drying coffee beans in front of their home on a small farm in the department of Caldas. (Courtesy of the National Federation of Coffee Growers of Colombia.)

in a static society where most people accept for granted the estate to which they were born and are permitted to receive few if any stimuli encouraging them to seek a higher one. But it is fraught with serious consequences in terms of personal frustration and social conflict within a mobile society, such as that in the United States, in which the channels of social ascension now are open to those who possess the physical characteristics which once were the identifying marks of those of a servile group. Under such circumstances the scrambling of class and caste relationships may bring untold suffering and misery to millions of human beings, even though they may be making tremendous progress from the standpoints of material well-being, health and levels of living. As the Latin American countries, including Colombia, are swept into the maelstrom of the modern world, the shattering of old patterns and the crumbling of traditional attitudes are likely to produce a chaotic situation with respect to the relationships involving class and caste.

In addition to the nature of the several social classes which has just been considered, two other matters should be kept in mind by those who deal with the class system in any part of the world. The first of these is the fact that it is necessary to make a distinction between an *intermediate* social level and a genuine middle social class. There always are various gradations in the economic, occupational, and socio-political statuses, even, for example, among the laborers on a sugar-cane plantation where all with much reason may be categorized as belonging in the lower social class; or, to mention just one other case, among the farmers in a district monopolized by family-sized farming units, where all certainly pertain to the middle social class. The failure to distinguish what is merely a stratum intermediate between two others from a middle social class as such is responsible, of course, for much of the tremendous variation one finds between the estimates of two or more writers relative to the importance of the upper, middle, and lower social classes in a given society.[7] Fortunately, there have been exceptions to this rule, of which a good example is Fals-Borda's study of the settlement of Saucio in Colombia. This perceptive sociologist sought to discover whether or not there were "strata within the peasant class in Saucio?" For this purpose he made use of a scale, based upon those developed by F. Stuart Chapin, William H. Sewell, and Louis Guttman; and this enabled him to indicate that among the 69 heads of households "excluding the *hacendado* who belongs to the terrateniente class" there were indeed four social levels among the humble inhabitants of the district he was surveying. The four levels or layers he identified and the relative importance of the households falling in each are as follows: upper, 19 per cent; middle, 17 per cent; lower, 42 per cent; and destitute, 22 per cent.[8]

7. For some examples of the great differences between the estimates of the relative importance of the different classes within the same societies, see the contributions in Crevenna, *Materiales para el Estudio de la Clase Media en la América Latina.*

8. Fals-Borda, *Peasant Life in the Colombian Andes,* pp. 160-61.

The second basic consideration that should be kept in mind by those who attempt to study and describe any society is that there is absolutely no reason for one to expect to find representations of all the social levels or layers in the population of any given locality, department, or nation. Geologists certainly do not expect to find examples of all the earth's strata in any one given location, and there is no more reason why the sociologist should expect to discover all of the social classes at a given place at any particular time. Indeed, in Colombia and most of the other Latin American countries the traditional pattern has been the two-class society, in which the middle social classes have been conspicuous by their absence; whereas in the family-sized farming districts of the midwestern part of the United States, all of the major socio-economic levels are subsumed in one genuine middle social class. In practical terms this means that the pyramids customarily used for the graphic portrayal of the class structure of a given society may be entirely inappropriate.

THE MIDDLE CLASSES

Most of the moot points with respect to the class structure of Colombian society revolve about the question of the extent to which a genuine middle class is evolving in the major cities and in certain of the rural zones of the country. Unfortunately the specific studies needed in order to settle the issues are still to be made. It does seem evident, though, that in parts of Antioquia and in much of Caldas the rural population has developed many of the characteristics that entitle them to be classed as genuine members of the middle class, albeit their farms are too small to permit most of their operators to attain a status near the top of such a class. It will require a great deal of study before the basic outlines of the process involved in this development will be known, but some of the most pertinent factors seem to be the following: (1) this was the most remote and inaccessible section of Colombia, so that it was the one to which it was most difficult for influences from the outside to make their way; (2) the Indians in these mountain fastnesses were less "civilized," that is they were in a less developed stage of social organization than those in many other parts of Colombia, and hence they were more cantankerous about accepting the Spaniards as overlords than the ones who lived in the high inter-mountain valleys of the eastern range; (3) as a result more of them were slaughtered, driven back into the mountain fastnesses or the jungles, and the land left devoid of inhabitants; (4) mining and other nonagricultural activities occupied the attention of the population to a far greater extent than they did in most other parts of the country; and (5) during the nineteenth century, after the removal of royal restraints, a tremendous epoch of self-propelled colonization activities got underway, one in which the family itself carved out a farm and made a home in the wilderness with fair assurance that its members would be able to enjoy the benefits of their labors. But irrespective of whether these are the factors or whether the causes were different, the fact remains that hundreds of individual farm properties and thousands of other small enterprises have been developed by the enterprising Antioqueños. Considering that they have lived and worked in a country where the many social restraints have operated against the evolution of a genuine middle class, what has taken place seems all the more remarkable.

But the case of Antioquia and Caldas is unique. Elsewhere in Colombia there continued to be well-defined and widely separated classes of the elite and the lower orders, with hardly anything deserving of the designation middle class present to help fill the great void between the two. It is true that there are in cities like Bogotá, Cali, and Barranquilla large numbers of office holders, professionals, merchants, industrialists, and those engaged in other white-collar activities. However, one should examine the actual situation rather carefully before he jumps to the conclusion that all of these people constitute a middle class in the society. This is most true of the office holders and professionals; and apparently less the case with the merchants and small industrialists.

Consider first the fact that most of those in the swarm of minor officials who occupy posts in the national, state, and local governments are the sons, grandsons, and great-grandsons of persons who once occupied positions at the apex of the social pyramid in Colombia. The same is true of the host of lawyers, who make up the overwhelming majority of the professional men, and who must seek every opportunity to gain a small added stipend by performing notarial services, teaching, and so on, in order to support their families on the modest scale to which they have been reduced. "Self-made men" in Colombia are not entirely lacking, but they are not numerous. A count would probably indicate that the overwhelming proportion of those who may at first glance appear to be of middle class status, and whose descendants eventually may help form a genuine middle class, are members of proud old families.

In this connection the observations of Eduardo Santos, former president of Colombia and publisher of the great newspaper, *El Tiempo* of Bogotá, are very much to the point. He has written as follows. "Systems other than the liberal one are impossible in a country of the middle class, in which the aristocrats are tumbling from their exalted positions to very modest posts. Everyone recalls the grand families of a century ago whose descendants today are in the lowest positions in the bureaucratic scale. Those who dominated the Savanna with immense latifundia, and possessed enormous landed estates, presently humbly earn 80 pesos a month in an office of secondary importance."[9]

The reasons for this state of affairs are not hard to find. Until educational opportunities are extended to the masses, only an exceptional child here and there will succeed in lifting himself by his own bootstraps out of the illiterate, disease-ridden, malnourished, ill-clothed, poorly housed, poverty-stricken, landless mass which constitutes the bulk of the Colombian population. The fact that most of them are of more or less colored descent does not aid the prospects of the members of Colombia's lower classes. Added to this is the stern reality that the factors affecting vertical social mobility create a movement in just exactly the opposite direction to the principal currents of circulation within our own social pyramid.

This last statement calls for an explanation. In the United States and most countries of western Europe, the members of the upper-middle and lower-upper classes fail to reproduce themselves. One generation of them does not leave enough offspring to carry on the work performed by its members, and in addition the number of highly paid and responsible jobs is expanding fantastically. This creates a kind of a suction which carries many members of the middle and lower classes to positions considerably higher in the social scale than the ones occupied by their parents. It does much to generate an optimistic outlook on life within the society, the hope and expectation that one's offspring will enjoy a higher social status than that of the person himself. But in Colombia, as in most Latin American countries, there seems to be no differential fertility favorable to the lower classes. Upper-class families produce as many children, if not more, than those in less fortunate circumstances.

9. *Una Política Liberal*, p. 32.

Furthermore, of the children born, undoubtedly the upper classes succeed in safeguarding a larger proportion through the tender years of life than do the lower classes. As a result one of high estate leaves not one heir to assume a position in society more or less equal to that of his own, but a flock of sons all of them "to the manor born." As a matter of fact, since the generations come along about 25 years apart, a single member of the elite may live to see the time when three generations of his descendants (not infrequently as many as 100 persons) are struggling desperately to maintain positions on a high rung of the social ladder. If, as in Colombia, the original social position and wealth are based upon land, since the institutions of primogeniture and entailed estates have been abolished, a few generations are sufficient to pulverize even the largest holdings. If the actual legal and physical subdivision of the land among the heirs is not carried out the situation may be even worse. Then one more great property is added to the already large number of haciendas or fincas on which operations are paralyzed because the number of owners is legion and no one of them may operate since all the others have a claim on what is produced by his efforts. Such a state of affairs is conducive to anything except an optimistic outlook upon life on the part of the sons, grandsons, and great-grandsons of the important men of the country. Inexorable forces are pushing them down the social scale, making it increasingly difficult for them to maintain the appearances of the type of life to which they were born and which they came to regard as their right. Their actual levels of living may make it clear that they enjoy no more goods and services than a person of middle-class status, but their standards, the amounts to which they feel entitled, are far greater.

Eventually the descendants of many of these old families may be expected to contribute to the formation of a genuine middle class in Colombia, although not a few of them may be debased to the very bottom of the social scale. But the transition will not be easily nor quickly achieved, and many of the persons involved may become so demoralized that they will forfeit all chances for themselves and their children. Others will continue to use their connections to obtain minor positions in the bureaucracy; and in a highly familistic society, where the practice of nepotism is almost a sacred obligation on the part of successful politician or statesman, such employment becomes available to not a few. Many will resort to the liberal professions, especially the law which equips them for notarial work, teaching, and other activities involving use of wit and lacking the stigma attached to the trades, the most skilled labor, and much of commerce. Never under any circumstances short of almost absolute starvation will they consent to engage in any activities involving manual labor, at least in its traditional forms, for that would stigmatize them as acknowledging a mean origin and position. This attitude toward physical labor, the utter impossibility of viewing it as honorable and ennobling, a mind-set which they share with all other peoples whose formative processes were shaped by the large-landed estate and its accompanying servile labor force and two-class system of social stratification, is the thing which makes it most difficult for tens of thousands of present-day Colombians to become full-fledged members of a genuine middle social class.

Since 1943, tens if not hundreds of thousands of well-built and well-equipped dwellings and apartments have been built in new residential districts of Bogotá, Cali, Barranquilla, and the other major cities in Colombia. My contacts have been for the most part with those who practice law or medicine, with those who hold governmental positions, and with those in the universities. I have had very little opportunity to know those engaged in commerce and industry. This means that my information has been derived mostly from Colombians of Colombian parentage, and only slightly from the immigrants and their children. With very few exceptions, moreover, the Colombians I know who reside in what would be judged to be middle-class residential districts, in homes that our sociological scales would identify as dwellings of those of the middle class, are the decendants of those who were unchallenged members of the upper class. Furthermore, even today they seem to identify themselves with the elite, although probably to a lesser degree than was the case in 1943 and 1944. But it seems evident that this state of affairs cannot continue indefinitely, and that the connections between each generation of the offspring of such families and actual elite social status, even when the latter is limited to the standing of a grandfather or great-grandfather, is becoming more tenuous.

The findings of one recent study of the Bogotá entrepreneur shed a few rays of light upon the nature of the changing class structure of Colombia's great capital city.[10] Its author generalizes that these entrepreneurs are "well-educated, urban, and . . . from a predominantly middle class background, in a society that is mainly rural, has

10. Lipman, "Social Backgrounds of the Bogotá Entrepreneur."

a low educational level, and an overwhelmingly large lower class."[11] His data were secured in interviews with 61 executives who headed 26 per cent of firms with membership in Asociación Nacional de Industriales, said to be roughly comparable with the National Association of Manufacturers in the United States. "In each case the person interviewed was the executive at the top of the personnel hierarchy in his particular firm."

One striking fact revealed by this study is represented by the finding that 41 per cent of his cases were foreign born, although the author correctly states that "Colombia has traditionally had a very low rate of immigration throughout the years."[12] Another is the indication that only five of the executives had fathers who belonged to the "working class," of whom four were "skilled workers," and that four of the five had fathers who were born in Europe and not in Colombia. Moreover, "in not a single instance had the entrepreneurs ever held any manual job in their previous occupational history."[13]

CLASS STRUCTURE THROUGH FIVE CENTURIES

It is hoped that the materials presented so far in this chapter, along with those given in the chapters dealing with land tenure and the size of the holdings or agricultural-pastoral units, are sufficient to bring out many of the more salient features of the class structure of Colombian society. As has been suggested above, though, there exists in a widely scattered manner, a number of highly valuable analyses and descriptions of this or that aspect of social stratification in Colombia as these have been observed and recorded from the early colonial period until the present. Unfortunately these fragments have never been brought together and organized into any consistent body of fact and theory, but they do constitute highly pertinent information for anyone who seeks to gain a sound understanding of social stratification in Colombia or in Latin America generally. Therefore it has been judged opportune to include as the concluding section of this chapter a few selected extracts which I believe to be the most reliable and informative of the available information on class and caste in Colombia from the days of the conquistadores until the present.

To begin with, two extracts are reproduced which give the de-

11. *Ibid.*, p. 227.
12. *Ibid.*, p. 231.
13. *Ibid.*, p. 234.

scriptions and generalizations of Bancroft, the prolific historian who wrote so voluminously on the history of the western United States and that of the countries below the Rio Grande. They pertain to the situation in Spain and in the Spanish colonies during the all-important formative period. These are followed by the widely copied description of Antonio de Ulloa, whose statements concerning race and social status at Cartagena seem to have been the source for what most of the general historical treatises have to say about social stratification in the Spanish colonies. Since much the same analysis is found in the writings of many eighteenth-century authors, a translation of another excellent summary account, that of Joaquín de Finestrad, is also given. Next is included a translation from the Spanish of an exceptionally fine treatment of social stratification as it existed on the Savanna of Bogotá about the middle of the nineteenth century. This is followed by the most pertinent excerpts from our own study of social status in the Municipio of Tabio which appeared in Spanish in 1944 and in English the year following. Fortunately, we have also been able to include liberal extracts from the most comprehensive investigation of social stratification in Colombia that has been done to date, that by Whiteford of the class system of the famous old colonial city of Popayán. Finally, at the last moment before the book went to press, a careful study of Cereté in Córdoba, appeared, and we have been able to use, in translation, a short but highly pertinent section of it.

THE SPANISH BACKGROUND

"Inequalities of power and wealth, unless arrested by extrinsic causes, ever tend to wider extremes. In Spain, the increase of wealth in the hands of priests and princes was checked by long-continued war. The products of the country must be used to feed the soldiery, and the power of the nobility must be employed against the common enemy. There was neither time nor the opportunity to grind the people to the uttermost. Though the war bore heavily upon the working classes, it proved to them the greatest blessing; while the masses elsewhere throughout Europe were kept in a state of feudalistic serfdom, the necessity of Spain being for men rather than for beasts, elevation followed. Further than this, race-contact, and the friction attending the interminglings of courts and camps, tended in some degree towards polishing and refining society. 'Since nothing makes us forget the arbitrary distinctions of rank,' says Hallam, 'so much as participation in any common calamity, every man who had escaped the great shipwreck of liberty and religion in the mountains of Asturias was invested with a personal dignity, which gave him value in his own eyes and those of his country. It is probably this sentiment transmitted to posterity, and gradually fixing the national character, that had produced the elevation of manner remarked by travellers in the Castilian peasant.'

"And yet there were caste and social stratification enough. The stubborn manliness of the lower orders did not make them noble. Royalty alone was divine. The nobles loved money, yet for them to traffic was disgraceful. The ecclesiastic, whose calling placed him on a place distinct from these, aside from his religious teachings, stood out as the earnest advocate of honest labor. Work was well enough for Moor, and Jew, and Indian; but he whose line of fighting ancestors had not beginning within the memory of man, must starve rather than stain his lineage by doing something useful.

"The several social strata, moreover, were jealously kept distinct. The first distinction was that which separated them from foreigners. In the days of Caesar and Cicero, Rome was master of the world; Rome was the world; were any not of Rome they were barbarians. So it was with Spaniards. To be of Castile was to be the most highly favored of mortals; to be a Spaniard, though not a Castilian, was something to be proud of; to be anything else was most unfortunate.

"The next distinction was between the Spaniard of pure blood and the Christianized native of foreign origin. In the eyes of the Castilian baptism could not wholly cleanse a Moor or Jew. Moriscos the Church might make; heretics the Inquisition might reconstruct; but all Spain could not make from foreign material a Christian Spaniard of the pure ancient blood. About foreign fashions, foreign inventions, foreign progress, foreign criticism, they cared nothing. And probably nowhere in modern times was this irrational idea of caste carried to such an absurd extent as in the New World. Children of Spanish parentage, born in America, were regarded socially as inferior to children of the same parents who happened to be born in Spain. To be born a Spanish peasant was better than *hidalgo,* or cavalier, with American nativity; for at one time the former, on migrating to America, was entitled by virtue of that fact to the prefix 'Don.' Under the viceroys native Mexicans, though of pure Castilian ancestry, were too often excluded from the higher offices of Church and State; and this notwithstanding that both canonical and civil law, if we may believe Betancur y Figueroa, provided that natives should be preferred in all ecclesiastical appointments from the lightest benefice to the highest prelacy. 'But notwithstanding such repeated recommendations,' says Robertson, 'preferment in almost every different line is conferred on native Spaniards.' Mr. Ward, English consul at Mexico in 1825-7, affirms that 'the son, who had the misfortune to be born of a creole mother, was considered as an inferior, in the house of his own father, to the European book-keeper or clerk, for whom the daughter, if there were one, and a large share of the fortune were reserved. "Eres criollo y basta"; You are a creole and that is enough, was a common phrase amongst the Spaniards when angry with their children.' Truly it was a good thing in those days to be at once 'of Christ' and 'of Spain.' It was positively believed by some that blood flowed in accordance with the majesty of law, and that the quality of one was inferior to the quality of another. The blood of the Indian was held as scarcely more human than the blood of beasts, and was often shed as freely."[14]

CLASS STRUCTURE IN THE SPANISH COLONIES

"The creoles, as the offspring of Europeans born in America were called, though descendants of the conquerors, and preserving in their veins the best blood of Spain untainted, were in many instances by law degraded, and made inferior to those shiftless chapetones who had lived in idleness at home. What policy could be more suicidal than this, which in effect debarred those entitled by their enterprise to the most honorable positions from any but a scanty lot in the institutions of the country, and made them by virtue of their devotion well-nigh ostracized. In the distribution of lands and natives, the conquerors and their descendants were supposed to be favored before all others, but men from Spain must manage the government and institutions of the country. Thus degraded and left to indolence and listless and luxurious indulgence, they sank into the strange position of wealthy and respected human beings, having homes but no country, having acknowledged rights but no voice in their vindication; they were lords of lands and vassals, and yet the most impotent of mankind. Thus was engendered hate between classes which subsequently lapsed into chronic civil wars.

"Attempts have been made to classify these several castes, though without pronounced success. Robertson places first the chapetones,

14. Bancroft, *History of Central America*, pp. 24-26.

or old Christians, untainted by Jewish or Mohammedan blood; second, creoles; third, mulattoes and mestizos, the former the offspring of an African and European, and the latter of an American and European; and lastly Indians and negroes unadulterated. Marriage with the natives was encouraged by the government, but few of their connections were ratified by any holier sentiment than lust. There was one only great leveller of rank, the church. Torquemada says that on Sundays and feast days the gentleman could not be distinguished from the plebeian, or the knight from the squire, all dressing alike in rich garments. And yet oidores and high dignitaries would fight over place and the position of their chair at church as quickly and as fiercely as over political preference."[15]

RACE AND SOCIAL STATUS IN CARTAGENA

"[The] . . . inhabitants may be divided into different casts or tribes, who derive their origin from a coalition of Whites, Negroes, and Indians. We shall therefore treat of each particularly.

"The whites may be divided into two classes, the Europeans and Creoles, or Whites born in the country. The former are commonly called Chapetones, but are not numerous, most of them either return into Spain after acquiring a competent fortune, or remove up into inland provinces in order to increase it. Those who are settled at Carthagena, carry on the whole trade of that place, and live in opulence; whilst the other inhabitants are indigent and reduced to have recourse to mean and hard labour for subsistence. The families of the white Creoles compose the landed interest; some of them have large estates, and are highly respected, because their ancestors came into the country invested with honorable posts, bringing their families with them when they settled here. Some of these families in order to keep up their original dignity, have either married their children to their equals in the country, or sent them as officers on board the galleons; but others have greatly declined. Besides these, there are other whites, in mean circumstances, and either owe their origin to Indian families, or at least to an intermarriage with them, so that there is some mixture in their blood; but when this is not discoverable by their colour, the conceit of being whites alleviates the pressure of every other calamity.

"Among the other tribes which are derived from an intermarriage of the Whites with the Negroes, the first are the Mulattos . . . Next

15. Bancroft, *California Pastoral, 1769-1848*, pp. 77-78.

to these are the Tercerones, produced from a white and a Mulatto, with some approximation to the former, but not so near as to obliterate their origin. After these follow the Quarterones, proceeding from a white and a Terceron. The last are the Quinterones, who owe their origin to a White and Quarteron. This is the last gradation, there being no visible difference between them and the Whites, either in colour or features; nay, they are often even fairer than the Spaniards themselves. The children of a White and Quinteron are also called Spaniards, and consider themselves as free from all taint of the Negro race. Every person is so jealous of the order of their tribe or Cast, that if thro' inadvertence . . . you call them by a degree lower than what they actually are, they are highly offended, never suffering themselves to be deprived of so valuable a gift of fortune.

"Before they attain the class of the Quinterones, there are several intervening circumstances which throw them back; for between the Mulatto and the Negro, there is an intermediate race, which they call Sambos, owing their origin to a mixture between one of these with an Indian, or among themselves. They are also distinguished according to the Casts their fathers were of. Betwixt the Tercerones and the Mulattos, the Quarterones and the Tercerones, & c. are those called Tente en el Ayre, suspended in the air, because they neither advance, nor recede. Children whose parents are a Quarteron or Quinteron, and a Mulatto or Terceron, are Salto atras, retrogrades; because instead of advancing towards being Whites, they have gone backwards towards the Negro race. The children between a Negro and Quinteron are called Sambos de Negro, de Mulatto, de Terceron, etc.

"These are the most known and common tribes or Castas; there are indeed several others proceeding from their intermarriages; but, being so various, even they themselves cannot easily distinguish them; and these are the only people one sees in the city, the estancias (Estancia properly signifies a mansion, or place where one stops to rest; but at Carthagena it implies a country house, which, by reason of the great number of slaves belonging to it, often equals a considerable village), and the villages; for if any Whites, especially women, are met with, it is only accidental; these generally residing in their houses, at least, if they are of any rank or character.

"These casts, from the Mulattos, all affect the Spanish dress, but wear very slight stuffs on account of the heat of the climate. These are the mechanics of the city; the Whites, whether Creoles, or Chapetones, disdaining such a mean occupation, follow nothing below merchandize. But it being impossible for all to succeed, great numbers not being able to procure sufficient credit, they become poor and miserable from their aversion to those trades they follow in Europe; and instead of the riches, which they flattered themeselves with possessing in the Indies, they experience the most complicated wretchedness.

"The class of Negroes is not the least numerous, and is divided into two parts; the free and the slaves. These are again subdivided into Creoles and Bozares, part of which are employed in the cultivation of the Haziandas (Hazianda in this place signifies a country-house, with the lands belonging to it), or estancias. Those in the city are obliged to perform the most laborious services, and pay out of their wages a certain quota to their masters, subsisting themselves on the small remainder."[16]

RACE AND CLASS IN COLOMBIA, 1783

The social scientist can hardly expect to find a more succinct description of the classes in any society, nor a more precise statement of the manner in which social status may be related to race, than is given by Joaquín de Finestrad in his *El Vasallo Instruido* (1783). Finestrad, a Capuchin priest, was thoroughly acquainted with the revolt of the Comuneros in Nuevo Granada during the second half of the eighteenth century and he offered the Viceroy in Lima his analysis of the causes of the rebellion and a program for correcting the sad state of affairs which prevailed.

This padre began his analysis of social stratification in the New Kingdom, which he designated as a *República,* by indicating that the inhabitants were first divided into Spaniards and natives. The former included only those "cradled in Spain" of parents who were Spaniards. (He then points out that while the British granted citizenship to children of foreign parents born in the Empire, in Spain children followed the condition of their parents.) Even among the Spaniards were the precise distinctions of a carefully arranged hierarchy. "The first rank is occupied by those of noble birth," and these

16. Juan [de Sancticilia] and Ulloa, *A Voyage to South America . . . ,* I, 30-33. Simliar analyses and descriptions of the populations of Quito and Lima are given in *ibid.,* pp. 275-78, and II, 54-57.

were the rulers, sometimes in positions of highest authority, sometimes in subordinate places.

"Second place is occupied by those who with royal consent have transplanted themselves to the New Hemisphere; and third place by those who as stowaways furtively left their native land and were naturalized in this country." In the New World the unequalled blessing of Spanish birth alone was sufficient to insure the most ne'er-do-well fugitive a place near the apex of the social pyramid. All creoles, irrespective of their parentage or personal accomplishments, merely because theirs was not the good fortune of being born in Spain, were automatically relegated to lower positions in the social scale.

Padre Finestrad continues by describing the status of persons born in the New Kingdom. Some of the Spaniards gladly embraced the married status, and "others assumed the obligations of parenthood without having any marital bond whatsoever. Both kinds of children have originated from Spain and enjoy the nobility which characterizes their lines. These are those who represent the most distinguished character of the American people, glorying in their European origin and citing in the courts the glorious deeds and distinctions of their ancestors, and their preeminent merits in the royal service."

In second place among the natives was another class also designated as "whites" because nature "did not care to stigmatize them with the ignominious brand which goes along with the blood of Negro, *zambo,* mulatto, and other castes of people which will be referred to, excepting the pure Indians." Of these "whites" by convention some were farmers "who are called *orejones* in the Kingdom, employing themselves in the cultivation of the land and the raising of cattle, and whose activities in addition to being very useful are also very honorable; they enjoy great prominence."

But the Padre indicates that there was also another "caste of people who exist in the greatest drunkenness and sloth, friends of unchecked liberty, without applying themselves in any way to the cultivation of the land, the most fertile and productive. Like the Arabs and Africans who inhabit the southern pueblos, such are the Indians, the mulattoes, the Negroes, the *zambos,* the *saltoatrás,* the *tente en el aire,* the *tercerones,* the *cuarterones* the *quinterones,* and the *cholos* or *mestizos.* The crosses of Negro and white are called mulattoes; those of mulatto and Negro, *zambos;* those of *zambo* and Negro, *saltoatrás;* those of *zambos, tente en el aire;* those of mulattoes, the same; those of mulatto and white, *tercerón;* those of a *tercerón* and a mulatto, *saltoatrás;* those of *tercerones, tente en el aire;* those of tercerón and white, *cuarterón;* those of *cuarterón* and white, *quinterón; quinteron* and white, Spaniard, now reputed entirely outside the Negro race; and likewise the crosses of Negro with Indian to the fifth stage are called *zambo;* also that of Negro and mulatto, *tercerón;* and finally that of Spaniard with Indian, *Cholo* or *mestizo.*"[17]

Social Stratification on the Savanna of Bogotá about 1850

"The inhabitants of each District may be divided into three sections or social classes: (1) the great capitalists, (2) the small proprietors, and (3) the proletariat (the Indians).

"The first class is made up of people living in Bogotá who possess valuable haciendas on the Savanna, managed by mayordomos, which they visit once or twice a week in order to ask an accounting from the administrators, to take note of the condition of their herds, the plantings, and the fences; to the great capitalists the moral and material progress of the population is a matter of indifference. These persons, because of their relations in the capital and on account of their financial positions, frequently are nominated as alcaldes or as members of the District Council; they do not accept the first responsibility in order to escape the work of going on market days to hear complaints and administer justice and for fear of losing the good will of the smaller proprietors; but they make use of their influences with the government to secure the naming of authorities whom they can influence in favor of their particular interests in the building of certain roads, deciding of controversies, etc.

"They accept membership on the Council and then do not attend the sessions except when they learn of a levy of direct taxation or of subsidiary personal labor, in order to make use of their powerful votes in favor of the improvement of the ways which lead to their haciendas. They do not participate in the elections because this would alienate sympathies and consequently clientele from their business negotiations. They are indifferent to public education because their children are in the academies of the capital. For them

17. The report entitled "El Vasallo Instruido en el Estado de Nuevo Reino de Granada y en sus Respectivas Obligaciones," has been republished in *Los Comuneros,* Vol. IV of the Biblioteca de Historia Nacional, Bogotá: Imprenta Nacional, 1905, pp. 1-204. The direct quotations are from pp. 103-4.

the priest is satisfactory when he does as they bid. They only demon-strate interest in the *pueblo,* and then with enthusiasm, when they protest against some lack of respect on the part of its civil or ecclesiastical authorities.

"Among this social class, there are not a few examples of the cor-rupters of the youths belonging to the lower social classes; and still more pernicious, among them are some, who because their children have given themselves to dissipation in the capital, believe that they can be reformed by being sent to the haciendas, where they propa-gate infections and teach vices to members of all classes.

"The second class, more numerous than the first, is composed of inhabitants of the District, whites, mestizos, and Indians, among whom are seen very large families, many of them exemplary in all respects; but generally from them come the great seducers of the parish, corrupters of every Indian woman whose graces distinguish her from the others; the gamonales, or caciques, despised persons who pillage and abuse the unhappy Indians mercilessly; the matones, men of the revolver and the bottle, who 'give the law in the chicharias' [saloons in which native beer or *chicha* is dispensed] of the District. From this second class, ignorant and poor in morals, the one known among us under the appellation of Orejones, of necessity come the authorities of the District. An alcalde, or a judge, is then the favorer of all the others of his class, through fear or because of kinship and friendship, and a tormentor of the proletariat. Among these individuals there are close ties of kinship and friendship due to the fact that the families are very large, and also at times they are divided into bands originating out of deep personal rivalry, from family dissensions, or in conflicting interests. As a class it is full of envy of the wealth and privileges possessed by the large landholders and of contempt towards its inferiors. Its members send their children to study a few years in the capital, with the result that 95 per cent learn only vices and bad ways of behaving, and who for sustenance occupy themselves almost exclusively in fomenting litigations which ruin the families and disturb the peace of the pueblo. Almost all of the individuals of this class live in run-down houses, many of them lacking living space for the family but containing large apartments for the services of the chicharias which they operate. Among them come forth from time to time notable soldiers and chieftains as sacrificing as they are enthusiastic.

"The third class, composed of Indians, is more difficult to classify:

it cannot be compared with the pariahs, with the helots, nor with the gypsies, because its members completely lack the spirit which animates those classes. They are unfortunate beings deprived of intelligence, of education, of moral and religious instruction and even of good sentiments; without aspirations; for whom nothing has been of interest since the Spanish government was expulsed from this country. This is a completely abject race, which, perhaps fortunately,

Personnel of the University of El Valle and the Candelaria Home for the Rehabilitation of Malnourished Children visit a lower-class village family which has just completed building its own bath-toilet-laundry unit. (Courtesy of the Rockefeller Foundation.)

is disappearing, owing to its bad habits and undernourishment. In it the families are small, there are no ideas of dignity, and filthiness is incorrigible; they are thieves, given to drunkenness, who place no value whatsoever upon the honesty or virtue of their daughters. A family of Indians lives in a roofless hut; the parents arise early, give the small children a little cornmeal with panela [crude brown sugar from which none of the molasses has been extracted] and water for breakfast; [then] the father and the mother go to work on the hacienda of the master and do not return to the hut until night, both drunk, and generally beaten up in the quarrels they have with each other; the woman prepares the mazamorra [a thick soup with a base of potatoes to which such grains as corn or wheat and some vegetables such as onions may be added] for the children, who have had no food since morning, and afterwards in a confused mass parents, children, and even outsiders lie down to sleep on the bare earth. In this manner they bring up their children in the most absolute state of abandonment without notions of religion or of

Dwellings of lower-class farm families in the lowlands of Colombia.

morals and lacking even in natural affection: for them the home does not exist and they develop physically and morally not like human beings but like plants. With such a life it is not strange that the race does not propagate itself, because children reared in this manner from the time they need the mother's breast, die upon being attacked by the first sickness or vegetate weak and incapable of perpetrating the species. Recruitment is another of the causes which diminishes the number of Indians: the Indians, poor friends to matrimony, once they are inducted into the army, almost never marry; and it seems that the Indian women prefer a criminal existence to an honest married life.

"Many other causes impede the progress of the populated places near Bogotá which is for them a great attractive force: almost every young person of any aspiration or medium advancement born in one of these pueblos comes to the capital in search of better social environment and broader horizons; and the girls made desperate by the bad treatment and worse examples that they receive from their parents take advantage of the first opportunity which presents itself to flee from their parents and to come here to hire themselves in a household or store, or to engage in prostitution.

"Government authority has very little prestige in these pueblos because in 20 years of a hateful domination they have become accustomed to look upon the authorities who have taxed them as enemies whom they should obey only when brute force obliges them to do so; thus it is that although the present authorities are acceptable to the pueblos they enjoy only their own personal prestige."[18]

Social Stratification in Tabio

a. *"Land and Social Status.* The class system of Tabio has its principal basis in the ownership and control of the land. The possessor of broad acreages automatically enjoys comparatively large wealth and income, he has great political prestige and exercises extensive political power, and he is entitled to expect from the members of the lower orders of society acknowledgments of his superior status in myriads of ways, some of them quite obvious and others extremely subtle. The large landowner is entitled to give orders; the lower classes must obey. This is the phenomenon generally designated as *caciquismo.*

"The two most obvious layers in the class structure of Tabio are the *terratenientes* and the *campesinos.* The former, quite limited in number, are the owners of large acreages. Without any doubt they occupy the apex of the social pyramid. The campesino class is not so homogeneous, and it includes the bulk of the population. This class embraces not only the large mass of landless rural workers, who are permitted to occupy small estancias on the margins of the haciendas and fincas, but the bulk of the small landowners as well. In wealth and income, political status, level of living, and social privileges and obligations there is no great difference between the man who rents a small estancia and the one who owns a couple of *fanegadas.* Between the two and the terrateniente there is a social

18. Translated from Gutiérrez, *Monografías,* pp. 90-92.

chasm. On the whole, though, the social differences in Tabio are less than they are in many parts of the Republic.

"Within the class of campesinos there is considerable variation. The landless agricultural workers no doubt occupy the bottom stratum of the social pyramid. Next come those who own a fanegada or two. At the top of this class are a significant number who have acquired enough land to carry on considerable agriculture, maintain some livestock, and employ several workers. Some of these higher members of the campesino class probably are the descendants of former terratenientes who have been reduced to campesino status through the continued subdivision of the estates among the numerous heirs of each succeeding generation. But some of them no doubt are people who have made their way up the agricultural ladder from a less enviable status. It would be interesting to know the extent to which a family is able to keep its upper-class status after it has lost its wealth, and also the vicissitudes encountered by the man rising from the ranks and attempting to become an accredited member of the terrateniente class.

b. "*Race and Social Status.* Although the ownership and control of the land form the principal basis of social stratification in Tabio, social status has other important determinants as well. One of these is race. There can be no doubt that the white population occupies a higher average social status than the mixed white and Indian, or mestizo class. Many of the data gathered in the survey may be brought to bear on this hypothesis. First, there is the indisputable fact that the whites tend to occupy the position of farm operators, whereas the mestizos, in much higher proportions, fall in the unenviable category of farm laborers. Headed exclusively by whites are 50.7 per cent of the households of farm operators and only 32.5 per cent of those of the farm laborers; headed exclusively by the mestizos are only 42.3 per cent of the former and 57.8 per cent of the latter. These data establish the fact that the white agriculturists of Tabio occupy a higher position on the agricultural ladder than their fellows of the mestizo class.

"In order to continue the analysis, a considerable number of indexes of social and economic status were computed and used for the purpose of comparing the 122 households of farm operators headed exclusively by whites with the 102 headed by mestizos; and for comparing the 61 farm-labor households headed by whites with the 108 headed by mestizos (see Table 17). The conclusions to be drawn from this Table are clear. Almost without exception on all the indexes of high social and economic status, the whites excel the mestizos, whereas on those indicative of low social and economic status the mestizos are represented in the higher proportions. Thus, in comparison with their white fellows, the mestizos live at greater distances from the village center, on smaller tracts of land. They own fewer livestock, and are less likely to possess wheeled vehicles. Their homes are smaller, of poorer construction, more likely to have

Dwelling of lower-class farm family in the uplands of Colombia. (Photo by U. S. Department of Agriculture.)

thatched roofs, wattle and daub walls, dirt floors, and to lack windows entirely. The homes of the mestizos are also less likely than those of the whites to contain such modern improvements as electric lights, running water, and other plumbing; and they are more likely to depend solely upon the *cocina de fogón* [three stones on the bare earthen floor] for cooking purposes, and to utilize the metate for grinding the flour which the family consumes.

"All these racial differences are more pronounced among the category of farm operators than they are for the farm laborers. The white family that has descended to the bottom of the social ladder, to the class of farm laborers, lives little better than its fellows of mixed white and Indian stock. Nevertheless, sufficiently pronounced are

TABLE 17

COMPARISON OF WHITE AND MESTIZO FARM OPERATORS AND FARM LABORERS WITH RESPECT TO VARIOUS INDEXES WHICH REFLECT SOCIAL AND ECONOMIC STATUS

Index		Farm operators		Farm laborers	
		White	Mestizo	White	Mestizo
Operators residing in village	Per cent	11.5	5.9	4.9	1.9
Average distance of home from plaza	Kms.	5.2	6.2	5.4	5.1
Operators living on a road passable for wheeled vehicles	Per cent	87.9	58.7	75.4	75.0
Operators possessing a supplementary dwelling	Per cent	19.7	10.8	6.6	5.6
Operators with holdings of less than 10 fanegadas	Per cent	59.0	65.7	—	—
Operators owning their fincas or estancias	Per cent	90.2	88.2	72.1	72.2
Average riding, draft, and pack animals owned	Number	1.3	1.1	.15	.22
Average cattle owned	Number	13.0	6.1	.87	.96
Average sheep and goats owned	Number	7.4	2.2	1.2	.7
Average pigs and hogs owned	Number	1.1	1.1	.93	.74
Average poultry owned	Number	13.3	9.1	7.0	4.3
Operators possessing no wheeled vehicles	Per cent	91.0	95.1	96.7	99.1
Literacy among heads of households	Per cent	72.1	52.9	57.4	46.3
Average rooms per house	Number	5.1	3.1	3.0	2.4
Homes with thatched roofs	Per cent	50.0	74.5	68.9	75.9
Homes with dirt floors	Per cent	46.7	75.5	78.7	82.4
Homes with wattle and daub walls	Per cent	39.3	69.6	65.6	63.9
Homes entirely lacking windows	Per cent	24.6	60.8	26.2	57.4
Homes that are ceiled	Per cent	73.0	51.0	60.7	41.7
Homes having electricity	Per cent	9.0	3.9	3.3	2.8
Homes having running water	Per cent	41.0	23.5	19.7	16.7
Homes having septic tanks	Per cent	3.3	0.0	1.6	1.9
Homes having indoor toilets	Per cent	13.9	3.9	3.3	0.0
Homes having estufas	Per cent	16.4	3.9	1.6	0.0
Homes having only cocina de fogón	Per cent	32.0	54.9	41.0	68.5
Homes having refrigerators	Per cent	1.6	0.0	0.0	0.0
Homes using metates	Per cent	92.6	97.1	95.1	94.4

the differences among the farm operators to make it evident that social stratification in Tabio is determined to a marked degree by racial factors.

c. "*Residence and Social Status.* There is also a definite tendency for the inhabitants of the pueblo to occupy a higher social and economic plane than those who live in the open-country portions of Tabio. In the first place, few of the farm laborers live in the cabecera of the municipio, only 5 of the 187 households. This indicates that when a family of farm laborers moves to the village it rarely con-

TABLE 18

Comparison of the Farm Operators and Non-agriculturists Living in the
Pueblo and in the Open Country with Respect to Various
Indexes which Reflect Social and Economic Status

Index		Farm operators		Non-agriculturists	
		Pueblo	Open country	Pueblo	Open country
Literacy among heads of households	Per cent	95.0	61.1	92.9	53.2
Average rooms per house	Number	7.1	3.8	4.2	3.0
Homes having tile roofs	Per cent	70.0	19.9	78.6	22.6
Homes having thatched roofs	Per cent	15.0	65.6	7.1	62.9
Homes having dirt floors	Per cent	0.0	66.5	21.4	59.7
Homes having wattle and daub walls	Per cent	5.0	57.0	7.1	56.5
Homes having glass windows	Per cent	31.7	8.6	50.0	9.7
Homes having electricity	Per cent	25.0	4.5	35.7	3.2
Homes having running water	Per cent	80.0	27.1	85.7	25.8
Homes having indoor toilets	Per cent	35.0	6.3	32.1	4.8
Homes having only the cocina de fogón	Per cent	10.0	45.7	7.2	50.0

tinues to work in the fields. In the second place, the farm operators who reside in the center live on a much higher level than those who dwell in the fincas, and the nonagriculturists who make their homes in the village live much better than their fellows who dwell in the surrounding area. Thus of the 20 farm operators residing in the pueblo all are farm owners, and only 88 per cent of the 221 living in the open country are proprietors. Furthermore, of the 7 operators with farms of 200 fanegadas or more, 4 are included among the 20 who reside in the village. But the material gathered (Table 18) brings out more clearly the sharp differences that exist between the farm operators who live in the center and those who reside on the farms, and also between the nonagriculturists dwelling in the pueblo and those living in the surrounding area. These data leave no doubt that the inhabitants of the village tend to occupy a higher social and economic level in society than do the persons residing in the open country."[19]

SOCIAL CLASSES IN POPAYÁN

"Social classes were real entities in Popayán. Frequent references to them were made in the newspapers, and individuals were almost invariably identified according to the class to which they belonged.

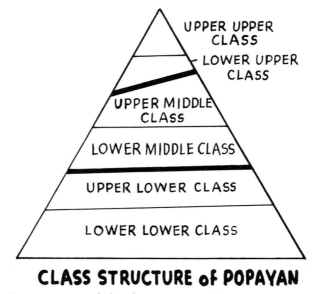

CLASS STRUCTURE of POPAYAN

Figure 7.—Representation of the class structure of Popayán. (From Andrew H. Whiteford, *Two Cities of Latin America: A Comparative Description of Social Classes*, p. 143. Reproduced with the permission of the author, Doubleday and Company, Inc., and the Natural History Press.)

In reporting upon fiestas or other social events the newspapers commonly referred to the members of *la aristocracia* (the aristocracy), *la flor-y nata* (the flower and cream) or *la vida alta* (the high life). The term 'class' was also often used and notices might appear telling of the departure for school of a son of a family of the *clase alta* (upper class) or an obituary was quite likely to lament the departure from this earth of one 'Ricardo Delgado, a respected member of the

19. Smith, Díaz, and García, *Tabio*, pp. 48-52.

middle class.' A variety of terms were used to refer to the group of people who were regarded as being at the bottom of the social hierarchy but newspaper notices dealing with such events as housing developments used the designations *clase obreros* (workers) or simply *los pobres* (the poor). They were also sometimes referred to as *el pueblo* (common people) or *la chusma* (rabble).

"The frequent use of class terminology was indicative of the general recognition and acceptance of the presence of class divisions in Popayán. Here social class was no theoretical construct conceived by the analyst, but a basic part of the social structure which defined each individual's mode of life and his relationships with the other members of the community. The city was small enough and sufficiently stable to enable a large percentage of the population to know each other and their family backgrounds. Change occurred of course and, as will be described later, some mobility between the classes was occasionally found, but the general pattern was one of a stable hierarchy, vested in historical continuity, generally accepted in the society, and exhibiting great contrasts in its extremes.

"Much of the flavor or the tone of Popayán was derived directly from its aristocratic old families. Most of them lived close to the central plaza in enormous homes which were built during the Colonial Period. They lived well, dressed in the fashions of the great cities, held most of the important offices, and owned large cattle haciendas in all directions. They were educated, highly literate, worldly wise, and proud. The city seemed aristocratic too; quiet streets and the simple beauty of colonial churches and balconied houses whose tiled roofs over-hung the narrow sidewalks and protected them from the rains.

"The market was always lively and the many people who stood in eternal conversation or who pushed through the crowds to get to the various stalls were obviously not all members of the aristocracy. Most of the people who worked here came from one of three sections on the outskirts of the city which were recognized by all as the barrios of the poor, the Lower Class. A great many of them were very Indian in physical type. The women wore long wide skirts and tied their hair in braids, and in the cool mornings many of the men wrapped themselves in the short dark ponchos called *ruanas*. Both sexes wore cotton *alpargatas* or sandals with braided fiber soles. Their homes were commonly small adobe houses roofed with straw thatch or corrugated iron and crowded together along mud streets which until recently ran between open sewers. Their education was scanty, their lives were simple, and the contrast which they presented with the members of the Upper Class was striking in every respect. Basically they derived from different traditions.

"Between these two easily discernible social classes lay the misty flats of the *clase media*—the Middle Class. To some extent this consisted simply of people who were not good enough to be Upper Class but too good to be Lower Class, but there was more to it than that. There were many families and individuals who were unerringly classified as Middle Class by everyone who knew them, and many of them not only recognized their position in the community but identified with others whom they regarded as their equals. As one informant said about his friends who belonged to this class, 'They have enough to eat but none to waste, they dress well but not with style, they have nice homes which are not fancy, and they live well without pretension.'

"Within this class striking differences were apparent as will be described in detail later. Rising members of the Lower Class climbed into its lower fringes by cadging white-collar jobs in the offices of the police or the government and, at its upper border wealthy tradesmen or successful professionals maneuvered for acceptance into the Upper Class by buying club memberships and courting the daughters of the aristocracy. Some were wealthy but many were desperately poor and, for them, the maintenance of the necessary facade of good, or at least decent, clothes, a house or apartment outside of the lower class barrios, an avoidance of hand labor, and the proper observance of the important celebrations, such as first communions, weddings and funerals, was a life-consuming effort. Failure of facade meant failure of acceptance for it was primarily upon the exhibition of exterior symbols that membership in the Middle Class depended.

"To exhibit the proper symbols of Middle Class status in the correct manner, or to strive toward their acquisition, a person first had to know what they were. And most Payaneses did. They knew how a Middle Class man should behave to avoid being considered, and therefore relegated to, Lower Class status. They knew what kind of work he should do, what kind of woman he should marry, where he should live, what he might do with his leisure time, what and when he might drink, how he must dress, and how he should treat members of the other classes. If he did all these things, and many others, correctly he was regarded as a good solid member of the

Middle Class but, if he failed in some, he was consigned to the bottom rungs of the society or dismissed altogether.

"Ascension from the Middle Class to the Upper Class was almost impossible. Although money, even in quantity, might be acquired through acuity, application and luck, the most significant symbols of the Upper Class, such as a family coat of arms, were very difficult or impossible to acquire through effort alone. As a result some of the most wealthy members of the community were still classified by their fellow-Payaneses as Middle Class.

"Social class was a way of life in Popayán. As in any ancient and stable community the presence and the knowledge of a traditional manner of behavior and interaction produced tranquility, grace, and security, but simultaneously it induced boredom, frustration, and stagnation. To a large degree the rigidity of the class structure was responsible for the city's lack of industrialization and progress in the modern era. For wealthy members of the aristocracy there was very little inducement to take financial risks or to make an effort to increase their fortunes; the poor aristocrats and struggling members of the Middle Class were forced to use every resource to maintain themselves, and the poor of any class who wished to improve their lives and were willing to take a chance or to work hard to accomplish it, left the city for the brighter lights and the brighter futures of the larger and more active cities."[20]

"In Popayán . . . when a family was referred to as an 'old family' it usually meant that some of the ancestors on one or both sides of the family had first arrived in the middle of the 16th century with the conqueror Belalcázar, or had come a short time later to hold offices in the colonial government and claim some of the surrounding mountains for their *encomiendas*. Some families still held lands which were deeded to them by the Spanish crown, and when a school boy in Popayán read his history text it was redolent with the names of local families which had played leading and decisive roles in the story of his country. The descendants or relatives of presidents, generals, archbishops, poets and heroes sat around him, and he knew intimately the houses where the Arboledas, the Mosqueras, the Valencias, the Velascos, the Caicedos, the Obandos, the Ayerbes, the Angulos, and others of equal fame and national prominence lived, where their family crests were carved in stone over the doors, and the family name still appeared on the mailbox.

20. Whiteford, p. 15-18.

"The enduring prominence of these families, their continuous leadership in national affairs, their power, possessions and eminence led to the development in Popayán of a true aristocracy. Regardless of the modern skepticism with which the claims of noble lineage by Spanish-American families is often regarded, all the elite of Popayán could exhibit their coat of arms (*escudos*) and the diplomas or parchments (*pergaminos*) which traced their lineage (*abolengo*)

Bedroom in the home of a middle-class family in the highlands of Colombia. (Courtesy of the Office of Foreign Agricultural Relations, U. S. Department of Agriculture.)

back to Spain and some distant noble ancestor. Their possession was commonly mentioned as a requisite for membership in the Upper Class. The fact that almost all Payaneses regarded membership in the Upper Class as practically impossible without lineage, and also recognized that this was something which was impossible to acquire during a lifetime, was an indication of the stability or rigidity of the social structure. Such continuity and stability, coupled with the small size of the city, made it possible for a large proportion of the Payaneses to know the leading families and to share common evaluations of them. There was no reason to question the existence of an ancient and powerful aristocracy."[21]

"For the Lower Upper Class families of Popayán their social position depended almost completely upon their social orientation. So long as they were able to maintain a socially acceptable appearance, to demonstrate a cognizance of intellectual cultural and political matters; and to remain unsullied by demeaning labor or indecent behavior, they and their children would be invited to the major fiestas, given assistance in attending the private schools, offered cut-rate memberships in the clubs, and generally regarded as the social equals of the aristocracy. If they abandoned the struggle to maintain facade, and their men began to take to work in the less prestigious occupations which would allow them to eat more regularly, they would soon cease to receive invitations from their Upper Class friends and would be absorbed into the Middle Class."[22]

"From the top to the bottom of the Middle Class the society of Popayán was an almost unbroken continuum marked by decline in income, subsistence level, housing, education, and social status . . . The Lower Middle Class in Popayán consisted largely of master craftsmen who owned their own businesses and employed other workers while they continued to work at their trade themselves: tailors, bankers, electricians, mechanics, masons, small merchants and school teachers. . . .

"A successful *ebanista*, a cabinet maker, might use his increased income to buy a house in a slightly better neighborhood, and to improve the quantity and quality of his family's dress and diet, but it is unlikely that he would even aspire to such a thing as an automobile or a television set. He might buy his son a bicycle, he might purchase a sewing machine for his wife, but more than likely he would use it to keep his sons in school until they had finished the *liceo* or high school and, if possible, he would try to send at least one of them through the university.

"Throughout the society of Popayán there was a particularly strong emphasis upon the value of education and the importance of good appearance and proper behavior. Many members of the Middle Class extended themselves to such extent to achieve these all important ends that they impoverished themselves and sacrificed their physical well being. It was sometimes necessary to skimp on food in

21. *Ibid.*, pp. 45-46.
22. *Ibid.*, pp. 49-50.

order to keep a son in school for, although tuition was determined on the basis of the family's income and was usually no great burden, he had to be provided with books, with a dark suit and white shirts, and probably with such prestige items as a Parker fountain pen, and a fancy cigarette lighter, to make him acceptable to his fellow students. The rest of the family also had to be dressed properly in order not to disgrace him and the public occasions of fifteenth birthday, saint's days, and first communions had to be properly observed with gifts and a fiesta, even if the family starved for a month and the father was forced to borrow from a money lender.

"The sons might surreptitiously help their father at his work but an effort was usually made to hide or disguise the working source of the family income. When the family had committed itself to a program of improvement through education, the young men and, to some extent, the rest of the family, tried to behave like gentry. These people, more than any others in the community were careful to be properly dressed at all times. This meant wearing a suit, being rigorously clean and properly behaved, and eschewing physical work of any kind in public, even if it only involved carrying a small parcel through the streets. Daughters were even more jealously guarded here than among the Middle Class in Querétaro. The entire picture was one of rigidity and conservatism, of a pattern so demanding that social acceptance meant constant restriction and sacrifice.

"Toward the very bottom of the Middle Class, where incomes were most meager, ambitions were also more restrained and pressure was somewhat relaxed. These poorer families also honored education and zealously maintained the façade of proper appearance to the best of their abilities. It was necessary to wear a suit to church, for both sexes to wear shoes instead of fiber soled *alpargatas* (sandals), to live in an acceptable section of the city, to be clean and to be circumspect in behavior. These were the chief symbols of differentiation from the Lower Class and they were abandoned or ignored only at the peril of social decline. These standards were rigorous but, for the Lower Middle Class, they did not preclude public appearance in working clothes, the enjoyment of a glass of beer or *aguardiente* at a favorite cantina, or a family picnic on the banks of the Cauca River. It was possible to remain in the lower ranks of the Middle Class without constantly striving to pretensions of wealth and gentility."[23]

23. *Ibid.*, pp. 71-72.

"Poverty was certainly one of the traits most obviously shared by the Lower Classes of Querétaro and Popayán. Which was the poorer of the two is unimportant. A comparison of the rate of exchange, or the relative purchasing power of their two pesos, or their incomes, is insignificant beside the simple fact that all the families in the Lower Classes of both cities found living difficult, prices high, and most goods beyond their reach. Their poverty was apparent in both cases.

Colombian school children at lunch in their cafeteria. Non-fat dry milk, flour, wheat, and vegetable and soybean oils are used under the U. S. Food for Peace program in the preparation of these lunches. (Courtesy of U. S. Department of Agriculture.)

In Popayán, as in Querétaro, they lived in crowded, inadequate, unsanitary rooms scattered throughout the city, or were concentrated in various undesirable areas on its peripheries. The Barrio Alfonso López Viejo, on the low flats along the sewer that was called the Río Ejido, was very similar to the Colonia España and El Mirador in Querétaro. It was located on property in which no one else was interested, its houses were small, poorly built, and almost totally without utilities. Most of them were built of unplastered, unpainted adobe blocks and, of 240 houses, 116 had only one window, and 65 had no windows at all; 134 had no running water, 188 had no toilets, and 191 consisted of three small rooms or less. As in Querétaro the people carried their water from neighborhood taps, and most of them washed their clothes and took baths in the nearby rivers. The Mexican Colonia España was more healthful, than the old Barrio Alfonso

López in Popayán because the latter was flooded by the Rio Ejido during the rainy seasons and, until 1950, the dirt streets were bordered with open ditches which carried off the waste of the barrio and polluted the air. . . .

"Furnishings in both countries were minimal. The Colombian houses rarely contained more than a table, two or three simple chairs, a bed, and some boxes or an old barrel to hold a few possessions. Fewer of these people slept on the ground than in Mexico and there was usually a bed or a cot of some kind, although it might consist of nothing more than a low platform on which slept three or four members of the family. The kitchen in Colombia usually consisted of an open extension toward the rear of the house where the cooking was done over a charcoal or wood fire set on an adobe platform. A crude rack or an old box held the few pottery plates and pots, and a metal tripod from which hung a cloth sack for coffee making completed the equipment. Tall fences of cane continued the walls of the houses toward the rear and gave most of them an enclosed yard which held the chickens, a small garden, the father's work shop, perhaps a pen for a pig, and almost always the family privy. House decorations were the same in both cities: a colored picture torn from a calendar, a colored litho of Our Lady of Sorrows or the Sacred Heart of Jesus, perhaps two or three family photographs, and some paper flowers. In 1949 the Colombian houses also contained political pictures and posters, particularly those depicting the visage of Jorge Gaitan, the assassinated Liberal Party leader."[24]

"For almost a century Mexico had extolled its Indian heritage and denigrated its Spanish conquerors. This did not convince everybody that it is better to be Indian than white, but it did make the Indian the symbol of the country and made it unpatriotic to discriminate against any person simply because he was a 'native.' Because of this feeling there was very little semblance of a caste system; and if a Lower Class boy, who might actually have been of pure Indian blood, succeeded in acquiring an education and an adequate complement of manners and money, he could have become a member of the Upper Class. If he was strongly Indian in appearance it might require rather better manners and a bit more money than otherwise, but standards of personal beauty always affect the conditions of social acceptance.

"The situation was quite different in Popayán, where many Indians

24. *Ibid.*, p. 108.

in a variety of native costumes could be seen in the streets every day, and the aristocracy prided itself on the purity of its noble Spanish blood. Even the members of the Lower Class in the city looked down on the Indians, in spite of the fact that many of them were of pure Indian blood themselves and were different only because they spoke Spanish, had discarded native costumes, and lived in the city. They were mestizos.

"There was no clearly defined caste line in Popayán, but a man who looked like an Indian was forced to work harder for an education and for social acceptance and would never be accepted in the Upper Class. Education, manners and the demonstration of good character might enable him to acquire a position in the Upper Middle Class, but for complete social acceptance and freedom from a very subtle suspicion of his worth he would be more successful in one of the larger cities. In Colombia there was no historical tradition which emphasized the culture and attainments of the native Indian civilizations; and, unlike Mexico, any relationship with a non-European ancestry was something to be ashamed of and to be concealed. Generations of racial intermixture had produced a delicately shaded scale from 'pure Indian' types to 'pure European,' and hardly anyone knew exactly where the line was drawn between them. This made racial discrimination difficult to apply and resulted in its use in a rather arbitrary manner, usually to exclude an individual who was not respected or admired, or to denigrate a person because of personal antipathy. Indian blood, Lower Class status, ignorance, and poverty were assumed to be categorically related to each other; there had been no Benito Juárez or Zapata in Colombian history—nor a Cuauhtémoc."[25]

"A very common form of social mobility which existed in both cities, but which was particularly well known in Popayán, was the use of political ties (corbatas) to secure appointments. Everyone associated with the business of government was appointed, from the governor of the department down to the clerks in the local police station and the women who swept the floors. Many Lower Class boys who were eager to escape a life of physical exertion and simultaneously to improve their position in the society, worked with the organization of one of the two political parties in the hope of being assigned to a desk job if they won the election. As a result the government offices, of whatever sort, were filled with poorly educated, untrained clerks who

25. Ibid., pp. 121-22.

preened themselves on their white-collar (*empleado*) status, and did as little as possible to validate it. They were poorly paid and not very well regarded in the community, but their office jobs gave them at least a tenuous toehold in the Middle Class."[26]

THE CLASS SYSTEM OF CERETÉ, CÓRDOBA

"In order to determine objectively the social classes in Cereté a number of 'key informants' residing in the municipio were interviewed. Each of these was asked to list 10 persons or families which were representative of the various social classes existing in the community.

"During this process it was observed that those in certain classes belonged exclusively to specific formal organizations or social clubs of the community. Hence it was possible to use the membership lists of these clubs for estimating the number of individuals in each class.

"Five social classes were found, namely: (1) the traditional upper class; (2) the new upper class; (3) the traditional middle class; (4) the new middle class; and (5) the lower class. It is interesting to note that the vocabulary of the local people contains only three distinctions. The traditional upper class and the new upper class are referred to as the *rich people* or the *people of consideration*. The two middle class groups are called the *middle class* or *middle people* and the lower class is known as *the poor*.

"The distinctions between the traditional upper class and the new upper class generally are imposed by the members of the traditional group. Thus the new upper class considers itself to be the upper class, although the traditional upper class does not identify with this group nor admit it to their social sphere. Therefore, it was necessary to divide it into two strata. . . .

"The *traditional upper class* (1.4 per cent of the population) is characterized, according to one of its members, by the features used to describe himself: 'I have the illustriousness necessary for a civilized man, with a primary and secondary education. My family is of the white race, traditionally Castillian and has a rigorously Catholic upbringing.'

"This stratum is made up of four family lines, presently intermarried, of Spanish origin, residents of the region for a minimum of four generations. They constitute a closed group which keeps itself apart

26. *Ibid.*, p. 123. Excerpts reproduced with the permission of Andrew H. Whiteford, Doubleday & Company, Inc. and the Natural History Press.

from almost all social and political activities, but which exercises a profound influence upon them. They consider themselves as responsible for the common welfare and accuse the rest of the upper class of being indifferent to it.

"Their economic position is most powerful. They are owners of large estates, cattlemen, and cotton planters. They constantly are preoccupied with the improvement of their technical and professional level. Almost all of the present generation are professional men: lawyers doctors, and engineers.

"Those belonging to this class are members of the Rotary Club, the center of their social activity is in Cereté. Other of their activities include family gatherings, travel, and social participation at the Country Club at Monteria. Most of them have travelled abroad and they maintain relationships with those of the upper class in other cities. In brief they are considered to be the leaders of the community. . . .

"The *new upper class* (6.3 per cent of the population) is made up largely of agriculturists who have acquired wealth by producing cotton, merchants, and immigrants of Syrian and Lebanese origin.

"The activities of those in this class consist of a series of demonstrations of their wealth with the objective of acquiring prestige. Among these activities are the fiestas at the Cereté Country Club, political activities (on the directing committees of the parties), and giving away bulls and money during the festivals on the days of the patron saints.

"Economic standing is the determinant for belonging to this class, and education and origin are unimportant.

"Sometimes the traditional upper class admits them to its circle, even though they are not considered as equals. Their indifference to the common welfare and their strictly economic power are the bases of their reputation among the lower class and serves to increase the prestige of the traditional upper class.

"The middle class (25.4 per cent of the population), despite their division into the traditional middle and the new middle, are generally viewed by others and even by themselves as occupying similar positions. However, their norms of conduct are different. The traditional middle class has an origin similar to the traditional upper, although they lack the economic resources of the latter.

"Its members are dedicated to commerce, are professionals, or have positions in the local government. The women of this group have a high educational level, are graduates of or have studied for some years in the Normal Superior del Carmen (Cereté). The children attend the local school for five years and then continue their studies in Monteria or some other city.

"Those in this part of the middle class are characterized by their strong social control and their support of the activities of the Church. It is, predominantly, a narrow or closed segment, composed of individuals who have accepted their position and developed their own models of conduct, without attempting to imitate the upper class as is done by the new middle class.

"The new middle class includes agriculturists with medium or small farms, but fundamentally it is composed of artisans and merchants. Most of its members are migrants from the rural areas who have benefited from their mobility because of the increased demand for their services. During the first years in their businesses they work as blacksmiths and carpenters. With the rapid introduction of jeeps and tractors, they have become owners of shops for woodworking, for mechanical activities, for leatherwork, and for building the bodies for jeeps. The increase in construction work also has influenced greatly the demand for artisans, especially the carpenters.

"Social control among those of the new middle class is less than among the traditional middle class, excessive drinking is more frequent on their part, and they are less formal in their activities.

"In summary, as a class, it is actively occupied in working in order to attain a higher social position; they imitate the upper classes as far as their economic circumstances will permit.

"*The lower class* (66.9 per cent of the population) consists of artisans, day laborers, and unskilled workers. It is composed largely of migrants from the rural districts to the city. The mode of conduct of those in this class is totally different from that of the classes previously described. Their economic level is precarious and may be considered as one of mere subsistence.

"In this class is where one encounters the majority of the common-law unions. Their families lack stability, where a man may abandon his woman and children for economic reasons.

"The practice of *buying the woman* has long existed, and it still persists although with no great frequency. This type of free union is formalized by means of a payment called a *dote* to the family of the intended wife."[27]

27. Havens, Montero, and Romieux, *Cereté,* pp. 91-96. Translated and published here with the permission of A. Eugene Havens.

10

Conclusion

During this half of the twentieth century social change is the order of the day throughout Colombia. For the most part the country is like a rudderless canoe pitched about down a turbulent stream by great uncontrolled forces thrusting and pulling upon Colombian society from all directions; and most of these forces give little indication of having expended any great portion of their energy. What is happening to Colombian society is the kind of change that was known as "development" prior to about 1950 or until the frequent, intimate contacts between the representatives of societies in all parts of the world made it essential to find some euphemism to substitute for the word "backward" when referring to peoples in many parts of Africa, Asia, and Latin America. Moreover, a minute part of the transformation going on in Colombia fully meets the requisites for being denoted as *development* in the sense of planned and directed social change, i.e. the movement from a known position to a purposely selected state or goal. Such telesis is the thing upon which Colombian leaders, as well as those in the "underdeveloped" or "developing" societies throughout the world, are pinning their hopes.

In this volume we have examined the situation and trends with respect to seven of the most important features or aspects of Colombian society, and also have given against a backdrop of four hundred years of history an analysis of the chief attack mounted to date, namely Agrarian Reform, on the principal endeavors to carry through a program of directed social change or development in the nation. The specific conclusions reached on the basis of those efforts are in most places in the chapters themselves, and no effort is made to bring them all together in this brief conclusion. Nevertheless, it seems well to restate, and possibly to amplify to some extent a few of the principal ones.

Colombia's social system remains essentially based upon large estates, discussed in detail in Chapter 2. However, the rapid urbanization of the country, to be treated in another volume, is bringing this to a stage of crisis; and all of the long-sustained efforts to change this system, to develop in Colombia a substantial rural middle class made up of the owner-operators of family-sized farms, so far have produced very modest results. Even the important factor of subdivision of the estates by inheritance has not changed the system essentially. However, many large landowners in Colombia have seized the opportunity offered by modern agricultural machinery and are transforming parts of their grazing estates into plantations for the production of sugar cane, cotton, and rice. In spite of this the vast majority of the large landed properties are devoted almost exclusively to rudimentary pastoral activities. Moreover, the benefits of modern scientific knowledge about agriculture, and even reasonable credit, are not available to the hundreds of thousands of farm families who are dependent upon minute plots, many of limited potential, for a livelihood.

Property rights in Colombia are in a chaotic condition due largely to the attempt to have two different legal philosophies of ownership rights in effect simultaneously. Traditionally, land was held in fee simple by means of a grant or deed from the crown or the Republic and transmitted from person to person by inheritance, sale, and so on. In 1936, however, Law 200 established "economic utilization" as the only basis for holding land, and allowed ten years for the owners to establish proof that they were making economic utilization of what they controlled. The foggy state of affairs growing out of these conflicting philosophies is being clarified, following the reestablishment of legislative bodies in the 1950's, as additional legal enactments are being made.

There are about 1,500,000 families in Colombia who are directly dependent upon agricultural and pastoral activities for a livelihood. Of these, by any reasonable criteria, only about 35 per cent can be considered to be operators of the farms on which they are dependent. This leaves almost two-thirds in the precarious condition of farm laborers. Herein lies Colombia's most acute problem—measures proposed or under way are entirely inadequate for the task to be done.

The system of surveys used in dividing Colombia's land among individual owners is defective in almost every respect. It is neither definite, determinate, nor permanent; and disputes over boundaries continue to generate hosts of protracted and expensive lawsuits and innumerable personal conflicts as they have done for centuries. Each year hundreds of thousands of acres of public domain are being claimed and patented under a haphazard, defective, and expensive system for dividing the land. And this system suffers acutely in comparison with ways of doing this job that have been known since the days of ancient Egypt. So far two separate attempts to get the Colombian Congress to enact an ordinance that will do for their country what the Ordinance of 1787 designed by Thomas Jefferson did for the United States, have not been successful. However, one of the most substantial parts of the agrarian reform program consists of the endeavor to return to the public domain the rights to huge expanses of land that are being illegally held by hundreds of large proprietors who have allowed the boundaries of their claims to ooze out in all directions so as to embrace areas greatly exceeding those to which they are entitled.

As mentioned above, a few of Colombia's large proprietors are moving rapidly to improve the system of agriculture employed on their estates, and more than a few high-grade sugar cane, cotton, and rice plantations are being developed. This definitely is not the case, though, with the small proprietors and other categories of farm operators, and the vast majority of Colombia's farmers continue to be dependent upon systems of agriculture that compare unfavorably with those the Egyptians were using at the dawn of history.

Currently much is being said in Colombia about community welfare and community development, and this of itself is a portent of changes to come. It may be that we are on the eve of witnessing substantial efforts to overcome the lethargic state in which Colombia's rural communities have been for centuries, to put an end to the debility of local government, and to develop genuine metropolitan, urban, and rurban communities.

Finally, largely because of the rapid growth of cities, the changing roles of the progeny of those of aristocratic standing, influence of many thousands of immigrants, and the agrarian reform program, Colombia's traditional two-class system is undergoing fundamental changes. There actually seems to be emerging a considerable number of middle-class people to fill the great void that long separated those of upper-class lineage from the huge mass of lower-class persons who constituted the bulk of the population. To the extent that the development process actually is carried on, the traditional two-class system must be modified to include a large and strong middle-class layer.

Bibliography

Amaya Ramírez, Guillermo. "Informe de Jefe del Departamento de Tierras y Aguas," *Memoria del Ministerio de Agricultura y Comercio.* 2 vols. Bogotá: Talleres Gráficos "Mundo al Día," 1937.

Ancízar, Manuel. *Peregrinación de Alpha.* Bogotá: Arboleda y Valencia, 1914.

Anonymous. *Geografía Económica de Colombia, Tomo V, Bolívar.* Bogotá: Editorial el Gráfico, 1942.

Anonymous. *Letters Written from Colombia, During a Journey from Caracas to Bogotá and Thence to Santa Martha in 1823.* London: G. Cowie & Co., 1824.

Anonymous. *The Present State of Colombia.* London: John Murray, 1837.

Bache, Richard. *Notes on Colombia Taken in the Years 1822-3.* . . . Philadelphia: H. C. Carey & I. Lea, 1827.

Backus, Richard C., and Phanor J. Eder. *A Guide to the Law and Legal Literature of Colombia.* Washington: The Library of Congress, 1943.

Bancroft, Hubert Howe. *California Pastoral, 1769-1848.* San Francisco: The History Company, 1888.

————. *History of Central America,* Vol. I. San Francisco: The History Company, 1886.

Bell, P. L. *Colombia: A Commercial and Industrial Handbook.* Washington: Government Printing Office, 1921.

Borda, José Joaquín. *Historia de la Compañía de Jesús en la Nueva Granada,* Vol. II. Poissy: S. LeJay et Cie., 1872.

Bowles, J. D., Esq. (Chairman of the Committee of Spanish American Bondholders). *New Granada: Its Internal Resources.* London: A. H. Bailey and Co., Cornhill; James Ridgeway, Piccadily, 1863.

Burton, Richard F. *Explorations of the Highlands of the Brazil.* 2 vols. London: Tinsley Brothers, 1869.

Camacho Roldán, Salvador. "La Agricultura en Colombia," *Escritos Varios,* Vol. I. Bogotá: Librería Colombiana, 1892.

————. *Notas de Viaje.* Paris: Garnier Hermanos and Bogotá: Librería Colombiana, 1897.

Carrasquilla H., Tomás. *Inmigración y Colonización.* Bogotá: Imprenta Nacional, 1906.

Cieza de León, Pedro de. *The Travels of Pedro de Cieza de León,* translated and edited by Clements R. Markham. London: The Hakluyt Society, 1864.

Cochrane, Charles Stuart. *Journal of a Residence and Travels in Colombia during the Years 1823 and 1824.* 2 vols. London: Henry Colburn, 1825.

Compton's Pictured Encyclopedia and Fact-Index, Vol. I. Chicago: F. E. Compton & Company, 1944.

Cooley, Charles H. *Social Organization.* New York: Charles Scribner's Sons, 1925.

Crevenna, Theo R. (ed.). *Materiales para el Estudio de la Clase Media en la América Latina.* 6 vols. Washington: Pan American Union, 1950-51.

Cuervo Márquez, Emilio. *La Cuestión Agraria en Colombia.* Bogotá: Editorial de Cromos, 1932.

Cunninghame Graham, R. B. *Cartagena and the Banks of the Sinú.* New York: George H. Doran Company, n.d.

Currie, Lauchlin, *et al. The Basis of a Development Program for Colombia.* Baltimore: Johns Hopkins Press, 1950.

Departamento Administrativo Nacional de Estadística. "Resumen Nacional," *Directorio Nacional de Explotaciones Agropecuarias* (*Censo Agropecuario*) *1960.* Bogotá: Multilith Estadinal, 1962.

————. "Resumen Nacional (Segunda Parte)," *Directorio Nacional de Explotaciones Agropecuarias* (*Censo Agropecuario*) *1960.* Bogotá: Multilith Estadinal, 1964.

Duane, William. *A Visit to Colombia, in the Years 1822 and 1823.* Philadelphia: Thomas H. Palmer, 1826.

Eder, Phanor J. *El Fundador: Santiago M. Eder.* Bogotá: Antares, Ltda., 1959.

Ellis, L. W., and Edward A. Rumely. *Power and the Plow.* New York: Doubleday, Page, and Co., 1911.

Facultad de Ciencias Económicas. *Censo Agropecuario del Valle del Cauca, 1959.* Cali: Universidad del Valle, 1963.

Fals-Borda, Orlando. *Facts and Theory of Sociocultural Change in a Rural Social System.* Monografías Sociológicas No. 2 Bis. Bogotá: Departamento de Sociología, Universidad Nacional de Colombia, 1960.

————. *El Hombre y la Tierra en Boyacá, Bases Socio-Históricas para una Reforma Agraria.* Bogotá: Ediciones Documentos Colombianos, 1957. (English text, *A Sociological Study of the Relationships between Man and the Land in the Department of Boyacá, Colombia,* presented as a Ph.D. dissertation to the Graduate School, University of Florida, Gainesville, Florida, 1955).

————. *Peasant Life in the Colombian Andes: A Sociological Study of Saucio.* Gainesville: University of Florida Press, 1955.

————. "El Problema de la Tierra Visto a Traves de los Linderos de un Resguardo Indígena," *Revista Bolívar,* XI (Marzo-Mayo, 1959), 459-71.

Farson, Negley. *Transgressor in the Tropics.* New York: Harcourt, Brace and Company, 1938.

Fermín de Vargas, Pedro. *Pensamientos Políticos y Memoria sobre la Población del Nuevo Reino de Granada.* Bogotá: Imprenta Nacional, 1944.

Finestrad, Joaquín de. "El Vasallo Instruido," in *Los Comuneros.* Biblioteca de Historia Nacional, IV. Bogotá: Imprenta Nacional, 1905.

Franco R., Ramón. *Antropogeografía Colombiana.* Manizales: Imprenta del Departamento, 1941.

Galpin, Charles J. *The Social Anatomy of an Agricultural Community.* University of Wisconsin Agricultural Experiment Station Bulletin 34, Madison, 1915.

García, Luis Roberto. "Notes on Land Tenure in Colombia," *Rural Sociology,* X (Dec., 1945), 416-18.

García y García, José Antonio (ed.). *Relaciones de los Vireyes del Nuevo Reino de Granada.* New York: Hallet & Breen, 1869.

Gosse, A. Bothwell. *The Civilization of the Ancient Egyptians.* London: T. C. and E. C. Jack, 1915.

Gutiérrez, Rufino. *Monografías,* Tomo I. Bogotá: Imprenta Nacional, 1920.

Guzmán Campos, Germán, Orlando Fals-Borda, and Eduardo Umaña Luna. *La Violencia en Colombia: Estudio de un Proceso Social.* Bogotá: Vol. I, Facultad de Sociología, Universidad Nacional, 1962; and Vol. II, Ediciones Tercer Mundo, 1964.

Hall, Francis. *Colombia: Its Present State, . . . , and Inducements to Emigration.* Philadelphia: John Grigg, 1825.

Hamilton, J. P. *Travels through the Interior Provinces of Colombia.* 2 vols. London: John Murray, 1827.

Haring, C. H. *The Spanish Empire in America.* New York: Oxford University Press, 1947.

Havens, A. Eugene. *Tamesis: Estructura y Cambio de una Comunidad Antioqueña.* Bogotá: Ediciones Tercer Mundo y Facultad de Sociologia, 1966.

Havens, A. Eugene, L. Eduardo Montero, and Michel Romieux. *Cereté: Un Area de Latifundio.* Informe Técnico No. 3, Bogotá: Facultad de Sociología, Universidad Nacional de Colombia, 1965.

Herrera y Tordesillas, Antonio de. *The General History of the Vast Continent and Islands of America, Commonly Called the West Indies.* Translated by John Stevens. 6 vols. London: Jer. Batley, 1725-26.

Hirschman, Albert O. *Journeys Toward Progress: Studies of Economic Policy-Making in Latin America.* New York: The Twentieth Century Fund, 1963.

Holton, Isaac. *New Granada: Twenty Months in the Andes.* New York: Harper & Brothers, 1857.

Irvine, Helen Douglass. *The Making of Rural Europe.* London: George Allen and Unwin Ltd., 1923.

Jiménez, Domingo. *Geografía Física i Política de la Ciudad de Corozal.* Mompos: Imprenta de "La Industria," 1873.

Jovellanos, Gaspar Melchor de. *Informe de la Sociedad Económica de Madrid al Real y Supremo Consejo de Castilla en el Expediente de Ley Agraria* (2nd ed.). Madrid: Imprenta de I. Sancha, 1920.

Juan [de Sancticilia], Jorge, and Antonio de Ulloa. *Secret Expedition to Peru.* Boston: Crocker and Brewster, 1851.

———. *A Voyage to South America. . . .* 2 vols. London: Davis and C. Reymers, 1758.

Koster, Henry. *Travels in Brazil.* 2 vols. Philadelphia: M. Carey & Son, 1817.

Leay, William. *New Granada, Equatorial South America.* London: Christian Book Society, 1869.

Lebret, Louis Joseph, *et al. Estudio sobre las Condiciones del Desarrollo en Colombia.* 2 vols. Bogotá: AEDITA, Editores Ltda.-Cromos, 1958.

Libro de Cabildos de la Ciudad de Tunja, 1539-1542. Bogotá: Imprenta Municipal, 1941.

Lipman, Aaron. "Social Backgrounds of the Bogotá Entrepreneur," *Journal of Inter-American Studies,* VII (April, 1965), 227-35.

López, Alejandro I. C. *Problemas Colombianos.* Paris: Editorial Paris-America, 1927.

McBride, George M. *The Land Systems of Mexico.* New York: American Geographical Society, 1923.

MacIver, R. M. *Community: A Sociological Study.* London: MacMillan and Company, Ltd., 1920.

———. *Society: A Textbook of Sociology.* New York: R. Long and R. R. Smith, Inc., 1937.

Maniño Pinto, Enrique. *Manual de Derecho Civil Colombiano para Uso de los Agricultores* (2nd ed.). Bogotá: Editorial Lumen, 1941.

María Henao, Jesús, and Gerardo Arrubla. *History of Colombia.* Translated and edited by J. Fred Rippy. Chapel Hill: University of North Carolina Press, 1938.

Martínez E., Marco A. *Régimen de Tierras en Colombia.* 2 vols. Bogotá: Talleres Gráficos Mundo al Día, 1939.

Maspero, Gaston. *The Dawn of Civilization, Egypt and Chaldea* (5th ed.). London: Society for Promoting Christian Knowledge, 1910.

Medina R., Juan (organizer). *Boyacá.* Geografía Económica de Colombia, No. III. Bogotá: Contráloria General de la República, 1936.

Mendoza, Diego. "Ensayo sobre la Evolución de la Propiedad en Colombia," *Repertorio Colombiano,* XVII (1897-1898).

Miller, Leo E. *In the Wilds of South America*. New York: Charles Scribner's Sons, 1919.

Mollien, G. *Travels in the Republic of Colombia in the Years 1822 and 1823*. London: G. Knight, 1824.

Morales Benítez, Otto. *Reforma Agraria: Colombia Campesina*. Bogotá: Imprenta Nacional, 1962.

Montero, L. Eduardo, and Dale W. Adams. *Algunas Consideraciones sobre Reforma Agraria en Regiones de Minifundio: un Ejemplo Colombiano*. Bogotá: Centro Interamericano de Reforma Agraria, 1965.

Nieto Arteta, Luis Eduardo. *Economía y Cultura en la Historia de Colombia*. Bogotá: Ediciones Librería Siglo XX, 1941.

Olmstead, Frederick Law. *A Journey in the Seaboard Slave States, with Remarks upon Their Economy*. New York: Dix & Edwards, 1856.

Ortíz, Sergio Elias. *Las Comunidades Indígenes de Jamondino y Males*. Pasto: Imprenta del Departamento, 1935.

Ossa V., Peregrino. *Medidas Agrarias Antiguas*. Bogotá: Tip. Voto Nacional, 1939.

Ots Capedequí, José M. *El Régimen de la Tierra en la América Española durante el Periodo Colonial*. Ciudad Trujillo: Editora Montalvo, 1946.

Páez Courvel, Luis E. *Historia de las Medidas Agrarias Antiguas*. Bogotá: Librería Voluntad, 1940.

Pardo Umaña, Camilo. *Haciendas de la Sabana*. Bogotá: Editorial Kelly, 1946.

Paris Lozano, Gonzalo. *Tolima*, Geografía Económica de Colombia, Tomo VII. Bogotá: Contráloria General de la República, 1946.

Parsons, James J. *Antioqueño Colonization in Western Colombia*. Ibero-Americana: 32, Berkeley: University of California Press, 1949.

Pearse, Arno S. *Colombia with Special Reference to Cotton, Being the Report of the Journey of the International Cotton Mission through the Republic of Colombia*. Manchester: International Federation of Master Cotton Spinners' & Manufacturers' Associations, 1946.

Peñalosa Camargo, Enrique, *et al. INCORA: Informe de Actividades en 1962*. Bogotá: Imprenta Nacional, 1963.

————. *INCORA, 1964: Third Year of Agrarian Reform in Colombia*. Bogotá: Imprenta Nacional, 1965.

Pérez Salazar, Honorio. "Emancipación Jurídica del Indígena," *Tierras y Aguas*, Año 6 (1944), pp. 3-11.

Pineda Giraldo, Roberto, *et al. Caldas: Estudio de su Situación Geográfica, Económica y Social.* . . . 2 vols. Bogotá: Empresa Nacional de Publicaciones, 1956.

Pino Espinal, Alfredo. *Conclusiones del Primer Ensayo de Explotación Agrícola por el Sistema de Aparcería de los Cultivos de Tabaco, Maíz y Millo en la Estación Agrícola de San Gil*. Bucaramanga: División Nacional de Agricultura, 1948.

Posada, Eduardo, and P. M. Ibáñez. *Relaciones de Mando*. Biblioteca de Historia Nacional, Vol. VIII. Bogotá: Imprenta Nacional, 1910.

Restrepo, Gonzalo. *Memoria del Ministerio de Agricultura y Comercio*. Bogotá: Talleres Gráficos, "Mundo al Día," 1937, 2 vols.

Rivas, Medardo. *Los Trabajadores de Tierra Caliente*. Bogotá: Imprenta y Librería de M. Rivas, 1899.

Rivas, Raimundo. *Los Fundadores de Bogotá*. Bogotá: Imprenta Nacional, 1923.

Rodríguez Freile, Juan. *El Carnero: Conquista y Descubrimiento del Nuevo Reino de Granada.* . . . Prólogo y anotaciones de Jesús M. Henao. Bogotá: Camacho Roldán & Cia., 1935.

Rodríguez Maldonado, Carlos. *Hacienda de Tena (IV Centenario), 1543-1943.* Bogotá: Editorial El Gráfico, 1944.

Rosales, José Miguel. *Histórias y Paisajes.* Bogotá: Editorial de Cromos, 1929.

Ross, Edward Alsworth. *South of Panama.* New York: The Century Co., 1915.

Rubin, Vera (ed.). *Plantation Systems of the New World.* Washington: Pan American Union, 1959.

Samper, José M. *Ensayo sobre las Revoluciones Políticas y la Condición Social de las Repúblicas Colombianas.* Paris: E. Thunot y Ca., 1861.

Santos, Eduardo. *Una Política Liberal.* Bogotá: Editorial Minerva, S. A., 1937.

Sauer, Carl O. *Agricultural Origins and Dispersals.* New York: American Geographical Society, 1952.

Simpson, Eyler N. *The Ejido: Mexico's Way Out.* Chapel Hill: University of North Carolina Press, 1937.

Smith, T. Lynn. *Agrarian Reform in Latin America.* New York: Alfred A. Knopf, Inc., 1965.

————. *Brazil: People and Institutions* (3rd ed.). Baton Rouge: Louisiana State University Press, 1963.

————. "Colonization and Settlement in Colombia," *Rural Sociology,* XII (June, 1947), 128-39.

————. "Conflicto de Teorías sobre la Propiedad de la Tierra en Colombia," *Revista Mexicana de Sociología,* XX (Mayo-Agosto, 1958), 371-84.

————. "The Cultural Setting of Agricultural Extension Work in Colombia," *Rural Sociology,* X (Sept., 1945), 235-46.

————. *Current Social Trends and Problems in Latin America.* Gainesville: University of Florida Press, 1957.

————. "El Desarrollo de Unidades Agrícolas Medianas," *Boletín Uruguayo de Sociología,* Año I (1961), pp. 39-47.

————. "Land Tenure and Soil Erosion in Colombia," *Proceedings of the Inter-American Conference on Conservation of Renewable Resources* (Denver, Sept., 1948). Washington: Department of State, 1949, pp. 155-60.

————. "Notes on Population and Rural Social Organization in El Salvador," *Rural Sociology,* X (Dec., 1945), 359-79.

————. "Notes on Population and Social Organization in the Central Portion of the São Francisco Valley," *Inter-American Economic Affairs,* 1 (1947), 50-52.

————. *Rural Sociology: A Trend Report and Bibliography.* Published as *Current Sociology,* VI (1957), 1-75.

————. *La Sociología y el Proceso de Desarrollo de la Comunidad.* "Serie de Desarrollo de la Comunidad y Bienestar Social," No. 2. Washington: Pan-American Union, 1964.

————. *The Sociology of Rural Life* (3rd ed.). New York: Harper and Brothers, 1953.

————. "Some Observations on Land Tenure in Colombia," *Foreign Agriculture,* XVI (June, 1952), 119-24.

Smith, T. Lynn, Justo Díaz Rodríguez, and Luis Roberto García. *Tabio: A Study in Rural Social Organization.* Washington: Office of Foreign Agricultural Relations, U. S. Department of Agriculture, 1945.

Solorzano Pereyra, Juan de. *Política Indiana.* Madrid: Gabriel Ramírez, 1739.

Spain. *Primera Parte de la Recopilación Historial Resolutoria de Sancta Marta y Nuevo Reino de Granada de las Indias del Mar Océano,* Tomo Primero. Madrid: Espasa-Calpe. S. A., 1930.

Spain. *Las Leyes de Indias.* 9 tomos. Madrid: Establecimiento Tipográfico de Pedro Núñez, 1889.

Spain, Ministerio de Trabajo y Previsión. *Disposiciones Complementarias de las Leyes de Indias,* Vol. I. Madrid: Saez Hermanos, 1930.

Steuart, J. *Bogotá in 1836-7*. New York: Harper & Brothers, 1838.

Steward, Julian H. (ed.). *Handbook of South American Indians*. 6 vols. Washington: Government Printing Office, 1950.

Suarez de Castro, Fernando. *Estructuras Agrarias en la América Latina*. San José, Costa Rica: Interamerican Institute of Agricultural Sciences, 1965.

El Tiempo. Bogotá, Oct. 7, 1943, and May 28, 1964.

Torre, Antonio de la. *Noticia Individual de las Poblaciones Nuevas Fundadas en la Provincia de Cartagena*. . . . Santa Maria: Luis de Luque y Leiva, 1794.

Torres de Mendoza, Luis. *Colección de Documentos Inéditos*, Tomo X, ... Madrid: Imprenta de Frias y Compañía, 1868. And Tomo XXIII, Madrid: G. Hernández, 1875.

Tylor, E. B. "On the Origin of the Plough and Wheel-Carriage," *Journal of the Anthropological Institute of Great Britain and Ireland*, X (1881).

Uribe Angel, Manuel. *Geografía General y Compendio Histórico del Estado de Antioquia en Colombia*. Paris: Victor Goupy y Jourdan, 1855.

Vautier, Ernesto E. and Orlando Fals-Borda. *La Vereda de Chambimbal: Estudio y Acción en Vivienda Rural*. Bogotá: Centro Interamericano de Vivienda y Planeamiento, 1958.

Veatch, A. C. *Quito to Bogotá*. London: Hodder & Stoughton, 1917.

Vicente de Oviedo, Basilio. *Cualidades y Riquezas del Nuevo Reino de Granada*, Edited by Luis Augusto Cuervo. Biblioteca de Historia Nacional, Vol. XIV. Bogotá: Imprenta Nacional, 1930.

Walker, Alexander. *Colombia: Being a Geographical, Statistical, Agricultural, Commercial, and Political Account of That Country*. . . . 2 vols. London: Baldwin, Craddock, and Joy, 1822.

Wallace, Alfred Russell. *Travels on the Amazon*. London: Ward Lock & Co., 1911.

Whetten, Nathan L. *Rural Mexico*. Chicago: University of Chicago Press, 1948.

Whiteford, Andrew H. *Two Cities of Latin America: A Comparative Description of Social Classes*. Beloit, Wisconsin: The Logan Museum of Anthropology of Beloit College, 1960.

Wissler, Clark. *The American Indian* (2nd ed.). New York: Oxford University Press, 1922.

Zabala C., Manuel. *Estudio Social sobre un Barrio de Invasión*. Cali: Universidad del Valle, Facultad de Arquitectura, 1964.

Zavala, Silvio. *De Encomiendas y Propiedad Territorial en Algunas Regiones de la América Española*. Mexico: Antigua Librería Robredo, 1940.

Author Index

Subject Index

A

Absenteeism, 56-57, 111, 130-31, 138, 140, 190, 263-64, 269, 298, 300, 323-24
Acción comunal, 315, 327
Advanced plow culture, 217-24
Agrarian reform, 1, 6, 80, 105, 133, 142, 236-86, 373, 375
Agrarian Reform Law of 1961, 27, 38, 88-89, 133, 241, 253-54
Agricultural extension, 324-25
Agricultural laborers, 11, 15, 16, 18, 19, 20, 23, 26, 36, 39, 40, 41, 49, 74-75, 76, 106, 108, 109, 110-14, 249, 315, 356-59, 374: types of, 114-24
Agricultural population, 105-6
Agriculture: lack of interest in, 31, 188-94; vs. pastoral activities, 189-95; minimum features of, 198
Alcalde, 77, 78, 275, 306
Antioqueños, 56, 183, 338-39
Aparcería, 119, 120-21
Aparceros, 57, 120-21
Arepa, 181, 188
Arrendatários, 25, 29, 40, 57, 74-75, 76, 104, 110, 115-20, 160, 228
Arrieros, 75-76

C

Caballerías, 92, 93, 95, 96, 150, 155, 156, 238, 270
Caciquism, 18
Capellanías, 60-61
Capitulaciones reales, 52
Caste, 7, 13-15, 242, 330-31, 335-37, 345, 346-47
Cédulas del Pardo, 94-95, 97, 237, 238
Churches, 78, 79
Class: system, 4, 6, 9-15, 16, 18, 328-72, 375; conflict, 7; structure, 26, 328-72

Colonization, 98-101, 102, 158-60, 246, 251-52, 255-56, 339
Colonos, 41, 75, 82, 84-86, 103, 114, 115, 140-42, 160, 204, 246, 250, 261, 283
Communities: of the Indians, 64; varieties of, 296-99, 305-14
Community, 4, 6, 287-327, 375: ownership of land, 142-46; organization of, 147-48, 316-17; development of, 253, 256, 289-90, 305, 315-27, 375; study, 290-91; nature of, 291-95; council, 316-17; score cards, 317-22
Comparative method, 4-5
Composición de tierras, 81, 94-95, 96-97, 237-38, 274
Concentration of landownership, 24-28, 245, 249, 253, 323: and the church, 60-61; and depopulation, 62-69
Concertados, 115-21
Concessions, 27, 28, 29, 56. *See also* Merced and Capitulaciones reales
Consacá Hacienda, 75-79
Consejo, 77
Conucos, 40, 111, 115, 118
Conuqueros, 115-21
"Consciousness of kind," 333-37
Coolies, 100
Corbatas, 369-70
Cortijo, 9
Cultural: norms, 16; lag, 147; heritage, 176, 179-95, 211-15

D

Development process: nature of, 1, 3, 6, 373
Díaz Rodríguez, Justo, 2, 75, 95, 120-21, 251
Differential fertility, 340-42
Digging sticks, 178, 206, 208
Domination and subordination, 10, 15, 18, 239-40, 242